CON THIEN

CON THIEN

THE HILL OF ANGELS

James P. Coan

The University of Alabama Press • Tuscaloosa

Copyright © 2004
The University of Alabama Press
Tuscaloosa, Alabama 35487-0380
All rights reserved
Manufactured in the United States of America

Designer: Michele Myatt Quinn
Typeface: ACaslon

∞

The paper on which this book is printed meets the minimum
requirements of American National Standard for Information
Science–Permanence of Paper for Printed Library Materials,
ANSI Z39.48–1984.

Library of Congress Cataloging-in-Publication Data

Coan, James P.
   Con Thien : the Hill of Angels / James P. Coan.
      p. cm.
   Includes bibliographical references and index.
   ISBN 0-8173-1414-8 (cloth : alk. paper)
   1. Vietnamese Conflict, 1961–1975—Vietnam—Con Thien Mountain
Region. 2. Vietnamese Conflict, 1961–1975—Personal narratives, American.
3. Con Thien Mountain Region (Vietnam)—History. I. Title.
   DS559.9.C66C63 2004
   959.704′342—dc22

                                                           2004004302

To the U.S. Marines and Navy Corpsmen who sacrificed all of their tomorrows at Con Thien.

They shall grow not old, as we who are left grow old:
Age shall not weary them, nor the years condemn.
At the going down of the sun and in the morning
We will remember them.

—Laurence Binyon, "For the Fallen"

Contents

Appendix C

Illustrations

Marines huddle in a trench at Con Thien

Artillerymen loading a howitzer

Soldier reaches for flak jacket

Author with tank platoon

MAPS

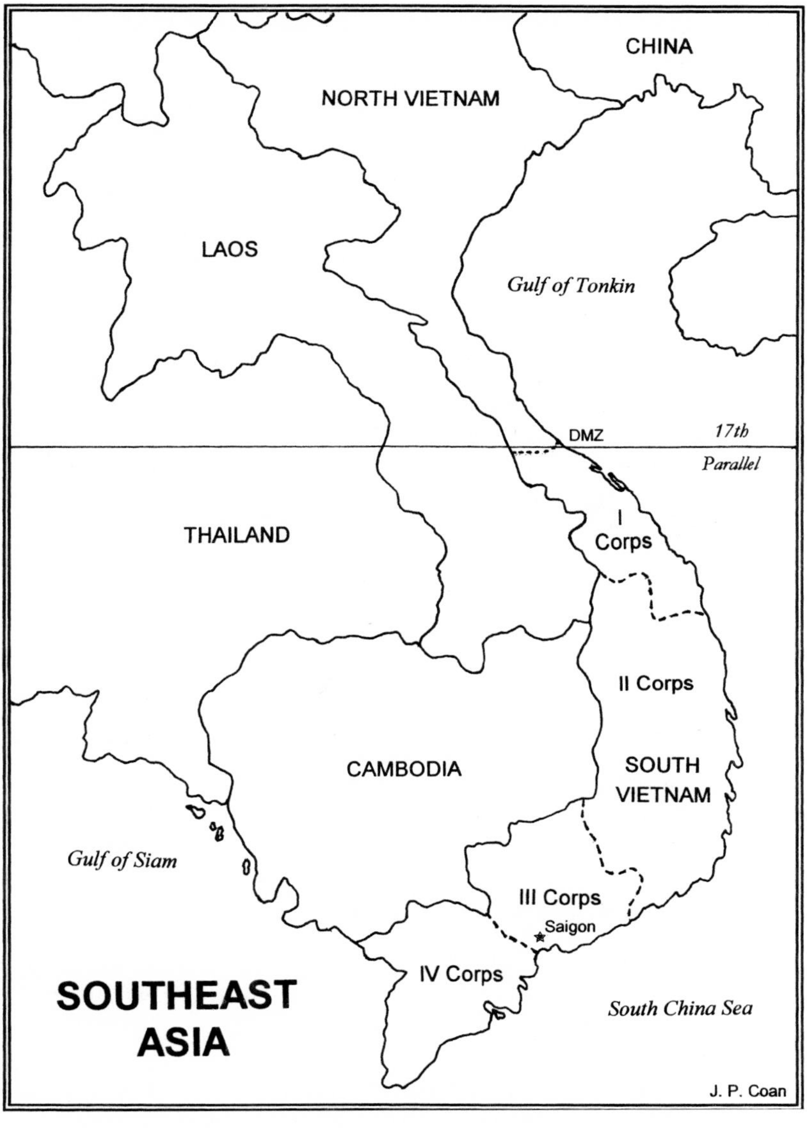
CHINA
NORTH VIETNAM
LAOS
Gulf of Tonkin
DMZ
17th
Parallel
THAILAND
I
Corps
II Corps
CAMBODIA
SOUTH
VIETNAM
Gulf of Siam
III Corps
Saigon
IV Corps
SOUTHEAST
ASIA
South China Sea
J. P. Coan

Southeast Asia

Preface

From September 1967 through July 1968, I was a tank platoon leader in Alpha Company, 3d Tank Battalion, 3d Marine Division. For eight of those months, my tank platoon operated out of Con Thien alongside various infantry battalions spending "time in the barrel" (as in the phrase "like shootin' fish in a barrel"). Con Thien was only two miles from the southern border of the demilitarized zone dividing North and South Vietnam, well within range of the entire arsenal of heavy weapons possessed by the North Vietnamese Army, and every square foot was zeroed in.

I have a deeply personal perspective about that red clay bull's-eye known as "The Hill of Angels," having survived the attempted siege of Con Thien in the fall of 1967. Hundreds of rounds of incoming artillery, mortars, and rockets pounded our beleaguered outpost daily. Monsoon downpours turned the laterite clay soil to oozing mud, flooded bunkers and trench lines, and made Con Thien a living hell. As our casualty list grew steadily into the hundreds, the news media latched onto our ordeal, referring to it as a "little Dien Bien Phu." We Marines knew otherwise, but we had the full attention of the entire military chain of command up to and including our commander in chief, President Lyndon B. Johnson.

In the years following my return to "the world," as we referred to home, I started writing as a form of self-therapy. Eventually, the faces of my dead comrades faded, and I could sleep through the night again. A decade passed before I resurrected my collection of Con Thien anecdotes and reread them. By then, the war was long over, and Con Thien had somehow taken a backseat to other major battles of the war: Khe Sanh, Tet, Dak To, and Hue, to name a few.

With no real purpose in mind other than curiosity, I embarked on a solitary sojourn to learn as much as possible about Con Thien's role throughout the entire war, besides what I personally saw and experienced during my year there. It soon became evident that the complete Con Thien story could not be told by describing one single battle, one operation, or even one year of the war. The United States Marine Corps and North Vietnamese Army had fought nearly three years for control of Con Thien. Thousands of young men on both sides gave their lives in this fierce struggle for a little piece of high ground that someone back in the Pentagon decided would anchor the infamous McNamara Line. Five Medals of Honor and thirty-nine Navy Crosses awarded to those Marines attest to the ferocity of combat that occurred at and around Con Thien from 1966 to 1969.

I determined that my own personal experience as an actual eyewitness, added to my insights garnered through years of research, placed me in a unique position to tell the Con Thien story before it got lost forever in the dusty archives of some military history research facility. I was initially unsure how to portray my own participation in several critical incidents that defined the Con Thien experience. The answer soon became obvious. The focus of this story is Con Thien, not this author; therefore, I chose to refer to myself in the third person whenever describing actions that I had personally witnessed.

I first had to decide where to draw the Con Thien area of operation limits for my research. The term *Con Thien* meant more than just a hill; it was the extended area being fought over to secure that hill. One key objective of all operations conducted in that area from Prairie III in early 1967 through Hickory, Buffalo, Kingfisher, and finally Kentucky in 1968–69, was to deny enemy access through the DMZ past Con Thien. Thus, I drew a rough circle around the Con Thien firebase that extended four miles in all directions. Any combat or noteworthy incident that occurred within this four-mile radius was considered Con Thien related. For purposes of continuity and to capture the full history of the DMZ fighting as it would subsequently relate to Con Thien, I chose to include brief descriptions of Operations Hastings and Prairie, even though those actions were outside of my self-imposed four-mile limit.

This plan worked well until events that occurred after January 1968, when the A-3 strongpoint was constructed 4.3 miles east of Con Thien, midway along the firebreak bulldozed out between Con Thien and Gio Linh. Thereafter, I considered actions as directly related to Con Thien only if they occurred less than two miles away.

From day one, my fellow vets let it be known that this story had to be told and that it had to be told not just from an infantry perspective. Thus, in addition to the infantry, the reader will learn about the others who played an important role in Con Thien's story: corpsmen, tanks, engineers, artillery, amtracs, Ontos, jets, and helicopters.

One substantial task facing me was to ensure that I was reporting fact, not fiction. Veterans have a way of embellishing their stories over time, plus memories fade; therefore, I included only eyewitness accounts supported by factual data from official records. Body counts and friendly casualty totals found in battalion command chronologies, combat-after-action reports, and medal citations were often close approximations, impossible to validate accurately. Nevertheless, I included these casualty totals anyway because they are a part of the official historical record maintained by our government.

I hesitated to criticize or second-guess decisions made in the confusion of combat by exhausted Marines operating under profound stress. I gave no such consideration to General Westmoreland and Secretary McNamara, however, who must shoulder the blame for a misguided barrier plan fiasco that resulted in the death and maiming of more than ten thousand American boys.

I must apologize in advance to any former members of the 1st Battalion, 9th Marines, the "Walking Dead" (a nickname that will be understood later) who might be offended by my references to them as a "jinxed" outfit. I was there with them, and to tell the full Con Thien story, I had to reflect how attached units felt and what we believed to be true at the time. In retrospect, we all realize such a denigrating label was offensive and demoralizing to the many brave Marines who fought so courageously with 1/9.

Last, and most important, this book is intended as a testimonial to the steadfast determination, valor, and sacrifice of the U.S. Marines at Con Thien from 1966, when they first set foot in the area, until 1969, when they turned it over to the South Vietnamese to defend. It is a story of courage under fire by young Americans, mainly teenagers barely out of high school, led by career NCOs and officers from a different generation, all of them aware that most business-as-usual civilians back home were neutral at best and that some were even openly hostile to their cause. Still, they carried out orders, called their officers "sir," and did their utmost to be good Marines, even at the risk of sacrificing all of their tomorrows. *Semper Fidelis!*

Acknowledgments

Grateful acknowledgment is made to the following for permission to reprint copyrighted material: *Dear America: Letters Home from Vietnam,* edited by Bernard Edelman for the New York Vietnam Veterans Memorial Commission, published by W. W. Norton and Company and subsequently by Pocket Books. Selections from *Operation Buffalo: USMC Fight for the DMZ,* by Keith William Nolan, Novato, California: Presidio Press, © 1991, Keith William Nolan, used by permission of Presidio Press. Selections from *Honor the Warrior,* by William L. Myers, Lafayette, Louisiana: Redoubt Press, © 2000, by William L. Myers, used by permission of the author. Selections from *Ambush Valley,* by Eric Hammel, Novato, California: Presidio Press, © 1990, Eric Hammel, used by permission of the author.

I also wish to acknowledge the following individuals who went the extra mile for me on this book project: Marine Corps University Research Center Archives staff at the Quantico Marine Base, particularly Dr. Ginther and Kerry Strong, archives director; Jack Dyer, Lena Kaljot, and Fred Graboske at the Marine Corps Historical Center at the Washington Navy Yard; Col. R. B. Losee, USMC (Ret.), and Maj. Frank Southard, USMC (Ret.), for their help with the 2/9 experience at Con Thien; Brig. Gen. Frank J. Breth, USMC (Ret.), for his assistance in getting the 3/9 story told; and Quynh-Du Ton-That and Tran Nguyen for assistance with translating Vietnamese into English. The aid of Ms. Debbie McCabe, Military and Veteran Search, was a most valuable asset in finding former Marine Vietnam vets. I am indebted to the former Marines and Navy corpsmen who took a risk and shared their personal papers with me: Sal Bafumo, Jim Cool, John H. Edwards, Jack T. Hartzel, Andrew Jones, James Kaylor, and Ron "Doc" Smith. Many veterans volunteered their experiences through letters and computer e-mails, by phone, and in person. I truly appreciate their help.

Last, I am eternally grateful for the enduring help and support from my wife, Sandra, and for all of her typing and proofreading assistance over the years.

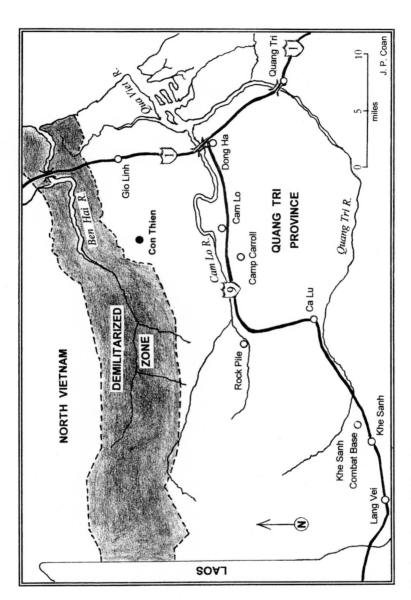

Northern Quang Tri Province

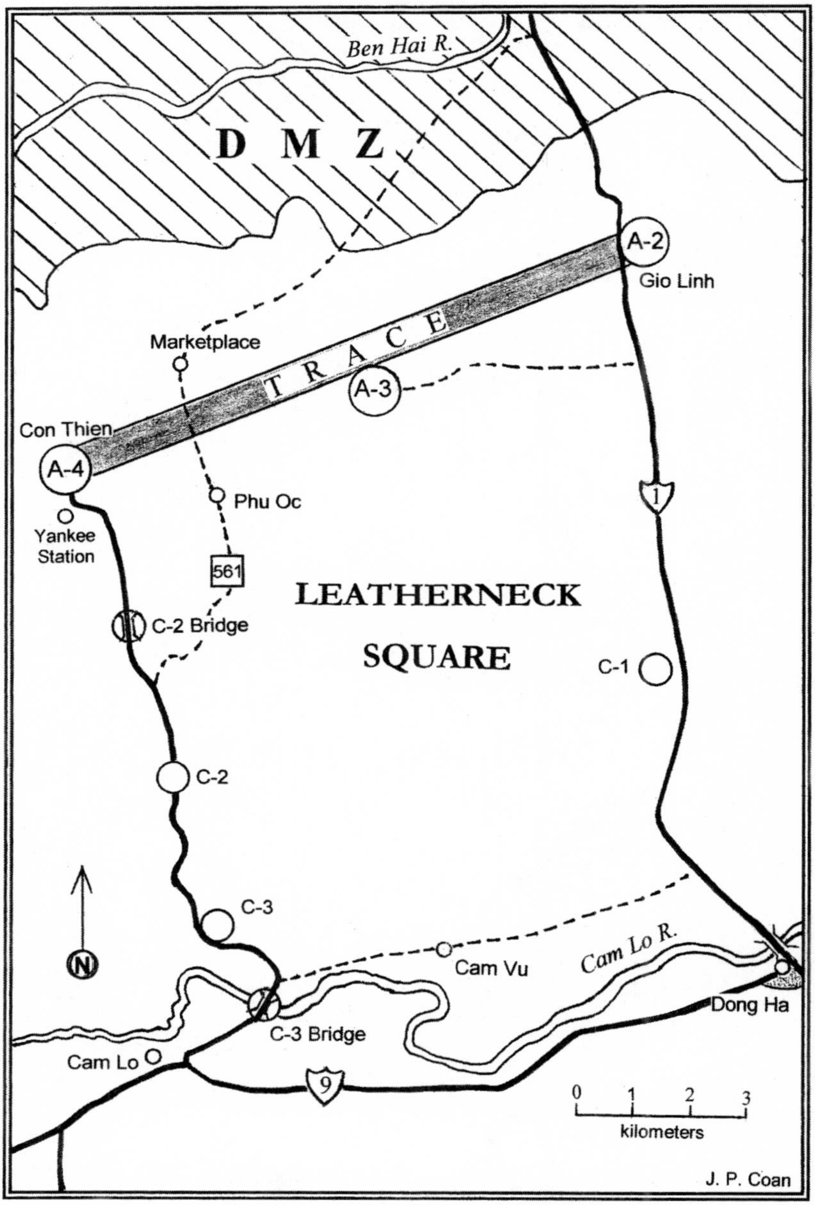
Ben Hai R.
D M Z
A-2
Gio Linh
Marketplace
T R A C E
A-3
Con Thien
A-4
1
Phu Oc
Yankee
Station
561
LEATHERNECK
SQUARE
C-2 Bridge
C-1
C-2
C-3
Cam Lo R.
Cam Vu
Dong Ha
C-3 Bridge
Cam Lo
9
0 1 2 3
kilometers
J. P. Coan

Leatherneck Square

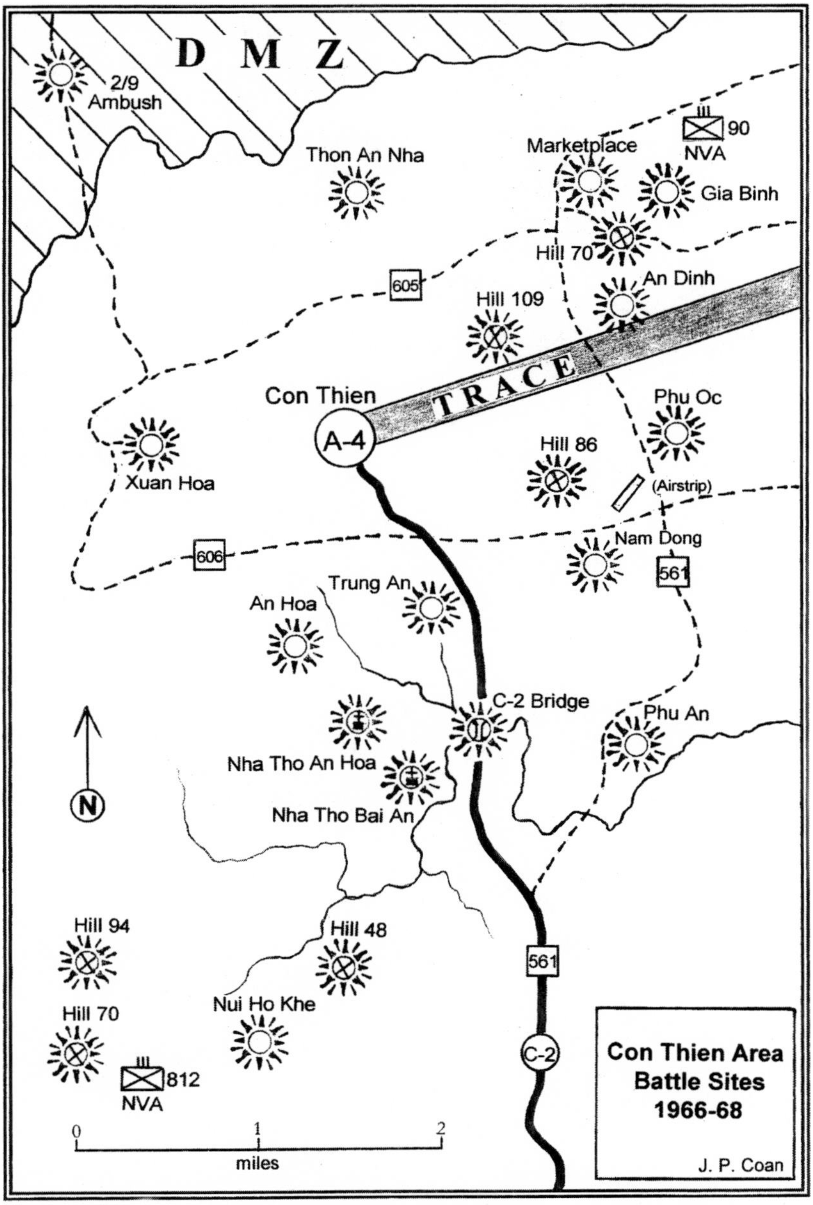
D M Z
2/9 Ambush
Thon An Nha
Marketplace
90 NVA
Gia Binh
Hill 70
An Dinh
605
Hill 109
TRACE
Con Thien
A-4
Phu Oc
Hill 86
Xuan Hoa
(Airstrip)
Nam Dong
606
561
Trung An
An Hoa
C-2 Bridge
Phu An
Nha Tho An Hoa
Nha Tho Bai An
N
Hill 94
Hill 48
561
Hill 70
Nui Ho Khe
C-2
812 NVA
Con Thien Area Battle Sites 1966-68
J. P. Coan
0
1
2
miles

Con Thien Area Battles, 1966–68

Prologue

Death at Ground Zero

Throughout much of 1967, a remote U.S. Marine firebase only two miles from the demilitarized zone (DMZ) separating North from South Vietnam captured the attention of the world's news media. Portrayed as a beleaguered, artillery-scarred outpost overlooking the fiercely contested DMZ, Con Thien was the scene of numerous savage encounters between the United States Marines and the North Vietnamese Army (NVA).

Military maps of the area indicated a prominent terrain feature 158 meters in elevation labeled "*Nui Con Thien,*" which in English means "a small mountain with heavenly beings," or simply "the hill of angels." In earlier, more peaceful times, French Catholic missionaries believed there was something angelic about that isolated hill that reached up toward the heavens. Years later, battle-hardened Marines came up with their own names for the place—"meat grinder," "hellhole," and "Dodge City." And they joked sardonically that DMZ meant "Dead Marine Zone."

In some circles, Con Thien came to symbolize America's failed military strategy of waging a high-tech war of attrition against the North Vietnamese Army. Far-removed White House and Pentagon planners devised a barrier system of firebase strongpoints (cynically labeled "McNamara's Wall") connected by a cleared swath of land sewn with barbed wire, mines, and anti-infiltration devices. This "Maginot Line" concept was supposed to deter northern invaders from moving across the demilitarized zone into South Vietnam. Con Thien was a key component of that much-maligned barrier plan and a linchpin in the defense of the entire northern border region.

Con Thien also came to represent the U.S. Marine Corps' resolve to persevere, to stand resolute against a dedicated, well-armed, and highly trained enemy. For nearly three years, the Marines never wavered in fulfilling their mission to hold that piece of high ground at all costs. But the cost was high.

Major infiltration routes traversed the demilitarized zone within sight of Con Thien, and the North Vietnamese desperately wanted to neutralize that key outpost. They brought to bear every heavy weapon they had in their arsenal to pound Con Thien's defenders. The NVA seemed to believe that, even if they could not take the base through a ground attack, they would make it untenable for the Americans to remain there.

Our government chose to consider the northern half of the DMZ inviolate territory; thus, through our own self-imposed rules of engagement, we were never authorized to move troops across the Ben Hai River. We limited ourselves to artillery and air strikes. The NVA knew they could emplace heavy artillery pieces north of the Ben Hai River and shell Allied firebases throughout the northern Quang Tri Province without fear of ground attack. The Marines at Con Thien, Gio Linh, and other bases below the DMZ, always vulnerable to enemy shelling from the DMZ, became human pawns in a bloody, stalemated war of attrition created by our own government.

July 27, 1967, was another broiling hot day around the DMZ. Gunnery Sergeant ("Gunny") R. B. English and his platoon leader, 2d Lt. John Brock, knew that their tanks badly needed preventive maintenance performed. Their platoon had been busy that entire spring and summer, operating in the heat and dust around Con Thien alongside various infantry units. First came Operations Prairie III and IV, then Hickory, Cimarron, Buffalo, and Hickory II in rapid succession. Their tank platoon had been involved in some of the heaviest fighting of the war. They had suffered extensive losses in personnel and equipment to mines, rocket-propelled grenades (RPGs), and incoming mortars, rockets, and artillery. RPG holes were patched; mine-damaged track, road wheels, and road wheel arms were repaired as well as one could expect in a combat zone. Blood and gore were hosed off the outside or wiped off the inside of the turret, and the tanks went right back out the next day.

As dusk approached, the fiery sun began to sink behind the slate gray western hills. Lieutenant Brock directed three of his fifty-two-ton, M-48A3 tanks to an open area behind the 105mm artillery battery just inside the southern perimeter minefield gate. He and Gunny English had decided to combine their platoon resources and do some much-needed preventive maintenance.

An expertly camouflaged two-man NVA forward observer (FO) team had waited patiently since dawn, concealed up in some densely leafed trees, waiting for a target of opportunity to present itself. They had to freeze, scarcely daring to breathe that morning, when a Marine patrol had passed close by their position, totally unsuspecting of their presence that close to the perimeter. But the mission of these NVA soldiers was to watch, not ambush.

From their vantage point six hundred meters southeast of Con Thien, they could look directly overhead and observe U.S. Marine Corps (USMC) helicopters making their landing approach runs from Dong Ha, following Route 561 north toward Con Thien. They noted that one helicopter landing zone (LZ) was located in a large, flat, bowl-shaped area next to a massive, mounded bunker where litter bearers entered and exited. Another LZ further to the east was where the resupply choppers, dangling fully loaded cargo nets beneath them, stirred up a whirlwind of thick dust each time they hovered over that LZ.

On the south side of the westernmost of the three small hills that made up Con Thien was another large bunker; row on row of bone white sandbags contrasted sharply with the bare, reddish brown earth around it. The FO team deduced that it was the command post (CP), the nerve center for Con Thien, but it was situated on the reverse slope of the hill, nearly impossible for them to hit.

Located at the flat base of the center hill was a battery of 105mm howitzers, each with a neatly laid, waist-high, sandbagged parapet encircling its five gun emplacements. A zigzagging, sandbagged trench line ringed the entire base perimeter just inside the minefield's inner band of concertina wire.

The NVA FO team paid particular attention to where the trucks, mechanical mules, and amphibious tractors (amtracs) traveled throughout the day. They would give away where the artillery ammunition bunkers were located. Even without their binoculars, the two North Vietnamese could see that Con Thien was a beehive of activity.

The FO team leader spotted them first—three tanks by the south gate. Excitedly, he radioed his artillery battery in the DMZ, north of the Ben Hai River, giving them the target description: "Three tanks in a group with their crews on the ground!" Key target locations at Con Thien were already preregistered, thanks to a few comrades who had months earlier infiltrated the Nung Civilian Irregular Defense Group (CIDG) and Army of the Republic of Vietnam (ARVN) detachments formerly occupying Con Thien. All he had to do was look at his chart and call it in. "Fire one marking round, I will adjust fire," he whispered confidently into his handset, struggling to keep his adrenaline-charged voice calm.

Brock's tank crewmen labored, dripping sweat in the sultry summer evening air. Most of the tankers had removed their flak jackets, and no one wore steel pot helmets. Tank crewmen wore hard-shell com-helmets, and they almost always kept them perched on their tanks when they climbed out.

A lone incoming artillery shell screamed overhead and impacted somewhere out in the southern minefield area. All the tankers paused momentarily, listening intently for the sound of any more rounds being fired. A few of the newer replacements, not savvy yet to incoming, scrambled under their tanks. But the old salts, the veterans who had survived five months of almost continuous combat, were used to periodic single rounds of incoming. They went right back to work, and the "new boots" followed their lead.

An artillery lieutenant from the nearby 105mm gun battery walked over to the tanks and said, "You tankers are all bunched up. Better spread 'em out or they're gonna nail you."

"It's almost sundown," replied the gunny. "Now is the only safe time we can do this. The gooks won't risk having our FOs spot their muzzle flashes this late in the day, sir."

"You tankers must think you're made out of steel like your tanks. . . . Well, you're not," the officer grumbled to no one in particular as he returned to his fire direction control bunker.

Then, in one terrible instant, a deadly barrage of NVA artillery bracketed the tanks. Three entire tank crews, a dozen Marines, were wiped out. The dead and dying boys, their young lives instantly blasted into oblivion, lay mangled in the dirt, appendages missing from bloody stumps, puddles of gore collecting beneath them. Killed outright were Cpl. David E. Flaningham, 22, Rockford, Illinois; Lance Cpl. Miles E. Jansen, 20, St. Paul, Minnesota; and Pvt. Raymond Ludwig, 19, Wilmington, Delaware. Corporal Manuel M. Garcia, Jr., 19, from Los Angeles, California, was standing in his tank commander's cupola, yelling something down at one of the men alongside his tank, when the incoming rounds hit. He would succumb to his grievous wounds the following day. Gunny English somehow ended up underneath his tank, riddled with shrapnel, but he would survive, as would Lieutenant Brock and the other six wounded crewmen. No one in the group escaped injury.

Lance Corporal Howard Blum, an Alpha Company flame tanker from Maryland, and two other tankers were taxied up from Dong Ha the following morning with instructions to retrieve the three tanks, still sitting in their triangle-shaped formation just inside the south gate. Blum chose the tank sitting at five o'clock and commenced loading scattered tools aboard. The grunts from the 3d Battalion, 4th Marines that manned the perimeter had not gotten to them yet, apparently leery of being seen by an FO near the zeroed-in tanks. Blum carefully skirted some large, purple red stains in the hard-packed clay soil where the lifeblood of dying young men had soaked into the earth overnight.

Blum noticed a four-foot-long pipe, five inches in diameter, lying in the dirt. He knew it was important; the pipe was used for leverage when adjusting track tension. As he picked up the pipe, stagnant blood and entrails poured out onto his boots. He recoiled in disgust, retching as he grabbed his K-bar knife and sliced through his bootlaces, kicking off his gore-soaked jungle boots. Thoroughly revolted, Lance Corporal Blum managed to drive his tank all the way back to Dong Ha barefooted. He later learned that Private Ludwig had been holding that pipe when he was ripped apart by an incoming shell blast.[1]

PART ONE

ROOTS OF CONFLICT

It is impossible for Westerners to understand the force of the people's will to resist, and to continue to resist. The struggle of the people exceeds the imagination. It has astonished us too.

> —Pham Van Dong, former prime minister
> Democratic Republic of Vietnam

1

Before the Americans Came

The Vietnamese people originated in ancient times from what is today south China. Thousands of years ago, this Mongoloid race of people was gradually pushed southward into the jungles of Indochina by the inhabitants of north China. Those early Annamites mixed with Thais and Indians along the way. They also intermarried with Indonesians. By the first millennium BC, they had created a home they called "Nam Viet," or "Land of the Southern Viet People." The western Indochina peninsula they came to call Vietnam comprised three large areas: Tonkin (north); Annam (central); and Cochin-China, the southernmost part of Vietnam.

For the first ten centuries AD, that portion of Vietnam known as Tonkin was ruled by the Chinese, but the Annamites continued to resist domination. For a thousand years, defeat after defeat did not deter them from resisting foreign assimilation. The Chinese ruled the country, but the Annamites maintained their language, customs, holidays, and religions. In the tenth century, the rebellious Annamites drove their Chinese governors out and declared their independence.

Kublai Khan sent a half-million Mongols south in 1284 to conquer the Viets. The Mongols were repulsed by a fanatical Vietnamese army made up of women, children, and elderly who took up arms and joined with their fighting men in a common stand that decimated the Mongol invaders. But their victory was a costly one, and a weakened Vietnam was again invaded by the Chinese, who conquered the Annamites in the fifteenth century. The Ming Dynasty governed ruthlessly, heavily taxing the populace and enslaving millions of men to clear forests and dig mines. A resistance movement arose, and within ten years they had evicted the Chinese once again.

The Annamites pushed south, defeating the Chams (Hindu Empire), then drove the Khmers back into what is present-day Cambodia. By the middle of the eighteenth century, all of Cochin-China had been conquered by the Viets. In 1789, Emperor Quang Trung surprised and defeated a Chinese army at Tet, while the Manchus were sleeping off the food and wine of a day's feasting. Still celebrated to this day, their victory was a major event in Vietnamese history.

Gradually, a new menace appeared on the scene: Europeans. First came the Portuguese, then the Dutch, English, and finally the French, who successfully forced out all other European competition. French colonial activity commenced in 1860, and by 1907 the entire Indochina peninsula was under its domination.

On September 22, 1940, three months after the fall of France to Nazi Germany in World War II, the Vichy French government capitulated to the Imperial Japanese Army in Vietnam. Up until mid-1945, the Japanese called the shots, gradually increasing their clout and dominance over the former French colonialists. This did not go unnoticed by the Vietnamese, who saw a former European power humbled by an Asian army. Even though the French later regained full administrative control over Indochina after the Japanese surrender that finally ended World War II, this perception weakened the French presence in the minds of the Viets.

The seeds of Vietnamese rebellion against the French, planted earlier under five years of Japanese rule, commenced to sprout under the tutelage of Ho Chi Minh. His Communist organization, the Viet Minh, grew from a poorly equipped band of resistance fighters into a modern army that vanquished their former French masters at the battle of Dien Bien Phu in 1954.

A central concept of Vietnamese military doctrine was that a weaker force handled properly could defeat a stronger one. For hundreds of years, their military teachings stipulated that the stronger force had to be worn down by protracted warfare. Vietnamese forces would employ hit-and-run tactics, morale-busting booby traps and ambushes, until the timing was right for a sudden shock offensive delivered with maximum surprise and deception.

The Vietnamese had always thought of themselves as giant killers, smarter and better organized than their enemy. Odds mattered little. They were used to beating the odds. They had repeatedly thrown back the Chinese, routed the "invincible" Mongol hordes, taken the remainder of their country from the Thais and Khmers, and soundly defeated the French. They never doubted that they would be victorious over the American "puppet government" in Saigon. "They were a people accustomed to war, a people who indeed defined themselves by war and struggle."[1]

Two Vietnams

After eight long years of struggle with the French army, the Viet Minh nationalists closed for the final kill in a remote valley in northern North Vietnam called Dien Bien Phu. A Vietnamese Communist force of fifty thousand troops commanded by General Vo Nguyen Giap surrounded and laid siege to a French force of thirteen thousand paratroopers, indigenous soldiers, and foreign mercenaries. The Viet Minh soldiers dug a maze of trenches and tunnels that surrounded Dien Bien Phu. Under Giap's orders, the Viet Minh had disassembled their Russian-made heavy artillery and antiaircraft guns and hauled them mile after tortuous mile over hundreds of miles of mountainous terrain, then put them back together in the hills surrounding Dien Bien Phu. It was a feat no one, certainly the French, believed possible.

On March 13, 1954, General Giap gave the signal to attack. For fifty-six days, the French fought back bravely, despite being outnumbered and outgunned. With their artillery emplaced on the high ground surrounding the valley, the Viet Minh pounded the once-proud French fortress to rubble. The beleaguered French garrison hung on tenaciously without relief or resupply. Finally, on May 7, 1954, with their medical supplies exhausted, and almost out of food and ammunition, the French commander radioed Hanoi for the last time: "Au revoir, mon general;

au revoir, mes comrades." Minutes later, hundreds of flag-waving Viet Minh soldiers overran the command bunker and hoisted the flag of the Democratic Republic of Vietnam. Ten thousand Frenchmen were taken prisoner. But victory had not come cheaply, as the Viet Minh suffered twenty-three thousand casualties.

Despite the loss by the French of many of their finest soldiers, the most important result of the battle was psychological. A demoralized French government faced escalating protests by a war-weary populace who demanded an end to the Indochina war. French leaders were resigned to negotiating a settlement.

In Geneva, Switzerland, a meeting called the Four Great Powers Conference was already under way to negotiate a Korea settlement. The day after the fall of Dien Bien Phu, an armistice conference convened with representatives in attendance from the United States, France, Britain, the USSR, China, North and South Vietnam, Laos, and Cambodia. Top priority was given to resolving the Vietnam situation.

Under pressure from both China and Russia to agree to the principle of partition, Vietnam's Pham Van Dong argued that the line should be drawn at the thirteenth parallel, which would have placed two-thirds of the country under Communist control. The French demanded the eighteenth parallel as the armistice line. Russia's Molotov, the wily old Bolshevik, arbitrated a last-minute solution on July 22, 1954. The line to divide North from South Vietnam was drawn at the seventeenth parallel, with a demilitarized zone five miles wide. Placing the demarcation line there won for the French the excellent port of Tourane (Da Nang), the ancient imperial capital of Hue, and the only direct land route between South Vietnam and Laos.

Another Molotov verdict allowed for elections in two years that would permit the people of Vietnam to finally determine their own fate, to live under either Ho Chi Minh and the Communists or Ngo Dinh Diem's American-backed government.

Hastily arranged and lacking formal signing by most of the participants, the Geneva Accords were primarily cease-fire agreements intended to buy time for the warring sides to disengage and withdraw their troops. The agreement was *not* a formal political settlement. The U.S. government did not join in the agreement, although it assured the other participants that the United States would not interfere with its implementation. Diem considered the provision for elections to be unfair and had no intention of carrying through with that part of the "agreement." Unforeseen at the time, the Geneva Accords laid the groundwork for many more years of bloody conflict in Vietnam.

CON THIEN

The demilitarized zone (DMZ) dividing the two Vietnams was sixty miles long and five miles wide. It started at the mouth of the Ben Hai River (Song Ben Hai) where it emptied into the South China Sea among barren expanses of sand dunes and occasional swamps. Inland a few miles from the coast, the lowland terrain becomes increasingly verdant and alive with rice fields, orchards, and occasional hamlets bordering the river. Another ten miles inland, the relatively flat ground gives way to rolling hills that soon merge into rugged limestone mountains covered in thickets of bamboo and fields of elephant grass, with triple-canopy jungle forests that could conceal an army. The Ben Hai shaped the northern and southern boundaries of the demilitarized zone, following the broad river's winding course west for thirty miles until it subdivided into narrow tributaries in the western mountains. Mapmakers followed the seventeenth parallel in a straight line the remaining distance across Vietnam to the border with Laos.

South Vietnam's northernmost province, Quang Tri, butted up against the demilitarized zone. Located in Gio Linh District, two miles south of the DMZ border and a dozen miles inland from the coast, was a place called Con Thien. Topographic military maps from that era by the U.S. Army Corps of Engineers indicate a surveyed horizontal control point 158 meters in elevation. Printed above it is the Vietnamese name for the hill, *Nui Con Thien,* which translates into English as "the hill of angels." The French army had appreciated its observation potential and built a concrete fort on the highest of three knolls on this small mountain rising up from the surrounding lowland countryside.

Con Thien's origin is volcanic. The soil covering the area is red laterite clay, rich in iron, and good for growing coffee, tea, black peppers, pineapple, and bananas.

This area of Vietnam experiences blowtorch hot days from May to August. Then, almost overnight, the weather changes into the fall/winter monsoon that blows in from the northeast, bringing typhoons that often produce flooding. Another facet of the monsoon is called the *crachin*, from the French word for "drizzle," and it consists of a light, steady, cold rain that lasts for two and three days at a time, accompanied by thick, blanketing fog. When not raining, the monsoon sky is often gloomily overcast. Even though temperatures rarely drop below forty-five degrees in the winter, the constantly damp chill in the air permeates one's very being. Northern I Corps is the rainiest place in Vietnam, averaging well over one hundred inches annually.[2]

Two dozen hamlets encircled the hill called Con Thien, but it was almost as if this high ground were off limits to the civilian inhabitants because the closest hamlet was a half-mile away. Connected by age-old cart trails and footpaths, this area of Gio Linh District was predominantly Catholic, as evidenced by the unusually large numbers of Catholic churches. Within two miles of Con Thien were six churches and cathedrals; some were elegant structures of concrete and brick and three stories tall.

It was not unusual to find areas of Vietnam with concentrations of Catholics. Prior to Geneva, numerous Catholic enclaves had supported the French and done battle with the Viet Minh. Those north of the demilitarized zone had good reason to be fearful after the armistice. When given the opportunity in 1954, an estimated six hundred thousand Catholics fled North Vietnam and resettled in the south.

Village life around Con Thien was typical of the Annamite people who had inhabited this area for many generations. In such a rural, agrarian society, the village was their cultural and political anchor. An old Vietnamese adage stated that "the authority of the emperor stops at the village gates."[3] Their daily lives revolved around working in the rice fields and tending to their animals and crops of vegetables, tea, and even tobacco. French-schooled missionaries and clergy played a central role in the village, often becoming community leaders and teachers. Attendance at Mass and other church activities was a fundamental facet of their lives.

Each village comprised a number of hamlets delineated by hedgerows and bushes. Individual homes were separated by small gardens and yards, often fenced to keep out their neighbor's animals. Most houses had thatched roofs with brick or bamboo walls and mud floors. Construction was rudimentary but comfortable. The people were not prosperous, but they were able to get by, feed their families, and have a little something left over. Surplus vegetables, potatoes, pigs, and chickens were taken to market and sold.

Cam Lo was a major trade center for merchants bearing salt, fish sauce, dried fish, ironware, silverware, and copperware in exchange for items brought from the Con Thien area such as rice, poultry, beeswax, tree bark spices, fabric, and cloth.

On a typical spring day, sun-bronzed boys sat astride water buffaloes out in the lush fields surrounded by tree- and shrub-crowned hedgerows. Barefooted children kicked up dust as they chased each other across paddy dikes and irrigation ditches. Wiry women dressed in black silk pajamas and white conical sun hats trotted off to market with their straw baskets of goods hanging from both ends of a pole riding on their calloused shoulders.

Life in the Con Thien area, though harsh at times, was enduring. Generation after generation had lived there and grown old, cognizant of their ancestors preceding them, secure in the belief that their children and grandchildren would continue to thrive on this peaceful land forever.

2

The Generals

Confuse the enemy. Keep him in the dark about your intentions. Sometimes what seems a victory isn't really a victory, and sometimes a defeat isn't really a defeat.

  —General Vo Nguyen Giap

AMERICA'S WAR

The national elections agreed to at Geneva in 1954 did not happen two years later, which was predictable. Diem believed it to be an unfair setup and had no intention of following through. Ho Chi Minh's revolutionary cadre then commenced organizing and carrying out a resistance movement against the Diem government they called "America's puppet state."[1]

In November of 1963, President Diem was assassinated in a coup, and an ongoing power struggle made the South Vietnam government unstable. The Viet Cong (VC), supported by their Communist brethren in North Vietnam, took advantage of that chronic instability and flexed their muscles, attacking South Vietnamese army (Army of the Republic of Vietnam, ARVN) units and American installations throughout South Vietnam. Riddled with corruption and nepotism, the South Vietnamese army was rendered ineffective. Newly elected president Lyndon B. Johnson wasted little time mobilizing support for a war against the Communists, despite strong reservations expressed by influential insiders such as the U.S. ambassador to South Vietnam, retired U.S. Army general Maxwell Taylor.

The U.S. 3d Marine Division was based on the island of Okinawa when elements of the 9th Marine Regiment landed at Da Nang, Republic of Vietnam, on March 8, 1965. They came ostensibly to provide security for the U.S. airbase at Da Nang. By July 1965, all three of the division's regiments (3d, 4th, and 9th) were operating in the southern and middle provinces of the I Corps zone.

For the remainder of the year and through the first half of 1966, units of the 3d Marine Division successfully fought the Viet Cong and forced them out of the Da Nang and Hue-Phu Bai tactical areas of responsibility (TAORs). General Westmoreland became concerned that the NVA/VC were maneuvering for an attack on the ancient imperial capital of Hue in Thua Thien Province. In April of 1966, Military Assistance Command, Vietnam (MACV) reinforced Westmoreland's suspicions with information that the NVA 324B Division was digging in above the DMZ and was likely to move south soon.

Westmoreland insisted the Marines move a battalion to Khe Sanh and conduct an operation to search for the NVA. He had plans for that former U.S. Army Special Forces camp. It lay astride Route 9, the major east-west corridor that he hoped to employ for his eventual incursion into Laos, where he could sever the NVA's supply lifeline called the Ho Chi Minh Trail. Although the Marines found no enemy forces at Khe Sanh, intelligence continued to indicate the NVA were up to something big in northern Quang Tri Province.

The Marines were doubtful, but they sent out reconnaissance (recon) teams anyway to find out whether the enemy was really hiding in the mountains south of the DMZ. They soon struck pay dirt. From July 4 to July 13, fourteen of eighteen Marine recon patrols in that area had to be lifted out because of enemy contact. An intelligence coup of the first order also occurred the first week in July, when two NVA soldiers from the 812th Regiment, 324B Division were captured near the Marine outpost north of Route 9 called the Rockpile. They divulged to interrogators that their mission was to liberate Quang Tri Province and then block ARVN relief forces coming up from the south.

GENERAL GIAP

North Vietnam's military commander was fifty-four-year-old Vo Nguyen Giap, architect of the French defeat at Dien Bien Phu in 1954. He was not exactly a polished son of the Vietnamese aristocracy. After having been imprisoned for three years as a teenager for participation in anti-French demonstrations, he earned a degree in law and political economics from the University of Hanoi and married the daughter of a dean. Giap barely escaped with his life in 1940, going into exile over the Chinese border to avoid an anti-Communist crackdown. His wife, however, was captured and sentenced to fifteen years; she died in prison. Giap's sister went to the guillotine.

General Giap was considered a brilliant field general in some circles, but others tended not to see him in that same light, noting that he was relatively unschooled in modern military methods and somewhat indifferent to his own losses on the battlefield. Noted military historian Eric Hammel was skeptical of Giap's reputation as a brilliant tactician. He gave as an example Giap's rigidity in thinking and trial-and-error solutions. This rigidness in thought and action carried down to field-unit command where quick adjustments due to unanticipated battlefield contingencies were often lacking.[2]

One talent Giap possessed that no one could dispute was his meticulous planning ability. He was able to set up tactical moves to carry out secret strategies unfolding years into the future. But his paramount virtue was an intensely burning revolutionary fervor. He had the gift of oratory to instill this spirit in young people who carried his message of revolution against the French and Japanese. From the earliest beginnings, Giap's cadres were taught that their war of liberation was a lifelong struggle, and it would only end with victory or death.

General Giap was once asked, "How long would you have gone on fighting against the United States?" He replied instantly, "Another twenty years, maybe a hundred years, as long as it took to win, regardless of cost."[3]

Giap was a plump man, small in stature, who, in the opinion of Western observers, lacked a general's commanding presence. Still, his forceful manner of speaking could and did surprise those who might have underestimated him. A reporter once remarked that his eyes glowed brightly with intelligence, even craftiness. The French had a nickname for General Giap: "Volcano under the Snow."[4]

Both Ho Chi Minh and Vo Nguyen Giap recognized that Vietnam's greatest strength as a people was its long history of fanatical perseverance against numerically superior forces. Ho Chi Minh once told a French officer: "You can kill ten of my men for every one I kill of yours, but even at those odds, you will lose and I will win."[5] Giap was of the same mind-set. He had witnessed the collapse of France's will to continue their eight-year-long war when the citizenry at home ran out of patience with the cost in lives and treasury. Dien Bien Phu was the final nail in the coffin. Giap had the utmost confidence that the same course of action would prevail against the Americans. His own casualties were of little concern to him. What mattered was the perception of American citizens. If he inflicted exorbitant numbers of casualties on American troops, then its citizenry would also conclude that their war against him was not worth the cost in lives and treasury, and they would sooner or later demand an end. To accomplish this, he must first learn how best to counter the Americans and their allies with their overwhelming numbers of airplanes and artillery and unending materiel resources.

GENERAL WESTMORELAND

General William Childs Westmoreland had been preparing his entire life for his role as the commander of American military forces in Vietnam. It had been an advantaged life. Son of a successful South Carolina banker, he was accustomed to having servants in the Westmoreland household. He excelled at polo as a young lieutenant at Fort Sill, and he wore a pink coat on Sundays to pursue the hounds with senior officers. His wedding to an eighteen-year-old Cornell University freshman was so noteworthy it made the front cover of *Cosmopolitan*. As first captain of his class at the U.S. Military Academy at West Point, he was in rather elite company with Robert E. Lee, John J. Pershing, and Douglas MacArthur.

Westmoreland's military bearing, his firm, assured sense of control called "command presence," was always present, whether he was playing tennis or entertaining dignitaries. It fared well for him as an artillery officer in World War II, where he won battle ribbons in North Africa, Sicily, France, and Germany. He later commanded an elite paratrooper regiment, instructed at the Command and General Staff College, and took management courses at Harvard. As the youngest major general in the U.S. Army, he made the perfect model for a post–World War II American general, excelling as a combat leader, manager, and executive. He was square-jawed, ramrod straight, and church going—a recruiting poster of a general.

When General Westmoreland assumed command of American forces in Vietnam in June 1964, he soon became convinced that more troops were necessary to prevent the collapse of South Vietnam's corrupt and dysfunctional government. He oversaw America's gradual buildup of men and materiel. Finally, with an army of a half-million soldiers, sailors, airmen, and Marines, he was convinced that his superior manpower and weaponry would crush the Viet Cong and their North Vietnamese masters and that he would soon be assuming the highly coveted post of General of the Army.

WESTY VERSUS THE MARINES

Lieutenant General Victor Krulak was a fifty-year-old bantamweight Marine who had won the Navy Cross fighting the Japanese in World War II. Because of his diminutive stature, five feet five inches in height, his fellow midshipmen at Annapolis nicknamed him Brute. His service in Vietnam dated back to 1962 when he accompanied Secretary of Defense Robert McNamara on his first visit to Vietnam.

During his almost thirty years of service, General Krulak had acquired the reputation, deservedly so, as an innovative genius. While still a lieutenant serving with the 4th Marines at Shanghai, China, in 1937, he observed a Japanese landing craft with a square bow and retractable ramp. He recognized this as the best solution to the Marine Corps' problem of landing troops under fire quickly and with minimum numbers of casualties sustained while exiting the landing craft. Thanks to his perseverance, which had to overcome traditional Navy reluctance toward innovation (especially from green Marine lieutenants), he finally got the ear of General Holland M. Smith, who adopted his idea. The retractable bow-ramp changed the old Higgins boat into the LCVP, our primary landing craft of World War II.

In 1948, when Brute was a lieutenant colonel at the Marine Corps Schools at Quantico, Virginia, he foresaw the helicopter as a future rapid insertion device for assault troops. He sketched out the first helicopter assault maneuver in history, with Marines being ferried off of an aircraft carrier by old Sikorsky helicopters to a landing site near Camp Lejeune, North Carolina.

America's war-fighting doctrine since 1965 emphasized attrition. In theory, our war machine would decimate the Viet Cong guerillas and kill sufficient numbers of NVA faster than the Hanoi government could send more men down the Ho Chi Minh Trail to replace their losses. Ultimately, in theory, the Vietnamese Communists would lose their collective will to fight and would withdraw their forces. Thus was born the "body count" as our way of measuring success on the battlefield. Westmoreland embraced this concept, envisioning a sky full of B-52 bombers and fighter planes, battalions of artillery, and masses of armor and infantry searching out and destroying the elusive enemy.

Lieutenant General Krulak was outspoken in his belief that such a war of attrition would fail "because attrition was the enemy's game." He advocated a strategy of pacification programs that would win the loyalty of the Vietnamese peasantry through social and economic reform. He considered the Vietnamese people the prize, because without them the clandestine guerillas and Communist regulars would be denied the food, taxes, and supplies they needed to survive. "The real war is among the people, and not among the mountains," said Krulak. His superior in Hawaii, Admiral Ulysses S. Grant Sharp, agreed with Krulak that this was the logical way to conduct the war in Vietnam, and the commandant of the Marine Corps, General Wallace M. Greene Jr., also supported Krulak's thesis.[6]

As a theater commander, Brute Krulak did not directly command Marines on the ground in Vietnam, but he convinced someone who did—Lew Walt. Major General Lewis "Big Lew" W. Walt was a legendary Marine Corps general awarded the Navy Cross twice in World War II, once at Cape Gloucester and again at Peleliu. The son of a Kansas rancher, he was a former football lineman who had worked his way through Colorado State University before joining the Marines.

Krulak shared his belief with Lew Walt of the efficacy of his pacification program ideas. Big Lew and Brute saw eye to eye on this concept, and they had the commandant's backing to boot.

County Fair and Golden Fleece were just a few of the innovative ideas implemented into successful civic action programs under Walt's leadership. County Fair was a basic cordon-and-search operation conducted in a village, but with a twist. While South Vietnamese government officials screened the village residents, checking ID cards and looking for possible Viet Cong, tents were set up nearby to provide the villagers with medical care, food and candy treats, and sweet drinks. The Golden Fleece program was established to prevent the villagers' rice crops from ending up in the hands of the Viet Cong.

Lew Walt soon picked up another star and became a lieutenant general. His initial efforts were directed at ridding the I Corps coastal and inland hamlets of their VC cadre. That objective was soon realized, and he then began infiltrating Marine rifle squads into Vietnamese Popular Force (PF) platoons in the villages, calling them Combined Action Platoons. Initially, they worked out well, but General Westmoreland was not satisfied. He was looking for body count, and the pacification programs did not produce the large numbers of enemy dead that Westmoreland and Washington sought to prove that America was winning. He believed those pacification programs should be run primarily by the ARVN and that the Marines should be out in force scouring the countryside for the enemy.

The impasse was settled by none other than General Giap. When he commenced moving his 324B Division across the DMZ in mid-1966, Westmoreland flew for the bait. He ordered Walt to find the NVA and engage them. Walt moved eight thousand Marines north to the DMZ area and established a main base at Dong Ha.

Giap's plan had worked perfectly. He was drawing the Marines away from their successful pacification programs along the heavily populated coastal areas into the sparsely populated mountains below the DMZ in northern I Corps, an ideal battlefield for the NVA. They would have shorter lines of supply by being in proximity to the DMZ, plus they would have the advantage of a nearby sanctuary for retreating units to refit and replenish their manpower losses. Giap would also be able to employ his vaunted artillery against the Marines within easy range of his big guns north of the Ben Hai River.[7]

Despite Lieutenant General Krulak's intense lobbying efforts to keep pacification as the primary focus, Admiral Sharp, commander in chief in the Pacific, did an about-face and bowed to pressure from the Joint Chiefs to support Westmoreland. The general was popular with the press and the public, and the president had confidence in him. He was *Time*'s Man of the Year in 1966. Caught in the middle between Krulak and Westmoreland, General Walt chose to give up his struggle with Westmoreland. To continue would have meant being relieved, and his premature departure would have incited even more internal dissent at the highest levels of command.

In October, Walt moved the 3d Marine Division north from Da Nang. Under orders from Westmoreland to establish strongpoints along the DMZ, Walt chose Gio Linh and Con Thien, the two former French forts just below the DMZ, and Cam Lo, Camp Carroll, the Rockpile, and Ca Lu along Route 9 leading to Khe Sanh. Westmoreland was growing ever more confident. He announced as he sent an Army division to take over the TAOR left vacant by Walt in I Corps, "We'll just go on bleeding them until Hanoi wakes up to the fact that they have bled their country to the point of national disaster for generations."[8] General Westmoreland had the ideal battlefield on which to wage his war of attrition . . . and so did General Giap.

3

McNamara's Wall

With these bastards, you'd have to build the zone all the way to India, and it would take the whole Marine Corps and half the Army to guard it. . . . Even then they'd probably burrow under it.
—Anonymous Marine Corps Officer

Infiltration into South Vietnam had been steadily increasing, from two battalions per month in late 1964 to an estimated fifteen battalions by early 1966. Through triple-canopied jungles in Laos coursed the Ho Chi Minh Trail, the primary people-mover path southward, but an increasing number of northerners were detected moving across the demilitarized zone through Quang Tri Province into South Vietnam.

In early 1966, a Harvard Law School professor, Roger Fisher, proposed the idea of a barrier to halt infiltration across the DMZ. Secretary of Defense Robert Strange McNamara agreed with the idea, envisioning a sophisticated approach to slowing the steady stream of infiltrators from the north. The idea was not new. As far back as the Indochina war, generals fantasized building a barrier across the narrow neck of Vietnam to separate warring factions.

Robert McNamara came to the Pentagon with an impressive business background. Shortly after his selection as president of Ford Motor Company in 1960, President Kennedy asked him to be his secretary of defense. McNamara had come to worship quantitative analysis and imposed these methods on the military. Military problems could be broken down into statistical factors, and those numbers would provide viable solutions. Like-minded analysts in the Pentagon with their MBAs were called his "whiz kids." A staunch supporter of McNamara was General Westmoreland, a graduate of Harvard Business School.

In March 1966, McNamara asked the Joint Chiefs of Staff to consider a barrier to halt infiltration across the DMZ. The Joint Chiefs formulated a plan and forwarded it to Admiral U. S. Grant Sharp, commander-in-chief of all American forces in the Pacific region (CINCPAC). The plan called for a barbed wire and mine barrier backed by reaction forces to run from the South China Sea below the DMZ through the panhandle of Laos to Thailand. To put it mildly, Admiral Sharp was less than enthusiastic about such a plan. He saw numerous flaws in the concept: enormous construction costs in dollars and manpower; a heavy logistical burden; an unduly large number of troops required to both secure and man such a system; and, most critically, the loss of maneuverability to friendly forces.

That should have been the end of it, but McNamara would not let it die. In September of that year, the JASON Group, a university consortium (think tank) conducting contract work for the Pentagon, proposed a barrier plan similar to McNamara's, only with air support. This barrier would consist of large numbers of antipersonnel mines, button bomblets, and acoustic intrusion detectors. Again, CINCPAC was unsupportive, arguing that such a plan would not be feasible.

Secretary of Defense McNamara, undeterred by his military brass detractors, appointed a three-star Army general, Alfred D. Starbird, to head up Task Force 728. On September 15, 1966, McNamara informed General Starbird that his top-secret task force's mission was "to provide an infiltration interdiction system to stop (or at a minimum substantially reduce) the flow of men and supplies from North to South Vietnam. It is . . . a matter of highest priority. You will have the system installed and in operation by September 15, 1967." Thus was born Project Practice Nine.[1]

General Westmoreland favored such a plan because he believed a barrier would eliminate the need for further troop reinforcements in I Corps, but he recommended to McNamara that it be toned down initially. Rather than an actual fence, he proposed clearing a strip of land below the DMZ supported by strongpoints. Observation posts and roving patrols would report any enemy attempting to cross the strip, and supporting arms would be brought to bear. Reaction forces would be stationed behind the barrier to respond to any breaches.

Westmoreland ordered the III Marine Amphibious Force (III MAF) to come up with a plan for implementation. A recalcitrant General Walt's only guidance to the 3d Marine Division commander, General Kyle, was to begin the report with a clear statement that III MAF disagreed with the barrier idea and preferred to retain the mobile defense tactics then currently being deployed. Walt added in a cover letter that "such a barrier was not worth the time and effort that would be put into it."[2]

Despite strong objections from the Marines, on November 26, 1966, General Westmoreland forwarded his own report to Washington recommending the barrier. It would lie south of the DMZ and extend inland from the coast for thirty kilometers to Dong Ha Mountain, be six hundred to one thousand meters wide, with watchtowers, electronic sensors, radar, minefields, and wire obstacles. Extensive on-call, preplanned artillery concentrations and aerial surveillance would back up the barrier. Ultimately, it would traverse all the way to the Laotian border. In addition, there were plans for civilian relocation out of the affected areas and establishment of bases for artillery and armor support.

Evidently, in a flight of fancy, Westmoreland even envisioned Route 9 becoming an international highway, running from the South China Sea across Laos to Thailand. He named it "Pan Sea Pike." A more-grounded Westmoreland, however, informed McNamara he was not supportive of a rigid deadline of September 15, 1967, for completion of the barrier.

In March 1967, McNamara ordered General Starbird to secure sufficient building materials, sensors, and surveillance devices to complete the first section of the Strong Point Obstacle System (SPOS) to be installed between Con Thien and Gio Linh. The Pentagon then put out contracts for fifty thousand miles of barbed wire and five million steel fence posts. The total cost for the entire system was estimated at between three to five billion dollars.[3]

In early April, Marines from the 11th Engineer Battalion quietly commenced clearing the strip from Gio Linh to Con Thien labeled

"Trace" on III MAF planning maps.[4] As the story goes, a staffer at III MAF, Maj. Donald Fulham, was "doodling" on a topographic map overlay and drew a line connecting two points of high ground on the map. After he had departed for the day, a colonel saw it, assumed it was the result of an in-depth study of the SPOS, and passed it on up through channels. According to Marine Corps lore, that was the origin of the Trace. Initially, most Marines working on it called it the "firebreak." Some later referred to it as the "death strip."[5]

Later that month, General Walt got the official bad news: Westmoreland indicated that the Marines would be tasked with building the SPOS using their own personnel. Walt was clearly disturbed. He knew that, unless he received additional resources to install and maintain the Practice Nine SPOS, he could no longer conduct adequate offensive operations in northern I Corps. Not only did III MAF and CINCPAC believe the barrier plan to be a flagrant waste of men and materiel, but Walt had to insure that the boondoggle was carried out—and with his own thinly spread resources.

General Walt relinquished his III MAF command to General Cushman on June 1, 1967. As the former deputy to Walt, Cushman was fully cognizant of the difficulty in attempting to construct the barrier system and defend it as well. A top-secret security breach forced the renaming of Project Practice Nine to Project Illinois City on June 13, but that name was changed a month later to Project Dyemarker.

The SPOS plan called for six eventual strongpoints to be given an "A" (Alpha) designation. Initially, Alpha 1 near the South China Sea would be occupied by ARVN soldiers. Alpha 2 would be at Gio Linh. Con Thien would become Alpha 4. Alphas 3, 5, and 6 would not come along until later. These strongpoints were backed by fire support bases located several kilometers to the south and given a "C" (Charlie) designation. The Marines were to build C-2 halfway between Cam Lo (C-3) and Con Thien (A-4). A dirt road identified on their maps as Route 561 would become the main supply route (MSR) between them. The four Marine positions at Con Thien, Gio Linh, Dong Ha, and Cam Lo formed a rough square; thus the name "Leatherneck Square" would assume a permanent place in Marine Corps' lore.

When McNamara removed the wraps and publicly announced his barrier plan in September 1967, the press quickly labeled it "McNamara's Line." As disgruntled Marines and others let their displeasure with the barrier plan be known, the name "McNamara's Wall" surfaced and became popular. The parallels in history were all too obvious: France's Maginot Line debacle in World War II and the Great Wall of China came instantly to mind. Unbeknown to McNamara and Westmoreland, the two great walls of Dong Hoi and Truong Duc that ran across Vietnam twenty-five miles north of the DMZ were built in the seventeenth century by the Trung Dynasty to keep out the invading Trinh emperors. They were not successful either.[6] Military historian and author Eric Hammel best summed it up when he wrote, "The barrier is one of history's best examples of what can occur when too much logic, too much intellect, and not enough experience are applied to the art of war."[7]

Westmoreland and McNamara had created a set-piece strategy that robbed the Marines of their mobility and valuable resources for bringing the war to the NVA. Strongpoints required troops to protect them from attack, thus reducing the numbers available for maneuver. Because our government leaders had deemed invasion of North Vietnam politically unfeasible, they chose to respect the demilitarized zone as a viable entity. Thus, we would build a barrier to keep the enemy from coming south.

This barrier concept would dominate American military strategy in northern I Corps for years, long after both McNamara and Westmoreland had left the scene. The Marines on the ground carrying out this misguided strategy within reach of Giap's big guns north of the Ben Hai would have to bear the brunt of it, bleeding and dying to ensure its success. The cornerstone of this barrier plan, Con Thien, would become the focus of protracted attention on both sides of the DMZ.

But why Con Thien? Many years before the Americans arrived, the French army had recognized the superior observation capabilities of that isolated little hill named Con Thien, rising up incongruously out of the surrounding countryside at the center of a gently sloping laterite clay plain. The French built a concrete and steel fort on that high ground. Eventually, it became an ARVN outpost, and the South Vietnamese placed numerous deadly mines on the northern slopes of the three hillocks that made up Con Thien. On February 20, 1967, Camp Con Thien was established by Captain Chamberlain's U.S. Army Special Forces Detachment A-110. Navy Mobile Construction Battalion 4 built roads, bunkers, and connecting trenches, cleared a landing zone, and put in barbed-wire obstacles.[8] It was now officially an American base.

U.S. Army 175mm guns, which fired a 147-pound projectile twenty miles, were emplaced at both Con Thien and Gio Linh to interdict enemy territory far into North Vietnam. This threat was more than the NVA could tolerate, and they retaliated by shelling those bases in February and March of 1967. The big guns were eventually pulled back to the Marine base at Camp Carroll, south of Route 9. The 1st Battalion, 4th Marine Regiment assumed responsibility for firebase security that spring, and the Marines were there to stay.

Project Practice Nine planners had identified Hill 158, Nui Con Thien, as a key strongpoint position. Other than being a high place surrounded by relatively flat terrain, there had to be something unique about the location that architects of the barrier plan realized, because one could never fully appreciate the importance of that position while flying overhead or by looking at a map.

The answer was readily obvious to anyone who actually set foot on the high ground at Con Thien. The view in all directions was magnificent. To the north, one could observe the terrain above the Ben Hai River for miles into North Vietnam itself. Looking east down the bulldozed-bare, fairway-like Trace, one had an unobstructed view of the firebase at Gio Linh six miles away. A few miles beyond Gio Linh, American warships could be seen cruising off the coast in the South China Sea. West of Con Thien was the open rolling piedmont that stretched for six miles before the ground rose gradually into hills and mountains. And, most crucial to the Marines, Con Thien overlooked the sprawling northern I Corps logistical complex at Dong Ha ten miles to the south, as well as Cam Lo and Camp Carroll along Route 9. Con Thien was an artillery forward observer's paradise, and that is the foremost reason why "the hill of angels" had to be held, even if the inane barrier plan had never been devised.

PART TWO

The DMZ War Unfolds

Soldiers of Vietnam, we go forward,
Ceaselessly for the people's cause we struggle,
Hastening to the battlefield!
Forward! All together advancing!
Our Vietnam is strong eternal.

  —*Doan Quan Viet-Nam Di* (March to the Front)

4

Nguyen of the North versus PFC Jones

The typical soldier in General Giap's North Vietnamese Army was an eighteen-year-old draftee. Draft age eligibility ranged from sixteen to forty-five, but those extreme age limits were rarely if ever tapped. Unlike his American counterpart, who signed up for a set number of years of service, Nguyen of the North was in it for the duration. He came from a rural, agrarian background and had little formal education. And he was small in stature by Western standards—five feet three inches tall and less than 120 pounds on average.

After induction, he underwent a three-month basic training and indoctrination course. The political indoctrination he received had as much emphasis as did tactics and weaponry. He and his fellow recruits were told every day: "The soldier's supreme duty is to fight on the side of the revolution. The revolution has given independence to one half of the country, but there still remains the other half . . . in the South [that] live in slavery."[1] Their political cadre drummed it into them constantly that they were fighting to expel the American imperialists and reunify their country.

Recruits selected to make the arduous journey south soon learned that they were ill prepared for the brutal reality facing them. They had not been trained in jungle survival; that would have to be on-the-job training. And even if they had been told about the American planes overhead, nothing could prepare them for the horror of a B-52 strike raining death down on them. Once they had completed their perilous journey down the Ho Chi Minh Trail or crossed the DMZ, they encountered villagers not happy to see them, and they often faced their ARVN cousins on the battlefield.

Recruits were often told by their veteran cadre that Americans killed and tortured prisoners and that American soldiers were cannibals who ate children. Many of the naive, uneducated recruits believed what they heard. The message received was that a horrible fate worse than death awaited them if they ever surrendered to the Americans. The indoctrination worked well, because few NVA soldiers ever gave themselves up unless wounded and unable to continue fighting.

The core unit was a three-man cell. Cell members shared food, cared for each other when ill, and fought together. If wounded they could depend on the other members to get them medical care, or if killed the others would retrieve their body. Three or four cells made up a squad led by a sergeant. Discipline was maintained by *kiem thao* sessions of criticism or self-criticism. Each day, soldiers had their performance and motivation discussed and critiqued both by peers and by leaders. Afterward, they acknowledged their own faults and weaknesses and promised to strive for improvement in those areas. *Kiem thao* was seen by all ranks as beneficial to their morale and discipline.

The basic uniform worn in combat was a green lightweight cotton shirt and trousers with large pockets from waist to thigh. Sometimes uniforms were dark blue, brown, or khaki. In addition to their trousers, belts held web harnesses and straps to carry ammo packets, canteens, weapons, and medical packets. Footgear was usually a pair of ankle-high, green canvas boots resembling tennis shoes. Occasionally, they wore sandals called *binh tri thien*, which were made from old tire treads held on the foot with rubber strips or cloth cords. Headgear was commonly a floppy cotton cloth "bush" hat or a sun helmet of pressed cardboard or cork covered with tan, brown, or green cloth. Many helmets had a five-pointed gold star emblem on a red background edged with a gold wreath of rice stalks. The helmet was no protection against shrapnel or bullets, but it did keep the rain and sun off.

The backpack made of dark green canvas cloth was actually preferred by some U.S. troops because it was lightweight and dried out quickly when wet. NVA equipped with the AK-47 assault rifle wore a vest with three large pockets in the middle to carry thirty-round magazines for their weapon. Extra pockets carried loose ammo and cleaning gear. Soldiers equipped with the SKS carbine wore an ammo pouch with ten pockets to carry ten-round clips. Even though each soldier modified or adapted gear to fit his needs for carrying grenades or special equipment, they all carried an entrenching tool with a six-inch-wide blade on a twenty-inch-long handle, essential for survival against allied artillery and air strikes.

The basic NVA infantry weapon was the Soviet 7.62mm assault rifle AK-47, which weighed 10.58 pounds loaded and fired a thirty-round magazine. It could be fired both on automatic or semiautomatic and had an effective range of three hundred to four hundred meters. The inventor of this assault rifle (Kalashnikov) intended it to function despite adverse combat situations such as rain, mud, dust, and snow without misfiring or jamming. His weapon was legendary for its ability to remain operable despite dirt, rust, or corrosion. The other rifle frequently issued was the semiautomatic SKS 7.62mm carbine (Simonov), which carried a ten-round clip and was accurate to four hundred meters. Officers, political cadre, and senior noncommissioned officers (NCOs) carried pistols, often of varied origin.

Infantry units had a 7.62mm light machine gun RPD or its Chinese Communist (Chicom) brother, Type 56. It had a 100-round drum mounted below the gun and a 150-rounds-per-minute rate of fire with an effective range of eight hundred meters. The NVA also possessed a larger, wheel-mounted 12.7mm machine gun that was employed primarily as an antiaircraft weapon. Their mortars varied from 60mm to 160mm, although the 60mm and 82mm were the most common. The 60mm mortar had a maximum range of one mile, and the 82mm could reach out three thousand meters.

One particularly effective weapon was the rocket-propelled grenade (models RPG-2 and RPG-7) employed against armor as well as personnel and other types of vehicles. The 40mm high-explosive antitank (HEAT) missile could penetrate six to ten inches of armor. The RPG-2 had an effective range of one hundred meters. The RPG-7, with its funnel-shaped rear tube opening, had an effective range of five hundred meters. Both had a gas escape vent on the right side of the weapon that would prove fatal to a left-handed shooter. The RPG proved to be a deadly accurate weapon against every type of armored vehicle the Allies used in Vietnam.

"Born in the North to Die in the South"

NVA soldiers were well armed, but could they fight? A misconception existed in America during the first year of the war that VC/NVA soldiers were neither well trained nor skilled enough to be a serious match for the Americans, and we tended to underestimate them. But that attitude changed, even to the point that some American soldiers stopped referring to their diminutive foe as "Charlie" and started calling him "Mr. Charles."

General Westmoreland wrote in his autobiography: "The North Vietnamese were wily, tenacious, persevering, and courageous to the point of fanaticism. . . . Many captured soldiers had tattoos bearing the slogan, 'Born in the North to die in the South.'"[2] James H. Webb Jr., former Marine platoon and company commander, best-selling author, and former secretary of the Navy, stated: "The NVA had great fire discipline and good marksmanship skills. They built excellent fortifications and incredibly impressive trenches and emplacements."[3]

Carlton Sherwood, who was a scout-sniper with Golf Company, 2d Battalion, 4th Marine Regiment in 1967–68, later became a successful journalist and Pulitzer Prize winner. He recalled an operation he went out on near Highway 1 in Quang Tri Province. His unit came across an NVA base camp complex with "barracks, cookhouses, latrines, bomb shelters, a hospital, everything picture perfect and spotless, but totally invisible from only a few yards away. . . . It was as if a master carpenter had designed and built everything to exactly the same proportions."[4]

Keith William Nolan, the prolific writer of numerous books on the Vietnam War, described the NVA light infantry as "highly indoctrinated, highly motivated, and well trained in the basic warrior skills, while their commanders, veterans of victories against the French . . . had learned through trial and error how to fight the 3d Marine Division. These lessons had become doctrine because there was no rotation in the North Vietnamese Army to short-circuit the institutional memory."[5]

PFC JONES, USMC

What about the U.S. Marines who served in Vietnam? The typical nineteen-year-old Marine was a volunteer (although later in the war some men were drafted into the Corps). He was better educated, larger, stronger, and blessed with superior firepower from his artillery, armor, and air support. He was well nourished, and his chances of surviving a battlefield wound were excellent due to rapid evacuation via helicopter ambulance (medevac) to a field hospital. He could also look forward to a definite rotation date to go home after his thirteen-month tour of duty; plus, he could leave the war behind for a week at some time during his tour of duty and travel on a Pentagon-sponsored flight to such exotic places as Bangkok, Singapore, Hong Kong, Sydney, or Hawaii.

Every Marine knew that, with each passing day, week, and month, he was getting closer to a ticket home. Nguyen of the North had nothing like that to look forward to. His only ticket home was a serious wound that disabled him so he could no longer fight the war. And he knew that, if killed in the south, he would be buried there (if his body was recovered by his comrades), not with his ancestors in the north.

The NVA soldier was prepared to sacrifice his life for a cause he totally believed in. The U.S. Marines thought less and less of their cause with each passing year of the war, but they fought for each other, ready to lay down their young lives for their buddies and for the honor of the Corps. Former secretary of the Navy James H. Webb Jr. also wrote:

> When I remember those days and the very young men who spent them with me, I am continually amazed, for these were mostly recent civilians barely out of high school, called up from the cities and the farms to do their year in Hell and then return. Visions haunt me every day, not of the nightmares of war, but of the steady consistency with which my Marines faced their responsibilities, and of how uncomplaining most of them were in the face of constant danger. The salty, battle-hardened 20-year-olds teaching green 19-year-olds the intricate lessons of that hostile battlefield. The unerring skill of the young squad leaders as we moved

through unfamiliar villages and weed-choked trails in the black of night. The quick certainty with which they moved when coming under enemy fire. Their sudden tenderness when a fellow Marine was wounded and needed help. Their willingness to risk their lives to save other Marines in peril. . . . I am alive today because of their quiet, unaffected heroism.[6]

The "old breed" Marines from World War II and Korea would have been proud to serve alongside Vietnam's PFC Jones, USMC. The fighting along the DMZ was some of the most difficult of the Vietnam War, and the Marines acquitted themselves well under incredibly challenging circumstances. Unfortunately, the American people and their government were sharply divided over the ultimate purpose and goals of this unpopular war. The longer the war dragged on, the louder and more vehement became the civilian voices of protest. Despite the riots and antiwar street marches occurring back home, PFC Jones and his young warrior comrades would conduct themselves courageously and professionally in the best tradition of the Corps.

5

Setting the Stage

ACT ONE: OPERATION HASTINGS

In the early morning hours of May 19, 1966, units of the North Vietnamese Army attacked two isolated ARVN outposts located just south of the DMZ, Con Thien and Gio Linh. Both outposts sustained heavy losses, but the ARVN defenders fought back bravely and managed to hold their ground. One captured NVA soldier informed his captors that he was part of the NVA 324B Division. Initially, no general alarm was sounded by this revelation. The Allies, slow to comprehend the significance of those two seemingly isolated events, were focused on events occurring elsewhere in South Vietnam.

By the time spring rolled into summer, intelligence was flowing into MACV and III MAF headquarters that the North Vietnamese 324B Division had infiltrated across the demilitarized zone and was lurking in the rugged hills of northern Quang Tri Province. Almost every Marine reconnaissance team that had gone out looking for the NVA the first week in July 1966 had found them, a lot of them.

The Allies were puzzled. What was General Giap up to? Why would he infiltrate and conceal a full division in a remote portion of Quang Tri Province below the DMZ, then make it obvious to the Allies where they were hiding?

Giap had a twofold purpose: first, create a *diversion* to draw the Marines away from the heavily populated coastal areas and their successful pacification programs into the hills and mountains, and then, to further his aim of *attrition,* inflict heavy casualties on the Marines. By luring the Marines into the rugged, jungle-covered terrain of the western mountains, Giap's all but invisible forces could wait in hiding, choosing the most advantageous time and place for them to do battle.

Westmoreland and MACV perceived at the time that Giap must be staging his forces for an eventual attack on Quang Tri and Hue in an effort to capture the two northernmost provinces of South Vietnam—a profoundly serious threat. The Americans took the bait and went on the offensive.

The 3d Marine Division assistant commander, Brigadier General Lowell B. English, met with the 1st ARVN Division's commanders to devise a joint USMC/ARVN operation called Hastings/Lam Son-289. The purpose was to counter the threat presented by the 324B Division in northern Quang Tri Province. English was headquartered at Cam Lo and would have four U.S. Marine infantry battalions, plus a battalion of artillery, to deploy. He chose to locate his logistical base at Dong Ha, where Highway 1 and Route 9 intersected. A large airfield located near Dong Ha was another determining factor.

The III MAF had learned that fifteen hundred men from the 90th NVA Regiment, one of three regiments from the 324B Division, had secreted themselves in the Song Ngan Valley, a hilly, lushly vegetated area located six miles northwest of the village of Cam Lo and six miles southwest of Con Thien. The Marines believed that the 324B Division command post was located at Hill 208, which offered a commanding view of the entire valley. A placid river named the Song Ngan (*Song* means river in Vietnamese) ran through the forested valley in a north-easterly direction directly toward Con Thien, then abruptly altered course a mile from there and meandered northward, ultimately flowing into the Ben Hai River.

The NVA main body appeared to be located in a triangle formed by Cam Lo, the Song Ngan, and an oddly formed geological anomaly aptly named the Rockpile. The Marines had earlier established an outpost atop that jagged, solitary little mountain situated just north of Route 9.

General English directed two of his battalions into the Song Ngan Valley in a helicopter assault on July 15, 1966. Thick black clouds roiled skyward from preliminary air strikes by A-4 Skyhawks and F4-B Phantom jets that pounded suspected NVA locations with napalm and 250-pound bombs. Then a heavy artillery bombardment shelled the area.

The 2d Battalion, 4th Marines, led by Lt. Col. Arnold E. Bench, proudly carried their nickname acquired during World War II, the "Magnificent Bastards." Bench landed his 2/4 unopposed three miles southwest of Con Thien and moved out in the stifling midsummer heat and humidity toward the Song Ngan Valley. (The designation "2/4" refers to the fact that Marine infantry and artillery battalions are commonly designated by a numeral representing the battalion number, a slash, and then a numeral representing the regiment. Thus, the 2d Battalion, 4th Marines is written 2/4 and pronounced "two four." The 2d Battalion's Company K [Kilo Company] would be K/2/4.) Lt. Col. Sumner A. Vale, commander of the 3d Battalion, 4th Marines, directed his battalion to land at LZ Crow, located in the middle of the valley between Hills 200 and 208. The mission assigned 3/4 was to set up a blocking force to trap any NVA fleeing from Bench's advancing battalion.

The first three waves of 3/4 Marines landed at LZ Crow in divisions of four dual-rotor CH-46A Sea Knight helicopters per wave. They disembarked their Marines with no resistance. While attempting to land the fourth wave, EP-155, flown by 1st Lt. Joe Roberts, dropped in almost on top of Major Gilbert from HMM-265. Losing power and lift, Lieutenant Roberts steered sharply to the right to avoid a collision. He almost succeeded, but his rotor blades ripped into a tree by the LZ, causing him to crash-land. Then, two more CH-46 helicopters from HMM-164 overshot the LZ while trying desperately to avoid some Marines on the ground, and their aft rotor blades intermeshed, bringing them crashing down in a cloud of dust and whirring rotor blades. Two Marines had been mangled and killed by the deadly rotor blades, and seven were injured—an ominous precursor of events to follow.

HMM-164 lost another CH-46 later that morning, hit by heavy ground fire from Hill 208. It managed to land northwest of Cam Lo but damaged its main landing gear in a crash landing. Of the twenty helicopters that started the operation, four were totally disabled, sitting immobile on the ground.

Later in the day, a flight of eight more CH-46s headed northwest from Dong Ha to LZ Crow with ammunition, water, and reinforcements from the 2d Battalion, 1st Marines. As they commenced their approach run at fifteen hundred feet, EP-171, flown by Capt. Thomas C. McAllister and 1st Lt. George C. Richey, was hit by 12.7mm heavy machine-gun fire, rupturing a pressurized fuel line. Its highly flammable jet fuel ignited, filling the helicopter with acrid smoke and searing flames. Horrified onlookers on the ground and in flight watched the doomed helicopter belching forth orange fire and smoke as the smoke-blinded pilot desperately attempted to land. Two Marines on board jumped out, one in flames, but they were too high up to have any chance at survival. EP-171 rolled over and exploded on impact. By some miracle, Captain McAllister and copilot Richey escaped with burns and minor injuries. Their door gunner, Sgt. Gary Lucus, survived despite third-degree burns received when he went back into the burning wreckage to attempt without success to save his trapped crew chief, Sgt. Robert Telfer. All twelve passengers from E/2/1 were killed. Henceforth, the Song Ngan Valley would always be known to the Marines as "Helicopter Valley."

Fierce fighting raged for the next several days over the area two miles south of the DMZ bordered by Hills 200, 208, and 362. On July 18, while providing security to engineers blowing up ammo and destroying the downed helicopters, K/3/4 was pinned down by a murderous mortar barrage. Then, several battalions of NVA blowing bugles and waving flags launched a massive attack.

First Platoon under Staff Sgt. John J. McGinty III became isolated from the rest of the company. In a four-hour battle in which his thirty-two-man platoon held off wave after wave of attacking NVA, McGinty was all over the battlefield, caring for his wounded and calling in artillery and air strikes. His Medal of Honor citation reads in part, "In one bitter assault, two of the squads became separated from the remainder of the platoon. . . . McGinty charged through intense automatic weapons and mortar fire to their position. Finding twenty men wounded and the Medical Corpsman killed, he quickly reloaded ammunition magazines and weapons for the wounded men and directed their fire upon the enemy . . . who left an estimated 500 bodies on the battlefield."

McGinty's company commander, Captain Robert J. Modrezewski, who would also be awarded the Medal of Honor for his inspired leadership and courage under fire, observed NVA attempting to remove ammunition from the downed helicopters and called for air strikes. One fiery napalm drop caught two dozen enemy around one helicopter, and then a second napalm run incinerated another group exposed in the middle of the LZ.

Marine casualties were heavy. Company K had incurred losses of fourteen dead and forty-nine wounded. McGinty's platoon alone had suffered losses of eight men killed and fourteen wounded. Hundreds of NVA had fallen on the battlefield that day, but official records only reported an estimated 138 dead.

Operation Hastings/Lam Son-289 officially closed on August 3. It was the largest and most costly operation of the war to that point, involving eight thousand Marines and three thousand ARVN. Both sides suffered heavy casualties in the brutal, close-quarters jungle fighting. The Marines had losses of 126 men killed and 448 wounded, and the ARVN had losses of 21 killed and 40 wounded. Enemy losses were more than seven hundred killed and seventeen taken prisoner.[1]

Operation Hastings was the opening round in the DMZ war that would enmesh the Marines in northern I Corps in large unit battles with the North Vietnamese Army for the next three years. General Giap had found a way to divert the Marines' focus away from the successful pacification programs they had developed in the heavily populated coastal areas. His new strategy would draw the Marines inland to battlefields more to his liking, close to his logistics centers and within range of his vaunted artillery secreted in the DMZ. Then, Giap could inflict greater casualties on the Americans and improve his chances of winning what would become a long, ugly war of mutual attrition. Undeterred by his own battlefield losses, he was certain that American citizens would soon grow disenchanted with the war's cost in lives and treasury and demand the withdrawal of American forces, just as the French had done in 1954 after their defeat at Dien Bien Phu.

OPERATION PRAIRIE

The defeated 324B Division pulled back into the DMZ at the end of July to regroup, but exactly where they retired was unknown. Intelligence reports indicated that two more NVA divisions, the 304th and 341st, were moving into the area immediately north of the DMZ. The North Vietnamese obviously had a plan, and the Marines had to take action to thwart their next move. The Marine Corps response would be called Operation Prairie.

On August 8, the NVA struck again. A team of recon Marines was surrounded and attacked by a large enemy force north of the Rockpile. In an all-night battle in which the outcome was often in doubt, the small band of recon Marines, reinforced after dark by a relief force from E/2/4, put up a valiant fight and turned back their attackers.

This heated action convinced the commanding officer (CO) of the 4th Marine Regiment, Colonel Alexander Cereghino, that the NVA had returned to northern Quang Tri Province in strength. In the first week in September, Colonel Cereghino decided to expand his TAOR to include the Con Thien area. New intelligence data revealed that a battalion of NVA from the 90th Regiment of the 324B Division had taken up residence in that vicinity.

By late summer of 1966, Con Thien was still an isolated DMZ outpost manned by a handful of ARVN soldiers and their U.S. Army advisors. Antipersonnel mines sewn liberally into its grassy slopes and a few strands of barbed wire were all that protected the South Vietnamese garrison if another ground attack came. Large numbers of North Vietnamese soldiers were regularly infiltrating across the DMZ, often within sight of Con Thien, but the reluctant ARVN were not inclined to leave their stronghold and interdict them.

Several factors made the area around Con Thien an ideal harbor site for the NVA. Densely wooded areas concealed their movements during daylight hours, few local civilians remained in the area to give them away, and several creeks provided a constant water source. Thickly overgrown hedgerows, many centuries old, bordered open rice paddy fields and created ideal ambush settings.

Lieutenant Colonel Bench was ordered to send his battalion north from Cam Lo on September 7 and to ferret out the NVA hiding amid the heavily vegetated hedgerow country surrounding Con Thien. Company H departed on foot, accompanied by a platoon of tanks from Company C, 3d Tank Battalion, while the remainder of 2/4 was ferried into landing zones around Con Thien by MAG-16 helicopters.

The following day, lead elements of 2/4 were advancing cautiously near Hill 109, less than one thousand meters northeast of the ARVN outpost at Con Thien, when they stumbled on an extensive enemy bunker complex that was so well camouflaged as to be nearly invisible to approaching troops. Sporadic small-arms fire greeted the Marines, who responded with a smothering barrage of return fire. After a fiercely contested three-hour firefight, the enemy fire subsided suddenly, and the NVA melted away, carrying their casualties with them and relinquishing the battlefield to the Marines. It was not a particularly newsworthy encounter, as DMZ firefights went, but five young Americans had forfeited their lives that day in what was the first of many bloody battles to be fought in the killing fields of Con Thien.

On September 9, Companies E and F of 2/4 entered the reportedly abandoned village of Gia Binh, another "klick" (kilometer) northeast of Hill 109 and only a mile south of the DMZ. They were greeted with neatly lettered signs posted in English that read "Death to the Americans" and "We Will Fight to the Last Man." What the alerted Marines had discovered was a completely fortified village skillfully interlaced with an elaborate system of interlocking firing positions and trenches, some extending almost up into the DMZ itself.

Cautiously they searched, mindful at all times of each footstep, eyes constantly scanning the ground for booby trap trip wires. Suddenly, streams of green tracer bullets tore into the Marines, spitting forth from numerous concealed enemy bunkers. The shocked infantrymen (called "grunts") went to ground but quickly recovered and returned fire. A torrent of Marine red tracers enveloped the enemy positions. Then, the five fifty-two-ton USMC tanks rolled into action, attacking straight ahead in juggernaut fashion, crushing many enemy bunkers. They fired point-blank into the remaining NVA positions, their machine guns chattering and 90mm cannons blasting away with cannister and high-explosive (HE) rounds.

When it was all over, twenty NVA bodies were counted in the smoking, destroyed remnants of Gia Binh and some nearby fortified hamlets.

The 2d Battalion, 4th Marines, its ranks depleted by months of near-continuous fighting, was pulled back to Dong Ha for a much-deserved rest. Another unit would have to finish the job of clearing the NVA out of the Con Thien area.

General Walt had confirmation that elements of the 90th NVA Regiment were south of the DMZ in eastern Quang Tri Province. He and his staff then sought and obtained permission to use the Battalion Landing Team (BLT), 1st Battalion, 26th Marines in a second search-and-clear operation in the Con Thien/Gio Linh areas of Operation Prairie. At 7:00 a.m. on September 15, the operation named Deckhouse IV commenced with Company A making an unopposed landing from the USS *Vancouver* in tracked landing vehicles called LVTs. The remainder of the battalion was ferried via helicopter to an LZ near Gio Linh, six miles inland.

For the next several days, the battalion made only light contact, advancing slowly inland toward Con Thien. Tangles of thickets amid dense woodland undergrowth made the going slow. On September 19, Company D came under heavy small-arms and automatic weapons fire just south of the village of Gia Binh, where, ten days earlier, Lieutenant Colonel Bench's battalion had discovered an extensive bunker–trench line system.

The lead squad, barely able to discern each other in the thick brush, had triggered a murderous L-shaped ambush. The remainder of Delta Company was immediately deployed to break up the ambush and rescue their pinned-down comrades. Twenty-two-year-old Navy corpsman Gollie Leo Grant, determined to save the lives of his wounded Marines, rushed forward into the kill zone. A bullet struck him as he aided one downed man. He crawled forward and was hit again as he applied a battle dressing to a second Marine. Despite his painful wounds, he bravely headed over to tend to another casualty when a third bullet found its mark and ended his life.

Delta Company pulled its casualties back out of harm's way and saturated the area with artillery. As the last friendly salvo detonated with a ground-shaking blast, the Marines attacked the village again, only to be met with an even heavier volume of fire from their determined foe. Delta's company commander ordered a second withdrawal and called in air strikes, producing several violent, secondary explosions. Enemy return fire ceased, and Delta was then able to enter the still-smoking, demolished village, but no enemy soldiers were visible, dead or alive. The dumbfounded Marines could not understand how the enemy had seemingly disappeared.

No sooner did their attached combat engineers set about placing charges to destroy the remaining fortifications than they began ducking heavy automatic weapons fire. The NVA had launched a counterattack. This time, the Marines pulled back several hundred meters and called in more air strikes plus naval gunfire. One jet unloaded his tumbling napalm canisters directly onto a trench line, sending up a chorus from hell as the searing conflagration engulfed an entire platoon of NVA.

When the NVA finally capitulated and broke contact before nightfall, Company D scoured the area, counting fifty-three NVA dead and estimating another forty-three probable. They found an immense network of tunnels and camouflaged trenches within the village complex, which explained how the enemy could seemingly vanish and then suddenly reappear in force elsewhere.

The NVA had outfoxed the Marines, but in the end, the Americans had too many trump cards—heavy artillery, air strikes, and naval gunfire—in their fire support arsenal. The NVA's stubborn tenacity in the face of devastating U.S. firepower had caused them to suffer heavy losses. Navy Hospitalman Gollie L. Grant, who sacrificed his young life to save his wounded Marines, would receive the Navy Cross for his heroism.

The sweep by BLT 1/26 continued north of Con Thien the following day without making any more contact. The NVA had vacated the area. Company B was less than one thousand meters below the southern boundary of the DMZ when they discovered a field hospital within a massive tunnel complex. One main branch was twelve feet wide by forty-five feet long; it contained five cases of medical supplies. Local civilians informed the Marines that a large group of NVA had been in the area recently, accompanied by Chinese advisors, but they had pulled out, whereabouts unknown.

BLT 1/26 Marines claimed to have killed more than 200 of the enemy during Deckhouse IV, and their own losses were 36 killed and 203 wounded in the ten-day search-and-clear operation around Gio Linh and Con Thien. No one at III MAF harbored any illusions that the operation had permanently eliminated the North Vietnamese from the area; it only forced them to withdraw. Giap's forces would return later when conditions were right.

Unbeknown to the combatants on both sides, the September 1966 fighting around Con Thien would become a template for several more years of bloodletting below the DMZ. Both 2/4 and BLT 1/26 had encountered extensive, expertly camouflaged fortifications in the Con Thien area that had always been the hallmark of General Giap's forces. The Gia Binh clashes had proved the NVA to be a worthy, determined foe who intended to remain in that area no matter what the cost.

Meanwhile, ARVN commanders at Con Thien seemed to be hiding their collective heads in the sand, apparently adhering to the credo that if they did not interfere with their North Vietnamese cousins building tunnel complexes and fortified trench lines less than a mile away, then the NVA would not bother them. But nearby civilians saw the handwriting on the wall, and gradually, one family after another, they packed up all of their belongings and herded their animals away from their ancestral homes and farms, hoping to avoid the holocaust certain to befall the Con Thien area.

Heavy fighting continued in the western sector of the Prairie operation area. Another regiment of the 324B Division had moved into the mountains north of the Rockpile at the Nui Cay Tre ridgeline in order to protect a key NVA infiltration route. The Marines knew they had to evict the NVA from their jungle-covered encampments on Hills 400 and 484 and that it would be a tough, bloody battle. The attack commenced on September 22 with the 3d Battalion, 4th Marines using machetes to hack their way through thick jungle undergrowth as they climbed steadily toward their objective, Hill 400. For four days, the determined Marines fought for every contested yard.

The Marines continued to lose helicopters. On September 25, a UH-34D helicopter from HMM-161, Marine Air Group 16, had just picked up a medevac casualty and was climbing for altitude when an explosion blasted the helicopter out of the sky, killing all five men aboard. The pilot, Capt. Philip A. Ducat, had called for a "Sav-A-Plane" (a request to the artillery fire control center for clearance to fly through their zone), but he was apparently too late because his craft was struck by an artillery shell in flight. That was the only proven incident in the entire war where our own artillery fire knocked a helicopter out of the sky.[2]

The resolute Marines from 3/4 conquered Hill 400 and were methodically inching their way over to Hill 484, which was three thousand meters to the west. The highly revered CO of K/3/4, Capt. James J. "JJ" Carroll (whose heroic leadership in the attack on Hill 400 would earn him the Navy Cross) arranged for direct tank fire the following day on Hill 484. He believed the flatter trajectory of the 90mm tank guns would be more effective than the high-angle fire of the supporting howitzers.

In one of those terrible "friendly fire" tragedies that invariably happen in war, a mislaid tank round impacted on Hill 400 instead of 484, killing Captain Carroll and two other Marines beside him. In his honor, an artillery firebase off Route 9 by Cam Lo would later be named Camp Carroll. Hill 484 was declared completely secured on October 5. Nui Cay Tre would thereafter be known as "Mutter's Ridge," named after the radio call sign of 3/4's new commander, Lt. Col. William J. Masterpool.

Enemy contact subsided sharply after the battle for Mutter's Ridge. By November, intelligence sources reported that the badly hurt 324B Division had retired north of the DMZ to wait out the winter monsoon season and regroup. Prairie would continue as an area of operation into 1967.

Operation Prairie had successfully prevented the NVA from establishing a major base south of the DMZ, but the cost to the Marines was high: 239 killed and 1,200 wounded. Enemy losses were put at 1,397 killed, plus 1,713 probable, and 27 captured.[3]

THE 9TH MARINE REGIMENT ENTERS THE ARENA

The 9th Marines had distinguished themselves in numerous battles long before Vietnam. Reactivated during World War II, the regiment fought valiantly against the Japanese in the northern Solomons, Bougainville, Guam, and Iwo Jima. Permanently stationed on Okinawa since the mid-1950s, the regiment had provided the first infantry combat units that President Lyndon B. Johnson sent to Vietnam.

On March 5, 1965, BLT 3/9 of the 9th Marine Expeditionary Brigade waded ashore unopposed north of Da Nang with the mission of providing security for the air base there. On June 17, BLT 3/9 was relieved of its airfield security duties by the 1st Battalion, 9th Marines, and BLT 3/9 sailed for a brief stay on Okinawa. A month later, the 2d Battalion, 9th Marines landed at Da Nang and was deployed south of the airfield. By this time, the other two regiments of the 3d Marine Division, 3d Marines and 4th Marines, had joined the 9th Marines, and the entire division was committed to the war effort in Vietnam.

When the 9th Marines first entered the eastern DMZ area early in 1967, carrying with them the distinction of having been the first Marine infantry unit to set foot on Vietnamese soil, they considered themselves the most experienced fighting unit in Vietnam. But few veterans of the early guerilla-fighting days around Da Nang were still present within their ranks.

Despite their two years of experience battling the enemy in Vietnam, the 9th Marines were newcomers to the DMZ style of warfare. They had many lessons to learn about fighting their resolute, highly disciplined, and well-armed new foe from the north. Existing war-fighting doctrine for dealing with Communist Viet Cong guerillas—peasant farmers by day, stealthy warriors by night—differed substantially when engaging in combat with North Vietnamese regulars, who could call in deadly accurate artillery fire support from the DMZ. The first unit from the 9th Marines to enter the DMZ arena and be bloodied in the killing fields of Con Thien would be 1/9.

❖

Operation Prairie became Prairie II on February 1, 1967, with the same mission of reconnaissance and screening actions. The Allies offered an olive branch during Tet, the lunar New Year festival so important to the Vietnamese people. From February 8 to 12, the U.S. halted all bombing north of the DMZ. The NVA showed their appreciation for that amicable gesture by using the respite to bring in tons of supplies and beef up their depleted divisions. Alarmed at the magnitude of their buildup, the assistant division commander of the 3d Marine Division, Brigadier General Michael Ryan, obtained clearance all the way up to the Pentagon and the Oval Office to fire artillery into the DMZ on February 25. Prior to this date, the NVA had enjoyed a safe haven in the DMZ.

In the mission called Operation Highrise, the Marines had four artillery firebases between Highway 1 and the Rockpile firing into the DMZ with twelve U.S. Army 175mm guns, eight Marine 155mm howitzers, and eighteen 105mm howitzers. For the next two days, they fired thousands of rounds. The NVA appeared stunned at first, and then they retaliated. First Gio Linh and then Con Thien came under heavy mortar, rocket, and artillery attack on February 27, with Gio Linh getting the worst of it. From that date forward, the Marine bases at Con Thien and Gio Linh (and later Dong Ha) became ground zero for deadly enemy shelling attacks.

March 5, 1967, was another bleak, gray, overcast day, chilled by an intermittent, cold rain—the tail end of a long monsoon season. The 1st Battalion, 9th Marines, led by Maj. James L. Day, was running a sweep through the abandoned hamlets of Thon An Hoa and Thon Trung An, both about one kilometer south of Con Thien. Once thriving agrarian communities, they had both been abandoned the previous fall. The arrival of war at their doorsteps had caused a mass exodus of civilians from the Con Thien area. Even the birds had taken flight elsewhere.

The telltale pop of an occasional sniper round kept the Marines on edge, especially in light of what had happened the previous day. While 1/9 had been advancing on Thon An Hoa from the west, two claymore mine booby traps were triggered, killing two men and wounding seven.

Seconds later, a sniper shot the platoon commander of Delta-1, 2d Lt. Robert N. Clark, killing him instantly with a bullet through the chest.

The NVA were close by. Telltale signs, fresh footprints in the wet earth, gave them away. Some Marines even claimed they could smell the enemy. Suddenly, a flurry of gunfire arose out of Company C's area. Several Marines had exchanged hurried shots with a group of fleeing NVA. One brief firefight followed another as the Marines pursued their elusive enemy. Company C's casualties kept mounting until, by afternoon, they had lost five killed and fifteen wounded in the hit-and-run skirmishes. Then Capt. William Keys's Delta Company came under fire. Keys's hard-charging Marines overran a bunker complex, killing seven NVA who had been defending an underground field hospital. Eight of their dead and wounded comrades were found lying inside.

By 4:30 p.m., Delta Company had arrived at a hedgerow-lined area near the deserted hamlet of Phu An, twenty-five hundred meters southeast of Con Thien. Dense groves of trees amid thick stands of bamboo and nearly impenetrable shrubbery limited visibility in places to only a few yards. Delta's weary grunts were foot-dragging tired, looking forward to finding a place to remove their packs and dig in for the night. The socked-in weather conditions had prevented bringing in medevacs, so the grunts were forced to lug their dead and wounded along with them, which only compounded their exhaustion.

An estimated forty to fifty NVA, hiding in well-camouflaged bunkers in a hedgerow, suddenly opened fire in a deadly ambush. A torrent of small-arms and automatic fire quickly enveloped Delta. Sixty "mike-mike" mortars (Marine Corps slang for 60mm mortars) and a 57mm recoilless rifle further pinned down the dirt-hugging Marines, desperately attempting to find targets to return fire.

The previous evening, a section of U.S. Army M-42 Dusters armed with dual-mounted 40mm guns and accompanied by a lone USMC M-48A3 tank had shown up unexpectedly at the 1/9 CP like manna from heaven. Not ones to look a gift horse in the mouth, battalion staff had welcomed them aboard. Now, their added firepower turned the tide. Concentrated fire from the Dusters plus the Marine tank firing cannister rounds shredded the camouflaged enemy positions, driving off the attackers, but not before four grunts and one tanker had been killed. Another fourteen Delta Marines were wounded.

As the grunts commenced loading their dead and wounded on the lone tank, more shots rang out. The tank was drawing enemy sniper fire like a magnet. All the wounded would have to either walk out or be carried. Former platoon sergeant Archie Echols of Delta-1 remembered: "It was late, and the rain had set in. I was called up to identify the dead. One of the sights I still see today is those four bodies under ponchos and the puddles red with their blood."[4]

Phu An was completely deserted the following day when 1/9 swept through again. The battalion was then ordered to return by truck to Dong Ha, their mission completed. They might search, and they might destroy, but the Marines did not occupy a place once they had taken it—manpower resources were too scarce. Phu An would continue to be 1/9's nemesis. The NVA would return, construct nearly invisible camouflaged positions, and then wait in ambush for those 1/9 Marines every time they swept through Phu An that spring.

Operation Prairie II ended on March 18. The Marines claimed 694 confirmed dead NVA and another 480 probable and had 93 of their own dead and 483 wounded. Deadly NVA mortar fire was to blame for one-third of the Marines killed and two-thirds of those wounded.

THE SECOND BATTLE AT PHU AN

Prairie III commenced March 19 with the same units carrying out the same missions as they had on Prairie and Prairie II. The Marines had in place five infantry battalions and three ARVN airborne battalions, plus one ARVN infantry battalion. As the winter monsoon season began to wane, Allied intelligence reports indicated that the NVA were once again moving large units south across the DMZ into northern Quang Tri Province.

On March 24, 1/9(-) (the minus sign indicating that the battalion was minus one or more of its normally assigned four companies) was conducting another sweep north toward the deserted hamlet of Phu An. This time, Companies A and C had the lead; Delta brought up the rear.

Bravo Company was elsewhere, about to be decimated at the Khe Sanh "Hill Fights." The Marines were alert, all senses fine-tuned. They did not have to be reminded that Delta Company had walked into a bloody ambush there three weeks earlier. As was the norm for an attack on an objective where enemy presence was suspected, the battalion prepped the hamlet area with artillery. Low clouds and inclement weather pre-empted air strikes.

What the doomed grunts in Alpha Company's point squad could not know was that they were heading into a massive NVA bunker complex with interconnecting trenches and mutually supporting automatic weapons positions. The newly dug fortifications were laid out with one branch running north to south and the other east to west, both branches about five hundred meters long. The khaki-clad regulars manning the complex were 120 in number, all wearing pith helmets, and they were well schooled in how to spring an ambush. The advancing Alpha point squad was only twenty-five meters from a skillfully camouflaged, bush- and tree-crowned hedgerow position when, on command, the NVA opened fire.

The shocked Marines embraced the ground where they dropped, unable to return fire or move out of harm's way. Then, round after round of 60mm mortar fire rained down on those pinned down as well as the rest of the platoon attempting to assault through the ambush kill zone. It was a hellish scene of total chaos and confusion.

Sergeant Walter K. Singleton, Alpha Company's supply sergeant, rushed forward to help when he heard that his company had suffered numerous casualties. He braved the firestorm of snapping bullets and impacting mortar rounds to rescue several wounded men lying helpless in the kill zone. He then grabbed an M-60 machine gun and fearlessly assaulted the hedgerow positions, delivering devastating fire where the greatest volume of enemy fire originated. He killed eight of the enemy and drove the others out before he fell mortally wounded. He would be awarded the Medal of Honor posthumously for his gallantry.

After two hours of furious battle, Company A was ordered to fall back so that artillery and air strikes could be brought in. But the NVA had another wicked surprise in store. As Alpha attempted to break contact and pull back, the NVA fired preregistered mortar barrages on all routes of egress they had anticipated the Marines would use. When it was all over, Alpha Company had incurred losses of seven men killed and twenty-seven wounded, including the company commander, Capt. Donald Festa, and three out of four platoon commanders. It could have been much worse had it not been for the valor and personal sacrifice of Sergeant Singleton and many others.

The night passed without any further action. All the wounded were located and medevaced out to Dong Ha Med. At first light on March 25, more air strikes were brought in on the still-smoking megacomplex. With the support of tanks, the Marines then swept the area and discovered how enormous the bunker-fortified stronghold was. It covered almost two acres of hedgerow-lined fields with mutually supporting fields of fire. Had the battalion come in from a different direction, Alpha's entire company would likely have been annihilated in the ambush kill zone.

Companies C and D found thirty-one NVA dead and one wounded while searching the area. Over the next two days, another nine bodies were located in the dense undergrowth by 1/9 patrols, but the main enemy force had pulled out after dark that first night. Official reports would later estimate that another forty-three NVA were probably killed.

One-Nine was learning how to fight these NVA, and the NVA were learning through trial and error how to inflict maximum numbers of casualties on the Marines. This brand of Communist was well trained, well armed, courageous, and cunning, and their mission was to shed American blood, regardless of their own losses. The term *meat grinder* was beginning to take hold among the grunts to describe Con Thien's killing fields.

THE M-16 RIFLE DISASTER

The first shipment of new Colt M-16A1 rifles began arriving at the 3d Marine Division the end of March, and the weapons were distributed to troops out in the field over the next month. The smaller, lighter-weight M-16 (7.6 pounds) would replace the heavier, bulky, but dependable M-14 rifle as the standard weapon for all of the armed services.

America's new service rifle would soon become the most controversial weapon of the war. The M-16 fired a .223-caliber bullet at a blazing fast muzzle velocity of 3,250 feet per second, and the bullet tended to tumble when striking human flesh, making it highly lethal, more deadly than a larger bullet that penetrated straight through the body without tumbling. And the weapon could be changed instantly from semiautomatic to automatic fire with the flip of a lever. Problems began to surface right away, however. It frequently jammed, often at the most crucial moment of a firefight when the Marines needed to establish fire superiority. Many Marines who died at Khe Sanh during the "Hill Fights" in early April were found with their jammed weapons broken down, attempting to clear misfeeds.

A letter published in the *Washington Post* on October 29, 1967, and later introduced into the *Congressional Record* by Senator Hatfield from Oregon illustrates the profound distress shared by the Marines over their new, jam-prone weapon:

> I am a Marine first lieutenant and have been serving in a rifle company in Vietnam since the 15th of May. Ever since my arrival, immediately following the battle of Hill 881, one controversy has loomed above all else—that of the M-16 rifle.
>
> . . . There is a basic mechanical deficiency with the weapon that causes a failure to extract. This failure to extract a spent casing from the chamber allows another round to be fed in behind the unextracted casing, causing the rifle to jam. When this occurs, a cleaning rod and precious seconds are needed to clear the chamber. A Marine in a fire fight does not have those precious seconds.
>
> We are constantly told that improper cleaning and unfamiliarity with the weapon cause any malfunction which may occur. Any rifle that requires cleaning to the degree they speak of has no place as a combat weapon.
>
> I believe that the cold, hard facts about the M-16 are clouded over by a fabrication of the truth for political and financial considerations. I have seen too many Marines hiding behind a paddy dike trying to clear their rifles to accept these explanations any longer.
> M. P. Chervenak, Executive Officer
> Hotel Company, 2d Battalion, 3d Marines[5]

The problem could be traced back to Secretary of Defense McNamara and his arrogant whiz kids in the Pentagon who wanted the new weapon *right now,* before it was fully tested under combat conditions. There was also a coconspirator in this weapons fiasco, and that was the U.S. Army Ordnance Corps.

The propellant was changed by the Army from the DuPont-manufactured IMR powder that was used so successfully with the M-16's predecessor, the AR-15, to the less-expensive, slower-burning "ball powder" produced by Olin Mathieson. Ball powder increased the muzzle velocity. With the increase in muzzle velocity came an increase in cyclic rate of fire from seven hundred rounds per minute to almost one thousand rounds per minute. But the M-16 was not designed to handle this drastic increase in rate of fire, causing it to misfeed and jam. Also, ball powder left a residue in the barrel and chamber that required constant cleaning to prevent jamming. The Marines were not informed of this.

Colt cleaning supplies were nonexistent. Incredulously, the Marines were told at first that their new weapons were "self-cleaning." They learned the hard way that they had a fussy weapon that needed constant meticulous cleaning and that their lives depended on it. Even then, cleaning was not enough. Ball powder was susceptible to moisture, and the cartridge could swell in the chamber overnight, causing the soft brass cartridge to rip when ejected. As if that were not enough, the magazine spring could weaken if the twenty-round magazine was kept full, and thus the Marines learned to put no more than sixteen rounds in the twenty-round magazines.

Gary D. Murtha was a Marine with F/2/7. He wrote, "You were guaranteed a jam after each shot. It was so bad that everybody carried their cleaning rods, fully assembled, in their belt. It reminded you of the Revolutionary War when the shooting started. One shot, then ram the rod down the barrel to free the jam."[6]

Initially, Army ordnance experts blamed the Marine grunts, going on record that any problems with the weapon were due to improper cleaning and maintenance. But a congressional inquiry in June would expose the M-16 program's shortcomings, resulting in a huge public outcry demanding that the weapon's problems be corrected. A subsequent report by a House Armed Services subcommittee in August, chaired by Representative Richard Ichord of Missouri, severely criticized both the Olin Mathieson Chemical Corporation and Colt Industries. The report left the brunt of its criticism for the Army, stating: "The M-16 is still seriously deficient" and that "the Army is guilty of 'unbelievable' mismanagement." The scathing report continued: "The Army's handling of ammunition procurement borders on criminal negligence."[7]

The fix would require several modifications, including a chromed chamber and a heavier buffer mechanism. Many Marines and other soldiers would die in the meantime because their primary infantry weapon had failed them.

CARVING OUT THE TRACE

That infamous anti-infiltration barrier between Con Thien and Gio Linh was begun quietly without any media fanfare in early April. The 11th Engineer Battalion was given the task of bulldozing a two-hundred-meter-wide strip from Con Thien to Gio Linh, six miles away, as the first step in the Strong Point Obstacle System installation. The official term used to describe the bulldozed strip was the "Trace."

Lt. Col. Theodore J. Willis's 1st Battalion, 4th Marines provided project security. Willis also had at his disposal a platoon of tanks from Alpha Company, 3d Tank Battalion; a platoon of U.S. Army M-42 Dusters; and a unit of ARVN to assist with moving civilians out of the path of the bulldozers. It was a harrowing task for the engineers, who were constantly faced with snipers, mines, booby traps, mortars, and artillery fire from above the DMZ. They could not hide where they were working or what they were up to. They had to labor totally out in the open, vulnerable to whatever obstacles the NVA could think of to deter them from their task.

One of the bulldozer operators, PFC George Snider, was new in country, having only arrived April 6. He was put right to work on a dozer scraping the earth bare of all trees, shrubs, bamboo, buildings, and whatever else stood in their way as he cleared the firebreak alongside another half-dozen bulldozers. It was scary, hazardous duty. He hated the naked feeling he experienced sitting atop his dozer, and the noise from his dozer engine prevented him from hearing incoming. He also knew that every time he started a new pass into the undergrowth, it could be his last. "Keep the dozer blade deep," everyone said. That would push any mines out in front of the dozer and keep the machine from running over them. One day, Snider did not keep his blade deep enough, and he ran over a mine. The estimated forty pounds of explosive destroyed his bulldozer. Snider got a Purple Heart and a one-way ticket home.

By the end of Operation Prairie III on April 19, more than half of the Trace was completed, despite the constant harassment. Prairie III had cost the enemy 252 dead, 4 captured, and 128 weapons seized. Marine losses totaled 56 killed and 530 wounded.[8]

Apparently, no one on General Westmoreland's staff or at the Pentagon had anticipated how strongly the North Vietnamese would eventually strike back in an attempt to disrupt McNamara's pet project. The barrier plan was a threat to their entire future war of liberation in the northern provinces.

Located less than two miles from the DMZ, with a panoramic view of the entire area for a dozen miles, Con Thien was taking on added significance with each passing day. The prominent little hill that rose up so incongruously from the surrounding flat, verdant countryside sat astride two of the NVA's favorite infiltration routes across the DMZ. Now it was going to anchor the SPOS barrier and become a key military installation. General Giap was ordered to direct his forces to take the offensive. The first objective would be to neutralize Con Thien.

PART THREE

THE BLOODY MONTH OF MAY

I have a rendezvous with Death
At some disputed barricade,
When Spring comes back with rustling shade
And apple blossoms fill the air-
I have a rendezvous with Death
When Spring brings back blue days and fair.

—Alan Seeger, "Rendezvous"

6

Battle for Con Thien

Commencing April 20, Operation Prairie IV, last in the series of Prairie operations, was a two-regiment search-and-destroy operation covering the same area of northern Quang Tri Province as Prairie III. In addition to the vital Marine base at Dong Ha, the 9th Marines had the responsibility of securing the area between Con Thien and Gio Linh, where the 11th Engineer Battalion was bulldozing a broad swath called the Trace through the fields and woods below the DMZ.

The DMZ war, as well as the weather, was heating up. The North Vietnamese seemed determined to disrupt the Strong Point Obstacle System. Both firebases anchoring the strip, Gio Linh and Con Thien, were being shelled regularly from NVA positions in the DMZ. Helicopter resupply was getting riskier with each passing day. The NVA targeted the landing zones, timing their incoming mortars to attempt to coincide with a helicopter's time on the ground.

By May 1, the initial two-hundred-meter-wide swath was completely carved out from Con Thien to Gio Linh. The next step was to clear a five-hundred-meter-wide strip around Con Thien that would eventually be filled with barbed-wire obstacles and antitank and antipersonnel mines.

May 8 Attack

Con Thien's defenses had to be beefed up to accommodate the Marines and their new mission. Former inhabitants, the ARVN and U.S. Army

Special Forces, along with their Nung CIDG mercenaries, had made a start at fortifying the base, but much work remained to be done. New bunkers had to be built according to specifications devised by MACV that would withstand direct hits from NVA artillery and rockets. Prior occupants had festooned the perimeter wire with a jerry-rigged assortment of hand grenade booby traps and trip flares, and it all had to be dismantled prior to the engineers putting in new minefield wire obstacles around Con Thien's perimeter.

The thirteenth anniversary of the fall of Dien Bien Phu was May 7, but no one at Con Thien had given that a second thought. It had been a day like every other scorching hot May day on the DMZ. Periodically, working parties were harassed by incoming mortars, and everyone had to scramble for cover. The dreaded cry for medical help would be heard, "Corpsman! Corpsman, over here!" Litter bearers carted another casualty off to the battalion aid station (BAS), and work resumed.

As the sun sank into the horizon, the hardworking detachment of U.S. Navy Seabees stopped their bunker building and looked forward to a few cold beers. The Seabees always had beer. They knew how to go to war. Seabees and the engineers—they always seemed to have showers, generators to provide electricity, and real cooking stoves. And they had *cold* beer!

Evening dusk faded into night. An almost tangible sense of relief could be felt by everyone on the hill. More incoming was unlikely after the sun set, and men could move about freely without becoming targets for any FOs or snipers lurking out among the surrounding bushes.

Stretching the length of the southern portion of the firebase, from roughly ten o'clock behind observer position (OP) #1 to four o'clock below OP#3, the easternmost knoll, was a fairly level hard-packed dirt airstrip. Situated around the east end of the airstrip were the Special Forces soldiers and their CIDG Nungs. The Marines did not trust them. They had put up a concertina wire barrier to separate themselves from "those fuckin' gooks." Nungs were mercenaries of Chinese extraction. Many generations earlier, they had settled in the rugged, remote Annamite mountains of Vietnam. A primitive people, most could not even read a map or use a compass. They were never intended to take on the

NVA in battle. Their original function was to provide limited local protection for tribal villagers.

Outside the perimeter wire in tree-covered staging positions a kilometer away to the northeast and southeast, a combined force of NVA soldiers and sappers from the 4th and 6th Battalions of the 812th NVA Regiment, 324B Division made last-minute preparations for an assault on Con Thien. They listened intently as their cadre went over the attack plan for the umpteenth time. The regulars would follow their highly trained sapper commandos through gaps blown in the perimeter wire and then quickly overrun the weak ARVN and CIDG forces they believed were manning the base. Each man with a satchel charge anxiously awaited his chance for glory by being the one to blow up a piece of construction equipment or demolish the main command bunker.

What they did not know was that the ARVN had been replaced recently by two reinforced companies from the 1st Battalion, 4th Marines, Companies A and D, plus a platoon of Marine engineers; moreover, the three tanks were manned by combat-savvy Marines from Alpha Company, 3d Tank Battalion, not ARVN.

At 2:50 in the morning on May 8, a green flare shot skyward from the tree line outside the southern perimeter, casting an ominous glow in the night sky. Almost immediately, sounding like dozens of kettle drums beating in the distance, the booming and thumping sounds of many artillery pieces and mortars firing could be heard all over Con Thien. Within seconds, a screeching roar descended on the Marines. The ground shook as round after round of incoming artillery blasted the battered slopes and valleys. Every man's fear—an all-out attack—was coming right at them. Hundreds of rounds of artillery and mortars came crashing down without letup.

NVA sappers sprinted in under the covering barrage and blew several huge gaps in the northern perimeter wire with bamboo bangalore torpedoes. The brunt of the assault was directed at the weakest section of the base, where the grunts from 1/4 tied in with the CIDG trenches. Once through the wire, sappers tossed satchel charges at the trench line bunkers, blasting them into piles of collapsed beams and sandbags. They marked their attack routes with small, red, pennant-shaped flags stuck into the ground as they moved ahead so that the following infantry would know where the defenses were weakest. While the sappers did their dirty work, the waiting infantry laid down a fierce covering fire with their automatic weapons.

Nearly all the young Marines had their heads down in a trench or were huddled inside a bunker. The sappers knew this. Creeping and crawling forward, they tossed one-quarter-pound blocks of TNT ahead of them, simulating mortar blasts. While the Marines had their heads down, the NVA sappers threw satchel charges in on them. Many Marines were killed this way.

About four in the morning, the main force attacked, pouring through giant gaps blown in the perimeter concertina wire. Three of the NVA were armed with flamethrowers; their blazing fuel suffocated and roasted several Marines crouched inside bunkers.

In the Special Forces area, the CIDG defense line collapsed, allowing a flood of NVA to charge through the breach. The detachment CO, Captain Chamberlain, and two of his Green Beret sergeants fought off repeated attacks against his command bunker. Then, to his horror, a stream of flaming liquid shot through a bunker aperture, but only partially ignited. He and his men retreated to the nearby Navy Seabee position, where they joined together in forming a defense line that fought off the NVA the rest of the night.

Three tanks were on the northern half of the perimeter, hunkered down in their firing slots when the attack began. Sergeant David Danner, the platoon maintenance man ("shit fister" in tanker jargon) was in the gunner's seat on the center tank. An RPG penetrated the turret and exploded with a searing flash, blasting the crew with molten steel fragments. Despite being hit and burned severely, Sergeant Danner got all of the wounded crewmen out of his tank and into a nearby aid station. He refused treatment, returning to his tank to retrieve the .30-caliber machine gun and as many boxes of ammo as he could carry. He continued to pour a heavy volume of machine-gun fire into the ranks of the attackers despite being wounded many more times by shrapnel from exploding mortars and grenades. On one occasion, when he saw a seriously wounded Marine lying exposed in the open, Sergeant Danner picked him up and carried him through intense enemy fire to the corpsman's bunker where he could receive first aid. Danner kept fighting until the attack subsided; then he allowed his wounds to be treated.

A second tank commanded by Corporal Charles D. Thatcher happened to be on the northeastern perimeter where the main assault came through the wire. Corporal Thatcher was asleep underneath his fifty-two-ton "iron monster" when the incoming hit. He stayed there. To climb out in the open would be suicide. His gunner, Lance Cpl. David Gehrman, took the attacking force under fire with his coaxially mounted .30-caliber machine gun. Suddenly, an antitank HEAT round pierced his turret and exploded. Choking smoke filled the turret.

Gehrman yelled, "Everybody bail out!" As he was leaning out of the tank commander's cupola, yelling at Corporal Thatcher to run, another explosion blew him out of the turret. The blast had mortally wounded the other two crewmen, Lance Cpl. John E. Young, 19, of Tigard, Oregon, and PFC James L. Lester Jr., 20, of Norfolk, Virginia. Gehrman was seriously hurt, but he managed to rise and stagger toward a nearby trench. Before he could reach safety, a bullet smacked into his leg, knocking him off his feet. He began crawling toward the trench, dragging his shattered leg, when a bullet struck him in his other leg. Two grunts reached out and grabbed Gehrman, pulling him into their bunker. He was out of the war.

The tank commander, Corporal Thatcher, was painfully wounded in the back and neck by shrapnel as he climbed back on his still-smoldering tank to pull out a crewman. He gave him first aid and comforted him as best he could. Then he reentered his tank and fired off all of his remaining .30-caliber ammunition, inflicting heavy casualties on the attackers. He climbed down from his disabled tank and retrieved a rifle from a dead Marine. Observing an RPG team about to fire at the third tank, which was the only one still mobile, Thatcher gunned them down before they could unleash their antitank rocket.

Gunnery Sergeant Barnett G. Person, the tank platoon sergeant, commanded the third tank. He was located on the northwest side of the perimeter, away from the brunt of the assault. He chose to button down his hatches and keep his tank moving, advancing to the main point of attack where his other two smoking tanks lay immobilized. While several NVA crawled atop his tank, attempting to disable it with satchel charges, he kept his 90mm gun blasting out cannister and "beehive" rounds; his two machine guns sprayed thousands of bullets into the determined enemy. His tank would be the only one of three still operable when daylight came.

Out of twelve crewmen on the three tanks, only one man survived the battle unscathed. Three tankers were dead. Sergeant Danner and Corporal Thatcher would survive their wounds and be awarded the Navy Cross.[1]

Company D was fighting for its life in hand-to-hand combat as the battle line surged back and forth. Capt. John Juul, Delta Company commander, went down hard, shot through both legs, but he was still firing his .45-caliber pistol as he lay there, calmly holding his radio handset up to his ear. Nearby, Sgt. Mailon Hall shouted to his men, "Stay put in your trenches! We're gonna kill anything that moves!"[2]

The engineer platoon, armed with their old reliable M-14 rifles, charged over to beleaguered Delta, plugging a breach in their lines to stem the tide of the enemy attack. They poured out a fierce volume of fire; their weapons did not jam like the M-16s. But the combat engineers were soon distressed to learn that their revered Navy corpsman, HM3 John C. Tate, a handsome, witty, all-American kid who liked to write his own guitar music, was grievously injured doing what he loved best, caring for some wounded engineers. A satchel charge had demolished his bunker. He succumbed to his wounds two days later.

Outside the southern perimeter, Alpha Company of 1/4 was crouched in their fighting holes listening anxiously to the thundering sounds of battle, the staccato chattering of numerous automatic weapons. Brilliant flashes lit up the night sky behind the hill.

One of the Alpha grunts, PFC David Lovewell, knew from the cacophony of battle noise coming from behind him that a major battle was raging, but all he could do was sit anxiously and await orders. Then, his platoon sergeant barked at the squad adjacent to Lovewell's, "Get aboard that amtrac over there!"[3] As that squad scrambled from their fighting holes into the awaiting amtrac, the remainder of Lovewell's 1st Platoon was ordered to prepare to attack. The 2d and 3d Platoons stayed in their fighting holes, guarding the southern perimeter.

Enough Delta grunts on the northern perimeter had survived the initial sapper attack to fight back fiercely, along with the tankers, and this slowed the momentum of the main attack. But they were running low on ammunition, and many of their jam-prone M-16s were useless.

By this time, the bulk of the surviving NVA attack force had passed between OP#2 and OP#3 and was headed toward the airstrip at the base of the hills. The 1st Platoon of Alpha Company was deployed along the southern perimeter, ready to charge across the airstrip in a counterattack. The tide seemed to be turning until the 81mm mortar platoon ran out of illumination rounds. The 175mm guns at Gio Linh were of no help; they were not equipped to fire illumination. What could have been a serious reversal did not last long, though. A flare plane came on station just then and kept the battle scene illuminated.

Seriously outnumbered, the 1st Platoon of A/1/4, accompanied by an Army M-42 Duster and two Marine amtracs, attacked across the old landing strip. An RPG struck the Duster, and it exploded into flames. The amtrac that was following caught fire when a satchel charge exploded underneath it, but the crew and its passengers managed to escape. The next amtrac was not so lucky. While trying to avoid the other two burning vehicles, the driver blundered into some barbed wire, entangling the wire around its left rear sprocket. It was stuck, sitting there as helpless as a beached boat. Another RPG flashed through the night, exploding inside the "flaming coffin," turning it into a death trap for the crew and squad of Marines. One man escaped as the amtrac exploded into flames, but he was shot down, riddled by machine-gun bullets. Horrifying screams from inside the blazing amtrac died down quickly. The ammunition inside continued to cook off and explode for hours.

The three blazing vehicles lit up the area, illuminating 1st Platoon. Two squads were pinned down by automatic weapons fire. Someone had to do something. People were getting shot lying there. Lance Cpl. Michael P. Finley, a grenadier, could stand it no more. He vaulted out from behind his cover and launched two grenade rounds from his M-79 "blooper" gun, scoring direct hits on an enemy machine-gun crew, killing them and putting their gun out of action. Then he was hit. Despite his wounds, he sprinted through a hail of enemy fire over to a wounded Marine and gave him first aid. He then exposed himself again to enemy fire and ran to his wounded squad leader's side, only to be struck again by a bullet and killed. He would later be awarded the Navy Cross posthumously.

Because of the courage of Lance Corporal Finley and many others, most of Alpha's 1st Platoon survived that frenzied charge across the landing strip. Those reinforcements, plus the platoon of stalwart engineers, halted the enemy's penetration and sealed off the breach in Delta's lines just before daylight. The NVA had waited too long to make an orderly withdrawal; now their routes for retreat were blocked.

As the morning sun rose in the smoke-shrouded sky, vengeful Marines attacked isolated pockets of NVA and shot them down as they tried to escape. With the perimeter sealed off, making escape impossible, it was either surrender or die. Most chose to die.

A relief force from B/1/4 headed out down the Trace from Gio Linh at first light. The grunt platoon was accompanied by a light section of two tanks and two Ontos. Gio Linh had been through hell. Incoming pounded them throughout the night, making a shambles of the base, collapsing bunkers and trenches, and shredding the perimeter wire. But they saw the black columns of smoke rising menacingly from Con Thien. Whatever they had endured that night was not as bad as where they were headed.

The relief force moved out at a rapid, forced-march pace; it was urgent they get there fast, but it was risky. Moving in column up the bald Trace only invited an ambush. Surely the NVA had anticipated a reaction force coming in that direction.

The platoon leader, Second Lieutenant Burke, wisely had his advancing force boxed in by artillery, calling it down along both sides of their route to screen off their advance. He halted his men a kilometer from Con Thien, suspecting a staging camp for the NVA was nearby. He guessed right. The tanks and Ontos blasted the trees along the southern edge of the Trace and flushed out a covey of NVA who were quickly taken under fire. The armor/infantry force then launched an attack and overran a bunker complex under the trees, finding twenty-six dead NVA.

Lance Cpl. Stephen Summerscales was hit by a dart from a tank beehive round. Despite his wound, he kept his gun firing throughout the attack. Later that morning, as the fighting ceased in his sector, he went to the corpsman's bunker to seek medical aid. He was stunned to find most of his squad mates lying outside on the ground, the wounded being attended to, his dead friends covered by ponchos, jungle-boot toes pointing skyward. He would write home later that day from a hospital in Da Nang, "I never want to go back to the DMZ, but I know I will. I want to live so much."[4]

General Lew Walt flew into Con Thien by helicopter later that morning, landing near the still-burning amtracs. He and three other passengers—two colonels and his aide, Capt. Bill Lee—had just passed a trench line holding three dead NVA when someone shouted, "Mortars, incoming!" Walt just made it to a bunker when the first round impacted. He was not hit, but Colonel James Barrett caught a piece of shrapnel in his cheek. That was the third time in ten days that Walt had to dodge incoming, both at Gio Linh and at Con Thien. Some isolated stragglers were still being hunted down and killed as late as eleven o'clock that morning, even as General Walt was assessing the attack damage.

Eight prisoners were captured and transported to Dong Ha for interrogation by 9th Marines Intelligence. What they were able to glean was that the first attack at 2:50 a.m. was a sapper company leading the way, followed at four o'clock by a combined attacking force from the 4th and 6th Battalions of the 812th Regiment. During and after the battle, casualty transportation teams carried their dead and wounded to an underground field hospital set up two thousand meters directly north of Con Thien. Their CP headquarters was also near there. They had been pre-registering their mortars during the day for weeks, one round at a time, gradually adjusting the settings until they could hit Con Thien's key strategic locations at night with pinpoint accuracy.

The NVA attack had been well planned and rehearsed. All soldiers wore a camouflaged jacket, cap, and shorts. Almost every man carried a satchel charge. Many of the bodies were found with bandaged wounds, which suggested that they had been wounded once and treated and then had continued on in the assault.

The human carnage was shocking. Approximately two hundred NVA bodies lay dead inside and outside of the perimeter. No doubt dozens more dead had been carried away by their "transportation unit" before dawn. The 4th Marines guesstimated that another two hundred had probably been killed, because large numbers of retreating NVA had been hit with air strikes and artillery and by tanks using the new beehive round.

Marine losses were heavy, with 44 killed and 110 wounded. Destroyed or damaged were two amtracs, three M-48A3 tanks, one road grader, one M-42 Duster, two dump trucks, two one-quarter-ton jeeps, and one Ontos. Attached units also suffered casualties: fourteen CIDG were killed and sixteen wounded; four Green Berets and five Navy Seabees were also wounded.[5]

PFC David Lovewell, a rifleman with the 3d Platoon of A/1/4, was part of the unlucky detail assigned to remove the remains of the dead from inside the still-smoldering amtrac. By midmorning, no more rounds of ammunition were cooking off. All he could see that remained of a once-vibrant group of American boys was a jumbled mass of unrecognizable lumps of charred bodies.

A relief crew of tankers came up that afternoon to replace the wiped-out crews from the three tanks and to see whether any of their equipment was salvageable. One tank driver replacement, Lance Cpl. Kenneth "Piggy" Bores, a rosy-cheeked teenager from Wisconsin who had not even started shaving yet, was put to work retrieving NVA bodies and going through their personal effects. Many had pictures of themselves with girlfriends and family. He then helped load the bodies on trucks and ride out with them to the burial site.

An engineer bulldozer operator had scooped out a wide ditch north of Con Thien in the newly cleared perimeter that encircled the firebase. Bores was part of the gruesome detail that tossed the bodies off the trucks into the ditch. He thought it was dug "kind of shallow," but he was not in any position as a lance corporal to be questioning those things.[6] Besides, his detached mind was in neutral, not allowing the piles of dead he handled to get to him. He had already witnessed a lifetime worth of nightmares in his five months in Nam, and he had learned to detach himself mentally at times like this. He watched in numbed silence as the dozer operator pushed dirt over the NVA corpses, noting that here and there a hand or shoe protruded up out of the mass grave.

For days afterward, whenever the wind was right, a dead-body stench descended on Con Thien like a putrid fog. Not soon enough for the Marines on the hill, another bulldozer was later seen at work out there pushing more dirt around, this time mounding the dirt higher over the NVA burial site.

The May 8 attack had been a disaster for the North Vietnamese. The better part of a reinforced battalion plus a sapper company had been sacrificed; half of their dead had to be left behind for the Marines to bury. Everything was planned down to the last detail, except what to do when they encountered a force of U.S. Marine grunts, tankers, and engineers who fought back like cornered badgers and thwarted their surprise attack plans.

The May 8 battle for Con Thien was a devastating defeat that would affect General Giap's future war planning. He learned that he would not be able to attack and overrun the U.S. Marines dug in at those barrier system strongpoints. Their tenacity and overwhelming fire support were too difficult to overcome. Instead, for the time being, he would carry out his war of attrition through ambushing patrols outside the firebases and by shelling the Marines with his artillery, rockets, and mortars. He planned to keep the Marines tied to defending their bases up by the DMZ, where his supply lines were short and he had a safe haven immune from ground interdiction. But all that would soon change, because immediately after the May 8 attack, Westmoreland's MACV authorized the III Marine Amphibious Force to commence planning a major ground operation into the DMZ.

THE "WALKING DEAD"

On May 10, in an ominous new development in the war, a Douglas A-4E Skyhawk was flying a radar-controlled bombing mission (TPQ) near the southern boundary of the DMZ above Con Thien. A Russian SA-2 surface-to-air missile (SAM), fired from a mobile launcher, tracked after the jet plane and blew it out of the sky.

On May 12, another air disaster occurred. This time, a UH-34D helicopter from the HMM-363 "Red Lions" was lifting off from the LZ at Con Thien when the unbelievable happened. Captain Richard Basinger's YZ-78 was about one hundred feet above the LZ when a mortar round struck the pilot's side of the craft, instantly killing him and his crew chief, Cpl. John W. Jackson. The helicopter crashed eight hundred meters south of Con Thien. The copilot and door gunner survived, barely.[7]

General Giap and his staff seemed even more determined than ever to disrupt the SPOS being constructed between Con Thien and Gio Linh. After May 8, Con Thien was bombarded daily by mortars or artillery firing from the DMZ. MACV was under orders from the Pentagon to ensure that nothing stopped the not-so-secret SPOS plan from being carried out as planned. McNamara's barrier plan had even been given the president's blessing. Nothing must interfere with its completion. To ensure that Giap's forces would not be able to disrupt construction of the SPOS, III MAF received the go-ahead from MACV to invade the southern half of the DMZ. However, planning and organizing such a large-scale attack would require some time.

The first step was to clear the NVA out of the area south of Con Thien. Intelligence sources indicated that a large force of NVA had moved in there again, planning to interdict Route 561, the main supply route north from Cam Lo. With the Marines preparing to launch an attack into the DMZ soon, they could not tolerate an enemy force lurking behind them. The 1st Battalion, 9th Marines had been in the area before. They were assigned the mission of eliminating that enemy presence.

As was the case throughout much of the war under General Westmoreland's strategy of finding, fixing, and destroying the enemy, the Marines were finding themselves mired down in endless patrols, one operation after another, killing and being killed. The Marines would search and find the enemy (or the enemy would find them), and they would destroy, but they would not physically occupy their objective for more than a day, usually even less. Then they would move on. The NVA would return days or weeks later, dig in even deeper, and wait for the Americans to return. When they were ready to strike, the cycle would be repeated, and more blood would be shed by both sides in this relentless war of attrition.

The same ground around Con Thien would be fought over again and again. The NVA liked the area. It was only a few miles below the sanctuary of the DMZ. The hedgerow-lined open fields made perfect ambush settings. Some of those hedgerows that delineated old family property lines were almost ten feet tall.

B-52 bomber strikes called "Arc Lights" were not permitted closer than three thousand meters from Allied forces. The North Vietnamese had figured this out, no doubt, which was another reason Con Thien had been ringed with NVA fortifications since the fall of 1966.

The NVA had staked out specific areas around Con Thien to fortify, and it seemed that, no matter how many young Marine lives were expended to destroy those fortifications, the NVA would return sooner or later and construct a new bunker complex nearby. That was the Achilles heel of the search-and-destroy attrition strategy so favored by General Westmoreland at this stage of the war. Gia Binh, the Marketplace, Phu Oc, Phu An, Thon An Hoa, and Thon Trung An were all blood-soaked killing grounds where the Marines would do battle with the NVA time and time again.

If their primary logistical resource, the sacrosanct DMZ, were ever denied to the North Vietnamese, they would not have been able to sustain those regiments so readily south of the DMZ. For the Americans, crossing the DMZ to invade North Vietnam was not politically feasible; thus, the United States and its ally, South Vietnam, blundered full speed ahead with what the Pentagon believed to be the next best thing, an anti-infiltration barrier.

Compounding the difficulty for the Americans was their own policy of rotating officers out of field command positions after three to six months. This policy created a lack of "corporate memory," and lessons had to be learned, and then relearned, over and over. Meanwhile, the grunts on the line paid with their own blood when "new-guy" mistakes were made.

The combination of the practices of rotating officers and replacing casualties with new arrivals in country was especially hard on battalions such as 1/9, which spent a lot of "bush time" making contact with the enemy. Yes, they had the highest number of enemy kills, but they also had a lot of their own people killed and wounded. Then they went out again looking for more contact, only in fewer numbers, desperate for replacements that were usually slow to filter in. And when they did show up—"those @#%*@! new guys"—no one even wanted to know their names at first. They were most likely to get themselves or somebody else killed the first month. If they survived and picked up some bush smarts, they would gradually be welcomed into the "old salt" grunt fraternity. Until then, every day for a new replacement was a lonely sojourn filled with hardships and fear.

The 1st Battalion, 9th Marines suffered so many casualties that they began calling themselves the "Walking Dead." Their reputation began to spread, so much so that other units labeled them jinxed. "If it could go wrong, it would go wrong with 1/9." That was the word.

On March 16, a squad from 2d Platoon of Bravo Company crashed on Hill 861 at Khe Sanh when their CH-46 helicopter overshot the landing zone. Eight men died. Then, on April 24, 2d Lt. Thomas G. King's 2d Platoon got ambushed on Hill 861. Subsequently, in a horrible friendly fire goof, one of our close air support jets dropped a bomb on them, obliterating one entire squad. Bravo fought toe to toe with the NVA for the next three days, incurring losses of twenty men killed and scores wounded, including their skipper, Capt. Mike Sayers. That was the opening round of what later came to be called the "Hill Fights" or the First Battle of Khe Sanh. When they were finally pulled out of Khe Sanh, what was left of the decimated company could easily fit onto a single C-130 for the flight back to Dong Ha.[8]

Phu An Revisited

On May 12, Companies A and C from 1/9 were trucked from Dong Ha to the Cam Lo area where they set in for the night. A platoon of tanks from Alpha Company, 3d Tank Battalion joined them. Their mission the next day was to move by foot and march six klicks north along Route 561 to Objective 1, the infamous hamlet of Phu An, twenty-five hundred meters southeast of Con Thien.

Phu An had a bad history. Ask any Marine who had been near that area in March, and the response was: "That damned place is fulla gooks." The NVA had attempted to ambush D/1/9 there on March 5; then Alpha Company had nearly walked into a company-sized ambush at Phu An on March 24. The battle-weary grunts from 1/9 had been bloodied twice there, and they did not need reminding that more trouble lay ahead.

Artillery prepped the objective the morning of May 13 from 9:10 to 9:25. Then, for the next two hours, air strikes pummeled the Phu An area. An ominous pall of dark gray smoke hung in the air over the target area. With the second platoon of A/1/9 in the lead, the Marines cautiously negotiated the thickly vegetated, bomb-cratered terrain without making enemy contact. The relieved grunts figured the NVA must have pulled out. Nothing could have survived a bombardment like that . . . they thought.

Perspiring heavily under a merciless midday sun, some of the men carried only the standard two canteens of water, not enough to last through a humid, one-hundred-plus degree day. That gross oversight was an indication of the lack of experience in the depleted battalion, its leaders unfamiliar with how swiftly the mild spring weather along the DMZ could jump right into stifling summer heat in May.

Then, just northwest of Phu An, a reinforced company of NVA hidden in camouflaged bunkers suddenly opened fire. Second Platoon had walked into a deadly U-shaped ambush. The NVA poured heavy streams of machine-gun fire into the terrified young Marines, many of them green replacements, and then dropped in mortar rounds to keep them pinned down in the kill zone. Dead and wounded alike fell atop each other. Bullets continued to rip into their bodies as they sprawled in the sun-baked dirt. Any unit leader who arose to use a radio or make a hand signal was an instant sniper target. The enemy's skillfully camouflaged bunkers, built out of logs, banana trees, and large beams, were almost impossible to see from ground level, which is where most of the pinned-down Marines had their heads—face down in the dirt.

A wide irrigation ditch stymied the tanks and prevented them from coming to 2d Platoon's aid. First Platoon vaulted the ditch in a valiant attempt to reinforce 2d Platoon, only to be pinned down by heavy automatic weapons fire coming from the right flank. The 3d Platoon and the tanks tried again to come to the aid of beleaguered 2d Platoon, but they were halted by a firestorm of RPGs and small-arms fire. Third Platoon was now in a world of hurt; they were being slaughtered.

Alpha's new company commander, Capt. Albert C. Slater, had been given the nickname "Captain Contact" by his salty troops who were not enamored with his "gung ho," hard-nosed demeanor. But he was a warrior—no one would deny that. One of his lieutenants, Al Fagan, captured the essence of his tough skipper with this pithy, bottom-line description, "He had brass balls."[9] With bullets and shrapnel flying all around him, Slater personally talked a tank over a spider hole to confuse an AK-47–wielding NVA and then ran out and shot him through the head with his .45-caliber pistol. Slater was then shot in the arm, but he refused evacuation until he was satisfied the battle was over.[10]

The 3d Platoon of Company C finally broke through the NVA force and connected up with the rest of Slater's Alpha Company. Captain Slater combined those forces into a cohesive tank/infantry assault team and quickly obtained fire superiority, overwhelming the enemy bunker complex. Five fifty-two-ton tanks rolled atop numerous bunkers, sometimes pivoting in a circle doing "neutral steers," crushing the bunkers along with their doomed occupants. When the last shot was fired and the smoke cleared, a head count revealed that the two 1/9 companies had nine dead and fifty-nine wounded, with the majority of those casualties being from Alpha.

After hoofing it from Cam Lo all day under the hot sun, Delta Company arrived and set in for the night west of the MSR. The 1st Battalion now had three out of four companies present. When newly rebuilt Bravo Company joined the battalion the following day, Major Don Fulham would finally have all four of his companies back together in one cohesive unit.

Church of Peace

Delta 1/9 conducted a cautious sweep to the west of Phu An on May 14, taking a few casualties from incoming mortars, but not making any significant contact. Late that afternoon, they encountered a dozen NVA loitering in the open north of the hamlet of Nha Tho An Hoa, about two kilometers west of Phu An. They gave chase, as gung-ho assault troops are prone to do, and ran right into an ambush.

Delta was in column with the CP and 1st Platoon in the lead. Deadly accurate, close-range machine-gun fire ripped into them from both flanks, east and west, quickly dividing the embattled Marines into three groups. Initially separated, 2d and 3d Platoons managed to fight their way through the ambush to link up and form a cohesive defensive perimeter, but they were still cut off from the lead group.

Jettie Rivers Jr., company first sergeant, was a no-nonsense Marine and highly respected by his troops as a first-rate leader. He did not disappoint. He was everywhere on the battlefield, directing fire, distributing ammo, leading fire-team assaults, and recovering his wounded. Despite being wounded himself, when he learned that all the other platoon leaders were casualties, he personally led the attacking force that made the difficult link up with 1st Platoon and the CP group.

But it was not yet over. No sooner had the evacuation of their wounded been completed when a dozen 82mm mortar rounds whooshed down from the night sky on to the exhausted Delta Marines. A wave of NVA firing their AK-47s from the hip and throwing satchel charges stormed right at Delta's lines. Inspired, First Sergeant Rivers's determined Marines fought off the charge and kept their lines intact throughout the night, despite incurring losses of six more Marines and corpsmen killed and sixteen wounded. Rivers would later be recommended for a battlefield commission, and he would also be awarded the Navy Cross posthumously (he was killed along with his company commander when an incoming artillery shell scored a direct hit on his bunker at Con Thien on July 6 during Operation Buffalo).[11]

While D/1/9 was fighting for its life at Nha Tho An Hoa that night, a UH-34D helicopter from HMM-363 landed near a church on an emergency medevac mission. As Yankee Zulu-77 lifted off from the LZ with its bloody human cargo of dead and wounded, heavy automatic weapons fire struck the craft, damaging the rudder control and causing it to spin out of control and crash-land two hundred meters north of the church. Some nearby Delta grunts ran over and, in concert with the medevac crewmen, carried the wounded and dead out, placing them on the ground. For some of the critically wounded, that abortive flight was likely their last chance to make it out of the battle alive.

The crew chief of YZ-77, Corporal Michael Tripp, had blocked the doorway with his body as the helicopter spun down to earth so that none of the passengers would be thrown out. He then exposed himself to hostile fire to remove weapons and ammunition, distributing them to the grunts, who were dangerously low on ammunition. Again exposing himself to enemy fire, he climbed atop his helicopter to fold the rotor blades, thus clearing the small LZ for other medevacs to land. Tripp's Navy Commendation Medal citation further read: "Throughout the night, he steadfastly remained in a fighting position on the defensive perimeter and, as a result of his effective suppressive fire, was instrumental in repulsing several vicious enemy assaults."[12]

Fortunately for Delta, another helicopter was able to land safely that night with much-needed ammunition and water, because early in the morning on May 15, the NVA went after them again with a mortar barrage near the church. At a quarter after four, the NVA began probing Delta's lines, looking for a weak spot to penetrate. But flares from artillery and a flare ship overhead kept the battlefield illuminated, thwarting attempts to sneak up close to the Marine lines. Delta held, despite probing attacks that continued throughout the night.

As morning dawned on the fifteenth, a most welcome sight greeted Delta's battered, exhausted survivors. Bravo Company had arrived at last. The two companies joined forces, securing an LZ to evacuate Delta's casualties. But the NVA had other ideas. Any time a resupply or medevac helicopter landed, mortars dropped on the LZ. The modest little church at Nha Tho An Hoa, which translates into "Church of Peace," thus became a sanctuary for the Marines to bring their dead and wounded that afternoon as fighting raged around them.

Photographer Frank Johnston recalled years later in a *Washington Post* story: "It was a butcher shop in that church. In the fading light, the moans of wounded Marines mingled with the explosions of incoming mortar rounds. Men were dying in one another's arms. Bodies lay on the floor. Shrapnel sprayed the cement walls outside like handfuls of nails hurled by a giant." Throughout that endless night, there were times when the occupants of the church were convinced they were going to be overrun. "We were in a house of God, and we were going to die. But there was a feeling in that church that if they couldn't survive, they were going to make it count. One guy who was seriously wounded said, 'Give me my rifle. . . . I'm going to fight until I can't fight any more.' He was hanging across a pew, he couldn't even walk. He died."[13]

May 16 dawned quietly. The bloodied grunts from Delta and Bravo loaded up their casualties and moved out of Nha Tho An Hoa one klick east across the MSR where the battalion had an LZ less vulnerable to small-arms fire and mortars. Companies A and C maneuvered out to search the shrub- and tree-covered area where they had been attacked three days earlier on the northern edge of Phu An.

Like a bad dream that would not go away, an identical scenario almost repeated itself. At 2:40 p.m., even though they were on high alert for any signs of enemy soldiers remaining in that area, a hailstorm of machine-gun bullets and mortars surprised them once again. At least a company of NVA had dug themselves into another hedgerow bunker complex with mutually supporting automatic weapons.

The tank platoon assaulted the complex with Captain Al Slater's Company A in the lead. One tank was hit by a 57mm recoilless rifle round that blew off a track as the five steel behemoths roared into the complex, firing point blank into bunker apertures. As a last resort, the tankers again employed their fifty-two-ton vehicles as steamrollers to crush the bunkers and their occupants. While the NVA were preoccupied with the tanks, the two infantry companies retrieved their casualties and pulled back. It was almost dark, and to remain there only invited further attack on the already depleted companies.

That fight had cost the lives of three more Marines and one of their corpsmen, and thirty-three others were wounded. Lying in and around the demolished bunker complex were twenty-three dead NVA and several machine guns. The tank platoon had destroyed six bunkers and was credited with ten of the NVA KIAs (killed in action).

The fierce battle to clear out the entrenched NVA south of Con Thien had lasted three days. Captured enemy documents revealed the NVA to be from the 6th Battalion, 812th NVA Regiment, one of the two units practically annihilated during their abortive May 8 attack on Con Thien. They were a tough, highly disciplined bunch, sworn to give no quarter. Surrender was apparently not an option.

Casualties were again heavy on both sides. The Marines from 1/9 had incurred losses of 28 dead and 245 wounded in that brutal three-day battle, nearly half the battalion. They claimed 134 NVA dead and another 209 probable. The 1st Battalion, 9th Marines had inflicted large numbers of casualties on their enemy, but the NVA were not retreating this time. Many more were still deployed among the hedgerows and woods around Con Thien, awaiting their next opportunity to kill more of the "Walking Dead."

Phu Oc

The 2d Battalion, 26th Marines, commanded by Lt. Col. Charles Figard, had been operating for some time south of Quang Tri in the Phong Dien area. Figard got the word in mid-May that his battalion was going to be placed under the operational control of the 9th Marines up by the "Dead Marine Zone." Few were excited at the prospect, to say the least.

The battalion had been involved down south in Operation Shawnee for the previous two weeks, where the action was minimal. To a man, they knew the gravy train was over. Their war was about to escalate. They would be among the lead elements of the ten-thousand-man allied force that would invade the southern half of the DMZ during Operation Hickory, commencing May 17.

Figard's battalion was moved by truck convoy up Highway 1 to Dong Ha on May 15. When he learned of the serious situation facing 1/9 near Con Thien, Lieutenant Colonel Figard loaded his anxious grunts back up and trucked them out to Cam Lo that same afternoon. The battalion then moved north on foot and set in for the night a few kilometers southeast of where 1/9 had been heavily engaged around the Church of Peace.

The following day, May 16, 2/26 had bypassed the 1/9 engagement area, advancing north about a mile beyond Phu An, almost to the Trace, when Company F walked into a devastating ambush. The NVA had upped the ante this time, because a full battalion was lying in wait in camouflaged bunkers, expecting 1/9 to come through the abandoned hamlet of Phu Oc. Instead, 2/26 had stepped into the well-laid trap.

The same sickening scenario occurred. Hidden in dozens of log-reinforced bunkers dug into thickly vegetated hedgerows, the NVA suddenly opened up with a murderous fusillade of automatic weapons on the lead platoon crossing an open paddy field. Then, they dropped mortars on the pinned-down Marines. Zinging bullets and blasting shrapnel tore into them. The scene was a living hell of desperate, terrified boys screaming for corpsmen, their buddies bleeding and dying. Officers and NCOs yelled out orders to pull back, but few dared to move, let alone raise up, lest they too became targets.

The bravest of the brave summoned up all of their courage and began to take action. Sgt. Ronald Curley was squad leader of 1st Squad, 1st Platoon, Company F. His squad was next in line behind the lead platoon when they came under attack. When his platoon leader went down wounded, Curley reacted instinctively and took charge of the remaining platoon members, exposing himself continually to enemy fire throughout the three-hour firefight. On two occasions, he single-handedly assaulted enemy bunkers, silencing their crew-served weapons. The LZ was four hundred meters away. Sergeant Curley made three trips carrying wounded men to the LZ while sniper fire peppered the ground around him, both coming and going.

Corpsman Raymond Mierzwa saw his Marines lying dead and wounded in the open amid exploding enemy hand grenades and snapping streams of machine-gun tracers. Without hesitation, he jumped up and ran forward into the firestorm, risking his own life to save the others. Despite being shot in the hand, he made numerous trips across the fire-swept terrain to administer medical aid and carry the wounded to safety.

While Foxtrot Company was fighting to stay alive, artillery and air strikes came crashing down on the Phu Oc bunker complex, keeping the NVA down in their bunkers, preventing them from maneuvering for a flanking attack. Company G then counterattacked with its platoon of tanks from the 1st Platoon of Bravo Company, 3d Tank Battalion.

Lance Cpl. Lloyd "Pappy" Reynolds was the driver on B-11, 2d Lt. Fred Rivero's tank. His five-tank platoon moved in column up a narrow dirt trail toward Phu Oc. Trees and underbrush grew so close to the trail that their 90mm main tank guns could not traverse left or right. All the tankers were tense, knowing how vulnerable they were to an ambush.

Two platoons of widely dispersed grunts from Company G were advancing cautiously up ahead of the tanks when a single shot rang out.

The adrenaline-charged grunts disappeared as one into the thick brush. Then all hell broke loose; that shot was the signal for all NVA in the area to open fire.

Lieutenant Rivero ordered Reynolds, "Make a hard right!" The tanks crashed through a tree-covered hedgerow into an open field. One hundred meters away was another tree line where they could see several NVA moving around and firing in their direction. The platoon of tanks came on line and opened fire, blasting away with their machine guns and cannister and HE rounds.

As they advanced across the open field "poppin' caps," RPG smoke trails crisscrossed the battlefield, seeking out the charging tanks. Rivero's first thought was, "Why is someone shooting flares at us?" It quickly dawned on him that those were antitank rockets and that he had better duck. Just then, an NVA rose up from his spider hole and sprayed B-11 with his AK-47. A bullet hit the open clam shell tank commander's hatch and shattered, grazing Rivero on both arms. Another bullet snapped off a radio antenna. Reynolds put his .45 pistol in his lap "to repel boarders." He made sure his overhead driver's hatch was closed but not locked; he might have to bail out fast.[14]

Reynolds's tank was almost on top of the NVA defense line when another NVA jumped up from behind a log and fired a burst from his AK-47. The tank gunner aimed his .30-caliber machine gun at him, but the NVA ducked out of sight. A few seconds later, he jumped up again to fire, but this time the gunner did not miss. A twenty-round burst blew him completely out of his hole. The tank's machine gun got so hot the loader was pouring water on it to cool it down. The broiling May sun had already made the inside of the tank feel like an oven; the steam coming off the gun turned the turret into a sauna.

One intrepid corporal, Richard Moffitt, led his fire team from Golf Company in a fierce counterattack on the cursed hedgerows. His fellow squad members looked on with a mixture of awe and amazement as the fearless young corporal, oblivious to the popping bullets and bursting mortars, charged an enemy machine-gun position and jumped into their hole, killing both occupants. As his fire team put down a base of fire to cover him, he continued his one-man attack, eliminating several more enemy positions. Corporal Moffitt's remarkable bravery under fire that day and the next would earn him the Navy Cross.

The Marines pulled back to allow air strikes to unload napalm on the NVA positions with punishing accuracy. The tank platoon and Company G then fought their way through the burned-out bunker complex, gagging from the overpowering stench of scorched human hair and flesh, reaching the decimated Foxtrot Company before dark.

The NVA withdrew from the battlefield at the end of the day, leaving behind seventy-nine dead. The killing ground belonged to 2/26, but Companies F and G had incurred losses of fifteen men dead and sixty wounded—a brief but brutal welcome to the DMZ war of attrition. As the weary Marines from 2/26 dug in for the night, their mood was one of restless anticipation mixed with dread. When the morning sun greeted them, they would commence another attack, crossing the Trace into a no-man's-land fraught with danger.

7

DMZ Invasion

A mighty Allied invasion force of ten thousand men sat poised to undertake the first-ever incursion into the demilitarized zone. The basic concept for the Allied invasion involved joint USMC/ARVN ground, amphibious, and helicopter operations in the eastern portion of the DMZ as far north as the Ben Hai River. Ground attacks by the 3d Marine Division and 1st ARVN Division would advance north on parallel routes commencing May 17–18. Operation Prairie IV would be suspended, and that operation area would become Operation Hickory for the Marines and Operation Lam Son 54 for the South Vietnamese. Lam Son was an ancient Vietnamese cultural hero for whom all 1st ARVN Division operations were named.

Newly formed Special Landing Force (SLF) Alpha would make an amphibious landing off the southern DMZ coast with BLT 1/3 and advance inland. That operation was named Beau Charger. On May 20, a second float battalion from SLF Bravo, BLT 2/3, would join the Hickory invasion forces in an operation code-named Belt Tight. They would be ferried in by helicopter to a landing zone in the southern DMZ, immediately east of Hickory, and then attack south, destroying all enemy supplies or forces they encountered.

A major objective was the removal of all civilians from the area to create a free fire zone from south of the Ben Hai River to Route 9, nine miles away. Project Practice Nine, McNamara's Strong Point Obstacle System, called for the removal and relocation of all indigenous personnel. Perhaps as many as ten thousand noncombatants would be uprooted from their homes and relocated to the government resettlement center being constructed at Cam Lo. The Vietnamese National Police were tasked with that unpleasant duty. Despite living in a battle zone, a surprising number of civilians would resist removal and have to be forced off their ancestral lands.

A buildup of Marine forces had been going on for several days prior to May 17. Lt. Col. Wendell Vest's 3d Battalion, 4th Marines came in from Okinawa. Lt. Col. Charles Figard's 2/26 had moved up from Phong Dien. Joining him was Lt. Col. John J. Peeler's 2/9, also coming north from Phu Bai. These three battalions joined three other battalions already engaged in Operation Prairie IV: 1/4, 1/9, and 3/9. Combined with the two float battalions, BLTs 1/3 and 2/3, eight Marine infantry battalions were ready to go on the offensive. In addition, the South Vietnamese provided five battalions, three airborne and two infantry.

Every U.S. Marine and ARVN soldier knew that this invasion was a major escalation in the war. Many wrote a last letter home to loved ones, fearing what fate might have in store for them in the coming days of battle. U.S. Navy chaplains noted a large turnout at their preinvasion religious services.

OPERATION HICKORY

The Prairie IV operation area became Operation Hickory at one minute past midnight on the morning of May 17. The Beau Charger and Lam Son 54 components would not get under way until May 18, and Belt Tight was not scheduled to begin until May 20.

The North Vietnamese realized soon enough that a massive Allied attack was coming their way. Were they aware that the objective was to invade the DMZ itself? Probably not, at least initially, but their spies in ARVN headquarters most certainly had apprised the North Vietnamese leaders that something big was up. General Giap dispatched his forces with orders to put up a fierce resistance around Con Thien.

D-Day: May 17

The first day of Operation Hickory saw the largest single mission fired by artillery during the entire operation. A massive preparatory fire mission was carried out in the predawn hours on 1/9's nemesis, the heavily fortified bunker complex northwest of Phu An. The 1st Battalion, 9th Marines had been trying to take that objective since May 13, when Company A walked into the first murderous ambush. On May 16, Companies A and C of 1/9 had partially overrun the complex after heavy fighting but chose to break contact and withdraw before dark to establish a night defensive position. The men were exhausted, and they had numerous casualties to evacuate.

Overnight, an outstanding FO team from 2/12 plotted the early morning D-Day fire mission. At 5:50 on the morning of May 17, five batteries of 105mm and 155mm Marine artillery opened fire. For forty minutes, the 1/9 grunts awaiting the word to move out sat hunched down in their fighting holes, hoping and praying fervently that all of the rounds screeching overhead were on target. They were right on target. All 685 rounds impacted precisely where they were supposed to fall. Something had finally gone off without a hitch for 1/9.

After the artillery ceased firing, extensive air strikes commenced. Eight sorties of two planes each dropped 1,000- and 750-pound bombs and napalm on the thickly vegetated objective, 250 meters by 300 meters in area. Sweeping through the blasted, smoking complex that had held out against 1/9 since May 13, Companies B and C were relieved to find nearly all of the seventy-five enemy bunkers damaged or destroyed. The only enemy activity was five off-target sniper rounds. Twenty-seven dead NVA were "officially" counted in and among the ruins. That was a body count guess, because there were so many body parts lying around that a realistic count was impossible.

The 1st Battalion, 9th Marines, now firmly established in the area, was assigned to protect the vital MSR from being mined or ambushed while the operation to clear the NVA from the southern half of the DMZ got under way. With its backside and major road supply artery both secure, Con Thien would now be able to play a vital role as a support base for the many Marine Corps and ARVN battalions involved in the DMZ invasion.

Throughout that long-awaited first day of Hickory, the 2d Battalion, 26th Marines continued to advance north along with the 2d Battalion, 9th Marines screening their right flank. The two maneuver battalions encountered only sporadic light contact. Then, disaster! At four in the afternoon, the 2/26 Battalion CP received forty-four rounds of 82mm mortar fire, wounding the battalion commander, Lieutenant Colonel Figard, the air liaison officer, artillery liaison officer, S-3 operations officer, headquarters commandant, and fifteen others. All had to be medevaced. The battalion executive officer (XO) assumed command until Figard's replacement, Lt. Col. William J. Masterpool, could arrive that evening. The edgy 2/26 Marines waited out the long night, knowing full well that many of them would be dead or mangled in the fierce fighting that lay ahead.

Landing at the Ben Hai

The sprawling logistics supply base at Dong Ha was a prime NVA target. The 3d Battalion, 4th Marines had arrived from Okinawa and set up its bivouac area at Dong Ha. The night of May 17–18, more than 150 giant 140mm rockets were fired at the base. A dozen rockets impacted in the 3/4 area, killing and maiming so many Marines from Kilo Company that only ninety men out of the company were unhurt.

Many casualties occurred in the ARVN sector where their command operations center (COC), which was not sandbagged, took a direct hit. Right next door, the Marines in their COC also took a direct hit, but they had only days earlier put up a tin roof over their sandbagged but leaky bunker, and, as lady luck would have it, that jerry-rigged roof prematurely detonated the rocket that had their name on it.

Dong Ha was devastated. Much equipment stockpiled for Hickory and the Prairie operations was destroyed. Several helicopters from HMM-363 had shrapnel damage but were still flyable. That was a stroke of good luck, because they were scheduled to lift the 3d Battalion, 4th Marines, the "Thundering Third," into the DMZ that day. Altogether, the shrieking, mind-jarring rocket barrage leveled at Dong Ha killed eleven and wounded ninety-one. Allied forces retaliated with a monumental show of counter-battery and air strike interdiction, bombarding the NVA throughout the DMZ.

In preparation for Operation Beau Charger getting under way on May 18, U.S. Navy ships dueled with NVA shore batteries that morning. No ships were hit. Dead-eye Navy gunners put the enemy shore batteries out of action with their five-inch guns, allowing the ship-to-shore landing of BLT 1/3 to proceed unopposed.

The helicopter-borne component of Beau Charger was not so fortunate. Only one platoon of BLT A/1/3 was able to land at LZ Goose due to heavy ground fire at the LZ. The remainder of the company was shifted to LZ Owl, eight hundred meters south. Accompanied by tanks, and with massive air strikes in support, the relief force fought their way through to the surrounded platoon before dark.

On the morning of May 18, according to plan, 3d Battalion, 4th Marines, commanded by Lt. Col. Wendell Vest, formed up by columns of companies and marched to the Dong Ha helipad a mile away. Most of the grim-faced grunts had leafy branches stuck into their helmets and packs for camouflage. The Marines were pumped with adrenaline, knowing their unit was going to be among the first Americans to invade the DMZ.

Support troops "back in the rear with the gear" lined the dusty road, watching the parade pass by. A battalion of Marines armed to the teeth and marching into combat is a truly impressive sight. None of the spectators cheered, but an occasional "Give 'em hell!" was heard. Their eyes said it all—a mixture of admiration and respect, plus a bit of "Thank God we ain't grunts."

After what seemed like a lifetime of waiting, baking under a relentless morning sun, the battalion's lead elements boarded helicopters and lifted off from Dong Ha at 11:20 a.m. They were ferried without incident to a landing in the DMZ at LZ Hawk, seven hundred meters south of the Ben Hai River. Once the LZ was secured, they would act as a blocking force to engage any retreating NVA being pushed north by 2/26 and 2/9. A worst-case scenario had them defending against a massive NVA counterattack coming at them from north of the Ben Hai River.

The apprehensive Marines, still a bit shell shocked from that rocket attack the previous night, were relieved to find the LZ uncontested. The battalion moved out in the stifling noonday heat to a deserted hamlet labeled Thon Cam Son on their maps and established a defensible position.

The Ben Hai area remained quiet overnight where 3/4 was encamped. In the morning, as 3d Platoon of India Company formed up and headed east along the dirt trail that ran by LZ Hawk, another tragic friendly fire incident happened. A new battalion FO called in a fire mission from the 81mm mortars, and four mortar rounds dropped out of the clear, blue sky, right on top of the men moving in column down the road. Agonizing cries for corpsmen went up: "Corpsman! Get a corpsman over here now!" Four Marines were killed outright, and twenty-seven others lay wounded along the blood-soaked trail.

Lance Cpl. Jim Cool ran over with his platoon to secure an LZ for the medevacs. He saw one anguished Marine in tears bend over one of the dead men and whisper, "Good-bye, Sarge." To compound the tragedy, men started falling out from heat exhaustion. Jim Cool helped carry two dead Marines to a CH-46 medevac chopper. It took four men to hoist and carry each body in the torrid heat. Cool noticed no wounds or blood and asked a nearby corpsman about this. The corpsman, who was nearly ready to faint from the heat himself, told him that the two men had died from heat prostration.[1]

Later that day, M/3/4 called in an air strike on a small cluster of buildings located just across the Ben Hai River at YD 078753 on their grid maps. Several fires and secondary explosions resulted. Being naturally curious, a squad of young Marines actually waded across the Ben Hai to search the area. In the process, they committed an act that could have had serious repercussions, but no officials on either side were the wiser. What they found was a major NVA logistics site with food, ammunition, weapons, and medical supplies. The grunts did not stay long because an aerial observer would logically assume those had to be *NVA* wearing Marine uniforms and bring friendly fire down on them.[2]

The Big Push North
Housed inside the perimeter at Con Thien was the 1st Battalion, 4th Marines. They would provide a reaction force in the event one or both of the maneuver battalions needed reinforcements. Patrolling south of

1/4 was the depleted 1st Battalion, 9th Marines, responsible for protecting Con Thien's rear and ensuring that the vital MSR from Cam Lo remained open. The 3d Battalion, 9th Marines guarded the Marines' flank southwest of Con Thien. The two maneuver battalions, 2/26 and 2/9, plus twenty tanks from Alpha and Bravo Companies of the 3d Tank Battalion, had pushed north across the newly cleared Trace and were headed directly into a bombed-out no-man's-land.

The North Vietnamese were determined to hold their ground. General Giap intended to make the Allies pay with their blood for every yard they advanced toward the DMZ. The Marines were equally determined to reach the DMZ, and they would not be deterred, but sudden death from snipers, booby traps, and ambushes was a cruel possibility every step of the way.

The terrain east and north of Con Thien was ideal for a defense-in-depth strategy. Densely wooded tree lines amid shrub- and bamboo-covered hedgerows provided perfect cover for the NVA lying in wait for Marine units to advance toward them across open fields. Acknowledged experts at camouflage, the NVA had learned how to capitalize on this skill and inflict heavy casualties on the Marines. The bloody battles at Phu An and Phu Oc were only the precursors of more brutal slugfests to come.

The four Marine tank platoons supporting the drive north had made a difference. They were usually able to keep attacking through the firestorm of popping bullets and blasting mortar shells, knocking out bunkers and suppressing the enemy's automatic weapons fire so that the accompanying grunts could assault through the enemy positions. But the tankers had suffered numerous casualties from RPGs, and antitank mines were also taking a toll on the armored forces.

"Pappy" Reynolds's tank, B-11, had hit a mine the previous evening, blowing off two sets of road wheels. He was towed back to the grunt CP where his tank commander, Second Lieutenant Rivero, took command of a different 1st Platoon tank so he could continue leading his platoon in the advance north. As Reynolds's tank and another mine-damaged Alpha Company tank were being towed back to Con Thien, the four armored vehicles came under attack. RPG trails zipped past them as they returned fire with their 90mm cannons and machine guns. Reynolds managed to climb up into the turret and get his cupola-mounted .50-caliber firing—three or four shots at a time until it jammed.

When the shooting died down, Reynolds heard someone rattling and banging the water cans strapped down on his tank. "What the hell you want?" he growled to the grunt. The man explained that his buddy had been gut shot and that he needed some water to put on his intestines that were hanging out. Reynolds gave him his last five-gallon can of water, the one he had saved under the gunner's seat. As Reynolds watched the Marine crawl away, dragging the water can, he disappeared in a dirty black and pink explosion. A mortar round had hit him right between the shoulder blades. His headless torso did a little flop and then lay still.[3]

By 4 p.m. of the second day of Hickory, May 18, battalions 2/9 and 2/26 had advanced one mile north of the Trace, reaching the road junction near the place indicated on their maps as "Market." The sun's heat was mind numbing in intensity as harassing sniper fire, mortars, and mines dogged the Marines all along their line of advance. No sooner was one enemy pocket eliminated, and friendly casualties collected and medevaced, than another enemy unit opened fire a few hundred meters further north. The resolute Marine tank/infantry force maintained the pressure, however, advancing steadily toward their main objective, the DMZ.

At nightfall, the sweat-soaked, dehydrated Marines pulled back to evacuate their wounded and bring in a much-needed water resupply. The casualty total for Hickory on May 18 added up to 5 Marines killed and 142 wounded, mostly from NVA mortars and artillery. The enemy tally was thirty-one actually confirmed dead. More killing and dying lay ahead, a harsh reality shared by both sides.

Later that night, NVA positions in front of the Marine lines were hit with seventy-five radar-controlled TPQ air strikes resulting in a spectacular fireworks show of secondary explosions. Few of the exhausted, sun-cooked Marines were awake to appreciate the spectacle.

Combatants along both sides of the DMZ were awakened early on the morning of May 19 by the sounds of artillery booming in from Gio

Linh to the east and from Cam Lo and Camp Carroll to the south. Massive preparatory fires had commenced at five in the morning because the Marines anticipated another day of bloody fighting to clear the NVA out of the Con Thien/DMZ area.

Lieutenant Fred Rivero had a French female war correspondent named Cathy Leroy sitting on the back of his tank taking photographs. She was a real curiosity out there in no-man's-land below the DMZ. Leroy was a vivacious, petite, pony-tailed blonde who wore jeans and had cameras dangling from her neck; it was hard to miss her. She refused to wear a flak jacket or helmet.

Because of the steady rumbling of the tank's powerful diesel engine, no one heard the telltale thump, thump, ka-thump sound of enemy mortar shells leaving their firing tubes. Two dozen mortar shells crashed down around Rivero's tank, seriously wounding Leroy along with eighteen nearby Golf Marines. As she lay on the ground, her shirt front soaked in blood, passing grunts could only stare and wonder who she was and what in the hell she was doing out there in no-man's-land with them.[4]

At 1:30 p.m., Capt. Robert J. Thompson's Hotel Company of 2/9, the easternmost company in the battalion, came under heavy attack by NVA hidden in camouflaged bunkers near the intersection of Routes 605 and 561 at the Market (later called the "Marketplace" by the Marines). Deadly small-arms and machine-gun fire tore into Cpl. Richard K. Gillingham's point squad. Several men shot down in the initial volley lay defenseless in the open. Without a second thought for his own safety, Cpl. Gillingham jumped up and ran through a hail of bullets and mortar shells to rescue one of his injured men. He was hit three times but refused to quit until he had dragged his wounded buddy out of the line of fire. Gillingham later succumbed to his many wounds.

Two Alpha Company tanks roared forward with their machine guns blazing, attempting to aid the pinned-down squad. Antitank rocket smoke trails zoomed in on the two tanks from a nearby tree line. The dozer tank, A-42 ("Earth-movin' Mama"), was hit first—dead center. Corporal Ratliff was killed instantly in the gunner's seat. The tank commander, Corporal Lozenski, was mortally wounded. PFC Kennedy and

PFC Summerlot, both unconscious, survived because a few heroic grunts risked their lives to pull them out of their smoldering tank before it exploded in flames.

The second tank came up to assist A-42. Within seconds, two more RPGs struck that tank, stopping it dead and putting it out of action. Altogether, three crewmen were killed and four wounded on the two knocked-out tanks.

Captain Thompson, the intrepid skipper who had been wounded the previous day but refused medevac, led his Hotel Company grunts forward in a fierce counterattack. They were able to lay down enough covering firepower to recover their casualties and pull them back. Thompson then called in air strikes and artillery to plaster the enemy stronghold.

Hotel Company had incurred the losses of seven Marines killed and twelve wounded in that attack. Enemy casualties were unknown. When Hotel later swept the area, the NVA had retreated, carrying off their casualties. Corporal Gillingham would be awarded the Navy Cross posthumously for sacrificing his life to save another. "Greater love hath no man than this . . . "

The next objective facing 2/9 was Gia Binh, a bomb-cratered, abandoned village located twenty-five hundred meters northeast of Con Thien and only a mile from the DMZ. Marines from 2/4 had done battle in that location the previous September during Operation Prairie. A sign reading "Death to the Americans" had first greeted them, followed by fierce fighting with NVA dug into a huge fortress of mutually supporting bunkers and trenches. One trench line, probably a former irrigation ditch, was filled with bunkers, reportedly extending clear up to the DMZ. BLT 1/26 had attacked the same complex later that September and driven out the NVA after a brief, violent encounter.

On May 20, 2/9 took its turn at the half-mile-long bunker complex off Route 561. The area was heavily prepped beforehand with artillery and air strikes. At 9:30 a.m., accompanied by two flame tanks and one gun tank, 2/9 started the attack. The flame tank crews fired two full loads of napalm (120 seconds), torching the bunker complex, while the M-48A3 gun tank crew blasted away with cannister rounds and its machine guns. Enemy resistance was surprisingly weak, much to the relief of the battle-fatigued 2/9 grunts. The main NVA force had apparently pulled out in great haste prior to the tank assault, leaving behind large amounts of equipment and ammunition.

Along with the Gia Binh bunker complex found deserted by 2/9, another huge vacated bunker complex was discovered by 2/26 right on the southern DMZ boundary line, two miles north of Con Thien. Constant pressure from allied air, ground, and artillery forces had ground down the NVA, forcing them to pull back from their numerous fortified enclaves surrounding Con Thien. Their sworn resolve to make a stand and fight to the death had not held up under the relentless Marine and ARVN onslaught. With the enemy's ability to resist broken, the way was cleared to enter the DMZ. Lieutenant Colonel Peeler's 2d Battalion, 9th Marines altered course and veered off to the east, paralleling the Trace. Lieutenant Colonel Masterpool's 2/26 continued the attack northwest into the DMZ.

The Fight for Hill 117

A cease-fire was declared throughout Vietnam on May 23 in honor of Buddha's birthday, and all Marine and ARVN units ceased advancing. The Marines, however, knew better than to sit around idly, cease-fire or no cease-fire. All units continued to patrol, ensuring that no surprises awaited them when the attack resumed the following day.

The 3d Battalion, 4th Marines had not encountered any serious resistance in their week-long advance south from the Ben Hai. One incident of note occurred with the 1st Platoon of Lima 3/4, led by 2d Lt. Robert McIntosh. His men located the crash site of an A4E Skyhawk jet while patrolling near the dirt road that ran north/south from the Con Thien area to the Ben Hai. The remains of the Marine pilot were flown out to Delta Med morgue.[5] The Marines believed they had located the jet fighter blown out of the night sky by a SAM missile on May 10. The bonus would be to locate the missile launch site, but that would be like finding the proverbial needle in a haystack.

By the eighth day of Hickory, May 25, the 3d Battalion, 4th Marines had located and destroyed tons of enemy supplies and demolished numerous fortifications while sweeping southwest from the Ben Hai River. Their objective on that scorching hot May day was to join up with 2/26 advancing northwest into the DMZ; then together they would continue sweeping south.

Three miles due west of Con Thien was a solitary, insignificant, tree-covered hill identified on the map as x117. Because the east-to-west DMZ boundary line meandered a few miles to the north above Con Thien to correspond with the flow of the Ben Hai River, Hill 117 was actually located one thousand meters inside the southern half of the DMZ, even though west of Con Thien.

On the morning of May 25, Hotel Company, 2/26, commanded by Capt. John J. Rozman, was patrolling just south of Hill 117, not anticipating any trouble. Supposedly, the NVA had left the area. Suddenly, Hotel was hit by a blistering barrage from a very large bunker complex hidden amid a tree line. A company or more of NVA had opened fire with small arms and automatic weapons from mutually supporting log bunkers.

Captain Rozman's Hotel Company fought back fiercely in the suffocating heat and humidity, killing twenty-six NVA before withdrawing to call for artillery and air support. He directed his company to circle back to the north, where he met up with Capt. John J. Flathman's Kilo 3/4, rushing to the sounds of battle. The two companies got on line together and attacked up Hill 117, but this time two companies of NVA defending from strongly built bunker fortifications awaited them. A former Kilo Company Marine, Hugh Kelley, remembered:

> When we got sent over to help out the Marines who were pinned down on the side of the hill, we had hustled all day to get there and were out of water. As soon as we crossed the top of this hill, we came under fire and had to fall back. Mortar rounds were hitting all around and we had several dead and wounded to deal with. I carried one of the platoon sergeants on my shoulder who had a gaping wound through his hip and abdomen. He lost so much blood that I'm sure he died before they could fly him out to Dong Ha Med. The hill caught on fire and several of the KIAs were burned badly as the fire swept over the hill. One dude, white as a ghost, asked me for some water. By the time I got back from carrying another wounded guy to the evacuation point, that heat

casualty had died of heat stroke. No one had water, and I was almost at the point where I hoped that I would get shot.[6]

The two companies, K/3/4 and H/2/26, pulled back to permit their artillery and air to soften up the objective. While they were waiting for their support fires to cease, an off-target artillery round landed amid Company K, killing and wounding several more men. Some began to lose it in all the bloody bedlam. The attack was delayed while Kilo got its casualties medevaced and its heat-exhausted, shook-up young Marines settled down.

The two companies joined in another attack but pulled back for good at 5:30 p.m. After having fought all day in the broiling heat, much of it without water, they had had enough. It was time to fall back, recuperate, repair their many jammed M-16s, and make plans for tomorrow. The day's brutal combat had cost the two Marine companies fourteen dead and ninety-two wounded.

All through the night, U.S. Marine and Army artillery pounded Hill 117. The following morning, the CO of 2/26, Lieutenant Colonel Masterpool, boarded a UH-1E Huey helicopter for a reconnaissance flight over the objective. Accompanying him were his XO, Major Landers, and the two company commanders from K/3/4 and H/2/26, Captains Flathman and Rozman.

As the Huey pilot circled high above Hill 117, hoping to avoid enemy ground fire, clouds of smoke floating over the lushly wooded hillside hindered visibility, preventing his passengers from sighting the layout of the enemy's fortifications and any likely avenues of approach. The pilot decided to drop down lower so his passengers could get a better look. Just then, a rapid *THUNK! THUNK! KA-THUNK!* rattled the sides of the helicopter. The Huey began to shudder and rotate wildly. The passengers and crew white-knuckled their cargo strap seats, praying for a miracle. Through some masterful flying and perhaps a bit of divine intervention, the stricken craft was able to crash-land without any fatalities. All four passengers were injured, but only Masterpool and Flathman required medevac.[7] This calamity, which could have easily been a major tragedy, forced a postponement of the attack until the following day. Lt. Col.

Duncan D. Chaplin III was choppered out to take over 2/26. He would become their third commander since Hickory commenced on May 17.

On the morning of May 27, Capt. Rozman's decimated Hotel Company pulled back, while two fresh companies from 2/26, Echo and Foxtrot, plus K/3/4, again attacked up Hill 117. This time, they advanced behind a wall of artillery walked up the hill ahead of them. By four o'clock their objective was declared secured. The NVA put up no more resistance. They were long gone. The Marines searched the hill, locating forty log and dirt bunkers, most demolished by the previous all-night bombardment. They recorded no NVA found, but the dead body stench coming from the rubble said volumes.

On May 29, H/2/26 was scouting around the woods six hundred meters northeast of Hill 117 when they made a very valuable discovery. It was that needle in a haystack. They found a Russian-made guided missile that was ten feet long and three feet in diameter and weighed five hundred pounds. All wiring and internal components were intact. Only the warhead was missing. One rationale for Operation Hickory had been realized. The Marines had found the phantom SAM missile site.

Relocation

A key aspect of Hickory called for the entire civilian population near the strongpoint-obstacle system to be relocated. That was an unfortunate but necessary evil in order for the grandiose barrier plan to work. More than twelve thousand people, twenty-seven hundred families, were uprooted from their ancestral homes within and south of the DMZ and then moved to a prepared site off Route 9 near Cam Lo. The relocation process was supposed to take a month, but heavy fighting along the DMZ caused the Vietnamese government officials to shorten the schedule to ten days.

Many villagers had no advance warning. As a result, they were forced to leave behind many possessions, taking only money, clothes, and a few tools. Most of their farm implements, livestock, and pets stayed behind. Their homes near the Trace were demolished. A census afterward found that only one family in five was able to bring even one chicken along with them.

Their new homes were in a cluster of tin-roofed huts constructed by the government on a barren plot of sun-baked, arid land. Water supply was a problem from the start and did not improve until the following year. A planned school for the children never materialized. The unemployment rate went up to 50 percent, whereas before it was nonexistent. Some of the more fortunate found work as laborers at American installations; others eked out a living selling items off the black market to American servicemen.

In his highly acclaimed book on the Vietnam War, *After Tet,* Ronald H. Spector summed up the bleak future facing those displaced civilians: "Uprooted from their ancestral lands, bereft of their meager possessions, unable to work at their traditional occupations or even work at all, apprehensive, confused, and depressed, these evacuees were the earliest casualties of the McNamara Line."[8]

Enemy contact diminished during the final days of Hickory and the other Allied operations. At midnight on May 28, all operations to clear the southern DMZ ended, and Operation Prairie IV resumed. More than fifty tons of rice and ten tons of ordnance had been destroyed or captured. Total enemy casualties for the combined Marine/ARVN operations were 789 killed, 37 captured, and 187 weapons taken. The Marines had 142 killed and 896 wounded, and the ARVN had 22 killed and 122 wounded.[9]

The Marines and their South Vietnamese allies had been extremely successful. Later assessments would conclude that it was one of the best-coordinated offensives of the war. Noted historian Eric Hammel believed that there was never a better time during the entire Vietnam conflict to carry the war into the enemy's backyard by crossing the Ben Hai River and continuing the attack north. The North Vietnamese had been caught off guard, unprepared to fend off a large Allied invasion force coming at them from across the DMZ.[10]

Capitol Hill politics prevented the Americans and their South Vietnamese allies from pursuing such a golden opportunity. Perhaps it was fear of Chinese intervention if the Allies crossed the DMZ en masse.

No one in the American government relished the idea of a repeat of that nightmarish Korean War scenario, when hundreds of thousands of Chinese troops counterattacked the United Nations' forces approaching the border with Manchuria in 1950. Another paralyzing worry was how far the Russians would go to defend a Communist ally, one that they were backing with a billion rubles' worth of supplies and armaments. America's leaders decided to exercise caution rather than risk fighting a wider war, perhaps even World War III; they stopped short of crossing the Ben Hai into North Vietnam.

Hickory was regarded as a daring escalation of the war at the time. In retrospect, the analogy could be made that the operation was only a Band-Aid when a tourniquet was needed to stem the flow of men and materiel from the north and neutralize the NVA's artillery capability from above the Ben Hai.

Despite stopping short of creating a serious setback for the North Vietnamese, Hickory did accomplish two goals: the removal of the local citizenry to create a free fire zone and the purchase of some time for work on the barrier to proceed with less disruption by General Giap's forces.

HILL 174

When the Marines on Con Thien faced west and peered off several miles into the distance, they would see terrain that changed markedly from generally flat land into green- and slate-colored hills and mountains. A distinct promontory about four miles away and a few degrees south of due west stood out from the surrounding hills. That high ground was Hill 174, a perfect spot for NVA forward observers to keep an eye on Con Thien. The Marines were inevitably drawn to that hill, and they knew it had to be taken.

The 3d Battalion, 4th Marines had been conducting its sweep through the DMZ in a southwesterly direction for much of Hickory. They had crossed the southern boundary of the DMZ and were back in South Vietnam when Hickory was terminated and Prairie IV was reinstated. The afternoon of May 28, about two thousand meters southwest of the now shell-cratered, fire-charred Hill 117, Mike and Lima Companies were advancing along the north finger of Hill 174 when several shots rang out, followed by a storm of automatic weapons fire coming from camouflaged positions in some woods.

Lieutenant Bob McIntosh ordered his platoon from Lima to lay down a base of fire to support an assault on the enemy bunkers. Most of his riflemen's M-16s jammed or misfired after the initial few rounds of fire. The only real fire coming from his unit was from his M-79 grenadiers and M-60 machine gunners. The two companies still managed to advance and had almost reached the crest of the tree-covered hill when they were opened up on from previously unseen enemy bunkers. Mortars, recoilless rifles, and automatic weapons "practically blew the Marines off the hill."[11]

Both companies pulled back to regroup and call in artillery and air strikes. The NVA launched nine shrieking 122mm rockets into Lima Company's area, inflicting numerous casualties. Then India, Kilo, and the battalion CP were on the receiving end of ten more rockets, causing additional casualties and rattling the nerves of the already-exhausted Marines. The battalion ordered its companies to hold in place for the night.

The following morning, a fresh India Company replaced shell-shocked Lima. Mike and India attacked up the hill. In a replay of the previous day's action, a sudden barrage of bullets and mortars descended on the Marines from another strongly fortified bunker complex hidden in a grove of trees.

Those NVA bunkers confronting them were solidly constructed out of sturdy, hardwood logs. Streams of green tracers sprayed out from narrow firing apertures. Sgt. Dominic Bilotta, the 60mm mortar section leader from M/3/4, watched in frustration as the Marines fired one LAAW (light antitank rocket) after another; they either misfired or bounced harmlessly off the bunkers. He tried taking the base plate off his mortars and firing them with a direct fire trajectory, but that did not work. They still could not get a mortar shell to go through a bunker aperture. Bilotta next hoisted a 3.5-inch rocket launcher and fired, barely missing his target. He reloaded the only round left, white phosphorus (WP). Taking dead aim, Bilotta's "Willy Peter" flew right through a bunker firing slot, burning to death the screaming enemy inside.

Clyde Petrella was a squad leader in 3d Platoon, Mike Company. His platoon had launched an attack directly into the heart of the bunker complex. Petrella remembered:

While we attempted to eliminate the bunkers to our immediate front, the NVA had snipers further up the hill using my squad for target practice. Myself and a lance corporal from Harlan County, Kentucky, can't remember his name, tried to knock out one bunker directly in front of us. I tried a LAAW but it malfunctioned. I then crawled up on the bunker and threw a grenade inside. The bastard threw it right back out. I crawled back up on the bunker and held another grenade until it was about ready to go before I threw it into the aperture. When we thought we'd killed everyone inside, I crawled around to the front aperture and the other Marine took the rear entrance. Somehow, an NVA had survived, and he fired off a clip with his AK-47 at the other Marine, wounding him several times in the left thigh, left arm and shoulder, and taking off two fingers and leaving a third dangling by a thread. All he said when I told him we had no one available to carry him off the hill was, "I'll walk. You take my canteen of water, Sarge, I'm goin' home." The last I saw of him he was limping back down the hill. I then made a satchel charge out of a block of C-4 explosive, crawled back to the bunker, and blasted the sonofabitch to hell! Nearby, other Marines from my squad were attempting to take out another bunker. They tried tear gas, but it blew back in their faces. One Marine, blinded by the gas, staggered in front of the bunker's main aperture and was gunned down. I could see an NVA inside watching me. Before I could react in time and swing my M-16 up, one of my fire team leaders, Cpl David Idle, shot him through the head.[12]

Sgt. Clyde Petrella was continuing to advance his squad up the hill when his point man was shot down thirty feet in front of a heavily camouflaged bunker. A burst from an AK-47 had ripped him right up the middle of his gut and chest. "I knew he was dead. Doc Crawford came up, but I told him there was nothing to be done for the man, that he would just get himself killed, and that he would be needed again for someone else who wasn't dead." But Navy corpsman Charles Crawford was not the kind of man who could stay down and not try to help a wounded Marine. "He had enough guts for three men." Petty Officer Crawford raced through the hail of deadly fire to the side of the downed Marine. Just as he reached his side, a bullet struck him in the head, killing him.[13]

Petrella also recalled, "After Doc was killed, a Black PFC was hit in the upper leg or buttocks by gunfire from the same bunker. While he was down, he would scream at the NVA in the bunker and call them 'stupid farmer mother fuckers!' Every time he screamed at them, they shot at him again."[14]

PFC Armand Thouvenell was a machine-gun team leader. He observed a fire team and a machine-gun team from another squad go down a ravine to reconnoiter two NVA bunkers. They immediately became pinned down in deadly machine-gun cross fire from the two positions. Knowing the Marines were running low on ammunition, several NVA had crawled in close enough to toss hand grenades. PFC Thouvenell grabbed his machine gun and nine hundred rounds of ammunition and raced in front of both enemy bunkers to provide covering fire to the pinned-down Marines. Under constant enemy fire, Thouvenell remained at his gun, laying down covering fire to ensure all the Marines had pulled back safely, until he was mortally wounded. He would be the third and last member of M/3/4 to be awarded the Navy Cross that day.

As darkness settled on the battlefield, the Marines held the western and northern slopes of Hill 174. The NVA still controlled the crest. Five Marines were dead, and thirty-three were wounded. Enemy losses were not known. The exhausted, sweat-soaked, grimy grunts knew what lay in store for them in the morning. They wondered who else would be dead after tomorrow's attack.

After another night of artillery bombardment, India and Mike attacked up the hill's rugged slopes. This time they had flamethrowers and an abundance of 3.5 rocket launchers, but they were still not able to reach the hill crest. The NVA were using a tactic the Japanese had employed against the Marines at Peleliu and Iwo Jima in World War II— situating their bunkers so that they were mutually supporting, connected by tunnels. When a force of Marines attacked one bunker, the NVA ran to another one and opened up on the Marines from the flank or rear. The tunnels were deep underground, practically impervious to our bombs and artillery. A small force of NVA holed up in bunkers at the top of the hill were prepared to fight to the death. Again the determined 3/4 grunts pulled back to blast the hilltop with air strikes and artillery.

On May 31, the Marines charged up the hill again, but this time the NVA were gone; they had pulled out overnight. A dozen dead NVA were left behind, lying among the demolished, bomb-blasted bunker complex. Three days and nights of continuous artillery bombardments and air strikes had apparently taken its toll on the defenders. The Marines had also paid a heavy price. Total casualties for the battle at Hill 174 were 12 Marines killed and 121 wounded.

Grunts and combat engineers from 3/4 combed the area thoroughly over the next two days, blew up any ammunition and bunkers they found, and then moved on to their next objective, just as they had after the other battles along the DMZ. What mattered to General Westmoreland, the Pentagon, and the Oval Office was the enemy body count. Holding on to hard-won terrain that had cost twelve young men their lives was not a high priority.

Manpower was another defining issue. The stretched-thin Marines did not have the luxury of providing troops to hold and then garrison their conquests. For a while after the Marines departed, harassing artillery shelling and radar-controlled TPQ bomb drops would follow, intended to deny the conquered hill to the enemy. Engineers also saturated the smashed bunker complex with chemical granules that would make the vacated terrain uninhabitable. In theory it sounded workable, but this enemy was doggedly determined to remain in that area.

Hill 174 was a key terrain feature. From Hill 174, the NVA could monitor all activity occurring at Con Thien and the other Project Nine strongpoints along Route 561, all the way south to Cam Lo and along Route 9 to Camp Carroll. The hill also made a perfect rocket-launching site. The NVA fully appreciated its value; it was only a matter of time until they reoccupied Hill 174.

With the taking of Hill 174 by the Marines on May 31, Operation Prairie IV ended. The next operation would commence June 1 and be named Cimarron. Prairie IV, like its predecessors, had been another round of hard-fought DMZ war slugfests. The NVA had losses of 505 dead, 8 captured, and 150 weapons seized. Marine losses were 164 killed and 1,240 wounded.[15]

The bloody month of May ended with the Con Thien area finally secured. What remained to be seen was how long it took the NVA to rebound from their setbacks suffered during Hickory and Prairie IV and once again present a serious threat to Con Thien and McNamara's barrier plan.

PART FOUR

SUMMER IN HELL

The Angel of Death has been abroad throughout the land:
You may almost hear the beating of his wings.

—Sir John Bright, Speech to House of Commons, Great Britain

8

Buffalo

General William Childs Westmoreland, COMUSMACV, helicoptered into lonely, little Con Thien. Major Danielson [1/9 XO] escorted Westmoreland around the perimeter. When a Marine pointedly asked, "General, I lost my best buddy to incoming yesterday—why can't we go into the DMZ after those bastards?" Danielson said, "The general's response was, 'Son, I wish we could, but the politics of the situation are such that we can't violate the DMZ.' Can you imagine how frustrating that response was to a young, dirty, unshaven, bleary-eyed, thirsty Marine?"
—Keith W. Nolan, *Operation Buffalo*

Operation Cimarron began June 1 on a quiet note for the Marines in the Con Thien area. Hickory had pretty much upset the NVA applecart, sending them reeling back across the DMZ to refit and regroup. Operation Cimarron would take place within the former Prairie IV area and continue to be a series of intermittent, minor clashes below the sun-baked DMZ, accomplishing nothing except to shed more blood in the futile, mutual war of attrition.

In the post-Hickory aftermath, both sides seemed to be taking a breather. But as June wound down and July was coming into view, enemy activity picked up again. Artillery shelling from the DMZ increased, and several sharp firefights occurred with scattered groups of NVA in the Con Thien area of operations (AO). Intelligence reports indicated clearly that the North Vietnamese were preparing for another offensive.

Meanwhile, work progressed steadily on the barrier system. Once the five-hundred-meter-wide perimeters around Con Thien and Gio Linh were completely cleared in early June, the 11th Engineers commenced widening the Trace from two hundred to six hundred meters. McNamara's Wall was becoming a reality, despite North Vietnam's efforts.

The 1st Battalion, 9th Marines under Lt. Col. Richard J. Schening had been assigned the Con Thien AO since taking over from 1/4 the last week in May. Capt. Richard J. Sasek's Delta Company manned Con Thien's perimeter lines. Housed inside the perimeter were the CP group and H & S Company. Alpha, Bravo, and Charlie Companies conducted patrols and set up night ambushes outside the perimeter.

Capt. Edward L. Hutchinson's Company C had been pulled back to Dong Ha the end of June for a few days of rest and relaxation (R&R) after they and Delta had completed an unproductive sweep two thousand meters northeast of Con Thien through the notorious Marketplace–Gia Binh area. Over the past year, the Marines had tangled repeatedly with company- and battalion-sized units of the NVA in this area labeled "Market" on their maps. The grunts always expected trouble when they went in there. Not finding anything amiss was troubling to some old salts who knew the area. That was a sure sign the NVA were up to something.

All was not well with 1/9 at Con Thien. Those eighteen- and nineteen-year-old kids holding down the fort were frustrated and angry at their role as live targets for the NVA artillery batteries up in the DMZ. Intermittent mortar and rocket attacks only added to the demoralizing situation. Day after day, more young 1/9 Marines became casualties, some riddled with shrapnel and some blown to pieces, and the only politically permissible response was to retaliate with artillery and air strikes. Unleashing our ground forces to go after the enemy gun batteries above the Ben Hai was not considered a viable option by our government.

On July 1, the last day of Operation Cimarron, Alpha and Bravo Companies were preparing to go back out into the same Marketplace area two thousand meters northeast of Con Thien that Charlie and Delta Companies had swept a few days earlier. The 9th Marines CO,

Col. George E. Jerue, wanted to foil the NVA pattern, which was to move into an area right after the Marines swept through and then dig in and prepare an ambush for the next Marine unit to come by on patrol weeks later. That night, Captain Al Slater's Alpha Company set in north of Con Thien, less than a mile from the DMZ near the deserted hamlet of Thon An Nha. Bravo Company had crossed the Trace that afternoon and set in for the night fifteen hundred meters to the southeast of Alpha along Route 561, the ten-foot-wide cart path that connected Cam Lo with the DMZ.

Bravo Company had a new skipper. Capt. Sterling K. Coates was a 1961 graduate of the Naval Academy. He came to 1/9 in June as the new S-3A, where he learned the ropes under the current S-3, Captain Curd, recipient of two Silver Star Medals in the March 5 and March 24 battles at Phu An. After two weeks as the S-3A, Coates took command of B/1/9. He was generally regarded as a levelheaded, dedicated officer of Marines, well respected by his peers. All he needed was some combat seasoning.

The plan for Alpha and Bravo entailed setting up patrol bases north of the Trace and then spending the next two weeks sweeping back and forth between Con Thien and the DMZ. The purpose was to detect the enemy's intentions in the area so the 3d Marine Division could shift its paper-thin manpower resources as needed to disrupt any plans for another invasion across the DMZ into Quang Tri Province.

The men were tired. A relentless pace of operations around Con Thien and the DMZ was taking its toll. After humping through the bush all day long in the blistering heat, each company had to conduct two ambushes a night. In addition, practically every level of command from platoon leader to fire team leader was undermanned and inexperienced. Heavy casualties, end-of-tour rotations, and R&R vacancies meant that Bravo Company took to the field with 150 men instead of their assigned complement of 200. Lance corporals were doing the job of corporals, corporals were leading squads instead of sergeants, and so on.

After the spring Hill Fights at Khe Sanh and the bloody month of May at Con Thien, many of the men in Bravo were "new boots," green replacements assigned to the "Walking Dead" who soon learned of 1/9's reputation as a hard-luck outfit. But they were combat Marines. They had a tough job to do, and they would do it to the best of their ability.

As the sun peeked above the horizon on July 2, 1967, the first day of Operation Buffalo, tension was almost palpable as Bravo Company formed up along Route 561 and headed north. Awaiting them in freshly dug, carefully camouflaged fighting positions were two fresh battalions of the 90th NVA Regiment, 324B Division, who were determined to seek retaliation for the mutilation of their dead by some 1/9 Marines during the earlier Prairie and Hickory operations.

THE MARKETPLACE MASSACRE

No sooner had Capt. Al Slater's Alpha Company started advancing north from Thon An Nha when three men from the lead platoon went down from trip-wire booby traps—an ominous harbinger of events to follow. Medevacs were called in, and the advance continued.

Captain Coates's Bravo Company, southeast of Alpha, continued advancing smoothly with no problems. By 9:00 a.m., the Marines were already perspiring from the oppressive heat and humidity. Lieutenant King's 2d Platoon had secured its first objective, a small trail intersection twelve hundred meters north of the Trace, without making any contact.

The entire area consisted of hedgerow-bordered paddies that were overgrown with sun-dried grass and crisscrossed with irrigation ditches and trenches. Here and there were thick clumps of bamboo and banana trees. An occasional unwrapped field bandage, battered helmet, or other flotsam and jetsam from battles past served as a constant reminder to the 1/9 grunts that they were once again venturing into the grim reaper's lair.

Third Platoon, led by Staff Sgt. Alfredo Reyes, who was new to the rank as well as to Bravo, took the point as Bravo continued north. Following them was the CP group, and then came 2d Platoon with the XO, 1st Lt. William F. Delaney, and the mortars. First Platoon under Staff Sgt. Leon R. Burns brought up the rear; they had instructions to secure an LZ for resupply later.

Three hundred meters up the road, where east-west Route 605 intersected with Route 561, was a place the Marines referred to as the Marketplace. Third Platoon had just reached the intersection about 9:30 when several shots rang out from the west. The platoon wheeled left and got on line, believing they were taking fire only from a squad of NVA armed with SKS carbines in a trench. While two squads from 3d Platoon lay down a base of fire, the third squad assaulted into what turned out to be a platoon of NVA armed with AK-47s. The Marines were soon overpowered and pinned down. M-16 jamming problems began to crop up, further limiting their return fire.

People wearing USMC helmets and flak jackets were shooting at them. Confused Marines shouted, "Stop shooting! We're friendlies!" From numerous concealed positions, the NVA quickly overran Staff Sergeant Reyes's 3d Platoon with their superior firepower. Huddled together in disconnected, isolated pockets, the outnumbered Marines were systematically surrounded, hit with grenades, and then overrun. The wounded were executed where they lay prostrate in the sun-baked dirt.

Captain Coates moved his command group up to support 3d Platoon, but the NVA fire intensified, bringing them to a halt. He ordered Second Lieutenant King to shift his 2d Platoon to the right of the road and attempt to flank the NVA, but overwhelming firepower from NVA attacking from the eastern flank drove King's men to ground. Cpl. Mike Hughes saw his squad just lying there, some not firing. He shouted, "Get up and move back!" Someone said, "We can't." Hughes retorted, "You want to live, you got to move!" Slowly they inched back to the road. Sgt. Richard Huff, mortar section leader, recalled that Captain Coates "was all up and down that line, shooting his .45. He told me to get my mortars firing. Then he ran back up front and that was the last I saw of him alive."[1]

Casualties began to mount. Snipers were situated to fire down into the Marines hugging the road. Captain Coates ordered 1st Platoon to move up. As they hustled forward, the point squad leader noticed movement on his right flank on Hill 70. His men took the figures coming their way under fire, even though at first glance they appeared to be a half-dozen Marines wearing USMC helmets and flak jackets. This was a common ruse used by the NVA to get in close while the Marines attempted to confirm their identity. Once in close, the Marines could not employ their air and artillery trump cards against them.

Captain Coates then ordered a two-squad assault, one squad each from 1st Platoon and 2d Platoon, against a tree line situated at the eleven o'clock position. They were soon pinned down by machine-gun and RPG fire from bunkers hidden in the tree line. The NVA could see them, but the Marines could not find any targets. Snipers up in trees fired down on the pinned-down Marines, picking off anyone with a radio or anyone who made a hand signal. The survivors tried to withdraw, but most were shot down. Few made it back alive. Several NVA ran across the road between 2d and 3d Platoons, taking the Marines under fire from both sides of the road. To make matters worse, mortars and artillery began crashing down, further cutting off the 3d Platoon and the command group from 2d and 1st Platoons. Bravo was getting murdered.

Alpha Company's Captain Slater was in contact with the 1/9 CP back at Con Thien. He was ordered to reverse direction and march south whence he had come and then turn east and come up to assist Bravo from the rear. Captain Hutchinson's Charlie Company, just starting to unwind and relax after a few days of relishing hot chow and showers back at Dong Ha, was alerted to mount up and make tracks to the helipad; they would be choppered in. At Con Thien, Delta Company was taking heavy incoming as they organized a tank-infantry relief force.

As Alpha closed the fifteen-hundred-meter distance between themselves and beleaguered Bravo, the point team walked into a claymore mine booby trap, wounding four more men. Alpha could not stop for a medevac. Captain Slater ordered his point platoon to pick up its casualties and keep moving.

Two F4B Phantom II jets and two Huey gunships arrived, finally. A propeller-driven O1-E "Bird Dog" observation plane circled overhead and then dove down firing white phosphorus rockets to mark targets. The Phantoms roared in and unloaded their 250- and 500-pound bombs, and some hit so close that the grunts were showered with dirt clods. As the jets flashed west over Alpha advancing from the east, heavy machine-gun fire could be heard coming from a tree-lined ridge to the north as the NVA attempted to knock the jets out of the air. One of the Marine Phantoms flown by Major Ray D. Pendergraft was hit. Trailing smoke, he turned east and headed for the South China Sea, but he crashed just as he cleared the coastline. Both he and his copilot were killed. Both Huey gunships circled overhead and poured torrents of machine-gun fire into the NVA positions.

Capt. Bruce Martin piloted an F-8 Crusader from VMF-232 that flew in from Da Nang. He watched Major Pendergraft's Phantom nose over and crash into the sea. Armed with eight five-hundred-pound snake-eye bombs, Martin, directed by the Alpha forward air controller (FAC), made his bomb run from the west. As he dove down and pickled his full bomb load, he felt something thumping into his fuselage. His fire warning light flashed on, so he also headed east toward the coast. When he saw clouds of black smoke pouring out from behind him, he bailed out, parachuting to a safe landing in the sea.[2]

Back at the Marketplace road junction, the situation was growing more desperate with each passing minute. Bravo's CP group and 2d Platoon fought back fiercely against the hordes of attacking NVA. Cpl. Margarito Garza kept his M-60 machine gun chattering, despite being wounded twice. Cpl. Mike Hughes helped prop up some of his wounded men so they could still fire. One man with a shattered arm asked for help loading his last round.

Bravo's forward air controller, Capt. Warren O. Keneipp, who two weeks earlier had also been an F-8 Crusader pilot with VMF-232, radioed XO Delaney to tell him that Captain Coates was down, that both platoon commanders were dead or wounded, and that he was also hit. Keneipp no longer had communication with 2d and 3d Platoons. He told Lieutenant Delaney, dizzy and disoriented from heat exhaustion, that Delaney was now in charge. Delaney urged Keneipp to hold on a little longer, that he was pinned down on the trail along with the mortars and the rear of 2d Platoon and could not move up but that Alpha would be there any minute.

Captain Slater doggedly pushed his Alpha Company forward toward Bravo, despite incoming mortars that were taking a heavy toll of his men—about thirty wounded. Captain Slater ordered Second Lieutenant Muller to deploy 3d Platoon around a hasty LZ at the rear of the company while he continued advancing with his CP group alongside 2d Platoon. He sent his 1st Platoon on up ahead with orders to link up with Bravo, but only a dozen men managed to break through. Amid all the chaos, two CH-34s managed to land and pick up Alpha's most seriously wounded. A few seconds after they had lifted off, NVA artillery zeroed in and blasted the LZ.

Heavily camouflaged NVA infantry, clumps of elephant grass tied to their backs and pith helmets, crawled to the edge of the LZ defended by Alpha's 3d Platoon. At a signal they rose up, charging through their own incoming, and penetrated the perimeter. A second group of NVA following the attacking force executed every Marine they found wounded. An M-60 machine-gun crew in a hedgerow kept firing until they were overrun. PFC Charles Ragland, the sole survivor of his three-man team, played dead while small groups of NVA rifled through the Marine packs, discarding equipment but taking cigarettes, canteens, and ammunition. They soon completely overran Lieutenant Muller's 3d Platoon at the LZ, killing him and many of his men.

The scattered survivors hurdled hedgerows and sprinted across paddies to make it back to where Alpha's 2d Platoon had dug in. Most were out of water, nearly delirious from the heat, and low on ammunition. Somehow, a handful of surviving NCOs managed to get the panicked stampede turned around and formed up into a tight perimeter around a paddy, braced for whatever was yet to come.

Smoke began to drift over the battlefield. Several NVA with flame-throwers had set the hedgerows and dried elephant grass aflame. Marines fleeing the fires were cut down by snipers and machine gunners. Those dead or unable to run were soon enveloped and roasted by the racing flames.

Back at the road junction where Bravo was fighting for its life, Captain Keneipp had run out of time. His last brave words to the 1/9 CP were: "I don't think I'll be talking to you again. We are being overrun." The entire Bravo CP group was killed: Captain Coates, Captain Keneipp, Lieutenant King, Corporal Garza, Corporal Demers, Corporal Haines, and Lance Corporal Bradley.[3]

Staff Sgt. Leon Burns and his men from Bravo's 1st Platoon had fought their way up the road toward 2d Platoon while holding off NVA reinforcements coming over Hill 70 from the east. Burns emptied four rounds from his shotgun into an NVA who ran by him using a flame-thrower. He then got up on the tactical air communication (TAC) frequency and contacted a Bird Dog spotter pilot orbiting overhead. The pilot said, "Who are you?" Burns replied: "This is Bravo One, Two, Three, Four, Five, and Six, and I need all the help that I can get. If you don't get somebody in here pretty soon this is going to be the Lost Command. I don't care if you get the Army in here, but we gotta get somebody in here."[4]

A flight of A-1 Skyraiders came on station just as several groups of NVA surged over the crest of Hill 70. Burns directed the first napalm run on the hilltop, which incinerated the attackers. He spotted another group of forty NVA up ahead at the road junction where Bravo's CP group had been overrun. He made an agonizing decision to have a bomb drop made there, certain no one was left alive. Burns and his men fought their way forward, finally reaching what was left of 2d Platoon and the mortars. As Burns ordered the remaining survivors from Bravo to withdraw, he heard tanks approaching. The relief force had arrived at last.

CAVALRY TO THE RESCUE

Shortly after noon, the 1/9 CO, Lt. Col. "Spike" Schening, dispatched a relief force from Con Thien consisting of the 3d Platoon from Delta Company and a four-tank platoon from Bravo Company, 3d Tank Battalion. The remainder of Captain Sasek's Delta Company had to remain on the Con Thien perimeter in the event that a full-scale attack such as the one on May 8 was coming next. Leading the relief force was the new assistant S-3, Capt. Henry J. M. Radcliffe. His instructions were to find Bravo Company, take command and reorganize the scattered units, and evacuate the dead and wounded.

First Lieutenant Gatlin J. Howell, the battalion S-2 intelligence officer, requested to go along. He was only weeks from rotating home to his wife and kids, but he knew the area out there, having been Bravo's 3d Platoon commander for more than eight months. A former enlisted man, he had gone to college after his active duty service in the Corps and then become a teacher and coach. He knew how to handle young Marines.

His men knew it and revered him as their leader: "Those were his Marines dying in the Marketplace, and there was no way he could abandon them. That's the kind of man he was."[5] Delta's 3d Platoon leader, Second Lieutenant Turchan, was brand new, as was Radcliffe; Gatlin Howell's experience would be needed. Captain Sasek volunteered his own senior radio operator, Cpl. Charles A. Thompson, to go along. He, too, knew the territory.

Turchan's grunts were already waiting aboard the tanks when Radcliffe, Howell, and Thompson mounted their one-quarter-ton jeep and moved out, leading the column east along the southern boundary of the Trace. When they reached the spot where Route 561 intersected the Trace, the column of tanks made a left flank turn and got on line headed north. Lieutenant Turchan's men dismounted and found some old fighting holes on the northern edge of the Trace straddling the road. Delta-3 settled in along there with their backs against the Trace, facing north. Captain Radcliffe ordered Lieutenant Turchan in no uncertain terms to hold that position no matter what might come their way.

Commanding the four tanks from Bravo Company, 2d Platoon was Gunnery Sergeant Norman Eckler in tank B-25. His platoon sergeant was Staff Sgt. Lemuel Sloan, commander of B-24. The other tank commanders were Sgt. Dover Randolph in B-22 and Cpl. James Holston in B-23. This was a gritty group of combat veterans. Many of the crewmen had participated in the Prairie and Hickory operations. They also knew this area well.

Accompanied by the four tanks, Captain Radcliffe and First Lieutenant Howell, with Corporal Thompson lugging the radio on his back, headed north on foot toward the sounds of battle. "When I heard those tanks, I cried," recalled Sergeant Huff later. "All around, men of Bravo Company lay dead or wounded, but when they saw Mr. Howell, they started to cheer."[6]

The relief force began to encounter dazed and wounded Marines struggling back south on the road. Radcliffe approached the XO, First Lieutenant Delaney, who was rambling incoherently, an obvious heat casualty. Radcliffe saw he was out of it and told him to keep moving to the rear.

Staff Sergeant Burns and his Bravo survivors had pulled back down the road about forty meters when they ran into Radcliffe, Howell, and Thompson moving north with the tanks.

"Burns, where's Bravo Company?" asked Captain Radcliffe.

"This is it."

"What?!"

Burns's emotions were getting strained. "Sir, this is your command. This is it. This is First Platoon and that's all there is left."

Radcliffe was stunned. The situation was drastically worse than anyone back at the 1/9 CP had realized. "Well, we're going up there and get 'em," Radcliffe told Burns. "You going with us?" The trio was joined by Burns, who preferred to leave his spent platoon behind. They continued cautiously along the road as stray bullets snapped and zinged overhead.[7]

Staff Sergeant Leslie, the Alpha-1 platoon leader who had earlier broken through to Bravo, approached the group. Radcliffe was dismayed to find that Leslie had less than a dozen men with him, but he ordered him to hold the left flank and not let any NVA through to the road. He then directed Staff Sergeant Sloan's section of two tanks to drop off to the right so he could protect his vulnerable right flank. With his flanks reasonably secured, Radcliffe and Gunny Eckler's other two tanks continued north.

What Radcliffe's men saw at the road junction shocked them. Dead Marines were lying everywhere. It was a charnel house of death. "Thirty, forty, maybe fifty Marines lay twisted along both sides of the road, clumped atop each other in spots, their weapons and gear strewn down the middle of the road for the length of the column."[8]

Bullets began kicking up dust and ricocheting off the tanks as the NVA attempted to surround Radcliffe's meager relief force. Gunny Eckler's B-25 and Holston's B-23 unleashed a torrent of cannister rounds, HE, and machine-gun fire, driving the NVA back.[9] A Bird Dog pilot told radioman Thompson that he had spotted a hundred NVA in a tree line up ahead. Burns called in an air strike, which saturated the target with bombs and napalm. But they were still taking fire from NVA positions closer to the road. Burns called in another napalm run so close to the road that it sucked their breath away. The Bird Dog pilot then said he needed to head home and refuel and that he had counted seventy to ninety dead NVA caused by the air strikes Burns directed.

Company C, commanded by Capt. Edward L. Hutchinson, began arriving by helicopter at the Trace around twelve thirty in the afternoon. They were only about one hundred strong; half the company's original strength were casualties from earlier battles not yet replaced. Captain Radcliffe was in communication with Hutchinson. He told him he needed a platoon to come up fast to help protect his right flank. Captain Hutchinson sent 2d Lt. Frank Libutti on ahead with his platoon.

Radcliffe, Burns, Howell, and Thompson went searching for any wounded left alive. They found dozens of men, mostly from 1st and 2d Platoon and a few 3d Platoon survivors, and carried them to the two tanks. Several of the dead and wounded were found with their M-16 rifles broken down where they had tried to unjam them before they were overrun. Many had been executed, shot in the face or back of their head as they lay there wounded. A few of those executed had battle dressings that had been placed on their wounds by corpsmen while still alive.

Lieutenant Gatlin Howell was everywhere, a man possessed, desperately searching for any survivors. He ignored the intermittent incoming mortar and sniper fire. Between himself and Corporal Thompson, they accounted for two dozen of the survivors being rescued. One man they rescued was Cpl. Domingo Trevino, a twice-wounded radio operator, who had been tied to a tree while barely conscious, presumably as ambush bait.

Radcliffe's team and the two tanks were attempting to reach 3d Platoon's furthest point of advance when they began taking heavy AK-47 and mortar fire. The situation was rapidly changing from bad to worse. The two tanks, loaded with all the casualties they could carry, headed back south, leaving thirty-four dead behind. That was a heartbreaking decision because Marines never leave their dead behind, but it had to be done to save the wounded.

Lieutenant Libutti and his 2d Platoon from Charlie Company had just met up with Radcliffe and the two casualty-laden tanks when an RPG scored a direct hit on Gunny Eckler's tank, impacting at the rear of the commander's cupola. Fortunately for Eckler, it was a dud. Captain

Radcliffe got nicked in the face by a piece of shrapnel from the dud RPG. He was unaware of it until Libutti mentioned the blood running down his sweaty face.

Libutti's orders were to continue north and guard the rear gate until Bravo's survivors and Staff Sergeant Leslie's Alpha-1 Platoon had pulled out. He was then to bring up the rear for the movement south to connect up with the remainder of Captain Hutchinson's Company C holding the door open to the Trace.

About 2:00 p.m., one of the two tanks left behind to protect Captain Radcliffe's right flank hit a mine estimated at forty pounds of TNT with a pressure fuze. There was no way to repair the damaged track and road wheels; it would have to be towed. Staff Sergeant Sloan then directed the connecting of tow cables from his disabled tank onto the rear of Sergeant Randolph's tank.

Corporal Holston's tank, B-23, loaded down with more than a dozen casualties, was approaching fast, only a few hundred meters from Sloan and Randolph, when his tank hit another mine, possibly a dud 175mm artillery shell, breaking a track and knocking some of the casualties off his tank onto the ground. An exasperated Captain Hutchinson yelled at the tankers to leave the tanks and keep moving on foot. Gunny Eckler would not hear of it. His crewmen heard him curse, "Tell him he can hang it in his poop-snapper," as he ignored the captain and hooked up his tow cables onto Holston's tank.[10] He was not about to leave any of his tanks behind. Again the column moved out, two tanks towing the two disabled ones loaded down with casualties.

The grisly caravan had traveled only a hundred meters when an RPG exploded on the right side of Holston's B-23. It penetrated the sponson box into the turret, wounding driver Lance Corporal Hunter in the back and PFC Martin, the gunner, in both legs. Then, another RPG team stood up at the eleven o'clock position and fired. Their antitank rocket struck the turret front and ricocheted up, detonating on the open loader's hatch. The blast knocked crewman Lance Cpl. Henry Brightwell unconscious. When he came to, his com-helmet studded with shards of metal, he saw the turret filling with smoke. Brightwell grabbed the fire extinguisher, but a crewman had wasted some of it the day before to cool down some beer, so it was almost empty. He discharged what remained in the extinguisher bottle, and it was enough to do the job—the smoke cleared. While Brightwell was putting out the turret fire, Corporal Holston drew out his .45-caliber pistol from his shoulder holster, took careful aim, squeezed off two rounds, and knocked down both members of the NVA RPG team that had just fired at them.

Back at Alpha's perimeter, the beleaguered force was holding together. Gunnery Sergeant Tony Santomasso did a masterful job of directing fire and organizing (and ass kicking) his Marines into a cohesive group. Captain Slater and his CP group had managed to join up with the 2d Platoon, and their combined fierce return fire had stopped the NVA advance. The artillery FO ringed their position with artillery, further solidifying their perimeter's chances for survival. The NVA were also directing artillery toward Alpha's position, but their rounds were falling short, landing on their own men.

At 3:00 p.m., Lieutenant Colonel Schening radioed the 9th Marine Regiment's CO, Colonel Jerue, informing him that all of his companies were engaged, that the situation was critical, and that he had no more reserves to commit. Colonel Jerue responded by ordering Major Willard B. Woodring's 3d Battalion, 9th Marines to prepare to be lifted by helicopter to the Trace to support 1/9.

Captain Radcliffe's remaining withdrawal to the Trace one thousand meters away was like running the gauntlet from hell. Snipers, mortars, and artillery dogged Bravo's survivors all the way. The tanks blasted away with their cannister rounds and machine guns, preventing the NVA from moving in close enough to penetrate the column's flanks. Some of the wounded riding on the tanks were hit by bullets or shrapnel and killed. Air strikes pounded the NVA with bombs and napalm, with some less than one hundred meters from the road. At last, at about four in the afternoon, Bravo and the tanks reached the Trace.

Chaos reigned at the Trace. Bravo Marines stumbled into the D-3 perimeter. They were exhausted and semidelirious from the heat and no water, and some were going into shock with serious wounds. Corpsmen labored to sort out who was who and to fill out medical tags.

The seriously wounded were brought to the center of the perimeter formed by Delta-3 where they could be the first ones loaded on the soon-to-be-arriving medevacs. No sooner was that done than a 130-round artillery barrage plastered the perimeter. Several of the more seriously wounded men lying exposed in the center of the perimeter took direct hits, and they were blasted to bits. Delta-3's platoon sergeant was killed, and Lieutenant Turchan was wounded. Amid all the chaos and carnage, someone made the decision to move the remaining casualties across the Trace to the southern edge, where they would be out of sight of the NVA FO calling in the accursed artillery. Everyone expected another NVA attack, and this new location would mean the NVA had to charge across six hundred meters of open ground to reach the casualties.

One CH-34 medevac made it in to the shell-cratered LZ. The pilot held up four fingers, the number of casualties he could safely carry. Ignoring him, men loaded six critically wounded Marines minus their helmets, flak jackets, and weapons. Somehow, thanks to skillful piloting and a few Hail Marys, the overloaded helicopter was able to struggle up over the trees and into the sky.

Back at the Con Thien CP, forty or so wounded were observed limping across the Trace. Lieutenant Colonel Schening ordered his XO, Major Danielson, to take every available vehicle out to retrieve those men and bring them back into the Con Thien perimeter. Danielson and his "Keystone Cops" convoy of one Marine jeep-ambulance, a "deuce-and-a-half" truck borrowed from the Navy Seabees, and his one-quarter-ton jeep roared down the Trace in a cloud of dust. The seriously wounded were loaded aboard the major's vehicles. Then two CH-46 Sea Knight helicopters arrived. The wounded men were transferred to the helicopters, but the pilots complained that they were overloaded and that some would have to come off. Major Danielson had to make many gut-wrenching decisions about who was in the most danger so they could remain on the medevac choppers. A dozen men had to be taken off and reloaded on the vehicles.

Meanwhile, this delay was putting everyone in jeopardy. Sure enough, the first rounds of incoming came in, but they were off target. The helicopters lifted off as Danielson's vehicles were unloaded again and the wounded rushed to safety in the woods. On the third try, Major Danielson was able to get his group of wounded back on board the vehicles and moving toward Con Thien before the NVA could find the range.[11]

Radcliffe and Burns moved the remaining Bravo troops, those still able to walk, back across the Trace and sat them down in several old fighting holes on Delta-3's perimeter. Company C had yet to fight its way back out, so Bravo's exhausted, barely coherent, heat-drained survivors would have to remain in place, guarding the vital south gate.

Lieutenant Libutti's platoon, pulling rear guard duty, went as far north as the Marketplace but came under fire before they reached Bravo's dead. They reversed course and were moving back to meet up with the rest of Company C when they got hit. A small unit of NVA, likely a squad or more, saw something they liked and attacked with AK-47s, getting in close enough to throw grenades.

Captain Hutchinson left his company in place and ran forward with a handful of volunteers to assist Libutti. Fighting back fiercely, scared as hell that they were going to be the next unit of dead Marines wiped out that day, the rear guard soon broke through the ambushers and joined up with the remainder of Charlie Company. But they were not home free yet. They still had to fight their way through a second ambush while carrying their own dead and wounded out.

It was almost dusk when Charlie Company's men looked up to see the sky full of helicopters bringing in the 3d Battalion, 9th Marines. The NVA could see them, too, and decided to break contact. It had been a close call. Perhaps the NVA were depleted in numbers; otherwise, Charlie Company would have been encircled at the Marketplace, and 3/9 would be coming to their rescue.

As soon as Capt. Jerry Giles's K/3/9 landed on the Trace, they pushed north, linking up with Captain Slater's A/1/9. Alpha's men were emotional at the sight of their relief arriving. They knew that they would not have survived through the night, that the NVA would be back in sufficient numbers to overrun them and then coldly execute them where they lay. Captain Giles and his Kilo Company men helped retrieve Alpha's casualties, many of the dead charred by the merciless flames that had swept across the LZ. Alpha's men trudged south to the Trace as night fell, carrying the bodies of their dead friends in ponchos.

Bravo's survivors and Delta-3 got the word to mount up on the tanks and head back to Con Thien. The dead were placed on the two tanks being towed. Captain Hutchinson's Charlie Company settled in for the night with I/3/9. Alpha Company, or what was left of them, joined K/3/9 in the 3/9 perimeter. After their horrendous, day-long ordeal, Alpha's battle-fatigued, dehydrated survivors wondered out loud why they were not being allowed to return to Con Thien along with Bravo.

It would be a long night. The enemy's full intentions were not known at this point. A major ground attack might yet be planned for Con Thien. Knowing that another Marine battalion might be headed their way in the far-off morning hours offered little cheer to the men from 1/9 and 3/9.

At the end of that terrible day, 1/9's casualties were 53 KIA, 190 WIA, and 34 MIA (33 bodies eventually found, 1 not recovered). Seven of those killed were U.S. Navy corpsmen.[12] Keith W. Nolan, author of *Operation Buffalo: USMC Fight for the DMZ*, wrote that what happened to Bravo 1/9 on July 2, 1967, was "the worst single disaster to befall a Marine Corps rifle company during the entire Vietnam War."[13] Only twenty-seven men from Bravo Company walked out of that battle un-scathed. It had been a costly battle for the North Vietnamese Army as well. Burns and Radcliffe estimated they saw eighty NVA dead. Alpha Company observed thirty dead outside of their perimeter. The tankers claimed another forty probably killed. Hundreds more were likely killed by air strikes and artillery, some by their own friendly fire. Still, the battlefield belonged to the NVA at the end of the day, and by anyone's definition, that meant it was their victory.[14]

When they were safely back in the Con Thien perimeter, the tankers and corpsmen unstacked the dead from their tanks and laid them gently on the ground, where they would have to remain until morning. The battalion aid station was overflowing with wounded men. The dead could wait. For the tankers, their ordeal was not yet over. The inescapable stench of death and charred human flesh permeated their senses all night.

An embittered Staff Sgt. Leon Burns would later remark: "We got very well chewed up. There's a lot of people dead out there who won't come back for various reasons, and one of those reasons is the M-16."[15] Staff Sergeant Burns and 1st Lt. Gatlin Howell would receive the Navy Cross for their heroic actions in the Marketplace.

Body Recovery

The following day, air strikes and Marine artillery prepped areas north of the Trace in anticipation of the ensuing attack to the north. At 9:30 a.m., an Air Force aerial observer reported spotting more than one hundred NVA advancing toward Con Thien. Battery E, 2nd Battalion, 12th Marines took them under fire, killing an estimated seventy-five.

Battalion Landing Team 1/3 under Lt. Col. Peter A. Wickwire had just come off of Operation Maryland on July 2 when they were ordered to join up with 3/9 north of the Trace on July 3. The airlift would be flown by helicopters from HMM-362 and HMM-164. Their mission was to land astride Route 561 just below the Trace, cross over and meet up with 3/9, and then attack north from the Trace and retrieve B/1/9's missing in action.

The liftoff from the carrier Okinawa went off at 10:30 a.m. on July 3 as scheduled. What did not come off like clockwork was the landing. Through a navigation error or communication error, no one knew for certain, the battalion was inserted three thousand meters below the Trace out in Leatherneck Square. They had to move north parallel to Route 561 through thick, tangled brush and shrubs bordering the road, and it took hours of valuable time to make the march safely. Thus, the attack with 3/9 to retrieve 1/9's dead was delayed a day. This was a most unfortunate foul-up. The NVA knew of the Marine Corps tradition about not leaving their dead behind; they now had another day to prepare their defenses for the attack they knew was coming.

Once the linkup was made between BLT 1/3 and 3/9 late in the afternoon, two full-strength battalions were on line north of the Trace, with the depleted A-C 1/9 contingent acting as their reserve. Route 561 was the north-south dividing line between them. To the left of the road was 3/9, extending over a five-hundred-meter front on a line extending to Hill 109. Alpha and Charlie 1/9 were dug in behind them. BLT 1/3 was right of the road with Alpha, Bravo, and Charlie Companies on line and Delta in reserve. Few men on the front lines slept that night. The sickening odor of death from hundreds of heat-blackened corpses, both friend and foe, wafted into their lines during the night. What would the morrow bring? Surely, more bleeding and dying awaited them in the killing fields.

D + 2, July 4

At 7 a.m. on July 4, 3/9 and BLT 1/3 commenced their joint attack on a six-company front to retrieve the dead from Bravo 1/9. This was the same area that 2/26 and 2/9 had previously attacked and cleared during Operation Hickory at the end of May, six weeks earlier.

At 9:15 a.m., just as Company K under Capt. Jerry Giles had advanced a half klick north of Hill 109, Kilo's lead elements were opened up on by NVA hiding in camouflaged positions laid out to intercept their advance. Captain Giles started losing men killed left and right due to sniper fire picking off his Marines. By 11:15, Kilo Company had incurred losses of twelve dead and seventeen wounded and had yet to see a single NVA. They were hidden in depth in spider holes and bunkers in the hedgerows. Kilo pulled back two hundred meters to the dirt cart trail labeled Route 605 on their maps so that the area of contact could be saturated with air strikes and artillery.

East of Route 561, A/1/3 made heavy contact with a force of NVA entrenched in camouflaged positions in tree lines two hundred meters to their front. Captain Jordan's lead platoon was almost one hundred meters from the Marketplace when their advance was halted by AK-47 and machine-gun fire coming out of the trees. Jordan's men placed air panels out in front of their lines to ensure that the jet pilots knew where the friendlies were. Marine A4 Skyhawks dove in and bombed the NVA positions.

It was not obvious at first, but a third Skyhawk seemed to line up differently from the rest, that is, much closer than the others. Then, as the disbelieving grunts looked up in horror, two 250-pound bombs were released from the diving jet's wing racks and sailed directly into the positions occupied by Lieutenant Kulhmann's 1st Platoon. One was a dud, but the other was not. The bomb blast concussion and falling rocks took their toll. Lieutenant Kulhmann and eight others had to be evacuated with broken bones and ruptured eardrums. One man had his leg blown off. He would eventually die on the hospital ship *Repose* days later.

At 4:30 p.m., K/3/9 plus two platoons from India Company moved forward again, this time with four tanks from Alpha Company, 3d Tank Battalion to retrieve their fifteen dead from the morning's fighting. Although only occasional sniper fire greeted Kilo, the two India Company platoons had two more killed and four wounded. Once all their dead and wounded were loaded aboard the tanks, Captain Giles pulled his force back to 3/9's position at the east-west road, Route 605, and dug in. Those Bravo 1/9 dead at the Marketplace would have to lie another day out in the broiling sun.

D + 3, July 5

The men of 3/9 and BLT 1/3 were awakened in the predawn darkness by a massive mortar bombardment. Hundreds of 60mm and 82mm mortars rained down, but casualties were light—only a half dozen were wounded. The Marines then opened up with a booming artillery response, prepping the areas in the path of the morning's planned advance as well as known and suspected artillery and rocket positions in the DMZ. Air strikes followed the artillery preparatory fires, and at 7:15 a.m., with 3/9 west of Route 561 and BLT 1/3 still east of the road, the second day of the body recovery operation commenced.

As both battalions advanced slowly, it became obvious that the NVA had pulled out during the night. Nevertheless, they had left numerous booby traps behind to bleed further the Marines coming for their dead. Lima 3/9 reported uncovering a minefield with twenty assorted mines, including one 250-pound and two 500-pound dud bombs wired for electrical detonation. Attached combat engineers detonated them where they lay.

With 3/9 providing security, BLT 1/3 drew the gruesome assignment of recovering the bodies from B/1/9. Major John C. Studt, the XO of 3/9, was sent forward to supervise the recovery. He described it as "a grisly task after 3 days in the hot sun."[16] Working parties wore gas masks as some protection from the ghastly stench. They had to remove grenades and other pyrotechnics from the bodies to prevent accidents later when gear was loaded on helicopters for removal. Personal effects were collected and placed in upturned helmets. The corpses were then placed in body bags and carried over and placed on the Alpha Company tanks. Many men retched and vomited.

Compounding the horror were the atrocities committed on the dead Marines. Several dead radiomen were found nailed to trees with engineer spikes through their shoulders.[17] PFC Robert Law, Delta Company, BLT 1/3 recalled the abomination he witnessed:

> The bodies were of white Marines, but the sun had turned their bodies charcoal black. Maggots had infested them and you could see them crawling through eye sockets and mouths. They were bloated, with the skin very taut, and one had popped open and spewed its contents from its midsection. One Marine had his genitals cut out and sewn to his face, with a picture of his girlfriend stabbed into his chest. Though I knew there were more live Marines from my own outfit with me, I felt as though I was the only one alive.[18]

Corporal David Gomez from 1/3/9 recalled a scene that could have come only from a perverted horror film:

> I remember seeing bodies that had superficial wounds—and bullet holes in the head, back of their heads blown off. I remember some of the bodies being mutilated, genitals cut off and put in the mouth. . . . I remember being very pissed. Very angry. I have never seen so many people ready to kick someone's ass. We wanted to fight. We wanted to even the score. We wanted to prove to the NVA that you just can't do this and fucking walk away.[19]

Many Marines with their own bayonets still in their scabbards retrieved the discarded bayonets from the dead and affixed them to their own rifles. Paybacks could not come soon enough to quench the hatred these Marines felt toward their enemy. By one o'clock in the afternoon, thirty-three bodies had been recovered and transported to the rear. The body of one Marine, Lance Cpl. Wayne V. Wilson, was not recovered. He was listed as missing in action.[20]

Both battalions pulled back to their original battle lines after the body recovery mission was complete. It almost seemed surreal, but the NVA were not ready to quit the battlefield. In midafternoon, an aerial observer spotted a large concentration of NVA three thousand meters northeast of Con Thien in the Gia Binh area. He called in artillery and air strikes and later radioed back that he had counted two hundred dead NVA lying in the open.

REMEMBER THE MARKETPLACE!

When the company commander of C/1/9, Captain Hutchinson, was wounded and evacuated, Capt. Al Slater was ordered to join Charlie up with his sorely depleted Alpha Company and lead them out the morning of July 6 on what seemed to his men to be a suicide mission. His task was to escort a force of 3d Recon Battalion Marines led by 1st Lt. Stephen M. Hartnett north about twelve hundred meters and set up a patrol base in the deserted hamlet of Thon Phuong Xuan. Then, from there, the recon teams would slip out and cross into the DMZ, barely a klick away.

The mission of the 3d Recon Marines was to determine the strength of NVA units north of the Trace and to ascertain the infiltration routes the NVA used in crossing the Ben Hai River. Mixing the recon teams with the regular infantry unit was a ploy to deceive any NVA scouts in the area who would believe it was just a normal patrol.

Following in the wake of artillery preparatory fires, A-C/1/9 and the recon platoon shoved off in broad daylight, but not a shot was fired. Either the NVA had made a total withdrawal the previous night, or they were caught napping. Captain Slater placed his men on a peanut-shaped rise of ground immediately south of Thon Phuong Xuan. They also had an added bonus: previous NVA inhabitants had built a bunker and trench line complex in the two-hundred-meter-long little hill, and it was made nearly invisible by the surrounding elephant grass and banana trees. Thus, despite having been blasted and bombed previously during Operation Cimarron in June, the men now had fantastic cover and conceal-ment. After the recon teams departed, A-C/1/9 spent the remainder of the day clearing fields of fire, digging in, rebuilding collapsed bunkers, and waiting, fully aware of their naked vulnerability being situated more than a klick out in front of 3/9.

All was not quiet on the eastern end of the two-battalion front. The 2d Platoon of Charlie Company, BLT 1/3, engaged an enemy unit several hundred meters in front of their lines. A 57mm recoilless rifle had inflicted numerous casualties. One platoon from Bravo Company, plus a three-tank section led by 1st Lt. Wayne Hayes, came forward to assist. Hayes blasted the recoilless rifle position with his 90mm main gun but apparently did not knock it completely out. Moments later, a 57mm round struck Hayes's tank right where the turret and hull joined—an incredibly lucky shot—penetrating the turret and setting the tank on fire. Hayes and his crewmen were rescued, but Lieutenant Hayes succumbed to his wounds before he could be medevaced.

Back at the main defense line, 3/9 and BLT 1/3 were put on alert. Russian-made PT-76 amphibious tanks had been spotted north of the Ben Hai. And SAM missiles were being launched from north of the Ben Hai River toward Marine A-4 Skyhawk jets attacking NVA positions. Major Ralph E. Brubaker's VMA-311 jet was shot down by one SAM strike, and his plane crashed in enemy territory. He was located the next morning, slightly wounded but okay, by an Air Force rescue helicopter.

Lt. Col. Wickwire ordered his engaged BLT 1/3 units back to the original perimeter—and not a moment too soon. About 4:45 p.m., that distinctive bass drum–beating sound of dozens of artillery pieces firing from the DMZ reached the ears of the Marines. The earth heaved and shook as six hundred artillery rounds and rockets crashed down on the hunkered-down troops from 3/9. Then, the firing abruptly stopped and shifted onto BLT 1/3's perimeter, where they were hit by nearly one thousand rounds of incoming. Casualties were surprisingly few. The Marines had dug in deep this time.

An AO reported four hundred NVA crossing the Ben Hai River in route march formation, which meant they were moving fast. Captain Slater wanted desperately to pull back, but he had to wait for the recon teams. One of Lieutenant Hartnett's recon teams confirmed the sighting of a large number of enemy troops headed their way, and Slater's Marines were directly in their path. All available weapons the Marines had were brought to bear as 60mm, 81mm, and 4.2-inch mortars, along with tanks and artillery, opened fire on the approach path reported by recon.

The CO of B/1/3, Capt. Burrell H. Landes, had climbed a tree to adjust air strikes and artillery fire in front of his position. When he heard that the AO had spotted a large force of NVA crossing the Ben Hai, he asked how many. The reply was, "I'd hate to tell you, I'd hate to tell you."[21]

Then, just before dark, a large group of NVA camouflaged with banana leaves and elephant grass charged toward the eastern sector manned by C/1/3, tossing one-quarter-pound blocks of TNT ahead of them to simulate incoming mortars. Combatwise NCOs and officers yelled at their Marines: "Keep your heads up! Be ready! They're comin' in on us!"[22]

These heads-up Marines were ready, opening up with a concentrated "mad minute" of firepower, stopping the enemy dead in their tracks. Farther west, where Alpha and Bravo tied in, was a seam in the defense line. The NVA were able to exploit it and penetrate the lines. However, reaction squads moved up and closed the breach. Artillery fire called down in front of their lines prevented more NVA from exploiting the original breakthrough.

Captain Slater's Marines could not believe their eyes. Hundreds of NVA in column formation were dogtrotting directly at them, weapons at port arms, helmets bobbing. They were clearly unaware of the Marines' presence in the bunker complex and were planning on carrying right on by them toward their attack objective. When they were within one hundred meters, the entire Marine line opened fire, mowing down the unsuspecting NVA (Captain Slater later called it a "turkey shoot"[23]). One NVA sounded out a bugle call, and survivors scattered in all directions. Two of the four recon teams had made it safely back to the patrol base. The other two were told to hide and wait because moving in the open would be suicidal.

Slater's Marines soon realized they were completely surrounded. The fighting raged at close quarters for hours, often hand to hand. The outnumbered A-C/1/9 men were fighting for their lives. Captain Slater, who was only four days from rotating stateside, was resigned to not surviving through the night without massive artillery support.

Lance Cpl. J. Larry Stuckey was in a bomb crater with two comrades furiously fighting off attacking NVA. They shot down eight men running at their position. Stuckey retrieved a stick-handled Chicom grenade that bounced in his crater and tossed it back. A second grenade bounced near him, and he threw that one out. A third grenade landed near him, and he picked it up to throw it when it exploded, blowing off most of his hand. He knew he had to get out of that crater or die. No sooner had he taken off running than he was shot in the thigh. Then more grenades landed nearby, peppering him with shrapnel. Nearly blind from his glasses being blown off his face, and having no weapon in his hands, he decided to play dead.

Captain Slater was all over the perimeter, sealing off a breach in the lines here, directing fire there. His FO was PFC David Sankey, an Arapaho Indian, and he was adjusting artillery fire masterfully in concert with his CO's directions. He called in more than three thousand artillery rounds, walking several in to less than fifty meters. The perimeter held. A few hours after midnight, firing from outside the perimeter slackened and then ceased altogether. Slater sent his corpsmen around to check for casualties. They found Lance Corporal Stuckey more dead than alive from loss of blood, but he would survive.

At 5:30 a.m., Captain Slater ordered his men to begin vacating their patrol base and head back to the main defense line. The last group had just left the complex and was some distance away when that alarming *boom-ba-boom-boom-ba-boom!* drum sound was heard off in the distance. A blistering NVA artillery barrage fell directly on Slater's empty hill position, but no one was home.

In Captain Slater's unit three men had been killed and twenty-one wounded that night. Slater and his platoon commanders originally estimated three hundred to four hundred NVA killed. That figure was later reduced for the record to 154. Major Woodring's 3/9 staff estimated 681 NVA dead. BLT 1/3 came up with an estimate of 490 KIA. They had gone out on a recon of the battlefield area in the morning and found a killing ground of mind-numbing proportions. Their official history reads: "The grisly carnage was beyond description. Hundreds of bodies covered the scarred battlefield, some half buried, others in pieces, all surrounded by a carpet of battered equipment and ammunition."[24]

No matter what the actual body count, the 90th NVA Regiment had been slaughtered. Revenge for the Marketplace massacre was finally realized. Captain Al Slater and Lance Cpl. David Stuckey would receive the Navy Cross for their heroism that unbelievable night; PFC David Sankey would be awarded the Silver Star Medal.[25]

FATE IS A FOUR-LETTER WORD

While the focus of the press and the generals during Operation Buffalo was outside of Con Thien, the Marines of Delta 1/9 and their supporting units inside Con Thien's perimeter wire were taking a daily pounding from NVA artillery, rockets, and mortars. From July 2 to 14, 1/9 incurred losses of twenty-six Marines KIA and seventy WIA at the Con Thien firebase. General Giap's artillery was becoming deadly accurate.

During the evening of July 6, while the preassault barrage was occurring in the 3/9 and BLT 1/3 areas, the highly regarded CO of Delta 1/9, Capt. Richard J. Sasek, was standing near his CP bunker watching the fireworks show. About to meet their fate with him were several spectators: 1st Sgt. Jettie Rivers, Cpl. Joe Barillo, Lance Cpl. Edward Brady, and two corpsmen, Hospitalmen Christopher Maguire and Michael Dotson. Without warning, an artillery barrage screamed in. One round scored a direct hit atop the Delta CP bunker, killing Sasek, Rivers, and all the others. First Sergeant Rivers had been awarded the Navy Cross for his heroism during Prairie IV in mid-May. The loss of Rivers and Sasek staggered Delta Company. Losing either one would be devastating, but both together was a total disaster—and not only for Delta but for 1/9 as well.

The following day, July 7, an even worse calamity befell 1/9. In a one-in-a-million shot, a 152mm artillery round roared in through the doorway of the 1/9 CP bunker behind OP#1 and detonated against a twelve-inch by twelve-inch upright timber. A five-foot layer of sandbags and huge support beams came crashing down. Those Marines not killed instantly by the blast were crushed by the collapsed overhead. First Lieutenant Gatlin Howell, the much-revered and respected leader of Bravo-3 during the Khe Sanh Hill Fights and hero of the July 2 Marketplace massacre, was sitting by the bunker entrance when the shell hit. He and fourteen others were killed. Among the twenty-five wounded survivors of the blast was Lieutenant Colonel Schening (his fourth Purple Heart from three wars). The fortunate XO, Major Danielson, was back in Dong Ha at the time. Captain Radcliffe, who had left the CP bunker only moments before the CP was hit, said, "If the NVA fired the rest of this goddamn century, they couldn't do that again!"[26]

There seemed to be no end to the agonies of 1/9 at Con Thien. Propaganda leaflets found later in the Marketplace area indicated that the hard-luck battalion had been targeted by the NVA for destruction. Recent events seemed to indicate the NVA were making good on their boast.

On July 13, the remaining "Walking Dead" of the 1st Battalion, 9th Marines, battered and demoralized, departed for Camp Carroll to re-build and replenish their losses. The fresh 3d Battalion, 4th Marines would be next in line to spend "time in the barrel."

Operation Buffalo, which began as a disaster for 1/9, ended in total de-feat of the 90th NVA Regiment. The operation was officially terminated on July 14. The Marines reported 1,290 NVA dead, whereas their own losses were 159 killed and 345 wounded. The heavy reliance on support-ing arms, artillery, air strikes, and naval gunfire seemed to have ac-counted for more than five hundred of the NVA dead. Marine aviation dropped 1,066 tons of ordnance. Conversely, NVA artillery and mortars accounted for half of the Marine casualties suffered during the opera-tion.[27]

Buffalo was brief but brutal—the DMZ war in microcosm. Ask any Marine or corpsman who was there, and the response would always be the same. It was pure hell. And many believed it was pointless. A lot of young men died, and they wondered to what end. When the last shot of Buffalo was fired, the Marines controlled not a single square foot of land they had bled for, except Con Thien, and the barrier-building folly would continue.

That awful spring and summer had taken a heavy toll on 1/9. They had severely punished the NVA, but it had cost them dearly, not only in numbers but also in experienced squad, platoon, and company-level leadership. Unfortunately for the 1st Battalion, 9th Marines, their unlucky moniker, the "Walking Dead," never seemed so justified.

9

Running the Gauntlet

Don't ever march home the same way. Take a different route so you won't be
ambushed.
　　—Major Robert Rogers, *Standing Orders, Rogers' Rangers*

Operation Buffalo had shown the Allies that General Giap was prepared to feed entire regiments into the DMZ meat grinder to thwart the
installation of McNamara's Line. Allied intelligence sources had located
the 31st, 803rd, 812th, and 90th Regiments of the NVA 324B Division
within and south of the DMZ. Along with the 324B, three additional
NVA divisions, the 304th, 320th, and 325C, were positioned in the eastern DMZ and around Khe Sanh. These army divisions, with an estimated twenty-one thousand troops, were controlled by the newly created DMZ Front Headquarters.[1] Staffers at III MAF were growing
increasingly concerned that Hanoi had upped the ante and planned to
commit an entire division to interdict the SPOS barrier.

After Buffalo ended on July 14, a new operation named Hickory II
was ordered by III MAF. This Hickory was similar in concept to the
original Hickory operation back in May, except on a smaller scale.
Hickory II was intended to destroy enemy mortar and artillery positions
and ammunition and resupply depots in the southern half of the DMZ.
Enemy territory north of the Ben Hai River was still off limits to the
Allies, so Giap's forces ensconced there would continue to enjoy immu-
nity from Allied ground attacks.

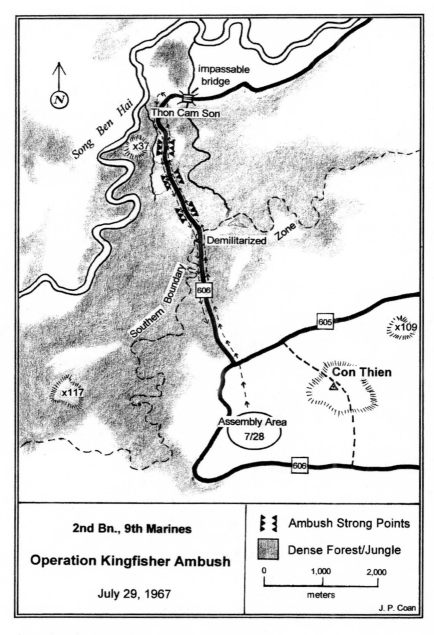

2/9 Operation Kingfisher Ambush, July 29, 1967

Commencing directly on the heels of Buffalo the morning of July 14, three Marine battalions—1/4, BLT 1/3, and BLT 2/3—plus their supporting tanks attacked north across the Trace. Three ARVN infantry battalions, including an armored personnel carrier group, attacked north from Gio Linh. Near the coast, the U.S. Marines 1st Amphibious Tractor Battalion rolled out through the sand dunes above the Qua Viet River. The Allies proceeded all the way to the banks of the Ben Hai without making any serious enemy contact. They then wheeled about and attacked in a southerly direction, reaching the Cam Lo River two days later without much to show for it.

Considering the fierce resistance faced by the Marines only a week earlier, every time they attempted to move north of the Trace, it was eerily quiet everywhere except in the amtrac's sector. Apparently, the NVA had pulled back to regroup and replenish their manpower losses after Buffalo, just as they had in May after Hickory I.

Hickory II ended quietly on July 16, and Operation Kingfisher began in the same general area. The mission was the same: stop the NVA from infiltrating across the eastern DMZ into Quang Tri Province while construction continued on the barrier.

Although the 90th NVA Regiment had been soundly defeated the first week in July during Operation Buffalo, and Hickory II had encountered little resistance, III MAF was receiving new intelligence reports that the NVA were preparing for another offensive. Posing that threat were the 31st, 803rd, and 812th Regiments of the NVA 324B Division. Marine brass decided to strike first.

Activity began to pick up around Con Thien at the end of July in preparation for another thrust into the DMZ. Trucks bearing ammunition for the tanks, mortars, and 105mm artillery battery rolled in one after the other, along with giant CH-53 Sea Knight helicopters dangling huge cargo nets crammed full with "beans, bullets, and band-aids." All that activity raised clouds of fine, pink-beige dust that settled on every exposed surface and permeated every crack and crevice on "The Hill," as the Marines who served at Con Thien purposely called this piece of land. Letters written and sent home from Con Thien that summer often had reddish-brown fingertip smudges from sweat mixed with the ever-present clay dust.

The plan, conceived at III MAF and developed by 3d Marine Division, called for an armored force to accompany a full-strength 2d Battalion, 9th Marines on a reconnaissance in force north through the DMZ up to the Ben Hai. Once that was accomplished, the combined force would advance in an easterly direction for several miles and then head south out of the DMZ toward the Trace. If Giap had replaced his forces in the area, 2/9 would take them from the rear. The mission was called a "spoiling attack," as in strike the enemy first and spoil his plans to launch an attack.

The men of 2d Battalion, 9th Marines, led by Lt. Col. William D. Kent, were no strangers to the DMZ war. They had played a major role in Operation Hickory in May. Since then, they had been operating continuously throughout Leatherneck Square. Lieutenant Colonel Kent's grunts were battle-tested, bush-wise veterans.

Accompanying 2/9 was a platoon of tanks from Alpha Company, 3d Tanks, led by Gunnery Sgt. Bernard A. Person. Gunny Person's tanks had helped fend off the bloody May 8 NVA attack on Con Thien. His tankers were not strangers to the DMZ war either.

Just before sundown on July 27, Lieutenant Colonel Kent's battalion, accompanied by five tanks, three Ontos, three amtracs, and a platoon of combat engineers, assembled in some woods one thousand meters southwest of Con Thien. Holding down the fort at Con Thien was the 3d Battalion, 4th Marines.

On the morning of July 28, which was destined to become another broiling hot DMZ day, the main body of 2/9 moved out in a column headed north along Provincial Route 606. Route 606 was nothing more than a well-worn dirt cart path that ran from Con Thien to the Ben Hai and then generally followed along the Ben Hai's eastward course through the DMZ.

After standing by all morning as battalion reserve in the event the main body of 2/9 stepped into something big, Company F, led by Capt. M. E. Rich, boarded helicopters. Shielded by a smoke screen laid down by fixed-wing aircraft, Foxtrot Company was hopscotched ahead of the battalion to an LZ near Hill 37, only a few hundred meters from the Ben Hai.

For the main body of the battalion, the terrain adjacent to the road soon became thickly vegetated jungle, which was very difficult for infantry flankers to move through in any kind of cohesive formation, much less tracked vehicles. The vehicles soon became trail bound in order to negotiate their way through the area. Another complication, somehow overlooked in the planning stages by regimental and division staffers, was that the route north was bordered on both sides by tributaries flowing into the Ben Hai River, further channeling the armored force onto the road.

No enemy contact was made during the move north, although flankers screening the road to the east and west reported numerous bunkers and spider holes dug along the perimeter of a wide clearing they encountered. Captain Frank Southard, CO of Hotel 2/9, filed that information away in the back of his mind, but he was not overly concerned because he knew he would not be returning that way.

The 3d Battalion, 4th Marines had preceded 2/9 in the area on May 18 during Operation Hickory, when they had been inserted into the Thon Cam Son area by helicopter. They traveled south along Route 606 without incident when they left the Ben Hai. But that had all occurred over two months earlier.

Kent's Marines set up their night defensive positions around the abandoned hamlet of Thon Cam Son. Tanks and the combat engineers proceeded to destroy a large number of vacant bunker fortifications before dark. The night passed peacefully, except that Hotel Company reported hearing truck traffic north of the Ben Hai. Company F, located five hundred meters south of Hotel in the vicinity of Hill 37, reported hearing digging noises.

The first thing Lieutenant Colonel Kent did in the morning was call his company commanders and armored vehicle leaders together for a powwow. Scouts had followed the road at dawn and found that a stream at the bottom of a steep-sided gorge, spanned by a narrow concrete bridge, lay just to the east. The narrow old bridge would not support armored vehicles, and there was no way to circumvent it. They would have to turn around and go back out of the DMZ the same way they came in.

The combatwise grunts and armored vehicle crewmen grew alarmed. A cardinal rule drummed into them repeatedly was that "you never return the same way you went out." Any unit that did so was asking for trouble, big trouble. And yet, they were going to do just that. In stunned disbelief, the leery warriors faced to the south and formed up in a column, not liking this turn of events one bit.

Captain Wolk's Echo Company, accompanied by the battalion commander and his CP group, led off the road march south in the midmorning heat along with three tanks, one Ontos, and the amtracs. Next came Hotel Company, followed by two tanks and two Ontos. H & S and Foxtrot Companies came next. Golf Company brought up the rear.

The first two platoons of Echo had just crossed a clearing about one thousand meters south of their night bivouac position when a command-detonated 250-pound bomb exploded near the road, killing and maiming a half-dozen men. What greeted those coming after was the sickening sight of entrails and body parts hanging in the tree branches overhead.

Farther down the road, alert combat engineers found a second dud 250-pound bomb wired for detonation, but they were able to rig explosives and blow it in place. That blast apparently was the signal the NVA had been waiting for, and they opened up on the road-bound Marines with a rising crescendo of small arms, machine guns, and mortars in a king-sized ambush. Some Marines dove off to the side of the road, only to land on booby traps emplaced there overnight. One amtrac got holed through one side and out the other by an RPG but kept moving.

Guessing correctly that the road-bound armor would be forced by the impenetrable jungle terrain to reverse course and exit the DMZ on the only way out, the NVA had set up three strongpoints along the road roughly five hundred meters apart. Echo and Command Group A, plus the tanks, amtracs, and Ontos, managed to fight past the first enemy strongpoint and continued to battle their way south through a thousand-meter-long gauntlet of fire.

When Hotel Company came on the clearing, the first thing Captain Southard noted was several dead Marines from Company E, including

2d Lt. Robert Kisch and his radio operator, lying in the grass beside the road. Six or eight other Marines from Echo, one seriously wounded, were lying in the undergrowth with Hotel's 1st Platoon (2d Lt. Robert Leary) along a narrow ridge on the west side of the clearing. Groups of NVA were attempting to attack along the small ridge leading toward the road, but Leary's men were stopping them.

Captain Southard remembered the empty bunkers and spider holes his flankers had spied on the edge of the clearing the previous day. Heavy enemy fire was coming from that area. He gave the coordinates to his artillery FO, Lieutenant Nighthammer, who attempted to call in the fire mission, but Sav-A-Plane was in effect. As long as aircraft were in the air overhead, no artillery could be employed. Southard was stymied. His CO, Lieutenant Colonel Kent, was prodding him to keep moving. Frank Southard recalled:

> During this period, Lt. Col. Kent . . . was urging me to move Hotel Company down the road. He, of course, had already cleared the clearing and was well down the road by now with the rest of Echo and most of the tracked vehicles. . . . I told him we were waiting for fire support before we would move. There was no way I was going to move the company across that clearing without fire support—I could see what had happened to Company E.[2]

Captain Southard then asked his FAC where the air support was. He was told the planes had just lifted off from Da Nang and would be there very soon. But Southard needed to take some action. He could not just sit and wait while the NVA were attacking the road from both flanks, attempting to cut off and isolate his company. Mortars were falling. Men were dying. He summoned the two Ontos from back in the column and instructed them to fire on the eastern tree line at the edge of the clearing. They each delivered a dozen rounds of 106mm. After each six-round salvo, a crewman with a lot of guts had to run out in the open and reload the six guns mounted atop the Ontos. An RPG struck one Ontos, killing two crewmen. The second was able to suppress the enemy fire long enough for them to limp back together, one Ontos still smoking. Three Ontos crewmen would be dead before that terrible day ended.

Captain Southard also sought the aid of the two tanks behind him to help him break through, but the tankers had witnessed what happened to the two Ontos. They lingered out in the clearing only long enough to fire a few rounds and then retreated to safety back down the road.

Southard then ordered Lieutenant Leary to pull his platoon out and join a flanking attack on the bunker positions to the east. Leary protested that the NVA would infiltrate into their positions from the west if they pulled out, but his captain overruled him. It turned out Leary was right. As soon as his platoon pulled out, the NVA moved in, setting up a machine gun to fire down the road. Captain Southard remembered, "It was scary as hell, to put it mildly. I was pinned down for what seemed like a long time, but was probably only a few minutes."[3] His FAC went down, shot in the head by a sniper as he walked along talking into his radio handset.

Lieutenant Clarke sent some of his men up to bail out the CP group. Corporal Alfred Gaspar, Lance Cpl. James Proctor, and Lance Cpl. James McGovern ran east across the road to retrieve several wounded, including the FAC, who were lying in thick brush. As they came back out attempting to drag several wounded men to safety, Captain Southard yelled at them—twice—to stop, but it was too late. All three of those Marines were shot down and killed.

Action was hot and heavy to the rear of Hotel Company as well. Foxtrot Company was ordered to establish an LZ for casualty evacuation. When tanks carrying dead and wounded from Echo and H & S Companies reached the zone, all hell broke loose. The NVA attacked the LZ with RPGs, mortars, and machine guns. One tank was hit by an RPG, wounding three crewmen and setting the tank on fire.

Corporal Miguel A. Rivera Sotomayor was a grenadier with 3d Platoon of Foxtrot Company. A 12.7mm machine gun had his platoon pinned down. Despite having received painful shrapnel wounds in the arm earlier in the battle, Corporal Sotomayor crawled out by the burning tank and opened fire with his M-79 grenade launcher, exhausting all of his ammo, but he knocked out the heavy machine gun position. With bullets kicking up dust around him, he ran out in the open to one of his own machine guns, saw that the gunners were badly wounded, and stood up with their M-60 machine gun to return fire at the enemy. When that ammo was exhausted, he grabbed a rifle and opened fire with a full magazine before he was wounded again. Bleeding heavily from numerous wounds, he returned to get another magazine, but corpsmen physically restrained him from going back out. Corporal Sotomayor would survive his wounds and later be awarded the Navy Cross for his heroism.

Fixed-wing aircraft finally arrived. The NVA knew the danger that air support presented and attempted to move closer to the Marine column, charging out of their bunkers across an open field. F4-B Phantom jets swooped so low over 2/9's grunts that they could see the Marine pilots giving them a thumbs-up as silver, cylindrical napalm tanks tumbled down toward the NVA positions east and west of the road. Lance Cpl. Richard A. Russell, a fire team leader with Foxtrot Company, later recalled: "The exposed NVA also saw their oncoming immolation and raised a cry of horror that went far beyond my wildest concept of fear, a cry I can hear right now and will hear till I join them."[4]

Echo Company and Command Group A were still leading the attack south. Lance Cpl. Jack Hartzel, a machine gunner with Echo, was walking as fast as he could and still aim his red-hot weapon at the enemy positions. He shot up everything that even looked like it might be NVA.

The cry went up, "Friendlies on the right, friendlies on the left!"[5] But those were not friendlies, because the Marines had no flankers out. A dozen NVA wearing flak jackets, helmets, and utilities and firing M-16s opened fire on Echo. Hartzel and his company returned fire, cutting them down, and then moved out again, firing as they walked. They had to keep moving or die. A group of combat engineers with Company E came across a wheel-mounted 12.7mm machine gun and attacked, killing the seven-man NVA crew and destroying the gun and its ammunition.

Bringing up the battalion rear was Golf Company led by Captain Horowitz. Golf was fighting a desperate rear-guard action, holding off numerous NVA encircling them like a pack of hungry wolves closing in for the kill. Golf fought back desperately to keep from being cut off and isolated from the main body—a certain death sentence. Horowitz's grunts killed two dozen NVA, and an attached scout-sniper team picked off another fifteen.

A final enemy strongpoint slowed the battalion exodus. A tank and an Ontos had been stopped dead by a flurry of RPGs. Mortar rounds crashed down around them, but the 2/9 grunts soon gained fire superiority, forcing the NVA back. Lance Cpl. Jack Hartzel helped pull a dead tank crewman, PFC Eric M. Dewey, out of the tank turret. The tank platoon leader, Gunnery Sergeant Barnett G. Person, Silver Star recipient at Con Thien on May 8, had been wounded again.

Most of Echo Company and Lieutenant Colonel Kent managed to break out of the ambush zone by late afternoon. Mike Company, 3d Battalion, 4th Marines had been sent over from Con Thien for support. They linked up with Lieutenant Colonel Kent's exhausted force at six thirty in the evening. By this late in the day, the remainder of the battalion had too many wounded and heat casualties to move farther and had to halt in place for the night.

Captain Southard pulled his Hotel Company back to join with Foxtrot and H & S Companies in setting up a night defensive position. Two separated squads from Echo and two squads from Company G joined them. But it was an all-infantry force, because all the armored vehicles carrying wounded had been with Company E when they broke free of the ambush to join up with M/3/4.

Company G, bringing up the column rear, had successfully fought off the NVA all day to keep from being isolated and probably overrun. But as night fell, they found themselves separated from the main battalion body by a thousand meters of jungle, bogged down with casualties, and unable to move. Fortunately for Golf Company, the NVA had already begun disengaging, dragging off their dead and wounded.

Mike 3/4, now under the operational control of Lieutenant Colonel Kent, moved back up the road at dusk with the colonel to attempt to rescue the two cut-off squads from Echo Company. Their mission succeeded, and Mike Company set up in a defensive perimeter for the night. The remainder of Echo, which was two thousand meters to the south and far removed from the kill zone, was able to call in medevacs for their wounded.

The night passed quietly until about 3:30 a.m. when some NVA sappers ran through Foxtrot's perimeter, throwing satchel charges and firing AK-47s. One Marine was killed, and three were wounded. Somehow, the sapper unit managed to pull off that brazen stunt and not be caught by the Marines.

Mike 3/4 and Lieutenant Colonel Kent moved north at first light on July 30, meeting no opposition, and linked up with the remainder of 2/9. The NVA were long gone, having faded away into the jungle as suddenly as they had appeared. Medevacs began arriving and lifted out 2/9 casualties all morning. The battalion had incurred losses of 23 men killed and 191 wounded and evacuated (45 of whom were heat casualties). Left behind on the battlefield were 32 NVA bodies by actual count, but the battalion estimated another 175 probable, most of them resulting from air strikes. By noon, all Marine units were out of the DMZ.

The 2d Battalion, 9th Marines had experienced a close call coming out of the DMZ. They were up against a unit new to the area, the 803rd NVA Regiment, which might explain the lack of artillery and rockets being employed against the Marines. These NVA soldiers were hard core, highly aggressive, and determined. One Marine could certainly attest to that; he had shot down an NVA soldier charging at him with an axe. Had the AO not been overhead to direct air strikes skillfully, the story could have had a much different ending.

The NVA plan had been to conduct ambushes at three separate strongpoints and then separate the column and overrun individual companies. Their plan had almost worked. The dud bomb detonated by Marine engineers seemed to have caused the NVA to initiate their ambush prematurely, that is, before the main body of 2/9 had moved into the first kill zone.

Blame for 2/9 being put into that perilous situation in the first place rested squarely on the shoulders of higher-ups at regiment and 3d Marine Division Headquarters. No essential reconnaissance seems to have been conducted in advance to ascertain whether armored vehicles could safely traverse the terrain on that particular route along the Ben Hai. Instead of providing infantry support, the road-bound armored force ended up having to be escorted out of harm's way by the infantry.

The surviving 2/9 grunts left the DMZ and returned to Leatherneck Square, harboring smoldering feelings of bitterness and betrayal. They believed that they had been hung out to dry on that abortive "spoiling attack." Serious doubts had begun to fester throughout the 9th Marines, from the grunts on the line all the way up the chain of command, over the stalemate that had evolved along the DMZ. Discontent, frustration, and even contempt were brewing. It required a long stretch of faith to believe that the brutal bloodletting around Con Thien that hellish summer of 1967 was part of some overall grand design for victory over General Giap's North Vietnamese Army.

U.S. Army Duster and USMC amtrac still burning after the May 8, 1967, attack on Con Thien. *(National Archives)*

U.S. Navy corpsman attends to a wounded NVA soldier during Operation Prairie II below the DMZ. *(National Archives)*

NVA flamethrower from May 8 attack on Con Thien, held by Maj. E. H. Boyd, XO of 1st Battalion, 4th Marines. *(USMC History Collection)*

Marine engineers string barbed-wire obstacle around the perimeter. *(USMC History Collection)*

Marines from 3/4 search a destroyed NVA bunker in the DMZ during Operation Hickory. *(USMC History Collection)*

Marines from 3/9 load aboard CH-46 helicopters at Dong Ha on July 2, 1967, to assist the embattled 1/9 at the Marketplace during Operation Buffalo. *(USMC History Collection)*

Cpl. Jim "Dead-eye" Holston, tank commander of B-23, during Operation Buffalo. *(Courtesy of Terry Hunter)*

Marines from K/3/9, plus tanks from Company A, 3d Tank Battalion, move forward to attempt recovery of B/1/9 dead on July 4, 1967, during Operation Buffalo. *(USMC History Collection)*

Marines from 2/9 return from the DMZ after fighting through a one-mile "gauntlet of fire" ambush during Operation Kingfisher, July 30, 1967. *(National Archives)*

Marines out on patrol take a break by a Catholic church, vicinity of Con Thien, July 1967. *(National Archives)*

Lance Cpl. Ken "Piggy" Bores with NVA skull on his tank's searchlight mount. *(Courtesy of Ken Bores)*

Marine sniper Dalton Gunderson. *(National Archives)*

Hooking up a cargo net to a hovering CH-46 Chinook resupply helicopter. *(National Archives)*

PFC Jennings looks over a bunker at Con Thien that took a direct hit by a 57mm recoilless rifle. *(USMC History Collection)*

Typical Marine ammo crate and sandbag bunker. *(National Archives)*

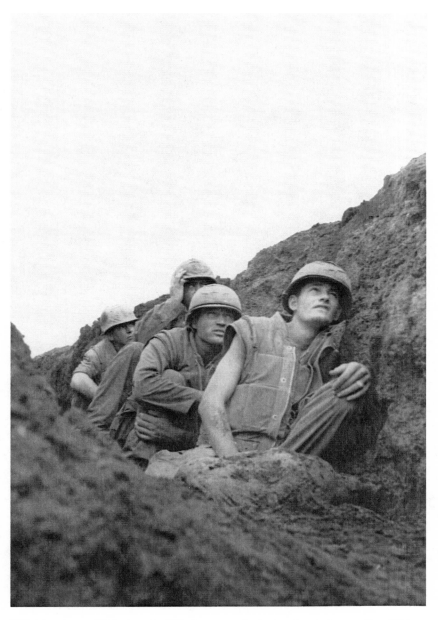

"Waiting it out." Marines huddle in a trench during incoming at Con Thien. *(National Archives)*

Artillerymen from 2d Battalion, 12th Marines load their 105mm howitzer at Con Thien, October 1967. *(Department of Defense, USMC History Collection, A421910)*

"Incoming!!" Cpl. Gary Miller reaches for a flak jacket as Lance Cpl. David Sullivan and Cpl. Gail Culp scramble for cover at Cam Lo, 1968. *(National Archives)*

Author *(far left, hands on knees)* with tank platoon at Con Thien, June 1968.

PART FIVE

GENERAL OFFENSIVE, PHASE I

Boys, they have us right where we want them.

—Lt. Col. "Chesty" Puller, USMC

10

The "Thundering Third"

A depleted, battle-weary 1st Battalion, 9th Marines had been pulled out of Con Thien on July 13 and reassigned to Camp Carroll for rest and refitting. Replacing 1/9 at Con Thien was the highly regarded 3d Battalion, 4th Marines, who had distinguished themselves in World War II at Guam and Okinawa. They fought commendably in the 1966 battles at Mutter's Ridge (where Capt. J. J. Carroll was killed tragically in a friendly fire accident) and Helicopter Valley and most recently in the battle for Hill 174. This proud battalion, nicknamed the "Thundering Third," was next in line to serve their "time in the barrel" at Con Thien.

Neither the Americans nor their South Vietnamese allies knew precisely what the North Vietnamese government was planning to do next. Dissent did exist among North Vietnam's leaders at the highest levels. Some factions advocated a return to guerilla warfare while they sought an accommodation with the U.S., whereas the "hawks" pushed for an all-out, spectacular blow against the Americans. What is now known for certain is that some time in late June or July of 1967, at a meeting of the Lao Dong Party Politburo in Hanoi, the party called for a decisive blow against the Americans to force them to accept a military defeat. What ultimately came out of that meeting was the "General Offensive, General Uprising" plan, which would culminate in the 1968 Tet Offensive.

Phase I was planned to commence in late August of 1967 and involve attacks on the periphery of South Vietnam along its borders and below the DMZ. This would draw U.S. forces away from the population centers. Phase II called for major battles with the Americans that would

Con Thien
Fall 1967
J. P. Coan
TRACE
To Gio Linh
3
9
USMC
1
OP
CP
2
OP
3
OP
81
4.2
105
Bn
Aid Station
LZ
LZ
LSA
N

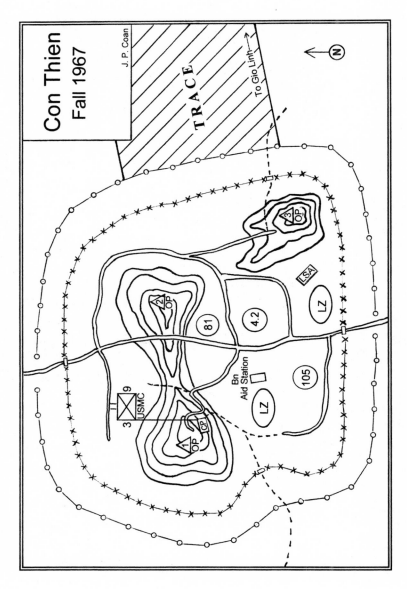

Con Thien, Fall 1967

weaken their resolve. Phase III was the longed-for "uprising of the oppressed masses in the South" *(Khnoi Nghai)* against the Americans and their puppets in Saigon. The people would then throw out the defeated Americans and demand reunification of the two Vietnams into one nation.

In I Corps, Phase I began with stepped-up pressure on Con Thien in late August and September. Allied intelligence was in the dark as to Hanoi's far-reaching motives. Most analysts logically assumed that the creation of the NVA DMZ Front and its focus on Con Thien and Gio Linh was due to the SPOS barrier activity there. However, one far-sighted Marine general, Victor H. Krulak, deduced that what the NVA were really up to was drawing the Marines' attention away from the populated coastal areas into more advantageous battlefield sites in remote areas below the DMZ. But Krulak was a voice in the wilderness, not given a serious ear at either MACV or the White House.[1]

At that point in the war, Allied efforts in northern Quang Tri Province were dedicated to completing the SPOS barrier regardless of the costs. We would refuse to alter that course of action for another full year, no matter what anyone believed motivated the North Vietnamese Army to go on the offensive below the DMZ.

If one of the goals of the General Offensive, General Uprising was to take over the two northernmost provinces in South Vietnam, Quang Tri and Thua Thien, then it made good tactical sense to continue to test the dominant military force in the region, the U.S. Marines. General Giap would resort to his preferred method—trial and error—to learn how the Marines would respond to large-scale attacks by his ground forces and vaunted artillery. The 3d Battalion, 4th Marines at Con Thien would be next in line to face this test.

DYEMARKER

On June 18, III MAF published Operation Plan 11-67, which outlined the SPOS concept. The first phase consisted of widening the Trace between Con Thien and Gio Linh to six hundred meters; installing a linear obstacle system along the Trace, including mines, radar, towers, barbed wire, and sensors; and constructing four strongpoints and three base areas. Also, Routes 1, 9, and 561 would be improved, and Dong Ha would develop a storage site for construction materials. The ARVN would complete strongpoints A-1 and A-2 and base area C-1. The target date for completion of this first phase was November 1, 1967.

The final phase was planned to begin when the monsoon season ended the following spring. That phase entailed completion of two more strongpoints west of Con Thien and continued Trace obstacle construction. The III MAF projected an overall completion date of July 1968.

The code name for the SPOS, "Practice Nine," was renamed "Dyemarker" on July 14. One other major change had occurred earlier in June when Lt. Gen. Robert E. Cushman Jr. replaced the commanding general of III MAF, Lew Walt. In his role as the former deputy commander at III MAF prior to this promotion, General Cushman was no stranger to the barrier plan controversy and problems that had faced Lew Walt.

The Marines still disagreed with Westmoreland that pacification was the sole responsibility of the South Vietnamese and that the large unit war was the U.S.'s responsibility. General Walt and General Cushman strongly advocated continuance of the joint Marine/South Vietnamese Combined Action Program (CAP) in the villages. In July 1967, General Krulak, another proponent of the CAP, expressed his displeasure with the way the war was going by stating: "We have seen what we sincerely believe to be a maldeployment of forces, a misapplication of power."[2]

On August 16, Lieutenant General Cushman sent an urgent message to General Westmoreland explaining that four infantry battalions plus supporting units were insufficient to both fight the NVA and construct SPOS bases. General Westmoreland concurred and moved an Army brigade up to I Corps. That move would ultimately enable Lieutenant General Cushman to move two battalions from the 1st Marine Division up to the DMZ area.

General Westmoreland directed III MAF on September 7 to prepare an estimate of the number of casualties the Marines would suffer by meeting the SPOS target completion date of November 1, 1967. He also ordered an alternate plan in the event Dyemarker could not be completed on schedule.

On September 10, III MAF presented its estimates if Phase I were to be completed within twenty-nine days. Total projected casualties, based on actual numbers of casualties incurred during previous operations related to SPOS construction, were 672 U.S. personnel killed and 3,378 wounded. Estimates of South Vietnamese casualties were 112 killed and 642 wounded. Not surprisingly, General Westmoreland came back three days later approving III MAF's alternate operation plan, 12-67, which recommended cessation of the Trace obstacle construction component until after the strongpoints and base areas were completed and the tactical situation stabilized.

MINES AND MINEFIELDS

Something almost always went wrong somewhere, somehow. It was always something vague, unexplainable, tasting of bad fate, and the results were always brought down to their most basic element—the dead Marine. . . . And you knew that, sooner or later, if you went with them often enough, it would happen to you too. . . . And the grunts themselves knew: the madness, the bitterness, the horror and doom of it.

—Michael Herr, *Dispatches*

Something Con Thien had in abundance besides rats, ants, mosquitoes, and incoming was minefields. One of the first features a visitor inside the perimeter noticed was the well-trodden paths through "death valley" bordered with rusty barbed-wire strands strung on old engineer stakes. Spaced every twenty or thirty feet, small triangular metal signs dangled from the wire strands. Barely legible, the weathered signs read MINES! DANGER! No one knew for certain who had emplaced the mines on Con Thien's grassy slopes. Some said the French were responsible, and others believed the ARVN and Special Forces had a hand in it. Most likely, they all had something to do with placing those cursed mines inside the perimeter. No one will ever know how many Americans later paid with life or limb in those minefields. And to the Marine engineers fell the perilous task of clearing some of those mine-seeded areas to permit construction of Dyemarker bunkers.

One of the most feared antipersonnel mines was the "bouncing betty" (also called "tomato can"). When its victim stepped on one of three prongs jutting up from the earth, he first heard a muffled blast, which was the firing device that propelled the main charge up about a yard into the air. It was the last sound he would ever hear. The main charge then exploded, typically chest high, taking off heads and arms and ripping out intestines. The victim was instantly dead, and anyone else in the near vicinity would be maimed. Bouncing betty mines were in abundance on The Hill. In his book *The Grunts*, Charles R. Anderson described an incident that occurred in mid-1969 when 2/9 occupied Con Thien:

> Everyone at Con Thien, including Roland Epps, knew there were minefields both around the outer perimeter and inside the wire in the fenced-in grassy areas. But those mines had been there over three years and probably didn't work anymore. . . . So, Roland Epps walked out into the grassy area behind his bunker with nothing more on his mind than finding the can of beans and franks he had thrown away two hours before. . . . Lance Corporal Epps's Bouncing Betty picked him up and, while he flew through the air, ripped off his clothes, legs, hands, and all of his head but the lower jaw, then dumped him on his back—stumps of thighs and arms raised in supplication to a garish sun. The first man on the scene told a corpsman that he thought he saw a pink mist hanging over the corpse for a few seconds. . . . Roland Epps had won his plastic body bag with the big long zipper. About one hundred twenty of their son's one hundred seventy-two pounds were sent home to Mr. And Mrs. Epps.[3]

Especially terrifying were those moments when one realized he was going to have to traverse one of those minefield paths after dark on a moonless night (flashlights were forbidden). More than one Marine knelt and recited a few Hail Marys before embarking on his perilous journey. Add in a howling monsoon rainstorm or some nocturnal incoming, and the fear factor quadrupled.

Mines and, just as pernicious, the threat of mines, tended to work on the psyche. Vietnam veteran and author Tim O'Brien wrote:

> When you step about these pieces of ground, you do some thinking. You hallucinate. You look ahead a few paces and wonder what your legs will resemble if there is more to the earth in that

spot than silicates and nitrogen. Will the pain be unbearable? Will you scream or fall silent? Will you be afraid to look at your own body, afraid of the sight of your own red flesh and white bone? You wonder if the medic remembered his morphine. You wonder if your friends will weep.[4]

Dyemarker called for extensive minefields to be installed around strongpoints and support bases. That task fell to the 11th Engineer Battalion once the five-hundred-meter-wide swath around each base perimeter had been cleared. Steady nerves and an abundance of courage were required to work around those mines and booby traps every day, all day long, out in a minefield, nakedly exposed to any snipers or FO teams who elected to conduct a little target practice.

The other inescapable hazard in all minefield work was human error. It was inevitable. Someone would make a mistake, and lives would be lost. That happened on August 15, 1967, at Con Thien. Ron "Doc" Smith, a Navy corpsman assigned to 1st Platoon, Kilo Company, 3d Battalion, 4th Marines, had just removed his boots to wash out his dirty socks in his helmet when he heard a loud explosion. That dreaded cry went up: "Corpsman, get a corpsman over here!" HM3 Smith, accompanied by another corpsman, Bob Wilson, ran barefooted over to the scene of the explosion. Both corpsmen had been through a lot that summer, but nothing could have prepared them for what they saw lying on the ground beneath a pall of smoke and dust. Two blood-covered Marines lay writhing in pain out in an old minefield. They were combat engineers clearing mines out of an area of Con Thien called "Death Valley" where some Dyemarker bunkers would be constructed.

The two Navy corpsmen never hesitated. They made two perilous trips through the deadly minefield to the side of the mortally wounded engineers and carried them to safety. One of the Marines, Cpl. Gerald B. Weaver, died in the arms of corpsman Bob Wilson while expressing concern for his family, asking over and over, "How can my mother make it without me?" The second Marine, Lance Cpl. Andre R. Latessa, held Navy chaplain Leo "Chappie" Stanis's hand tightly, reciting the Lord's Prayer over and over, while the two corpsmen worked rapidly to save his life. He would later succumb to his grievous wounds.[5]

Another deadly error happened two months later at Charlie-Two (C-

2), the artillery firebase four miles south of Con Thien. In this September 13 minefield tragedy, engineer Staff Sgt. James W. Savage was taking his new lieutenant, Ronald S. Sweet, on a tour through the C-2 minefield. There were "safe" lanes laid out in the minefield that were clearly indicated on the minefield map. But, inexplicably, one of them made a fatal mistake and set off a mine, killing them both. It was tragic enough to trigger an enemy mine—that was expected in this war. But to be killed like that in a "friendly" minefield was almost unspeakably appalling. It was often said with typically blunt Marine Corps cynicism that "our damned minefields killed more Marines than they ever did 'gooks.'"

Phase I Begins

Hanoi's new offensive did not begin with a bang, but rather with a noticeable increase in enemy activity all across the DMZ in late August. Occasional salvos of incoming were common all summer at Con Thien and Gio Linh. That was not new. What changed dramatically was the ferocity of the enemy's artillery directed at Dong Ha. On August 26, 150 rocket and artillery rounds destroyed two helicopters and damaged twenty-four others. What compounded matters further was that a valuable fuel storage area was set ablaze.

In a second attack geared to coincide with South Vietnam's September 3 elections, forty-one 130mm artillery rounds hit Dong Ha again, this time destroying the ammunition storage area, bulk fuel farm, and seventeen helicopters from HMM-361. The column of smoke that rose into the sky could be seen as far away as Phu Bai. Four hours of herculean effort by damage-control teams finally brought the conflagration under control. By some miracle, no fatalities resulted, but seventy-seven men were injured. As a direct result of that September 3 attack, Dong Ha would no longer be used as a permanent helicopter squadron base. HMM-361 was moved south to the Marble Mountain facility.

❖

The 3d Battalion, 4th Marines, commanded by Lt. Col. Lee R. Bendell, were no strangers to incoming. Since their mid-July arrival on The Hill, the "Thundering Third" had come to expect and even anticipate occasional recoilless rifle and mortar fire and even sporadic artillery fire. Hardly a day passed without them taking some incoming. But life on The Hill became more perilous as August rolled into September. Staying alive, always the prerequisite motivational drive shared by men in war, became even more of a contest. The Marines could no longer count on the usual incoming times, early morning, noon, and late afternoon, to be inside or near a bunker or trench. Death could fall from the sky at any hour, any moment.

The September Battalion Command Chronology for 3/4 clearly indicates when the pressure from the NVA escalated. Log entries for the first day of September indicated tension was building around The Hill. Patrols located several freshly dug bunkers to the south of Con Thien, and incoming mortars peppered the Marine position at unusual times throughout the day.

The daily routine at Con Thien involved a morning mine sweep of the MSR from Con Thien's south gate a little over three miles to the north gate of Charlie-2. With the engineer mine-sweep team in the lead, a squad or more of grunts provided flank security. Two tanks brought up the rear, trailing the engineers down the road. Once the detail reached the Charlie-2 north gate, they mounted the tanks and headed back up the road to Con Thien.

Everything went routinely the morning of September 2 until the returning mine-sweep detail reached a fork in the road one thousand meters southeast of Con Thien. They were near the abandoned hamlet of Thon Trung An, site of bloody fighting during Hickory. As the mine-sweep detail dismounted the tanks, an alert grunt spotted freshly turned dirt beside the road up ahead. He investigated and spotted two wires running west along the ground into the tree line that paralleled the MSR. The team was cautiously following the wires when two explosions rocked the Marines. The prematurely detonated mines caused no casualties, but triggered an attack from the tree line that erupted into a crescendo of small-arms fire.

One of the two tanks, A-13, was driven by Lance Cpl. Ken "Piggy" Bores. Out of the corner of his eye, Bores picked up a flash of light and then saw a glowing red ball rocketing directly toward him. Reacting instinctively, he threw his tank into reverse and stomped on the throttle.

The RPG missed. His tank commander, Corporal Aranda, ordered his crew to open fire and attack the tree line. Lance Cpl. Bill "JJ" Carroll loaded cannister rounds as fast as he could slam them into the tank cannon breech. Both tanks advanced on the tree line, hosing it down with their .30-caliber coaxial machine guns and blasting out cannister rounds.

Lance Corporal Bores saw two wounded grunts lying in the grass to his front. Bullets were zinging overhead like angry hornets. He undid the escape hatch on the tank floor and steered his tank directly atop one of the injured Marines and hauled him inside. Bores repeated this maneuver a second time. Reaching down through the escape hatch with one arm, Bores grasped the second wounded man's belt, threw his tank into reverse, and dragged him out of harm's way as bullets bounced harmlessly off the steel behemoth.

A-13 unloaded the two casualties and, joined by grunt reinforcements from K/3/4, resumed advancing toward the tree line. The tankers were so close to the air strikes being run on the NVA positions that they could feel their breath being sucked away by the vacuum pressure inside their turret. Driver Ken Bores recalled:

> As we approached the tree line, I saw an RPG team getting ready to fire at us. I yelled, "One o'clock! One o'clock!" The tank commander grabbed the override handle and swung the turret to about one o'clock and fired the cannister round that Lance Cpl. Carroll had just loaded. The gook RPG team and several riflemen vaporized in front of my eyes, but they got their RPG round off just as we fired at them.[6]

The antitank rocket struck the front of the turret on the gun shield right above Bores's head and exploded inside the turret. Loader Bill Carroll was instantly "flash-blinded":

> I looked out of the loader's hatch and it appeared like I was floating in a red cloud. I thought the tank was on fire. "Maybe they got us with a satchel charge?" I climbed out of the tank and rolled behind the turret. The NVA were attempting to pick me off with rifle fire.

A grunt jumped on the back of the tank when he noticed I was bleeding all over the place. The artery in my right calf was punctured and blood would shoot out every time my heart beat. Some grunts dragged me off the tank to a knoll where they had set up a hasty aid site.[7]

The rest of the crew of A-13 all suffered flash burns and were peppered by bits of shrapnel, but only Carroll was hurt seriously.

The abortive NVA ambush was quickly quashed, and the attackers fled the scene. It was a minor incident, with five grunts and one tanker wounded and medevaced, but it was the precursor of more savage fighting to come as the NVA attempted to cut the vital resupply lifeline to Con Thien.

Election Day, September 3

It began at three in the morning. A half-dozen rounds of 82mm mortar fire woke up the Con Thien garrison, but no casualties were reported. At first light, Marines on the eastern perimeter discovered a gap in the wire had been blown by a bangalore torpedo. At one in the afternoon, an alarming *booom!* from north of the Ben Hai reached the ears of 3/4's Marines, followed seconds later by a sound like a jet screaming overhead and then an earth-shaking blast. Bunker-busting 152mm artillery rounds began impacting, blasting craters in the earth so huge that a man could stand in one of them and barely see over the edge. Added to the bunker busters' destructive impact was their range, ten and one-half miles, which outreached our 105s and 155s. Our 175mm guns returned counter-battery fire, and air strikes were called in, but to no avail. Before the day was over, Con Thien had been clobbered by seventy-two rounds of 152mm artillery and more than one hundred rounds of assorted smaller-caliber artillery and mortars.

Dong Ha appeared to have been hit hardest that day, as evidenced by a towering pillar of smoke visible for many miles. The most deadly accurate weapon in the NVA arsenal, Soviet-built 130mm field guns, had done the damage. They had been directed precisely where they would hurt the Marines the worst—logistically. Ammunition, fuel supplies, and helicopters bore the brunt of that attack.

The 130mm gun fired a seventy-four-pound shell up to thirty-one thousand meters with stunning accuracy. America's only comparable weapon was the 175mm gun, which could reach out 32,800 meters, but it could deliver a round only every two minutes. The 130mm had a maximum rate of fire of six to seven rounds per minute. Because of the gun's enormous range, all Allied bases in northern Quang Tri Province from the Cua Viet on the coast to Camp Carroll and the Rockpile inland were within the 130mm artillery fan. Our bases could be reached any time the NVA chose to unleash that weapon from above the Ben Hai. By establishing our own ground rules that the northern DMZ was off-limits to U.S. ground troops, the NVA needed to be concerned only with our counter-battery fire and air strikes.

Outside the Con Thien perimeter, India and Mike Companies cautiously revisited the site of the previous day's encounter near Thon Trung An, expecting more trouble, but the NVA had withdrawn during the night. Eight freshly dug bunkers with four feet of overhead protection were all destroyed with C-4 explosive by the engineers. Later that same afternoon, India Company destroyed thirteen newly constructed bunkers adjacent to the MSR and only two hundred meters south of the previous day's road ambush.

For the time being, the NVA had pulled back from these areas. But they rarely stayed away for long. Those Marines from 3/4 would experience what all the other Marine battalions had learned previously about Con Thien. The NVA could be bombed, blasted, and burned out of their bunkers, but they would eventually sneak back. Recent enemy contacts indicated the NVA had infiltrated in force to the An Hoa–Trung An area south of Con Thien that 1/9 had fought so fiercely over the previous spring. The question now was "when" the NVA would strike next, and no longer "where."

Marine intelligence analysts had previously warned that the NVA might attempt to sever the MSR lifeline to Con Thien and then attack the base itself once it was cut off. Recent events had lent credence to those warnings. Lieutenant Colonel Bendell and his battalion staff prepared to counter any such interdiction moves by the NVA. The vital road artery to Con Thien had to be kept open.

Counterattack at An Hoa

On September 4, Captain Richard R. Young's India Company patrolled all morning without making enemy contact in the thickly wooded hedgerow country near Thon An Hoa, barely a klick southwest of Con Thien. On their return route, the company point squad was suddenly taken under fire by an unknown-sized enemy force. Bullets whizzed and snapped overhead from several directions. Before anyone could figure out for sure what was happening, the entire company was receiving heavy fire from numerous nearly invisible bunkers and spider holes.

Captain Young radioed his predicament back to the Con Thien CP. Lieutenant Colonel Bendell rounded up his command group, and together with two tanks from the 1st Platoon of Alpha Company, 3d Tanks, they hurriedly joined up with Mike Company and moved out to launch a counterattack.

After prepping the NVA position with artillery fire, Mike Company and the two tanks rolled in against the enemy's left flank while India Company provided a concentrated base of fire to keep the NVA pinned down in their bunkers.[8]

Attacking relentlessly, knocking out one bunker after another in concert with the two tanks commanded by 2d Lt. Thomas C. Barry, Mike Company routed the enemy, taking the pressure off India and trapping a number of NVA between the two companies.

Taking advantage of the enemy's disarray, Captain Young commandeered the two tanks and led India Company in a frontal assault. Lieutenant Tom Barry, a short, wiry, taciturn young Marine officer from Maryland, had been the tank platoon leader at Con Thien for only two weeks, but he had already picked up two Purple Hearts from incoming shrapnel on The Hill. Though not exactly the recruiting-poster type of Marine officer, Tom Barry soon showed any skeptics that he was fearless under fire. He recounted his tank's role in that attack:

> I went with the grunt captain, and the other tank went with another unit from that company. We began catching heavy automatic weapons fire and mortar rounds. The grunt fire-team around my tank had a couple of M-16s jam. One of them asked to use my

.45-caliber M-3 "grease gun." Instead of passing it down to him and probably never seeing it again, I used it myself on several NVA I spotted in a hedgerow ten meters from my tank, then we drove over them, crushing that NVA position. We must have fired 90% of our .30-caliber machine-gun ammunition that day. The tanks really poured it on, which made the grunts exceptionally happy. When we finally halted, we found some Marine MIAs from a previous battle. Their bodies had been mutilated—skin peeled off, castrated, and other unpleasantries I'd prefer not to mention. I remember thinking that I hoped they were dead before they were mutilated. Some of us ate C-rations while we were loading the bodies on the back of our tanks. I know I was starving. I hadn't eaten since the previous day, so I had some canned turkey while sitting right beside those poor dead Marines.[9]

Lieutenant Colonel Bendell had led a highly successful counterattack, almost textbook for tank-infantry coordination. The Marines claimed thirty-nine NVA killed and ten more probable. Their own losses were six killed and forty-seven wounded (nine medevaced). Most of the Marine casualties that day had been caused by enemy artillery.

An Hoa Again
The NVA had moved back in on all sides of Con Thien, just as they had done previously in March, May, and July. On September 6, an AO circling overhead spotted a large number of NVA, perhaps a company, in trenches and bunkers one thousand meters northeast of Con Thien near Hill 105. He called in artillery, results unknown. Later that same morning, a wire-laying detail found three breaches in Con Thien's northern perimeter wire blown by bangalore torpedoes. The next morning, September 7, some Marines found four more breaches in the northeastern portion of the perimeter wire, all blown by bangalore torpedoes. A sense of urgency percolated through the ranks at every level of command on Con Thien.

Lima 3/4 had responsibility for manning the base perimeter, and Lima's Marines were getting shell shocked. Ground-shaking blasts from 152mm artillery and 140mm rockets crashing into the earth had their nerves jangled. "I can't stand that artillery," one shaken Marine confessed. "There's no . . . rhyme or reason to who gets hit and who doesn't."[10] Only fate determined who lived or died during increasingly frequent bouts of incoming.

Lieutenant Robert McIntosh had the 1st Platoon of Lima. His platoon had been on the north side of the perimeter since mid-August. At 11:02 a.m. on September 7, he and several of his men were sitting on some sandbags outside their bunker when they heard that dreaded sound—*boom-ba-booom*—from north of the Ben Hai. They had seconds to act. McIntosh dove into a trench. A corpsman and two grunts dashed into the bunker. An ear-splitting explosion blasted their bunker into a pile of ripped-open sandbags and splintered wooden ammunition crates. The lieutenant ran over, ears still ringing from his near miss, to find both Marines dead. His corpsman died in his arms.

That afternoon, Mike Company was again sweeping through the Thon An Hoa area, scene of savage fighting on September 4, when they came under automatic weapons fire from what they assumed was an enemy squad hidden in bunkers along an east-west trail. Second Lieutenant Jim Singer's 2d Platoon was in the lead when the ambush kicked off. While Singer was talking on his radioman's handset, a mortar shell exploded nearby, killing his radioman. Singer luckily suffered only a concussion.

Mike Company returned fire and maneuvered for a flanking assault. Before they could launch their attack, however, the volume of enemy fire increased dramatically. They were up against much more than a squad. Mike Company had triggered an L-shaped ambush. Mortar and artillery shells began to explode around them. Mike Company was pinned down, being blasted mercilessly by incoming mortars and artillery, and unable to move.

Kilo was within two hundred meters of Mike Company when they started taking incoming as well. Navy corpsman HM3 Ron "Doc" Smith remembered that terrible day in a letter to his former platoon commander, Peter Wymes:

> We were just "shootin' the shit" when we heard the first gun fire across the DMZ. . . . It seems like the screaming started after that

first round hit. I got up and grabbed my unit one and Jeffries reached up and grabbed me by the nap of my flak jacket and pulled me down. He said, "Wait, Doc, you're no good to us dead." . . . Every time a round came in there was more screaming for corpsmen. Shrapnel was tearing the limbs off the tree over us. Some of the rounds were so close the impact bounced us a few inches off the ground. After the chopper came in, we were throwing the wounded in like crazy. I went over to where you were and gave you the names and types of wounds for the casualty report. I went to light a cigarette. My hands were shaking so bad I couldn't light it. I was hoping you didn't notice. My fingers were so bloody they were sticking together, and by then, I didn't even care.[11]

Sergeant Dominic Bilotta was in charge of the Mike Company mortar section. When the ambush began, Bilotta was hit in both arms by fragments from a grenade. A bullet had struck him in the left hand, severing two fingers. He lay in a bomb crater for hours, drawing enemy fire from a tree line to his front every time he raised up his head. He was bleeding profusely and believed he was going to die in that crater. He prayed that his buddies found his body before the NVA did.

Just before dusk, Bilotta heard the beautiful sound of a tank rolling to a stop alongside his crater. He thought at first he was hallucinating, but it really was a "Zippo" flame tank. He watched with mixed fear and fascination as the flame tank unleashed a long fiery tongue of flaming napalm, enveloping the tree line up ahead where the NVA machine guns were located. With the enemy threat silenced, two of the flame tank crewmen jumped down and hoisted Bilotta up onto the back of their tank. He and several other wounded rode the tank back to the LZ, where they were given a helicopter ride back to Delta Med. That was when Bilotta learned that every man in his mortar section had either been killed or wounded.[12]

Company I had arrived on the scene with a five-tank platoon from Alpha Company, 3d Tanks late in the afternoon. By six o'clock it was all over. Mike Company had taken the brunt of the incoming and suffered the majority of casualties. Together with India, they incurred losses of twelve men killed and thirty-five wounded and evacuated. Once again, deadly accurate NVA artillery and mortar fire had taken its toll.

When the NVA broke contact at dusk, the Marine companies were ordered to pull back closer to Con Thien's perimeter. The battalion CP had learned that another Marine Corps battalion had made heavy contact with a large force of NVA only fifteen hundred meters south of the Thon An Hoa encounter, and that battle was still raging.

11

Into the Valley of Death

Theirs not to make reply,
Theirs not to reason why,
Theirs but to do and die.
Into the valley of Death
Rode the six hundred.
  —Alfred, Lord Tennyson (1809–1892),
   "The Charge of the Light Brigade"

The commanding general of the 3d Marine Division, Major General Bruno Hochmuth, was deeply concerned over intelligence reports that the NVA were intending to sever the Cam Lo to Con Thien MSR and then launch a major attack on that firebase. Additional forces would be required to prevent that situation from becoming a reality. The 5th Marine Division's 3d Battalion, 26th Marines had been operating at Khe Sanh since June 13. They drew the short straw.

On September 5, all 3/26 elements at Khe Sanh were airlifted by CH-53 helicopters to Camp Carroll. Lima Company had been pulled out of the field weeks earlier and assigned to "Rough Rider" supply convoy escort duty out of Dong Ha. They were due to rejoin their parent battalion shortly.

The following day, 3/26(-) moved by truck convoy to their drop-off point on the MSR, about halfway between Charlie-2 and Con Thien. From there, they hiked a half-mile west to an abandoned hamlet, Nha

3/26 Battle
Nui Ho Khe
September 10, 1967
81mm mortar
NVA .51-cal.
landing zone
Mike withdrawal
NVA attack
Ontos
rice paddy
tank
0
100
200
meters
J. P. Coan
N
III
812
NVA
II
3
26
K
26
LZ
x48
M
26
B-22
L
26
26
LZ
Nui Ho Khe

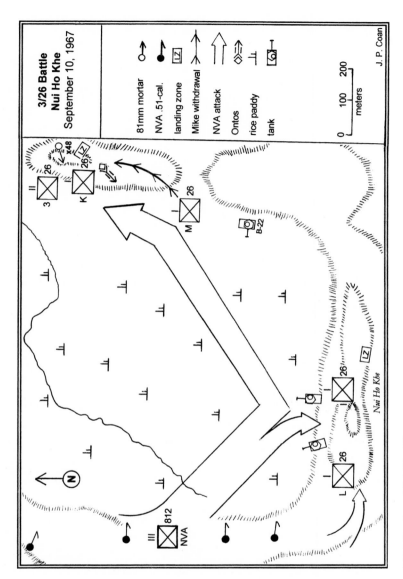

3/26 Battle at Nui Ho Khe

Tho Bai Son, located three thousand meters south of Con Thien. The plan was to join Mike Company at the churchyard and set up a battalion perimeter there for the night. Lt. Col. Harry Alderman, their newly assigned battalion commander, would be with them at the churchyard while Major Carl Mundy, battalion XO, would set up the battalion rear in Dong Ha.

Two companies from 1/9 and a platoon of tanks from Bravo Company, 3d Tank Battalion had been patrolling in that area for two weeks with zero enemy contact. The weather was overcast and drizzling that evening as 3/26 moved into positions in the churchyard just vacated by 1/9. The unofficial word among the grunts was that this area was quiet, that nothing was happening. As far as the men from 3/26 knew, they were there only to patrol around the area for a few days, familiarize themselves with the terrain, and then become the next Marine battalion to do "time in the barrel" at Con Thien.[1]

THE CHURCHYARD BATTLE

India Company's Patrol

The battalion's first night around the churchyard was quietly uneventful. The morning of September 7 dawned sunny and clear, and there was not a cloud in the sky. The 1st and 2d Platoons of India Company headed out on patrol northwest of the churchyard. Lieutenant Bill Cowan's 3d Platoon remained at the churchyard to secure the company position.

Captain Wayne Coulter, CO of India, was an aggressive and burly former football player from Kansas. His XO, 1st Lt. Robert Stimson, was more the quiet, cerebral type of officer. Both went along on the patrol. Negotiating the undulating terrain with alternating flat rice paddies and thickly vegetated hedgerows was slow going and tough to move through. Danger lurked out there, causing the company to move cautiously.

Staff Sergeant Russell P. Armstrong, 1st Platoon commander, was a no-nonsense former drill instructor who had six years in the Corps, much of that time spent with 81mm mortars. His unit came across a grassy clearing and found four fresh trails where a military unit had apparently marched through four abreast. He believed that it had to be the

4th Marines but wondered how they could be that close to them. It did not make any sense.

Captain Coulter directed his company to keep moving northwest. Suddenly, flankers on the left received some automatic weapons fire. Second Platoon had three men hit and wounded in the first flurry of shots. First Platoon had a man killed. The Marines could not see any NVA through the thick brush and trees, but they continued to return fire at muzzle flashes. A squad of NVA was firing and moving, probably attempting to learn how many Marines were facing them.

As suddenly as it began, the NVA fire slackened and then ceased. Staff Sergeant Armstrong took inventory and realized he was missing one man. He found the missing man lying in a bomb crater where he had crawled after being shot. No one could reach him because of the intense enemy fire. He was dead by the time Armstrong reached him.

Ninety minutes after the first shots were fired, a medevac was brought in to evacuate casualties. The UH-34D helicopter crew would take only the three wounded, not the two dead. No more medevacs would come for the KIAs. That meant the worn-out, combat-weary men of India had to carry out the bodies of their two comrades, six men to a bag, and they were royally pissed off. The AO circling overhead called in air strikes after the medevacs departed, reporting four NVA killed.

At 2:00 p.m., as the India patrol was returning to the battalion perimeter, the AO reported seeing a squad of NVA and finding numerous new bunkers southwest of India's original contact. He called in an artillery mission on them with unknown results.

Kilo Company was sent out along with four tanks from Bravo Company, 2d Platoon, commanded by 2d Lt. Paul Drnek, to intercept India and escort them back into the churchyard perimeter. Even though Drnek was new to Vietnam and this was his first command as a tank platoon leader, his platoon had been operating in the area with 1/9 for the past two weeks. Prior to Drnek's arrival, the tank platoon had been with 1/9 at Con Thien on July 2, 1967, and was part of Captain Radcliffe's reaction force that went out to rescue Bravo 1/9 during the infamous Marketplace massacre.

When Staff Sergeant Armstrong was almost within sight of the tanks and Kilo Company, he looked to his right across a four-hundred-meter open paddy area and saw a man standing by a tree line in a flak jacket and helmet, motioning to come his way. When Armstrong noted that the "Marine" had no weapon, his intuition kicked in, making him suspicious. Because of his concern that an NVA who spoke good English could be on his radio frequency and remembering that Kilo had a Rumanian staff sergeant who had an accent he would readily recognize, Armstrong contacted him on his radio and asked directions to his position. The Rumanian sergeant told Armstrong to continue straight ahead, that he was just on the other side of the berm to Armstrong's front. Armstrong ignored the man by the tree line to his right and continued forward. Fortunately for India Company, as it later turned out, Staff Sergeant Armstrong did not alter his course toward that "Marine" by the tree line.

The linkup was completed at 5:00 p.m., and India's two dead Marines were loaded on board one of the three gun tanks (the fourth tank was a flame tank). The tanks kept their main guns pointed northwest, the direction where India was coming from, in the event the NVA were following them in.

Captain Coulter climbed aboard one of the tanks and ordered Second Lieutenant Drnek to fire some rounds out where India had made contact earlier. Drnek hesitated and expressed concerns about whether all of India Company was clear of that area. He was overruled and ordered to "start shooting now." Sergeant Frank Vining, a tough, mouthy Irish kid from Boston, was on Drnek's tank, B-21. He shouted over at the captain: "For Christ's sake, whatever you do, get the troops the hell out of the open!"[2] Vining was on his second tour in Nam and a DMZ combat vet, and he feared that the captain's order was going to invite incoming. Despite their misgivings, the tankers carried out the captain's orders and fired several HE rounds, praying they were all going over the heads of any India Marines that might still be out there.

Kilo Company had turned Drnek's tanks over to India's control and then made an about-face and left, leaving India to fend for themselves. Kilo was almost back to the battalion perimeter, but the bulk of India was still five hundred meters away, when all hell broke loose. A volley of 140mm rockets and 82mm mortars rained down around the tanks. Captain Coulter was one of the first casualties. RPGs and small-arms fire opened up on India's men exposed in the paddies. Simultaneously, a probing attack was launched at the 3/26 battalion perimeter back at the churchyard.

Drnek wanted his tanks out of the open. They were drawing fire like a magnet. He led them out of the open paddy area south about a hundred meters to be near a thickly wooded tree line.

A second volley of rockets and mortars came crashing down. Staff Sergeant Armstrong had a piece of shrapnel tear into his face. A second shard ripped a gaping hole completely through his leg. His radioman was knocked on his back unconscious, riddled with shrapnel from his crotch to his face. Armstrong could scarcely believe what he saw next. A dozen NVA, or even perhaps twenty, were assaulting across the paddy area through their own supporting arms fire. He thought, "This is crazy; you don't do it that way." And then it really sank in—he was going to die. He remembered thinking:

> I have never been religious, but I distinctly thought I needed to say a prayer. . . . Then I began thinking about my son, who was just starting kindergarten that week in San Diego. . . . I was struck by very hard remorse, by guilt. I wasn't going to be there for my son; I wasn't going to be around to get him going in the right direction at that important juncture in his life. . . . I had seen so much death, had weathered so much grief, had come so close; and now I was going to die violently at the end of a day that had started out in beautiful sunlight, with the sound of birds singing and the vision of flowers growing.[3]

Lieutenant Stimson had no idea where Captain Coulter was, but he knew he was down and had to find him. The company was fragmented. First and 2d Platoons were cut off from each other about one hundred meters apart. Someone had to pull them into one defensive perimeter. Stimson and his radioman went looking for their captain, covering as much ground as they could while dodging incoming mortars and avoiding any of the NVA infantry moving around them. Stimson located Captain Coulter lying prone in the middle of a paddy, badly injured by a piece of shrapnel in his head. He had a pressure bandage on the wound and was still conscious. As Lieutenant Stimson lay prone beside the captain, attempting to figure out where members of his unit were, a mortar round impacted beside them. A piece of shrapnel sliced open Captain Coulter's forehead, only inches from Stimson's face. A nearby corpsman responded and bandaged the wound on the captain, who had passed out. Stimson knew then it was his company to command.

The tankers had seen Kilo Company move out, leaving them and India behind. In less than a minute after the last man from Kilo had disappeared from sight, the tanks began taking fire from the trail and tree line. The NVA had maneuvered across the trail between themselves and Kilo.

The tank commander of B-22, Cpl. Jack Wilder, radioed that there were fifty NVA on the trail. Gunnery Sgt. Harold Tatum (he had replaced Gunnery Sergeant Eckler a few weeks after Buffalo) on B-25 was new to Vietnam and new to the platoon. He told Wilder not to fire because those had to be Marines. Corporal Wilder replied, "I know NVA when I see NVA, and I'm firing!" He cut loose with his coaxial .30-caliber machine gun. The flame-tank commander, Cpl. Guy Wolfenbarger, came up on the radio and said, "For Christ's sake, they're all around me!" "Are you sure they're not Marines?" Lieutenant Drnek asked. He could not fathom that the NVA could be that close to them. "Yes, sir," said Wolfenbarger. "Those are definitely gooners. Can I zap them with the flame?" Lieutenant Drnek refused that request to fire the flame tank, uncertain as to what it could do and not willing to risk roasting some Marines by accident. "No, fire your .50-caliber if you're sure they're not Marines."[4]

Drnek got on a PRC-25 radio that he kept in his tank and raised someone on the infantry net, although he was not sure who it was. He wanted to form up with the grunts and fight their way through to the battalion lines. The reply was negative. India had too many casualties to move—seven dead and twenty wounded. Their only hope was to consolidate into one defensive position. Sergeant Vining then exhorted: "We better get the hell outta this brush. We're sitting ducks."[5] Drnek agreed and directed his driver to move out into the open paddy. They had gone only about twenty-five meters when the tank stopped. It would not move. An RPG had gone through the engine compartment, taking out his transmission.

Drnek glanced out through the rear commander's cupola vision blocks and spotted an RPG team getting ready to fire at his tank. He yanked the tank commander's override handle and swung the gun tube around 180 degrees. A cannister round was already in the breech. He pulled the firing trigger on the handle and literally blew the RPG team away. There was nothing left when the dust cleared. Drnek and his four-man crew disabled all the radios and weapons on their crippled tank and dispersed themselves among the other two gun-tank crews. His two remaining tanks and the flame tank moved to where India's men were attempting to form a defensive perimeter, blasting the attacking NVA with thirty-five rounds of 90mm cannister and thousands of rounds of .30-caliber and .50-caliber machine-gun fire.

First Lieutenant Stimson radioed Staff Sergeant Armstrong, knowing he had once been the 81mm mortar chief. Stimson desperately needed artillery called in on the attacking NVA, but his artillery FO, 2d Lt. Charles Ryberg, had been killed in a freak accident back at the LZ. Shrapnel from an exploding rocket round penetrated an M-60 machine-gun ammunition can, and it exploded, killing the FO.

Despite his painful wounds and loss of blood, Staff Sergeant Armstrong was able to radio in the correct grids and call down artillery fire on the NVA. This bought time for Stimson and his NCOs to push and prod India into a semblance of a defensive perimeter. At least the two platoons were no longer separated. Wounded men who could still fire a weapon were placed on the perimeter. Stimson saw a corpsman get shot in the throat, wrap a pressure bandage around it, and keep on working over the wounded.

Heavy machine-gun fire was coming from the north, west, and southwest. The tree line where Staff Sergeant Armstrong had earlier seen the "Marine" waving at him to come that way was where one of the 12.7mm machine guns was located. Lieutenant Stimson managed to contact the AO circling overhead, and the AO directed two F-4B Phantom jets down to their targets, finally silencing the heavy machine guns. Another bombing run to the north wiped out an NVA mortar crew.

As the sun went down, the beleaguered, understrength India Company began to believe the worst was over. They had the tanks with them inside their perimeter, the AO was overhead, and they were boxed in by friendly artillery. Staff Sergeant Armstrong was calling some rounds in as close as fifty meters. Literally dragging himself from position to position, he distributed ammunition and ensured that his men had good fields of fire. He would refuse evacuation that night, knowing his FO skills were needed to fend off any more NVA attacks. Lieutenant Stimson later said of Staff Sgt. Russell P. Armstrong, "He was an inspiration. We owe him our lives."[6] Armstrong would receive the Navy Cross for his heroic actions that day and night.

Churchyard Attack

From 5:20 p.m. to 5:49 p.m., the battalion perimeter at the churchyard received three volleys of assorted rocket, artillery, and mortar fire. Sixty of the huge 140mm rockets screamed down on the battalion. Kilo, Mike, and H & S Companies suffered three dead and twenty-five wounded.

At dusk, Mike Company, led by their volatile, hard-boiled skipper, Captain Andrew DeBona, encountered a large force of NVA assaulting their portion of the perimeter. He moved his second platoon over to cover the positions vacated by India's two platoons earlier that day. As 3d Platoon moved over to cover behind 2d Platoon, a strong force of NVA attacked through their own assault barrage, heading right for that weak spot in the perimeter.

Corporal Peter Fossel, a squad leader in 3d Platoon, ran over to help plug the gap with his platoon leader, 2d Lt. John Manzi, his radioman, and a grenadier. Fossel recalled:

The grenadier and I ran forward to the tree line the moment the attack started, and all I remember was that no matter how much fire I put out, they kept coming; not running, but advancing low and slow, relentless, and so many you couldn't begin to count. I remember thinking "Oh, shit" a lot that day. My M-16 jammed about the time the grenadier took a round . . . so I borrowed his M-79 and began shooting point-blank into the trees until I ran out of ammo. I crawled back to borrow a weapon from the lieutenant and found him dead a few yards behind me. He didn't have to get out of his foxhole. It cost him his life. I remember thinking, "I hope you don't mind me borrowing this, sir," and took his .45 and M-16 and went back to business. . . . Instead of firing on automatic, I had the good sense to aim single-shot at one target after another, one after another, and another. It went on for so long I can't even tell you. It was dark when the shooting let up.[7]

Snipers were picking off NCOs and officers or anyone using a radio. Someone reported a muzzle flash coming from the church steeple, and a grenadier pumped a few M-79 rounds into it.

Captain DeBona noted gunfire flashes coming from a tree line sixty meters away. He estimated eight to ten NVA. DeBona organized a reaction force led by the 60mm mortar section chief and ordered the group to go clean them out. They gave him an "aye, aye, sir" and departed. Moments later, a flurry of small-arms fire and grenade blasts originated from the tree line. Then it got quiet. The reaction team leader returned ten minutes later, a bullet hole in his shoulder, stating, "We got them all, sir."[8]

Chief Warrant Officer Richard Holycross was the 81mm Mortar Platoon CO. He moved among his men, repeatedly exposing himself to hostile fire, to direct their return fire. He commandeered an Ontos and directed the Ontos crew to open fire with their .30-caliber on a tree line where several NVA were spotted. Four NVA were killed by the Ontos machine gunner.

Enemy offensive action began to slacken noticeably. Both perimeters had held. The battalion S-3, Captain Wildprett, and Capt. Tom Early, communications officer, were credited with having done a masterful job of holding the tenuous situation together. While Wildprett coolly ran the show from his radio, Early was all over the churchyard perimeter directing fire, keeping the Marines supplied with ammunition, and ignoring the green tracers zipping overhead. After the firing had died down, medevacs began arriving and lifted off the seriously wounded first. One of the priority medevacs was Captain Coulter. The dead would have to wait until morning.

India Company reported thirteen men missing. That total was revised when they realized that six men had latched onto Kilo and had followed them back to the perimeter earlier. Occasional bursts of fire shattered the nighttime stillness until a "Puff" gunship arrived overhead, bathing the area in flare light the remainder of the night. (The nickname "Puff" came from a popular song of the time by Peter, Paul, and Mary called "Puff, the Magic Dragon." The tremendous volume of fire from this kind of gunship looked like a stream of fire or molten lava pouring down from the sky at night.) The NVA were dragging back their dead, which was a good sign they were through. Captain Tom Early recalled:

> The NVA dragged away their dead with meat hooks that had ropes attached. They threw the meat hooks and pulled the dead back so they wouldn't be hit with the same direct fire that had killed the dead. I think they also did it to demoralize us. We could hear the noise of the hook going into a body and the body hitting other objects as it was being dragged.[9]

At dawn, the men from India Company could scarcely believe the gruesome sight that greeted them. Dozens of dead and dying men, Marines and NVA, lay sprawled where they had fallen. Kilo Company went out to help India retrieve their dead and wounded.

Six of the missing men were located behind a dike, and all were dead—shot and bayoneted. They had been part of the linkup squad from Armstrong's 2d Platoon that followed behind Kilo Company when they turned over the tanks and left. The seventh missing man was found alive, having been bayoneted several times. Somehow, he had willed himself to live through the night.

The survivors stood around stunned at first, gazing blankly with that "thousand-yard stare"—that faraway look common to people in shock—and moving in slow motion. Then, NCOs started barking at their men to get moving, to get the gear policed up, and to load the dead and wounded on the tanks.

Lieutenant Drnek and his three tanks, loaded down with casualties, stopped to tow his disabled tank. Because the brakes were gone, B-21 was hooked up with crossed tow cables and a rigid tow bar to F-23. Slowly they rolled across the paddies toward the battalion perimeter, stopping from time to time to hoist aboard a dead Marine found lying along the way. There were signs of enemy dead everywhere: blood pools, drag marks, and torn equipment and uniforms.

Captain DeBona sent out his 2d Platoon to sweep the area through the tree line where his reaction force had fought during the evening. They found seven dead NVA and another one wounded; he had been shot in the ankle. He was just a kid, begging for mercy, and the only POW taken during the battle. When 2d Lieutenant Cowan asked what unit he was with and where his headquarters was located, he kept saying, *"Nui Tan Than, Nui Tan Than."* That meant Hill 88 or Mountain 88. Cowan tried to find it on his map but could not.

Altogether, 3/26 claimed 108 NVA killed, the majority being probables. The churchyard battle had cost the lives of twenty Marines and corpsmen; another seventy were wounded. Lieutenant Colonel Alderman's 3/26 had encountered two battalions of the 324B Division's 812th Regiment. They were in the enemy's backyard but had not been apprised of it. Now they knew this would not be easy. The 812th Regiment had even more in store for 3/26.

CHARGE OF THE 812TH BRIGADE

Capt. Richard D. Camp, the CO of Lima Company, had been a Marine officer for five years, leading a variety of platoons—infantry, reconnaissance, and most recently the prestigious ceremonial platoon at the Marine Barracks in Washington, D.C. He had taken over Lima a month earlier, in August. His company was released from Rough Rider convoy escort duty and came up the MSR by truck convoy to join 3/26 on September 8. Volunteering to join Lima were eight men from Mike Company and a large number of short-timers from the battalion rear who heard that their battalion had run into trouble and needed help. Altogether, 270 men made the trip out to beef up their battalion's lines. Kilo accompanied Drnek's tanks with the dead and wounded and met the convoy on the MSR shortly before noon.

As the replacements dismounted, Kilo's Marines unloaded casualties from the tanks and put them in the "deuce-and-a-half" trucks. The tanks, trucks, and hundreds of Marines out in the open made an irresistible target. Capt. Tom Early approached Captain Camp, frantically shouting, "Spread 'em out, Dick, spread 'em out! They're gonna get you." Captain Camp tried to calm his normally reserved friend, not understanding why he was acting so out of character. Seconds later, that *boom-ba-boom* sound was heard coming from the north. Marching down the length of the truck column, twenty 140mm rockets screamed down on the stalled convoy. The men scattered, looking for any hole or depression in which to dive. Luckily, there was a drainage ditch running along the eastern edge of the road, and many men found shelter there. When it was all over, one man was dead and twenty-eight Marines and corpsmen were wounded.[10]

The battalion CP group, plus H & S, Kilo, and India Companies, had moved one mile south of the churchyard that morning to an unnumbered hill at YD113659, about twenty-five hundred meters northwest of C-2. Mike Company had to remain at the churchyard to provide security for a downed helicopter that had crashed into a tree while lifting off with medevacs that morning. Captain Camp's Lima Company, bloodied but wiser, made the march from the drop-off point to the new CP in a widely dispersed formation.

Lieutenant Drnek dropped off his damaged tank at C-2. His tank crewmen badly needed to take time to replace their expended ammunition, but he was under orders to make the trip to C-2 quickly and get right back. There was no time to reload. His tanks rejoined the battalion within an hour.

All was quiet later that night except for intermittent H & I friendly fire believed to be from Camp Carroll. One round, an airburst, detonated right over India's lines, killing a man lying next to First Lieutenant Stimson. He was the only casualty. Camp Carroll denied responsibility, but after a lot of cursing and threatening over the artillery radio communication net, the mystery shelling stopped.

On September 9, the battalion CP was moved another klick south to Hill 48. Patrols were run to the south and southwest that day without incident. India Company was introduced to its new CO, Captain Matthew P. Caulfield, and Lieutenant Stimson reverted to XO. Captain Wildprett was replaced as battalion S-3 by Major Mundy, who in turn had been replaced as battalion XO by Major Joseph M. Loughran Jr.

Attack at Nui Ho Khe

The battalion was moving deeper and deeper into dangerous territory, unaware of the history and reputation of that area labeled "Nui Ho Khe" on their maps. Earlier that spring, two fierce battles involving 3/9 were fought at Hill 70—in March and May—only a klick or so west of Hill 48. Just beyond Hill 70 was Hill 94, scene of a large firefight on June 1, again involving 3/9. BLT 2/3 had also fought several times in that area during Operation Buffalo in July. Two months later, the 3d Battalion, 26th Marines was sweeping blindly toward the 812th NVA Regiment's headquarters.

The battalion objective for September 10 was an elongated hill labeled Nui Ho Khe, which was one thousand meters southwest of Hill 48. That ridge formed the southern rim of a V-shaped valley eight hundred meters long and bordered on both sides, east and west, by low ridges covered with thick brush and shrubs. A narrow streambed ran through the valley floor, which had once held a dozen acres of rice paddies but which had lain fallow for years and was now overgrown with weeds and bushes. Hill 48 was situated at the northern apex of the valley.

Captain Camp's Lima Company moved out at seven thirty in the morning to lead the battalion march, and they followed the ridgeline along the east side of the valley. The going was tough as they negotiated the thick brush. It took all morning to travel eight hundred meters to reach their first objective. Baking under the noon sun, Lima halted and awaited further orders.

Captain Camp sent out a squad-sized water detail from 2d Platoon to an apparent stream several hundred meters west that ran through the valley floor. An hour later they returned with full canteens. The platoon sergeant who had led the water detail, Sergeant Peck, approached Captain Camp and said, "Skipper, I smell gooks in that rice paddy." Captain Camp looked out there, saw nothing out of the ordinary, and dismissed it, jokingly accusing the sergeant of having something stronger than water in his canteens.[11]

Once the battalion's resupply had been completed, Captain Caulfield's India Company finally commenced moving from the CP. India traveled in the same direction as Lima, but west of them and closer to the valley floor where the underbrush was not as thick. Mike Company moved out next, followed by Second Lieutenant Drnek's three tanks carrying food and ammunition resupply for Lima. Kilo and the battalion CP group with the two Ontos were the rear guard.

By three in the afternoon, India Company, with 2d Lt. William V. Cowan III's 3d Platoon in the lead, had reached the battalion objective of Nui Ho Khe and was moving further west across the ridge toward another hill when a sudden barrage of small-arms fire from that hill enveloped the platoon lead elements. Two men went down wounded, one shot in the stomach. Lieutenant Cowan, a Naval Academy graduate, engaged the enemy force that he first estimated as a squad.

Captain Caulfield had started to maneuver a platoon around to come up on the enemy flank but thought better of it when the volume of enemy fire began to accelerate. Then mortars and RPGs started to impact around him. He prudently decided to wait for Lima and Mike to join him and proceeded to set India in around the crest of the hill. There were numerous fighting holes already there, dug months earlier by another Marine unit. His two platoons on the hill laid down a base of fire so that 3d Platoon could disengage and pull back to join the rest of the company.

Captain Camp requested of Major Mundy that he release the tanks to come up and support India. The two gun tanks and the flame tank had made it halfway to Lima's position when B-22, with Second Lieutenant Drnek aboard, broke a track. The platoon maintenance man, Sgt. Charles Witkamp, informed Drnek he had a serious problem that would take some time to repair. Drnek sent his other two tanks on ahead to support Lima's hookup with India. His disabled tank remained with Mike Company.

A flight of F-4B Phantoms arrived on station and began strafing runs on the enemy position. The NVA had several .51-caliber machine guns in place on the western ridgeline, concentrating their fire on the jets. In all the confusion, a UH-34 helicopter managed to land in a little LZ located by Lieutenant Stimson, and the two wounded India men were lifted out.

As Lima was preparing to move out toward India, a jet suddenly streaked in from the wrong direction and released a half-dozen bombs on the hill behind them, almost atop 2d Platoon. When the smoke cleared, by some miracle none of the grunts had been killed. While Lima was moving out toward India a few hundred meters away, a barrage of 140mm rockets came crashing down on the ridge Lima had just vacated. Only one man from the rear guard element was hit—another miracle.

Lieutenant John "Little John" Prince, a former University of Arizona football lineman from Phoenix, led Lima-2 along the crest of the ridge, tying in with the right flank of India. The two companies were situated along an east-west axis, separated by a rocky outcropping, looking down at the huge paddy area to their north.

Prince observed a dozen men in green uniforms, wearing flak jackets and helmets and double-timing across the paddy to his front only thirty meters away. He first believed they were Marines and then thought, "What in the hell are Marines doing out there?" When he noticed they had on clean clothes, he knew they could not be Marines. Prince shot four of them with his M-16 before it jammed. He called for an M-60 machine-gun team, but both of the gunners went down, blasted by a grenade. Then, either a grenade or mortar round landed next to Prince. A piece of shrapnel struck him by one ear, causing a lot of bleeding, and the side of his head went numb, but he shrugged it off. He was too busy taking care of his platoon.[12]

About 5:00 p.m., the astonished Marines could not believe their eyes. "The rice paddy stood up," recalled Sergeant Albert Peck, Lieutenant Prince's platoon sergeant who had smelled the NVA earlier on the water run.[13] A young corporal with India Company jumped up and screamed, "God, the whole mountain is coming!" A full battalion of NVA, hundreds of them, rose in unison from their hiding places in the paddy and charged directly at the two companies of Marines on the ridge. They were coming in waves right at them. Every Marine with a weapon opened up. It reminded Captain Caulfield of the bears in a shooting gallery. "The only problem was that as soon as we shot one, two more seemed to take his place," Caulfield said later.[14]

Lance Cpl. Chuck Bennet from India-1 could see them "kind of jogging, firing from the hip, and yelling at the same time. Some hit the deck and fired from the prone position, while others kept coming at us. I thought they were stoned."[15]

Another force of NVA was attacking India's left flank, coming through the draw where Lieutenant Cowan's 3d Platoon had first encountered the NVA. The FAC, 1st Lt. Ron Zappardino, was with Captain Caulfield at India's CP. He had constant air support overhead. When Second Lieutenant Cowan spotted an FO position (the NVA soldier was wearing binoculars) in a bamboo thicket two hundred meters from his position, he radioed the information back, and within a minute an F-4 roared over and dropped napalm right on target; it was so close that Cowan could feel the heat.

Captain Caulfield saw some of his 2d Platoon pulling back past his CP. He feared the northern perimeter had collapsed. He and his XO, First Lieutenant Stimson, jumped out of their holes to halt the pullback before it became a stampede. It took some cajoling and even some ass kicking, but the Captain and Lieutenant Stimson got them turned around, facing in the right direction. Lieutenant Zappardino recalled:

> Some of the young Marines broke. . . . Bob Stimson was on them right away, shaking the shit out of them, grabbing them, throwing them around. . . . Stimson got one kid by the shirt collar and almost shook his skin off his bones. Bob was a good leader, but very mild mannered. I couldn't believe how strongly he reacted. . . . Stimson straightened their heads right out. When he was done, he talked to me for a minute, very calmly.[16]

A little cheer went up from the lines when the two tanks arrived at Lima's position. They were going to save the day. The lead tank, B-25, was commanded by Gunnery Sergeant Tatum. He went partway up the hill and then turned back toward the paddy. He was right near Lima-2's lines. One round of 90mm HE exploded out of his main gun tube with a loud *KRAACK!* Captain Caulfield saw the tank machine guns open up, and twenty to forty NVA were mowed down.

Fifty meters behind the gun tank and lower on the hill was the flame tank, F-23, commanded by Cpl. Guy Wolfenbarger. His gunner, Lance Cpl. Wayne Chapman, was working the .30-caliber coaxial machine gun back and forth across the paddy. Wolfenbarger alternately fired his tank commander's .50-caliber and an M-79 grenade launcher at the charging figures in the rice paddy.

India Company's gunny ran over to Captain Caulfield and yelled, "Captain, get away from that tank."[17] Seconds later, a tremendous explosion occurred. Smoke and flames shot out of B-25's turret. First one man, and then a second, dropped to the ground on fire. Nearby grunts grabbed the two tankers and rolled them on the ground, attempting to extinguish the flames. Others risked their lives to climb atop the flaming tank to retrieve and throw down cases of ammunition stacked on the tank. The driver, Lance Cpl. Louis Ryle, put the tank in reverse and calmly backed the burning tank down the hill so that no grunts would be injured by exploding ammunition. Gunny Tatum and his loader, Cpl. Gary "Whitey" Young, had been critically burned when an RPG penetrated the turret and detonated a white phosphorus round in the ammunition ready rack. PFC James Wilson, the gunner, was killed instantly.

Corporal Wolfenbarger's flame-tank machine gun was firing so fast and furiously that the barrel turned cherry red. Wolfenbarger told his gunner, "Light the tube." He was getting ready to torch the paddy to his front when B-25, smoke boiling up out of the turret hatches, rolled backward and came to a stop near the flame tank. Wolfenbarger related what happened next:

> Things were getting worse. I saw NVA running between B-25 and me. As my gun tube was being elevated to the max, I saw what appeared to be two glowing footballs coming at me in slow motion. The whole tank rocked. Two RPGs had hit the tank, one of them setting the secondary fuel line on fire. Before the fire had a chance to spread, we all bailed out. As I jumped off the back of the tank, I still had my com-helmet on and the cord yanked me back. I unhooked it, and Ryle, the driver on B-25, ran up the hill with me to a bomb crater holding five or six other Marines. The only weapon I had was a .45 pistol with one clip.[18]

Just as Corporal Wolfenbarger and his crew made it to the crater, F-23 exploded. All 450 gallons of napalm and gasoline roared up in a fiery conflagration. Ryle, Wolfenbarger, and the other two flame-tank crewmen huddled in stunned resignation as their two tanks burned while the fighting raged around them. It had also been a demoralizing blow to the grunts, losing their armor support.

But in times of great need, ordinary men step forward and perform incredible feats of bravery. One of those brave men was Sergeant David Brown, platoon sergeant from Lima, 3d Platoon. He was a short-timer, due to fly out for home that very day. He led his men fearlessly, barking orders here and directing fire there. Captain Camp watched him stand upright at one point, take his M-16 in the offhand position, and calmly pick off a half-dozen NVA making their way up the reverse slope along a trail toward Lima's CP. He then grabbed an M-79 from a grenadier frozen with fright and squeezed off a round, striking an NVA soldier squarely in the chest. Then, holding M-26 frag grenades in each hand, the spoons pulled, he leapt out of his foxhole and charged down the hill, unleashing them at the last second at the NVA coming up through the thick brush. He did it a second time, and again and again, followed all the way down each time by his company gunny, Staff Sgt. Marvin Bailey, firing his .45-caliber pistol and shouting, "Goddammit, Brown, don't do that!"—*bang-bang*—"Get back, Brown!"—*bang-bang-bang*— "Jesus Christ, Brown, cut that out!" Captain Camp even yelled at Sergeant Brown to get down. Then he heard the terrible sound of a bullet striking a man in the head. Sergeant Brown finally went down—dead. Captain Camp, who truly believed he would not have survived that day without Sergeant Brown's gutsy heroics, put him in for the Medal of Honor; however, "men who were far from that nameless little hill and who did not see what I saw awarded David Brown's spirit a Navy Cross."[19]

Another of the bravest of the brave was Cpl. James J. Barrett, a squad leader with India Company. His Navy Cross citation reads in part:

> In the initial attack, numerous casualties were taken and the company was forced to withdraw to a more advantageous position. Undaunted, Corporal Barrett courageously maintained his squad's position and directed accurate counter fire against the hordes of

assaulting enemy. . . . He rallied his men, reorganized the platoon and led them in an effective counterattack against the enemy. . . . During the six hour ordeal, he repositioned his men five times to thwart the enemy advance and inflicted numerous casualties on the enemy force.[20]

Sergeant Marshall Jesperson, a squad leader in 3d Platoon, Lima Company, was in the middle of a grenade fight with some NVA in a thicket outside their position. He told his troops that the next time some NVA got close enough to throw grenades, they were going in there and clean them out. Some more NVA came up the trail and reoccupied the thicket. As promised, when the Chicoms started flying, Jesperson led his squad into the thicket.

Captain Camp heard the fighting. "It was horrible. Ghastly. There are no rules in a fight in which you could end up dead. Jesperson and his men did it any way they could—bullets, knives, bayonets, rifle butts, whatever. . . . The squeals of agony were almost too much to bear."[21] Soon after they cleaned out that thicket, another group of NVA foolishly challenged Sergeant Jesperson's squad of Marines. They met the same fate as the others.

With their ammunition running low, casualties growing worse by the minute, and nearly everyone out of water, it was looking bad for India and Kilo Companies. They were being attacked from all sides. But another unbelievable sight then befell the Marines on the ridge. The entire mass of NVA in the paddies made an oblique left turn and headed in the direction of Mike Company and the 3/26 CP. To Captain Caulfield, that was a pivotal mistake. "It was too good to be true—the enemy was offering me his flank."[22]

Battle at Hill 48
Capt. Andy DeBona's Mike Company had moved three hundred meters out from the battalion perimeter near Second Lieutenant Drnek's disabled tank when rockets started hitting Hill 48. It was about this time that India and Lima first came under fire. Major Carl Mundy, 3/26 XO, then saw "coming across from the high ground to the west of us . . . was

an almost perfect formation of NVA. It looked somewhat like what Andrew Jackson might have encountered in New Orleans as the British came toward him."[23]

When the NVA battalion had made its oblique left turn and headed for the 3/26 CP, their path of attack brought them right past the guns of Company M. Captain DeBona had his company in an inverted "V" formation, with the right arm of the V just outside the paddies and parallel to the NVA axis of attack. Two of his platoons, M-1 and M-2, had open fields of fire into the enemy flank. Third Platoon, the other side of the V, was behind and above them on the ridge. The Marines hesitated for a moment because a dozen NVA in the lead wave wore USMC helmets and flak jackets, but they were not fooled. Both platoons opened fire at the same time, shooting down many of the charging enemy, but not enough to halt the determined NVA, who were still advancing across the flat paddies by fire and maneuver toward the Hill 48 CP.

Lieutenant Drnek and his disabled B-22 tank crew opened up with their .30-caliber machine gun. He had no HE rounds left. His decision not to reload at C-2 after the churchyard battle had come back to haunt him. He decided to fire his "Willy Peter" rounds out in the paddies. The two WP rounds he fired exploded with clouds of white smoke that inadvertently provided the NVA with a smoke screen. Then his .50-caliber cupola-mounted machine gun jammed. Thoroughly frustrated, he dropped the .50 to the steel turret deck and stuck an M-14 rifle out of the machine gun's firing port, shooting off several magazines at the enemy running past his tank.

Mortars and artillery fire rained down on Mike Company. Casualties began to mount. The 2d Platoon, led by 2d Lt. Robert Gall, was at the apex of the V formation. The main NVA charge slammed into Gall's platoon first and then bounced into 2d Lt. Chad Crangle's 2d Platoon on his right. But the two platoons were not properly tied in and got separated. Fighting was at close quarters and vicious. The company gunny, Gunnery Sgt. Gleason Norris, a Native American from Sells, Arizona, was hit numerous times by shrapnel as he moved up and down the line directing fire, repositioning his men, and shouting encouragement. After his third wound, he was brought to a medevac zone. There he took charge of the walking wounded and integrated them back into the perimeter.[24] Mike Company had repelled the initial charge, but at a price. Lieutenant Gall and his platoon sergeant, Staff Sgt. Edward Gaytan, were KIA. Dozens more lay wounded. But the NVA were after the CP and continued to attack in that direction.

Several F-4 Phantom jets streaked low across the valley, unloading their bombs and napalm. The NVA had positioned five .51-caliber machine guns on the western ridge, firing at the jets during their bomb runs. Some of the Phantoms flew in so low that the NVA gunners were actually firing down at them. The antiaircraft fire was so heavy that it almost seemed that the pilots flew into a solid curtain of green tracers at times. One jet was hit and started to disintegrate, but the pilot somehow managed to steer his smoking craft away from the battlefield before he ejected.

Major Mundy sent for the two Ontos back at the battalion CP. They chugged forward into the lines with Kilo Company. One Ontos opened fire with its .30-caliber machine gun, "mowing those rows of NVA down like they were corn, like he was chopping corn," recalled the India Company gunny, Staff Sgt. Charles Owens.[25]

Just as he fired a salvo of 106mm rounds into the massed enemy, a close-in RPG team unleashed an RPG round that struck beside the driver and ricocheted into the Ontos commander, Sgt. Leroy Davis Jr., killing him instantly. The second Ontos, commanded by Lance Cpl. Randall Browning from Alpha Company, 3d Antitank Battalion, moved forward without hesitation, realizing they were the only tracked vehicle left running. Despite being wounded earlier by artillery shrapnel, he maneuvered his vehicle through intense hostile fire to a firing position. He would fire, duck behind a hill and reload, and then pull forward and fire again. His flechette and HE rounds scored numerous casualties. Browning's Navy Cross citation reads in part:

> [Browning] began delivering highly effective machine-gun and recoilless rifle fire against the enemy. Successfully repulsing the first of several human wave assaults, he remained undaunted by the vicious enemy fire and steadfastly continued to deliver a heavy volume of fire during ensuing fanatical enemy attacks. . . . When his recoilless rifle ammunition was expended and his machine gun

became inoperable, Corporal Browning unhesitatingly manned a sub-machine gun and continued to deliver devastating fire on the enemy.[26]

Captain DeBona requested permission to pull Mike Company back to the battalion CP. He had no fighting holes where he was, and NVA mortars were creating havoc among his men. He knew there were fighting holes where his company had been the previous night.

Most of his company withdrew in good order, taking their dead and wounded with them. Captain DeBona and his radio operator, Corporal Schneider, brought up the rear. He wanted to ensure that none of his company got left behind. The men in one squad from his 2d Platoon had to fight their way through the NVA to their new company perimeter while carrying a dead comrade with them, but they finally made it back to friendly lines with less than an hour of daylight left.

The tank crew soon realized that Mike Company had pulled out without a word, leaving them unguarded. Lieutenant Drnek had no choice. He knew the NVA were out there still attacking. He and his crewmen disabled B-22 by dropping the breech and removing all the machine gun firing pins; then, they bailed out and sprinted toward the nearest Marine unit they could see, shouting, "Don't shoot! Marines! We're Marines! Don't shoot!"[27] The tankers all scrambled safely back to Mike's perimeter.

Captain DeBona found the battalion CP in a state of confusion. An unwieldy number of wounded lay in bomb craters and holes. Mike Company had only one corpsman left uninjured. Intermittent artillery fire and small-arms fire were hitting all around Hill 48. Getting Kilo and Mike sorted out amid the thick brush and in position to hold off the enemy was top priority.

Captain DeBona learned that a large number of wounded were in a bomb crater about fifty meters to the west of Hill 48. They were pinned down, fighting for their lives. A group of NVA twenty-five meters farther from them in another crater was tossing grenades at the pinned-down Marines, but neither side could quite reach the other. DeBona and his radioman, Corporal Schneider, accompanied by Lance Corporal

Burke, who was carrying a case of grenades, sprinted through the brush and trees to the huge bomb crater. Fifteen men were crouched down in there, and half of them were wounded. A dozen inoperable M-16s and a broken M-60 machine gun lay at the bottom of the crater.

The Marines in the crater gradually got fire superiority, and DeBona devised a plan. Because all of the wounded except two could walk, the others would lay down a base of fire to cover the walking wounded while they made a break for the battalion perimeter. Then, everyone remaining would run back carrying the two serious casualties while DeBona covered them. The grunts looked uncertain. Then DeBona had a burst of inspiration. He gave the order as if they were on the rifle range firing line: "All ready on the right? All ready on the left? All ready on the firing line. Watch your targets. Targets!"[28] His plan worked like a charm. Everyone made it back to the perimeter. Captain Andrew DeBona would receive a Navy Cross for his heroic leadership under fire.

The word had traveled up through all levels of Marine command that 3/26 was engaged in a major battle with at least two battalions and possibly an entire regiment. The garrisons at Con Thien and C-2 had changed hands that day and were in the process of moving into their new homes. Despite any confusion and uncertainty inherent in taking over responsibility for a major strongpoint, 3/9 had a reaction company (reinforced) on standby at Con Thien, and 3/4 had a reaction company standing by at C-2. In the event 3/26 was not able to get the upper hand in their battle with the 812th NVA Regiment, they were ready.

By seven o'clock that evening, the NVA attack on the battalion CP had lost momentum. Incoming was sporadic, and only occasional sniper rounds were zinging by. The Marines began to take stock of how they were situated and how many able-bodied men were left.

The 81mm mortars on the reverse slope of Hill 48 had been hit especially hard by incoming rockets and mortar fire. Many of the mortarmen were dead and wounded, including Gunner Holycross, who had distinguished himself on September 7. He was killed by a direct hit while carrying out a fire mission.

A helicopter LZ was set up on the reverse slope, and a number of UH-34s were able to land, kick out supplies, and load casualties aboard.

Glowing green tracers from the NVA .51-caliber machine guns chased after them as they lifted off. After dark, "Puff" arrived on station, working over the ridgeline where those heavy machine guns were emplaced.

The Longest Night

The situation for Lima and India was still tenuous. Both companies had numerous casualties, with some critical. India had five emergency medevacs, and Lima had four. Helicopters were needed immediately, but the heavy antiaircraft fire from the ridgeline presented too much of a threat. The last thing the FAC, Lieutenant Zappardino, wanted was a flaming helicopter full of aviation fuel and ammunition to get shot down and crash on their heads, not to mention the lives of the helicopter crew that would be sacrificed.

The men were down to ten rounds each. Captain Camp convinced Zappardino to ask for a pilot who would volunteer to make an emergency ammo run. One pilot risked it and came in fast and low over the LZ, taking numerous hits while the crew chief kicked out several cases of ammo. All five NVA .51-caliber machine guns opened up on that chopper. There was no time to load any casualties. Somehow, the pilot got his craft out of the LZ without crashing. To the dismay of the grunts, most of the ammo was linked .50-caliber, which they could not use because they did not carry .50-caliber machine guns in the field.

A corpsman told Captain Caulfield that two of the emergency cases would die if he did not get them out in an hour and that the other three would probably die before morning. Everyone had seen what had happened to the last helicopter. The decision was made—no medevac. The captain knew it was the right decision, "but when the corpsman came during the night to tell me that one of the men had died, I learned what responsibility was all about."[29]

Captain Caulfield was able to get another resupply around midnight. Besides ammo, water was critical. He saw to it that most of the water went to the corpsmen for the wounded. But the SNAFU bug struck again. Most of the ammo crates were for 81mm mortars. All the 81s were located back at the battalion CP on Hill 48.

The two critically burned tankers, Gunnery Sergeant Tatum and

Cpl. Gary Young, lay on a poncho in agony all night. No one could do anything for them. A medevac was too risky. Lieutenant Bill Cowan recalled: "It was frustrating to know all night that I had a man there who was not complaining, who was hurting bad, who was conscious the whole time, who was willing to be quiet and lie there patiently while we tried to sort out the problem."[30]

Several grunts were getting nervous about the gun tank, B-25, parked in front of Lima's lines. Flames were still visible, occasionally licking up from inside the turret, causing the .50-caliber to cook off a round every now and then. Someone even reported NVA climbing around on the tank. Captain Caulfield agreed to send a rocket man (someone who carried a 3.5-inch rocket launcher as his weapon) down with his last remaining LAAW and attempt to blow up the tank. That seemed to make sense at the time to the starving, dehydrated, battle-fatigued infantrymen.

The grunt went out in front of the lines to get a better shot. His LAAW ricocheted off the turret, doing no damage. On his way back in through the lines, he drifted off course, and a jumpy A-gunner on a Lima machine-gun team shot him in the chest with his .45. Luckily, the rocket man had his flak jacket buttoned up, and the bullet ricocheted off, breaking only his collarbone. Grunts on the lines heard him cursing and yelling a blue streak at the man who shot him.

Enemy activity became less noticeable with each passing hour. Both groups, Lima-India and Hill 48, had been boxed in by artillery and illumination rounds. At 1:30 a.m., a feeble ground probe in Kilo's area was beaten back with no Marine casualties. One NVA was killed. As the night wore on, it became more and more obvious that the attack was over. There would not be another round of assaults to fight off. By early morning, men on the front lines reported hearing the NVA using meat hooks to impale and drag off their dead.

Aftermath

Just before daybreak, Captain Camp had his company fire a ten-second "mad moment" in the event any bad guys were roaming around outside his perimeter. A scene from a horror movie awaited the Marines. The dead and pieces of the dead lay everywhere. Men went out to check all of the Marine bodies to see who they were, and they were also hoping that some were still alive. Captain Camp recalled that "the smell of blood tinged with singed tissue and hair was almost overpowering."[31] Helicopters began arriving to carry out the wounded, some of whom had waited sixteen hours for a medevac to arrive.

Captain DeBona went out to the bomb crater where he had previously retrieved the pinned-down Marines. Then he approached the NVA bomb crater. He found three lines of enemy dead lying in the crater, stitched together with a meat hook. All their weapons were gone. Apparently, the weapons had a higher priority than their dead. He counted thirty-nine bodies lying in the crater.

Marines checking out the battlefield, which was strewn with dead NVA, were surprised that all of the NVA had clean clothes, new boots, and fresh haircuts and were clean shaven. They looked much better than the bedraggled, dirty, unshaven Marines who had defeated them.

While Mike Company's 2d Lt. Chan Crangle and some men were checking around the area where the NVA charge on September 10 had plowed into his platoon, an NVA FO ran from cover, *banzai* style, firing his pistol wildly. He was quickly shot down. The dead FO turned out to be an intelligence bonanza. His map showed Hill 88, which was the location the POW gave on September 8 as the site of his regimental headquarters. On the American maps, that location was YD946642, only a klick west of Nui Ho Khe. Air strikes and artillery were called in on the area. The FO's map was also helpful in plotting counter-battery fire.

Lieutenant Drnek went back to his abandoned tank that morning and was surprised that it had been left alone during the night by the NVA. His crew got the track fixed and started up the engine. Of the four tanks that he had started out with on September 7, his B-22 was the only one still operable. At midmorning, a tank recovery crew and several LVT amtracs showed up. Lieutenant Drnek and the recovery team leader determined that B-25 seemed capable of moving under its own power, even though the turret was burned out. They decided to tow the still-smoldering flame tank to the rear with the tank retriever.

The amtracs were loaded up with equipment and more wounded, and then they left. It was not a moment too soon. An NVA FO had them in his sights, and artillery began to crash down again. The tank retriever by Lima/India seemed to be drawing fire like a magnet.

A wiser course of action was decided. The flame tank was a burned-out hulk, and attempting to retrieve it was not worth the risk. It was left behind, and the retriever made a rapid withdrawal back to C-2. Air strikes were called in to bomb the flame-tank hull. Lance Corporal Ryle and Corporal Wolfenbarger were able to get B-25 started, despite the charred turret, and drive it to C-2. But Ryle did not stop there. He drove it all the way to Camp Carroll, barreling through every Marine guard post and security gate along the MSR and Route 9 without stopping until he reached his tank company headquarters area.

The 3d Battalion, 26th Marines hiked back in the late-morning heat to C-2, totally drained, dehydrated, and numb with battle fatigue. No one had to remind them to keep their distance from each other. A horde of news media folks awaited them at C-2, sticking microphones and cameras in their faces. Major TV network and newspaper reporters from all over the country were there. "How was it?" "What was it like out there?" were among the questions. And then there were the inevitable enraged Marines grabbing film out of the cameras of insensitive photographers taking pictures of the dead.

India and Mike Companies immediately mounted trucks and were convoyed back to Dong Ha. Kilo and Lima remained behind to man the perimeter until 2d Battalion, 4th Marines could relieve them.

The next day, September 12, the convoy carrying 2/4 arrived at C-2. The trucks stopped at the top of the knoll, lined up bumper to bumper. Lima's artillery-wise grunts could not believe that the convoy commander could be so oblivious. What a lucrative target he was offering the NVA FOs! They yelled at the truckers to spread out, but it was too late. *Boom-ba-booom* sounds echoed from the north. Lima and India went for holes and trenches like prairie dogs ducking a cattle stampede. As Lima Company had done only four days earlier, many 2/4 grunts stood around confused until the screeching rockets hit, and then they paid the price for their new-guy unawareness, becoming unnecessary casualties.

The September 10 battle had cost the 3d Battalion, 26th Marines 34 Marines and corpsmen killed and 192 wounded. From September 7 through September 10, the battalion, plus attached tanks and Ontos crewmen, had total losses of 56 killed and 290 wounded. That was more than 40 percent of that battalion's strength. Granted, many of the wounded were treated and returned to duty, but in other wars a battalion was considered decimated if losses of 10 percent were incurred.

A photo reconnaissance flight during the night of September 10 brought back pictures showing more than three hundred NVA bodies lying on the battlefield. The official count 3/26 sent up channels was 144 NVA KIA. Major Mundy insisted on reporting only what his men actually counted.

Many of the officers and men from 3/26 grew angry later when they started asking, "Why were we out there, uninformed that we were facing a regiment, with no prep fires and no reinforcements with us?" Major Carl Mundy, who would ultimately become the thirtieth commandant of the Marine Corps, commented:

> The NVA very apparently had every piece of ground in that operating area targeted with rockets, mortars, and artillery. The result was that, even when we moved to another hill, they could target us. They could pick any target they wanted to, lay in on it, and inflict significant casualties. . . . My belief is that the NVA . . . took advantage of the move of 3/26 in daylight on September 10 to attack us as we were strung out. That conclusion is not glamorous, but it was clearly we who received the incoming prep fires followed by an on-line infantry assault. . . . We were successful in blunting that attack and giving no ground. . . . But the notion that there was well-thought-out strategy or tactical brilliance in the design of the action is not something I can support.[32]

Despite the fact that 3/26 had proceeded more or less blindly into a regimental-sized trap set by the 812th NVA Regiment at Nui Ho Khe, they had acquitted themselves well. Many of the men were new arrivals after the September 7 encounter at the churchyard, and it was their first taste of combat.

A heavy toll was taken of the battalion's senior NCOs and officers, including the three-striper platoon sergeants. Nearly 25 percent of the battalion's dead came from that leadership pool. Coupled with the large number of short-timers who were due to rotate stateside in a few weeks or a month, 3/26 had some major rebuilding to complete before they would again be back to strength, not just in numbers but in veterans who could lead the way. The battle for Khe Sanh would be their next major test.

It is not known whether the lessons learned from this battle were disseminated up through higher levels of command. One major problem encountered by that battalion, as well as by others in similar circumstances, was the "Sav-a-Plane" rule. Under this rule, when the AO was in the area bringing in close air support, an artillery check-fire went into effect, prohibiting Marine forward observers from calling in fire missions. A lot of bad things could happen to a pinned-down infantry unit in the fifteen to thirty minutes it took for the air support to arrive.

With so many batteries of 105s, 155s, and 175s located at Con Thien, C-2, Cam Lo, Dong Ha, and Camp Carroll, a veritable firestorm of VT-fuzed air bursts should have been delivered over every square yard of those paddy fields once the NVA charge commenced. But, for reasons known only to the participants who were there and their higher-ups at regiment and division, that crucial artillery and mortar support did not come until later in the battle.

The suicidal tactics employed by the NVA in this battle have raised questions that will probably never be answered. U.S. intelligence analysts reported that, as part of Phase I, General Giap had planned to cut the MSR from Cam Lo, isolate the Marine garrison at Con Thien, and then launch an attack to overrun the base. Did 3/26 trigger a premature response from the 812th NVA Regiment while it was forming up for a major assault on the MSR and Con Thien? It seems that 3/26 did just that, and they blunted what was surely a major ground attack planned for Con Thien.

To the men of 3/26 who survived the battle, it may have seemed to serve little purpose. But there is no doubt, as future developments would prove, that the garrison at Con Thien owed a debt of gratitude to the 3d Battalion, 26th Marines for their tenacity and fighting spirit.

PART SIX

THE SIEGE

Dear Doug,

. . . The monsoon has been late up to now, but this day it rained in torrents. The jungle and the rice paddy we'd been wading around in wasn't affected much, but waist-deep streams we had waded [through] coming out were now impossible swamps 300 yards wide. . . . We were cut off from our base and requested a helicopter evacuation with priority for 30 cases of immersion foot, many of which had begun to bleed because of the constant water. We were all in sad shape now. I know that at one point, my feet about to crack open, my stomach knotted by hunger and diarrhea, my back feeling like a mirror made of nerves shattered in a million pieces by my flak jacket, pack, and extra mortars and machine-gun ammo, my hands a mass of hamburger from thorn cuts, and my face a mass of welts from mosquitoes, I desired greatly to throw down everything, slump into the water of the paddy, and sob. I remember a captain, an aviator, who, observing a group of grunts toasting the infantry in a bar, said, "you damned infantry think you're the only people who exist." You're damned right we do.

Love,
David

—Excerpt from a letter by 1st Lt. Victor David Westphall III

12

3/9's Turn in the Barrel

The 3d Battalion, 9th Marines, commanded by Major Gorton C. Cook, replaced Lieutenant Colonel Bendell's 3d Battalion, 4th Marines on September 10 and assumed full responsibility for Con Thien and the immediate vicinity. By September 11, the transition was complete. All of 3/4 had moved out of Con Thien and relocated to Charlie-2. Bendell's battalion also had responsibility for the Cam Lo artillery position (C-3) and Cam Lo Bridge.

The "Thundering Third" was not exactly reluctant to pull up stakes and leave Con Thien. NVA shelling attacks had grown increasingly deadly since the end of August. Ambushes, snipers, and antipersonnel mines had worn down Bendell's Marines. By the time 3/4 relinquished the reins to 3/9 on September 10, a full-scale siege was gathering momentum.

Lt. Col. John J. Peeler's 2d Battalion, 9th Marines had been operating in the Leatherneck Square area throughout most of August. In early September, his battalion minus Company F (OPCON 12th Marines at Gio Linh) was pulled in closer to protect Con Thien's eastern flank. The 2d Battalion, 4th Marines, commanded by Lt. Col. James W. Hammond Jr., was due to arrive in the Con Thien area a few days later. Thus, a full regiment of Marines plus supporting arms would be in place to meet whatever plans General Giap had in store for Con Thien. The 3d Battalion, 4th Marines at Charlie-2 constituted a battalion reserve that could also be deployed if needed.

Three regiments of the NVA 324B Division—812th, 803d, and

90th—were arrayed to the southwest, north, and northeast against Con Thien. Additional NVA divisions were garrisoned within and above the DMZ. The total number of enemy soldiers within a day's march of Con Thien was conservatively estimated at twenty thousand.

Facing General Giap's forces were a thousand-plus Marines dug into an area the size of two large city blocks. But 3/9 was by no means alone. In direct support and physically located on The Hill was a five-tank platoon from Alpha Company, 3d Tank Battalion; a platoon of 106mm-armed Ontos; a section of three U.S. Army truck-mounted quad-fifties; a section of two U.S. Army twin-40mm Dusters; and a section of three LVT amtracs from 1st Amtrac Battalion. Direct fire support was also present on The Hill proper in the form of a 105mm howitzer battery from 2/12, a 4.2-inch mortar battery from 1/12, and 81mm mortars. The outpost also had four .50-caliber machine-gun strongpoints and a number of 106mm recoilless rifles. When other supporting elements such as shore party and combat engineers were added in, the outpost presented a formidable challenge.

Con Thien in September was a much better defended firebase than previously on May 8 when it was attacked by two NVA battalions. A partial minefield with barbed-wire obstacles had been installed, and many strong Dyemarker bunkers had been constructed. But the Marines knew that, if the NVA wanted to pay the price, and a horrific price it would be, Con Thien could be overrun. The mission of the Marines was to make the NVA fully aware of the exorbitant price to be paid for that little piece of red clay real estate.

THE PRESSURE MOUNTS

Life on The Hill was growing increasingly hazardous. Intermittently throughout the day on September 12, Con Thien was shelled by more than one hundred 60mm and 82mm mortars. A dozen Marines were hit by flying shrapnel, but none were killed. The first round in the salvo was the most deadly because by the time one heard it whooshing down, it was too late to duck for cover.

The morning mine sweep of the MSR from Con Thien to C-2 had met with tragedy. A mine planted beside the road was triggered by one of the infantry security team, killing him and wounding two others. One of the engineers was also a casualty. With the added threat of snipers and ten-foot-wide holes blown in the outer perimeter wire by bangalore torpedoes, every man on Con Thien was feeling the stress of knowing something bad was coming their way. The increased pressure was mirrored in their faces.

The Probe

As the sun dropped below the horizon to end another perilous day on Con Thien, each attached unit prepared to play its role as part of the outpost's night defensive scheme. The little Ontos scooted out from behind daylight berms to positions along the perimeter wire. An infrared searchlight was uncovered and made ready for use, as were the starlight scopes along the perimeter and inside the three forward observer positions located at the crests of each of the three highest knolls on Con Thien: OP#1, OP#2, and OP#3.

Each night, one of the tanks took a turn on the northern side of the perimeter aptly named "Dodge City." At least one, sometimes two, NVA recoilless rifle teams were hidden among the bamboo thickets and hedgerows somewhere outside the northern perimeter, and they loved to snipe at tanks or other lucrative targets that presented themselves. Somehow, they were able to hide the backblast dust and smoke from searching FO eyes.

A-12's driver, Lance Cpl. Bert Trevail, a former Canadian with mischievous blue eyes and red-orange mustache, settled his fifty-two-ton iron monster into its predug firing slot facing north. Each of the four crewmen stood a two-hour watch during the night, commencing at ten o'clock. Corporal Sanders was scheduled for first watch, but he was feeling drowsy. The tank platoon leader, Second Lieutenant Coan, agreed to swap shifts and stand first watch. That way he might get an uninterrupted four or five hours of precious sleep after his watch ended at midnight.

Unusual reports began arriving at the battalion CP shortly before midnight. Mike Company reported some harassing sniper fire and movement to their front on the northeast perimeter. About the same time, the FO on OP#2 observed lights moving south across the Trace three klicks east of Con Thien and blinking lights on the southern edge of the Trace. An artillery fire mission was called in, and a spectacular fireworks show of twenty secondary explosions resulted in brilliant orange and red bursts of fire shooting hundreds of feet into the air. A follow-up TPQ air strike in that same area ninety minutes later resulted in two more huge secondary explosions.

Then, all was eerily quiet for the next three hours. Those secondary explosions along the Trace had been unsettling. The predominant thought shared by those witnessing the blasts was, "What the hell was that out there?"

Sleeping soundly on the rear steel deck of his tank, a folded blanket for his bed, Second Lieutenant Coan was startled awake about three in the morning by the snapping and popping of glowing green tracers barely clearing the top of the tank turret. An NVA heavy machine gun northwest of Con Thien was spraying the slopes of Con Thien. "We're being attacked!" he thought. With his heart pounding in his throat, he crawled over the gypsy rack onto the top of the turret and jumped down through the tank commander's hatch. Mortars and artillery began exploding in the minefield and along the wire to his front with blinding flashes. It was impossible to tell whether it was an assault barrage by the enemy or final protective fires by Marine guns. He traversed the turret to the northwest where the heavy machine-gun fire originated, estimated the range at eight hundred meters, and gave his fire command: "Gunner, one round HE. . . . enemy machine gun . . . eight hundred . . . FIRE!

"Up!" shouted Corporal Sanders, the loader, as he flipped the safety switch off.

"On the way," said Corporal Johnson, gunner, followed a split-second later by *WHAMM!!* The tank recoiled sharply as the 90mm HE projectile blasted out into the blackness, its red phosphorous tracer element glowing brightly, streaking toward the target. An expended brass cartridge clanked loudly on the steel turret deck. Acrid cordite propellant fumes permeated the close turret atmosphere. Sanders slammed another round of HE into the breech and shouted, "Up!"

The first round exploded with a dazzling flash just beyond the target. "Depress the gun tube, Johnson, we're too high." A humming noise indicated the gun tube was being depressed electrically a few degrees. "Stand by . . . FIRE!" A second round streaked out into the night, right on target. No more green tracers came from that area.

Shadowy figures silhouetted by exploding mortars and flare light sprinted toward the outer perimeter wire. Coan's tank spewed .30-caliber bullets at the charging enemy. "Fire more HE at 'em!" Six more 90mm cannon rounds split the night air with their high-velocity KRACK!

A U.S. Army truck-mounted quad-fifty from 1/44 wheeled into action from behind a berm and opened fire, its four .50-caliber machine guns spitting a stream of glowing tracer rounds into the attacking enemy's flank. Red tracers from numerous M-60 machine guns along the perimeter crisscrossed the battlefield.

The attacking force veered to the northwest for some reason and unleashed a volley of RPGs into the Marine lines at the base of OP#1. But it was too little, too late. They never made it through the wire. By 3:45 a.m., no more shadowy figures were seen moving toward the lines.

At four o'clock, two red flares shot skyward from the trees outside of the northern perimeter wire. Cries of "Cease fire! Cease fire!" were heard up and down the line. Moments later the first shouts for "Corpsmen up!" rang out.

An FO in OP#2 reported to the battalion CP that enemy troops were assembling one thousand meters north of Con Thien and called artillery fire down on them. At four thirty, a group of NVA was observed withdrawing to the northwest toward the DMZ. Artillery and air strikes continued to dog the retreating enemy force.

At dawn, daylight revealed the devastation wrought earlier. Great gaps had been blown in the inner and outer perimeter wire, and numerous fresh craters pockmarked the minefield. But to everyone's amazement, not a single enemy body was lying in sight. Had their eyes played tricks on them during the attack? Many a Marine began to doubt his own perceptions of what he had just experienced. But that ferocious barrage of incoming was no illusion. It appeared the NVA had attempted to blast paths through the minefield with a concentrated shelling attack.

The CP estimated five hundred rounds of all types and calibers of incoming had impacted on Con Thien during the one-hour attack. Smashed bunkers and poncho-wrapped dead Marines lying on stretchers would attest to the devastating intensity of the NVA bombardment. The Marines suffered fourteen wounded and four dead in the attack. NVA casualties were obviously heavy, but none were officially recorded.

The Marines were puzzled. A reinforced NVA company had attacked the northern perimeter and apparently been beaten back easily by the superior firepower on the perimeter as well as by the awesome artillery fire support from Gio Linh, C-2, Cam Lo, and Camp Carroll. If two NVA battalions had not been able to take Con Thien the previous May, when it was not as heavily defended, certainly a company-sized attack was a suicide mission.

Was it merely a large probe intended to ascertain 3/9's defensive capability? To the Americans, such a waste of human lives to gather intelligence was unthinkable. Or had some unforeseen disaster such as a lucky American TPQ strike or TOT artillery bombardment disrupted the NVA plans by hitting their main attack force? A likely possibility was that a major attack was still waiting in the wings to be unleashed on Con Thien. Not if, but when, was on the minds of Marines at all levels of command.

Incoming!

After September 13, pressure on Con Thien intensified in a variety of ways. Mortars ranging from 60mm to 120mm dropped on Con Thien at all hours of the day and night. No longer was there any pattern to the incoming. If fortunate, one heard the rounds as they thumped out of the tube and had several seconds to dive for cover. But with other noises, such as our own artillery or 4.2-inch mortars firing, helicopters or jets overhead, and tracked vehicles and trucks going by, the first warning that mortars were falling—an explosion—came too late to find cover.

Mortars were the silent killers feared by everyone on The Hill. Preventing them was nearly impossible. A camouflaged mortar crew could sneak into position before dawn, wait until the time was right, drop several rounds down the tube rapid fire, and be gone with their tube and baseplate before the first rounds impacted. Thus, counter-mortar fire with our 81s and 4.2-inch mortars was, more often than not, only for morale purposes. Chances of actually hitting any of the NVA mortar crews deployed around Con Thien were slim, especially those with lighter-weight 60s. Good success was had, however, by the battalion's 106mm recoilless rifles, tanks, and Ontos. They had the advantage of scanning the horizon with their binoculars, waiting with an HE round in the breech, ready to fire as soon as they saw flashes or puffs of smoke off in the distance. Many secondary explosions resulted this way.

NVA artillery was another curse. The unrelenting daily shelling increased despite thousands of rounds of artillery counter-battery fire; thousands of tons of bombs dropped by A-4 Skyhawks, F-4B Phantoms, F-8 Crusaders, A-6 Intruders, and B-52s; and tons of ordnance fired from the Seventh Fleet's cruisers and destroyers.

Vietnamese artillerymen, with centuries of history behind them, were experts at camouflage and deception. A favorite tactic was to build phony gun positions and then set off small explosive charges to simulate muzzle flashes for Marine observers. Some of those fake batteries even had simulated SAM sites nearby. The real guns, mortars, and rocket launchers were hidden in deep pits and tunnels some distance away. At irregular intervals, the camouflage netting was pulled back, the weapon was fired, and then it was wheeled back into its cave or tunnel and covered over again.

Heavy mortars were placed at the bottom of a nearly vertical shaft dug into a hillside. The crew and ammunition were protected by tons of earth above them. When the mortars were fired, both the telltale smoke and firing report were difficult to detect.[1]

To be a mortarman or artilleryman on Con Thien was an exercise in raw courage. They commanded everyone's respect for their unfaltering bravery during mortar and artillery duels. Each gun in a battery was situated in a scooped-out depression and encircled by a sandbag-lined parapet to protect the gun crews from flying shrapnel. Nothing but their maker could help them if an enemy shell exploded within the parapet confines. This brutal fact did not prevent Marines from carrying out fire missions in the midst of enemy artillery and mortar attacks, completely ignoring the crashing shells impacting nearby.

When a counter-battery mission call came in, a gun crew sprinted out from the safety of their bunkers to their 105mm gun, even as NVA shells or rockets screamed down out of the sky, detonating with ear-splitting blasts as they ripped into the earth. One Marine sighted in the gun while another with earphones crouched alongside. A third man cradled a shell in his arms and stood by the breech, anxiously awaiting the signal to load. If a man was hit by incoming shrapnel and went down, another Marine would run to his fallen comrade's side, drag him out of harm's way, and then assume the wounded man's role on the gun crew. None flinched from their duty; they continued the fire mission without letup until the enemy guns were silenced.

Artillery forward observers had a particularly rough go at Con Thien. Their bunkers situated at the crests of the three hilltops were zeroed in on by the enemy. Periodically, an 82mm recoilless rifle would find the range and score a direct hit on the FO bunker, killing and wounding all the occupants. Engineers would rebuild the bunker, and another brave, resolute FO team would continue the mission.

Mike Company of 3/9 was led by Capt. Frank J. Breth. His company had responsibility for the northern perimeter including OP#1. Frank Breth remembered the night that the FO bunker on OP#1 took a direct hit by a recoilless rifle round: "The FO from F/2/12 was a young Marine named Harry Hutchinson. He worked really well with us. When his bunker took a direct hit by an 82mm recoilless rifle round, he was badly wounded, but he survived. He was fortunate. The same couldn't be said of the FO bunker on OP#2. They took direct hits four nights in a row."[2]

The unenviable task of repairing the perimeter-wire obstacles and re-placing mines in the minefield fell to the combat engineers. That somber, vacant stare, as if the body was there but the spirit was not, was common among the combat engineers at Con Thien. It was a peculiar look in the eyes of brave men who had faced death often, witnessed too much bleeding and dying, and resigned themselves to not making it out of Vietnam alive. Their job put them in constant danger, and the more one was exposed to danger, the lower the odds of survival.

All the engineers were aware that every morning when they awoke there was good chance of being mortared while working out in the minefield that day. They were totally exposed, and there was no place to hide should an enemy FO decide to take them under fire. Bouncing Betties were all interconnected with trip wires. Incoming meant lying still and praying. Running for safety was not an option for survival in a minefield.

The engineers had a crucial job to do, albeit a nasty one, and they performed that job admirably under the worst of conditions. Very few Marines on The Hill would have traded jobs with them, not even for one day.

The Washout

The Hill was on high alert. Intelligence reports coming in from the 9th Marines indicated a regiment-sized attack was looming. The 2d Battalion, 9th Marines(-), operating out in Leatherneck Square, was ordered to snug in closer to Con Thien. On September 15, the battalion moved to a position two thousand meters south of Con Thien, just off the MSR. Taking responsibility for Con Thien's eastern flank was the 2d Battalion, 4th Marines. Con Thien had a full regiment of Marines prepared to do battle if the enemy attack came as predicted.

It began to rain in the middle of the night. At first, a gentle shower filtered down through the leaves in a foglike mist. Then raindrops began to fall, harder and harder, until by dawn on September 16, rain was pouring down in buckets. The two tanks assigned to the road-sweep detail had a problem meeting up with the engineer-grunt sweep team that morning because they were not waiting at the usual spot by the road. Soaked to the bone, the grunts had taken refuge under some trees. After some heated words between the grunts and the tank section leader to get a move on, the mine-sweep detail departed some thirty minutes late.

Lieutenant Coan had taken over A-11 when the previous tank commander rotated home a few days earlier. Following behind Coan's tank south on the MSR was A-13, commanded by Sergeant Osborne, a pudgy southerner who was one of several new replacements to the tank platoon.

The miserable grunts slogged through liquid mud and rivulets of water beside the road as the rain pelted down even harder. The crushed-rock road supported the weight of the tanks easily. If anything happened to force the tanks off the road, however, they would probably get bogged down in the porous paddy country. As the mine-sweep detail rounded a bend in the road a mile from Rocky Ford, they came upon two columns of grunts from 2/9 moving south on either side of the road.

It was a most welcome sight for two reasons: an ambush was not likely with all that firepower, and the men in the mine-sweep detail realized for the first time that 3/9 was not alone on Con Thien.

By the time the mine-sweep team reached Rocky Ford, the rain had slowed to a light drizzle. Rocky Ford bore that name even though it was no longer necessary to ford the creek where it intersected with the MSR. Marine engineers had installed a culvert the previous summer that permitted the creek water to flow unimpeded beneath the graded road. Only a few days earlier, an engineer road-repair team had been called out to shore up the roadbed at the culvert because water erosion had undermined it.

The early morning downpour had left a lake on the western side of the built-up dirt road. The culvert's twin corrugated steel conduits were not large enough to accommodate that tremendous volume of rapidly accumulating runoff. Two huge fountains of muddy water sprayed out of the culvert on the east side of the road. The roadbed appeared solid enough to the tankers, and they crossed over the culvert, continuing their road sweep south to Charlie-2 without incident.

The grunt squad and engineer mine-sweep team rode atop the tanks on the return trip once the morning mine sweep was finished. As the two tanks approached Rocky Ford, the tankers observed that perhaps 20 percent of the dirt road on the side backing up the flood waters had crumbled away since they had crossed over an hour earlier. Two columns of grunts were still walking across without pause, despite gushing torrents of muddy water shooting out from the culvert. The backed-up runoff was level with the road, threatening to overflow the damlike obstacle at any moment.

"Hold it up, DuBose," said Lieutenant Coan to his driver. "I want to take a closer look. That roadbed looks pretty shaky; it might not hold us." He climbed down from A-11 and jogged over to the culvert for a closer look. The road's capacity for withstanding the rapidly multiplying volume of water surging against it was growing more tenuous with each passing minute. Not taking a chance of crossing over meant being cut off from Con Thien and the rest of the tank platoon. Coan went back to his other tank and inquired of the driver, Lance Cpl. Piggy Bores, who had a year's experience driving tanks over every type of terrain possible in Vietnam, "What do you think, Piggy, can we make it over?"

Bores replied without any hesitation, "Let's go, Lieutenant. We can do it if we go now. It's not gonna hold up much longer."

"That's what I'm thinking," said the lieutenant, as he climbed up into A-11's tank commander's cupola. "Okay, DuBose. We're gettin' ready to give 'er a go." As he reached back to retrieve his fallen com-helmet from the gypsy rack, Coan looked directly into the intense, searching stares of a half-dozen alarmed grunts. He hesitated. That old Marine Corps adage from Officer Candidate School echoed in his mind—"Hesitate and you're dead!" But he could not make himself give the order to move out. Just then, with a mighty *KAWHOOSHHH*, the Rocky Ford culvert was no more—washed away in a torrent of pent-up water pressure.

In shocked silence, they gaped at the mighty surge of water as it flipped two enormous steel conduits end over end like paper straws. Then the horror of it all registered. Marines from Echo 2/9 were walking across that culvert when it washed away. Men began to shout. Two Marines instantly shed their equipment and flak jackets and jumped into the muddy, churning, swift-moving water to rescue one man who had somehow grabbed onto some tree branches near the bank. They pulled him to safety. Others sprinted along the bank looking for any others less fortunate. One man was missing and presumed drowned. "Doc," their Navy corpsman, had met his fate that morning. Weighted down with all of his equipment, he never had a chance. Heavy jungle undergrowth fifty meters from the roadbed prevented rescuers from going any farther downstream without machetes to hack their way through.[3]

What had been a lazy, meandering creek a day earlier was now a raging river, ten feet deep and one hundred feet wide. Rain commenced falling again as NCOs and officers physically restrained several grief-stricken men from stripping down and diving into that deathtrap to search for their revered corpsman. Others stood helplessly along the riverbank, cursing with rage and frustration. Vietnam itself had claimed the life of another American boy.

With one hard downpour, Mother Nature had accomplished what the NVA could not. Con Thien was cut off and isolated. No more resupply runs could be made on the MSR until the washout was repaired. There was nothing for Second Lieutenant Coan to do but take his two tanks and the mine-sweep detail back to C-2 and attempt to find a place out of the rain. The monsoon season had arrived.

13

Monsoon Misery

Alarmed that Con Thien and the regiment of Marines deployed there were cut off by the MSR washout, 3/9's CO, Major Gorton C. Cook, was ordered by Colonel R. B. Smith to move his two maneuver companies inside the Con Thien perimeter. A full-scale ground attack by the NVA seemed imminent. Con Thien was never intended to house more than two reinforced companies of Marines, and now its residents had to find room to house double their original number on the lines. Tankers were kicked out of their bunkers; they could live in their tanks. And some bunkers intended to house a squad of infantry were taken over by a platoon.

Gene Miller was a grunt with 3d Platoon, Kilo 3/9. When the rains came, a cart path that ran by his company position outside the perimeter wire became a muddy river five feet wide. Several fighting holes filled with water. Then his company was ordered to move inside the perimeter. Miller's squad took over a leaking bunker overlooking the minefield. Scrounged wooden pallets kept the soaking-wet Marines off the muddy floor.

Miller found the firing handles for several claymore mines and a fifty-five-gallon barrel of napalm that had been buried in the wire outside the bunker. He asked his sergeant, "What do I do if the gooks are in the wire and I need to fire the napalm?" "Lay down on the floor, hold your breath, kiss your ass good-bye, and let her rip," he was told. The sergeant was not kidding.[1]

The engineers had constructed sturdy bunkers that were nearly "bomb

2d Bn., 4th Marines
Battle at Phu Oc
September 21, 1967
CLEARED TRACE
Con
Thien
An Phu
Phu Oc
E/2/4
H/2/4
F/2/4
G/2/4
NVA
2
4
561
Thon Nam Tan
Nam Dong
(Abandoned Airfield)
MSR
N
0
500
1,000
meters
J. P. Coan

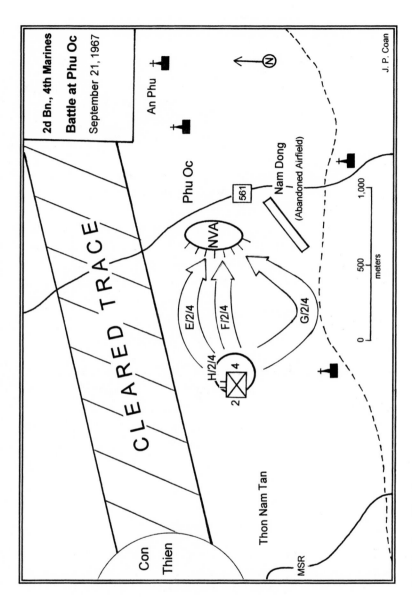

2/4 Battle at Phu Oc

proof" for the battalion CP, aid station, and other key locations. But what all too often passed as a "bunker" built by the troops manning the lines was an ungainly structure made of dirt-filled wooden 105mm artillery shell crates laid one atop the other to build the walls, with steel fence stakes hammered into the ground for support. Overhead cover was provided by two or three layers of sandbags, depending on the strength of ceiling material that the Marines were able to scrounge. The fortunate ones had twelve-inch by twelve-inch upright support beams holding up the bunker overhead, and the really lucky ones had a tarp over the top to keep out rain. When a unit pulled out and new arrivals took over a bunker, they would set about piling on more sandbags, digging deeper trenches, and doing whatever else they could think of to improve their odds of surviving a shelling attack. Always the realists, the Marines knew that if anything larger than an 82mm mortar shell scored a direct hit on their primitive bunkers, they were dead. Many preferred to ride out a storm of incoming in the fighting holes and trenches outside their ramshackle bunkers.

NVA sappers took advantage of the foggy mist blanketing the perimeter at night to sneak in close and blast holes in the wire with bangalore torpedoes. During daylight hours, when visibility was better both for the Marines and for the NVA, snipers took aim at the Marines manning the northern perimeter, occasionally hitting someone. No one could relax. Nerves were on edge. Perhaps that was the purpose of the round-the-clock harassment.

Mud Marines

The incessant downpour continued. In one twenty-four-hour period, division headquarters at Dong Ha recorded a rainfall total of 17.39 inches. Flooding became a serious problem at bases all around the DMZ area, especially Con Thien. Trench lines at the base of each hill were awash in cold, muddy water. Marines standing watch on the lines at night attempted to use their steel pots and whatever containers they could find to bail water out of their trenches and fighting holes. Packs and cots floated in two feet of runoff that had poured into some bunkers before the inhabitants could fill enough sandbags to barricade the entrance.

Some bunkers collapsed. The LZ was such a mud bowl that helicopters dared not set completely down for fear of getting swamped.

Roads and paths around The Hill soon became churned into quagmires of chocolate brown mud by tracked vehicles and trucks. More than one Marine was heard yelling for help when he sank down in the muck and could not extricate himself. On the plus side, incoming rounds tended to penetrate several feet into the mud before detonating, thereby funneling their deadly spray of shrapnel straight up.

An artilleryman was coming back from an errand to pick up a few cases of C rations one day when he sank up to his crotch while crossing the main perimeter road. The more he struggled, the more stuck he became. While he was attempting to extricate himself from the muck, mortars started impacting on that portion of the perimeter. The terrified Marine had only one chance for survival: bend forward and sink further into the morass. When the shelling ended, some grunts nearby heard loud cries for help. Expecting to find a wounded man somewhere, they saw instead a mud-covered creature with only his torso showing, frantically waving his arms. They laid out a path of wooden ammunition crates across the road and pulled the shaky man from the quagmire. As he rinsed the caked clay mud off his face and body with water from a shell crater, the Marine was shivering, but not from the cold. He had been bracketed by exploding mortar shells that walked right over him. The deep mud had protected him from getting hit by any shrapnel.

Vehicles, particularly tracked ones, created the problem of knee-deep mud in the perimeter roads, and they also fell victim to it. One tank got so bogged down in that chocolate mud morass that the only vehicle successful in extricating it was an amtrac. Somehow, the amtrac, perhaps due to its lighter weight, was able to obtain enough traction to dislodge the tank and break the suction that was holding the tank down.

"Otter" Frustration

The 2d Battalion, 9th Marines was deployed to the southeast of Con Thien. On September 16, the battalion S-4 had requested a food and ammunition resupply, but no truck convoy could get beyond the washout. Arrangements were made to attempt to use Otters, Marine Corps tracked amphibious vehicles, to swim the stream at the washout with the ammunition resupply. Lieutenant Robert McIntosh from L/3/4 was assigned to accompany the Otters on their resupply mission.

At midafternoon, five Otters loaded down with supplies left C-2 and traveled north on the MSR to the washout. The first Otter had Second Lieutenant McIntosh aboard. Once he glimpsed the rampaging river of brown, churning water, Lieutenant McIntosh could only hope and pray the Otter driver knew what he was doing. His Otter made it about ten feet from the bank when the river's current swept it away, causing it to capsize in the rough water. All the crewmen and the lieutenant managed to save themselves by grabbing on to overhanging branches and were rescued, but it had been a close thing. There was no retrieving the Otter; it was completely submerged somewhere downstream, along with all the ammunition. The other Otters returned to C-2 with the nearly drowned survivors, all thankful to still be alive.

Disbelieving Marines back at C-2 could not fathom how an amphibious vehicle could be sunk crossing a stream. But the washout was no longer the little stream 3/4 had crossed over a few days earlier when the battalion pulled out of Con Thien. Any more supply runs north of C-2 were going to have to be made by helicopter.

The Cam Lo Bridge Incident

Farther south at the Cam Lo Bridge, flooding problems were brewing. On the second day of heavy rainfall, September 17, Cam Lo Bridge, a key point along the MSR to Con Thien, was reported under water. Two amtracs attempting to ferry supplies across the Cam Lo River at the bridge became entangled in barbed wire and could not climb up the riverbank. It required two hours of frantic work to free the two stuck amtracs and get them out of the river.

As the day wore on, the Cam Lo River continued to rise. The first alarming reports from Lima Company's CO, Captain Carr, came in to 3/4's CP at C-2 early in the morning on the eighteenth. The river was overflowing, and many positions were under water. First the water was ankle deep and then became knee deep. At three thirty in the morning, Lima's CO reported to battalion that his position was untenable. He was directed to move his men to higher ground.

In the darkness, on unfamiliar terrain, and in a heavy downpour, several men wandered into their own concertina wire and were ensnared. Hearing their panicked cries for help, several NCOs and officers reacted instinctively and attempted to rescue their men, but they, too, got caught in the tangled wire obstacles. The swiftly rising water engulfed them before they could extricate themselves. By midmorning, four drowned Marines from L/3/4 were located: 1st Lt. Henry D. Babers, who had been wounded three times at Con Thien; Staff Sgt. John W. Boyer; Sgt. Harrison Ball; and an artillery FO, 1st Lt. Thomas F. Regan. Four more men from Lima were confirmed missing and presumed drowned. A search effort by the remainder of Lima Company went on throughout the day without success in finding the missing men. At one point, part of the search party itself got trapped by rising water and had to be lifted out by helicopter.

On the nineteenth, local Vietnamese villagers reported finding four Marine bodies on the south side of the Cam Lo River, two hundred meters south of the bridge. Two additional drowning victims were discovered the following day farther downriver at Cam Thai by villagers. The 3d Battalion, 4th Marines had lost nine men by drowning, eight from Lima Company. The tenth drowned Marine was from another unit not attached to 3/4.

Several senior officers from the 9th Marines descended on the scene of the tragedy. They could not do much besides shake their heads and wonder at the calamity that had befallen Lima 3/4 during the night. Mother Nature had become as much of an adversary to the Marines as the North Vietnamese.

2/9's Ordeal

After their near disaster at the end of July, when 2/9 had to fight its way through a mile-long ambush coming back out of the DMZ, Lt. Col. William D. Kent's battalion had spent most of August operating in Leatherneck Square. There were no major actions, just day after blistering hot day of patrolling through the deserted former agricultural area, digging fighting holes before dark, and going out on ambushes at night. Periodically, one of those ambushes would be triggered, and, more often than not, there would be nothing to show for it but a blood trail or two and possibly a weapon found. It was the lull before the storm . . . literally. Action began to intensify in September all around Con Thien, and 2/9 would invariably be caught up in those events.

At dawn on September 12, a few hundred meters south of Phu Oc near the abandoned airstrip labeled Nam Dong on their maps, 2/9 was greeted with a deadly wake-up call of eighty rounds of 82mm mortars, which wounded a number of men. The medevacs had barely commenced arriving when a second barrage of 60mm and 82mm mortars hit the battalion, most of whom were up out of their holes attending to the wounded. Lieutenant Colonel Kent and Major Murphy, the XO, were seriously injured. A staggering total of seventy-two Marines were hurt badly enough in that mortar attack to be medevaced. Through some whim of fate, none were killed. Counter-mortar action was taken, but results, as usual, were unknown.

Lt. Col. John J. Peeler, who had been the CO of 2/9 throughout the first six months of the year, replaced the wounded CO, Lieutenant Colonel Kent. After that September 12 mortaring incident, 2/9 stayed on the move. Each company would make a show of digging in and setting in for the night. Then, after dark, the entire company would silently relocate a few hundred meters away and really dig in for the night. It was an exhausting drill and required strict discipline for the bone-weary grunts to carry it off each night, but the ruse worked, and it saved lives. On more than one occasion, a nocturnal mortar attack struck the vacated position.

Under orders from the 9th Marines, 2/9(-) moved in closer to the MSR to protect the route better from interdiction after the company probe of Con Thien's perimeter. But after the washout occurred on the sixteenth, protecting the MSR became a moot issue. On the eighteenth and nineteenth, as the deluge continued without letup, the battalion CP was established only a few hundred meters south of Con Thien's outer wire at Yankee Station. There they would remain for the next week, pummeled and pounded by NVA mortars, rockets, and artillery, just like 3/9 on The Hill. However, 2/9 did not have Dyemarker bunkers and deep trenches to provide some protection from the incessant incoming. Moreover, they slept in the mud, defecated in the mud, and suffered in the mud, day and night, never getting completely dry or warm. Mosquito bites and scratches became infected, leaving open, weeping sores. And an epidemic of fungus rashes and immersion foot cases (trench foot) overwhelmed the medical capabilities of the corpsmen. Jack Hartzel, a machine gunner with 1st Platoon of Echo 2/9 at Con Thien, recalled his unit's ordeal:

> I don't remember a day in which we didn't get hit with incoming rounds of some sort. We also suffered something that was almost unheard of elsewhere in South Vietnam. It was called "shell shock" and it was not unusual. The constant pounding every day could make you go nuts. You would sit there on edge, wondering if the next round that came in would have your name on it. We were in holes in the mud. Our holes would fill with water; we'd have to bail them out four or five times a day. We also had immersion foot and your feet would bleed and hurt like hell. Then there was the damned mud! You walked in it, you sat in it, you slept in it and you even ate it. There was just no escaping it.[2]

With the MSR cut off, the only means of resupply was by helicopter. It was not worth the risk to make a resupply drop when the LZ was being shelled or rocketed. The highest priority was evacuating the wounded, and the choppers did brave the incoming to get casualties out. The next priority was ammunition, and last came food. Hartzel further remembered:

> Not only did we run out of chow, but that also meant no C-ration toilet paper. So we started to tear strips of cloth from the bottoms of our trousers to wipe with. We once went over three days without resupply. During that time, we actually scrounged around in our own trash pits trying to find something to eat. The door gunner on the chopper that finally brought us chow saw the look in our eyes and knew he'd better drop chow out of that door. There is nothing in the world meaner than a 20-year-old Marine, hungry, angry, with a loaded machine gun in his hands![3]

A platoon of tanks from Alpha Company, 3d Tank Battalion, led by Gunnery Sgt. R. B. English, was attached to 2/9. During the downpour on the sixteenth and seventeenth, two tanks with H/2/9 sank down in an old rice paddy and became stuck in mud up to their fenders. The remaining three tanks with the battalion CP and Company G also got bogged down trying to negotiate the rain-saturated fields to come to the aid of the other two mired vehicles.

For the tankers, it was a nightmare. Most of the grounded tankers came down with immersion foot. Gunny English injured his back attempting to get his tank unstuck and had to be medevaced. On the nineteenth, when Hotel was ordered to move with the battalion closer to Con Thien, their two stuck tanks had to be abandoned. The other three tanks also had to be abandoned when the battalion CP relocated. An entire platoon of five tanks was mired down in the mud and abandoned. For the 3d Tank Battalion, it was an unprecedented calamity. But the constant rain was also affecting the NVA. Their foot mobility was curtailed, apparently, because they did not bother with the abandoned tanks.

The near-constant downpour did not deter the NVA's artillery, mortars, and rockets. Taking advantage of reduced visibility that hampered Marine spotters, the NVA bombarded The Hill around the clock. One of the heaviest days of incoming was September 19, when 3/9 was shelled by nearly five hundred rounds, killing three men and wounding forty-three. Outside the perimeter, 2/9 was on the receiving end of 132 rounds of deadly accurate artillery, and they had one man killed and six wounded.

DISASTER AT PHU OC

While 2/9 was being bloodied by incoming outside of Con Thien's wire, and 3/9 was taking a pounding inside the perimeter, the 2d Battalion, 4th Marines had completed its move north from Charlie-2. The CO of 2/4, Lt. Col. James Hammond, directed the deployment of his battalion twelve hundred meters to the east of Con Thien near the deserted hamlet of Phu Oc.

Lieutenant Colonel Hammond received orders on September 20 to conduct a battalion search-and-destroy mission to the east of his position but to remain south of the Trace. The colonel requested tanks, but the rain-saturated terrain negated that option.

That thickly overgrown area around Phu Oc had an evil history. The day prior to Operation Hickory on May 16, F/2/26 had walked into a well-laid, multicompany ambush there. Golf came up with tanks, and after a three-hour firefight, 2/26 was able to overrun the bunker complex. They incurred losses of sixteen Marines killed and sixty wounded. On September 6, Hotel 2/9 had walked into an ambush set up in the tangled thickets, incurring losses of seven killed and twelve wounded before they were able to disengage with the aid of tanks, artillery, and air strikes.

On the morning of September 21, 2/4 prepared for another day of searching the rain-drenched countryside, hoping to spoil any ideas the NVA might have for an attack on Con Thien. The plan called for Foxtrot Company to move three hundred meters due east to a position near Hill 86 and wait; then, Company E would circle north around Foxtrot, keeping just below the Trace, and come up on line beyond them. When the two companies were aligned abreast, they would sweep south through Phu Oc toward Company G, set in southeast of the battalion position. When all three companies linked up, they would continue sweeping south.

At seven o'clock in the morning, after twenty minutes of preparatory fire from the battalion's own 81mm mortars, Echo and Foxtrot moved out. Movement was cautious and deliberate. Dense thickets in their path were almost impenetrable. At 7:50, lead elements of Company F advancing eastward began receiving sniper fire. The lead platoon charged across an open rice paddy in an attempt to attack the sniper positions—a fatal decision. Enemy automatic weapons opened up on the recklessly charging Marines from their front and left, trapping them in a murderous cross fire from heavily camouflaged bunker and trench-line fortifications—a skillfully designed L-shaped ambush.

Mortars began to fall on the pinned-down platoon, sending shards of shrapnel tearing into the prostrate Marines. Some of the critically wounded lay only yards from the nearly invisible enemy bunkers, preventing supporting arms from being called in.

Lance Corporal Jedh Colby Barker was wounded in the initial burst of fire. Lying out in the open, he bravely kept his machine gun firing, delivering a devastating volume of fire into the enemy positions. The NVA focused their return fire on him. He was hit again, this time in the right hand, which prevented him from firing his machine gun. An enemy grenade landed nearby in the midst of several wounded men. Lance Corporal Barker threw himself on the grenade, absorbing the blast with his own body. He then crawled to the side of a wounded comrade and was administering first aid when he succumbed to his many grievous wounds.

Corporal Tiago Reis, a fire-team leader, was in the point squad. He was the only man not hit. He began dragging his team members out of the line of fire, treating their wounds, and then going back out to retrieve more wounded. Inevitably, he was struck down by a bullet, but he would not quit. Despite his wound, he was continuing to attempt to rescue his many wounded buddies when a second bullet found its mark and killed him. Lance Corporal Jedh C. Barker would receive the Medal of Honor, and Corporal Reis would receive the Navy Cross, both awarded posthumously.

Echo Company was taken under fire at the same time. As they advanced to the left flank of Foxtrot, automatic weapons suddenly opened fire. Two mortally wounded Marines fell within ten meters of the entrenched NVA. PFC Mark W. Judge, the point man of the lead fire team, was hit several times in the initial burst of fire. He continued to fire his weapon despite being wounded again. Realizing the enemy was maneuvering toward his flanks in order to cut off the remainder of his squad, he provided devastating covering fire that allowed his comrades to pull back. He was finally shot down and killed. PFC Judge's Navy Cross citation reads in part: "Through his extraordinary initiative and inspiring valor in the face of almost certain death, he saved his fellow Marines from injury and possible loss of life."[4]

One of the two seriously wounded men lying in front of the NVA position was rescued. After several Marines were wounded attempting to save the second man, no one else tried; he would die where he lay.

Incoming artillery shells from the DMZ began to explode amid Echo and Foxtrot Companies as they tied in together, killing and maiming more Marines. The battalion CP and Hotel Company also became targets. Then, to compound the chaos, a medevac chopper lifting off with wounded was hit by ground fire; the stricken craft was last seen headed for Charlie-2 trailing a plume of black smoke. Lieutenant Colonel Hammond ordered Company G to stop its advance to the southeast and counterattack northward.

Located between Hill 86 and Route 561, 2/4 had run into a major fortification four hundred meters long and just as deep. At least two reinforced companies of NVA, possibly a battalion, were dug in there. The AO brought in fixed-wing air to suppress the enemy artillery fire from the DMZ, but no bombing runs could be made on the Phu Oc bunker complex with dead and wounded Marines lying so close. The NVA had learned their lesson well—"hugging the belt"—that keeping our casualties in close to their positions nullified our use of bombs and napalm.

While advancing quietly north toward the sounds of battle in an attempt to flank the NVA position, lead elements of Golf Company blundered into a booby-trapped hedgerow, resulting in numerous casualties. Then, with the NVA fully alerted, they faced 150 meters of open paddy field to assault through. Golf charged anyway, "hey diddle diddle, right up the middle" (Marine Corps slang for a straight-ahead charge). Thirty meters from their objective, the brave but futile attack faltered and ground to a halt. Mortars again rained down on the exposed Marines, taking a terrible toll of the wounded lying out in the paddy. Golf Company was pinned down and dying.

Lieutenant Colonel Hammond later recounted, "The enemy was observed to direct automatic weapons fire on those wounded who attempted to crawl to safety as well as to periodically riddle those lying motionless in the open."[5] With the aid of Echo and Foxtrot laying down heavy covering fire, Golf Company was finally able to disengage. Still, several Marines were not accounted for when they took a head count.

Shortly after noon, alarming news was relayed from the AO overhead. Two groups of NVA, each with as many as four hundred men, were converging on Phu Oc from the north and southeast in an attempt to surround 2/4. Artillery, fixed-wing, and Huey gunships responded immediately, blasting away at the NVA reinforcements before they could move close enough to launch an attack.

Prior to the operation, the division commander had warned Lieutenant Colonel Hammond: "If you get in a big fight, I haven't the resources to commit to help you. You are all I have in the area for some time. Good luck!"[6]

With only a few hours of daylight left, Hammond ordered his company commanders to retrieve their wounded. Echo, Foxtrot, and Golf set up a hasty defense around an LZ to bring in medevacs. Sixteen Marines and corpsmen were killed, and 118 had been wounded, but 15 of the dead had to be left behind to prevent any more casualties from attempting their retrieval.[7] Battalion staff claimed 39 NVA killed, but division later estimated 350.

Marine intelligence officers identified the enemy force as part of the 90th NVA Regiment, the same regiment that had wiped out Bravo 1/9 at the Marketplace massacre on July 2.

Leaving their dead buddies behind was the worst thing imaginable. "Marines don't leave their dead behind!" was the solemn oath of every Marine who ever wore the uniform. It rankled those grunts. They knew that TPQ bombing runs would be carried out on the bunker complex and that artillery would pound the area once the Marines left. And their dead friends were still lying out there. The nagging ache in their hearts and minds would not leave until those bodies were recovered.

Where was the "corporate memory" that could have warned Lieutenant Colonel Hammond and his operations officer that Phu Oc was a dangerous place, likely to be heavily defended? The 2d Battalion, 9th Marines had been in that area for months and even fought a brief but bloody battle at Phu Oc on September 6. Phu Oc had an evil reputation, and someone back at regiment apparently failed to convey that to Lieutenant Colonel Hammond and his staff. In the absence of that awareness, 2/4 had stumbled into an NVA buzz saw and been decimated.

14

Living in the "V" Ring

A letter from a father reprimanded one of our Marines: "Don't *ever* send a picture like that home to your mom again." It seems our Marine took a picture just as he took cover from incoming and unknowingly got a photo of "Mouse" Roberts being blown into the air by the shell that killed him.
—John H. Edwards, H & S Co., 3/9

The news media was becoming critical of the Johnson administration for placing U.S. Marines in harm's way at bases along the DMZ such as Con Thien. As reports of the escalating shelling attacks on Con Thien began to reach home, a heated debate took place in Congress. "Con Thien is Vietnam's special kind of hell," wrote Karl H. Purnell. Purnell was a former assemblyman from Pennsylvania on special assignment to Vietnam and had spent time with the Marines at Con Thien. Congressman Schweiker introduced his writings in the House of Representatives. Purnell's theme was that the Marines at Con Thien were victims of dubious policy formulated at the White House and Pentagon and that poorly constructed bunkers at Con Thien were getting Americans killed and wounded unnecessarily.[1] Some overzealous reporters and editorial writers even began to make comparisons to the French defeat at Dien Bien Phu.

General Westmoreland was determined to erase any perception that Con Thien could become another Dien Bien Phu. He acknowledged that the artillery fire concentrated against Con Thien was the heaviest since Giap's forces defeated the French in 1954. However, he tried to put a happy face on the increasingly dour reports coming out of northern I Corps, stating at a South Korean troop ceremony in Saigon on September 25: "The Allies in Vietnam are now in a position from which the picture of ultimate military success may be viewed with increasing clarity."[2] Not in any mood to appear indecisive at this crucial juncture in the war, when McNamara's entire SPOS project appeared to be in jeopardy, President Johnson unleashed Westmoreland to conduct what he called "the heaviest concentration of conventional firepower in history."[3] That may have been an exaggeration, but what followed was certainly one of the greatest concentrations of firepower in the history of the Vietnam War.

OPERATION NEUTRALIZE

The code name for the combined U.S. Air Force, Army, and Navy operation to relieve the siege of Con Thien in September and October was Operation Neutralize, launched on September 11. General William Momyer, commander of the Seventh Air Force, developed an approach code-named SLAM (seek, locate, annihilate, and monitor). It involved a coordinated series of attacks from air, land, and sea involving naval artillery bombardment, tactical air support, B-52 bombing, and artillery fire.

In one nine-day period, Con Thien (including 2/9 and 2/4) was hit with more than three thousand rounds of mixed artillery, rockets, and mortars. Operation Neutralize responded with 790 B-52 Arc Light missions "right in front of Con Thien" during September, dropping twenty-two thousand tons of bombs.[4] The III MAF artillery units fired 12,577 rounds at known or suspected enemy positions in the region; ships of the Seventh Fleet fired 6,148 rounds at the same area. Marine, Navy, and Air Force jets flew fifty-two hundred close air support missions in support of Con Thien.[5]

A particularly awesome weapon was the giant B-52 Stratofortress. A typical payload carried by one of those behemoths was twenty-seven tons, or 108 mixed 500- and 750-pound bombs. One plane could easily wipe out a grid square. A formation of six B-52s dropping their bombs from thirty thousand feet could churn up the earth and totally devastate all human life within an area one-half mile wide by two miles long.[6] To prevent a disastrous incident such as errant bombs falling on our own forces, the military imposed a three-thousand-meter buffer zone. The NVA around Con Thien soon realized this and bivouacked their ground forces inside that buffer zone whenever possible. But the North Vietnamese supply depots and artillery and rocket positions within and north of the DMZ took a relentless pounding from the B-52s.

To the Marines on the ground, huddled in their bunkers and trenches, nothing cheered them up more after a bad day of ducking incoming than feeling the ground shake and bounce during an Arc Light bomb strike. One could hear the falling bombs whistling a loud chorus of doom if the strike impacted within a few miles of Con Thien. If dropped farther away, there was no sound, just a sudden trembling and shaking of the earth beneath their feet that went on for half a minute. To be on the receiving end of such a devastating attack was a horrific experience. The internal hemorrhaging resulting from the concussion alone was often fatal. It was not uncommon, after a B-52 strike had annihilated an enemy force, to find a few incoherent survivors staggering around in shock, bleeding profusely from the nose and ears.

Another mighty weapon in Westmoreland's arsenal was ground-controlled radar bombing that could be carried out at night or during the worst weather conditions. Ground controllers were situated many miles to the rear in a heavily protected van that housed sensitive computers and the TPQ-10 radar to guide jet fighter bombers to their targets. The radar emitted a narrow beam that detected and locked onto the aircraft, typically an A-4 Skyhawk or A-6 Intruder. The ground controller programmed into the computer the enemy target coordinates provided by the fire support coordination center (FSCC), ballistic characteristics of the bombs, wind velocity, and so on. Connected to the radar, the computer provided corrections in airspeed, altitude, and heading to take the bomber over the target. At a predetermined release point, the ground controller told the pilot to release his bombs. Specially equipped aircraft such as the A-6 Intruder could have their bombs "pickled" automatically by ground control. The A-6 was the controllers' favorite because it packed a wallop, normally carrying twenty-eight five-hundred-pound bombs.[7] TPQ strikes were legendary for their accuracy. Many a Marine on the lines or in an FO bunker at night witnessed numerous secondary explosions that resulted from TPQs.

During the day, aerial observers circled like buzzards north of Con Thien, waiting for an enemy artillery piece to open fire so they could bring in Phantom, Crusader, and Skyhawk jets to unload their ordnance. Some 130 NVA artillery positions had been identified by Allied intelligence as early as the previous July, so there was no lack of targets. Discerning which were real and which ones were bogus was the catch. The NVA went all out to deceive Allied pilots by constructing fake gun batteries and SAM sites. Those deception tactics were fairly successful, as evidenced by intelligence estimates that indicated only forty artillery sites had been destroyed by the end of the year.[8]

In spite of the disastrous September 3 artillery attack on Dong Ha's fuel and ammunition depot, Allied artillerists had little problem fulfilling their end of the SLAM concept. Marine Corps eight-inch howitzers and Army 175mm guns blasted away night and day from Camp Carroll and Cam Lo. New Marines on the ground at Con Thien had to become acclimated to the sounds of their own outgoing shells. The "old salts," those who had been there more than four or five days, carried on without flinching when they heard that distinctive sizzling sound, like bacon frying, as a large-caliber shell whizzed overhead toward its target somewhere in the DMZ. Anyone who appeared to freeze or even pause when they heard that sound was immediately dismissed as a "new guy."

THE "SWORD OF DAMOCLES" SYNDROME

Despite an avalanche of ordnance blasting the North Vietnamese, the amount of incoming received daily at Con Thien continued without letup, slacking off only at night. On September 21, 3/9 received 368 rounds of assorted incoming, including ninety-five 122mm rockets, killing one Marine and wounding sixty-three. The next day 3/9 received 122 rounds of assorted incoming, with losses of fifty-eight men wounded and six killed.

One's chances for survival were no better outside the perimeter wire. On September 21, 2/9 received 206 rounds of incoming, killing five

Marines and wounding twenty-eight. Day after abominable day, the murderous shelling continued with no relief in sight.

For the rain-soaked, mud-coated Marines, their nerves stretched taut from the periodic blasts of incoming, staying out of harm's way was the uppermost priority. That was not always possible, because a myriad of routine tasks had to be performed throughout the day. Officers and NCOs had to check on their men and attend briefings. Supplies had to be unloaded from helicopters by working parties and moved to areas away from the LZ. Supporting arms had to carry out fire missions. And the "shitters" had to be burned daily—an ugly chore, but mandatory.

John H. Edwards, a member of H & S Company during the siege, recalled what it was like on Con Thien:

> The most noticeable first impression of Con Thien is mud, and a unique smell of mud, human waste, and decomposing flesh—not overwhelming, but there all the time. . . . One can not go very far without seeing (and smelling) various small body parts. . . . We are really back in 1917 for all intents and purposes. There is no electricity; not only can the wheeled vehicles not move through the mud, there are no unpunctured tires or radiators left. We illuminate our bunkers with diesel lamps made from C-ration cans with wicks made from web belts—a smoky, but adequate solution.[9]

Always present was the sense of impending doom, a sense of dread that one feels when serious danger is at hand. In an ancient fable, a king ordered a dinner guest to sit at a table and eat while a sword hung by a thread from the ceiling, directly over his head, ready to drop at any moment. That describes precisely how it felt to walk out in the open at Con Thien, knowing that an artillery shell or mortar round could drop out of the sky at any moment and have your name on it.

After a few days on Con Thien, one developed a peculiar way of walking out in the open. Some called it the "Con Thien Shuffle." Doing the "shuffle" meant striding quickly with a forward lean, knees slightly bent, eyes constantly scanning the ground for the nearest trench, rut, mound of dirt, or anything to dive toward at the first millisecond of warning sound that a shell was incoming. Some defiantly tempted fate and strolled calmly upright. They believed in that old adage, "It's the one you don't hear that gets you." They were convinced that "when your number's up, it's up. If it has your name on it, you're dead. Ain't nothin' you can do about it."[10] Even so, few were foolish enough to tempt fate further by not knowing at all times where the nearest hole or trench was located.

An artillery forward observer team was killed one night when a 152mm artillery shell scored a direct hit on their bunker, a sandbagged steel Conex box located on the saddle between OP#2 and the battalion CP behind OP#1. Replacements were brought in two days later by helicopter. The LZ was still too soggy for a landing, so the passengers had to jump off while the craft hovered a few feet over the LZ. Suddenly, the craft lifted up and banked sharply away to the south. Being new to Vietnam and never having set foot on Con Thien, one of the new lieutenants was still standing there, gawking at his surroundings, when the LZ was bracketed by incoming. He was killed instantly. All new arrivals to Con Thien were told that story to bring home the dangers of tarrying too long out in the open.

As perilous as daily life could be on The Hill, there was still a war to fight. The Marines had a clearly defined mission—hold Con Thien at all costs—but elite assault troops are neither trained for nor accustomed to huddling in one place, taking a pounding day after day. But their discipline would not break; these were Marines. They would continue to carry out their orders, despite the frustration they were feeling. Not surprisingly, the mood of these beleaguered Marines was growing meaner with each passing day as casualties mounted. Their patience for just sitting there and taking it was long gone.

The perimeter wire had to be checked daily. On the morning of September 23, a squad patrol from India 3/9 was ambushed near the northwest perimeter. A command-detonated explosive device killed two men, Cpl. Paul Price and Lance Cpl. Claude Smith, and wounded two. Then, the remainder of the squad came under small-arms fire. A fierce firefight soon developed.

India's CO, Capt. William "Wild Bill" Conger, had a reputation for being a "John Wayne" type—a risk taker who was fearless in battle. When he heard about the attack on his Marines, he snapped. He rounded up another squad of Marines, commandeered an Army Duster, and marched over to Sergeant Carter, tank commander on A-12. "You're going with me!" he barked at Carter in no uncertain terms. The Duster and Carter's tank roared out the south minefield gate ferrying Conger and his squad of vengeful grunts on board.

As soon as they reached the scene of the ambush, A-12 and the Army Duster opened fire. Captain Conger leapt off the tank, rushing the NVA position and emptying his M-16 and .45-caliber pistol as he ran. Conger's wild, one-man charge ended the firefight. The captain and his radioman then located their shrapnel-riddled dead and wounded men and hoisted them up on the tank.

The tankers came back inside the perimeter that morning applauding the captain's gutsy actions and claiming that he had single-handedly killed several NVA and driven off the others. The Vikings had a term for their warriors who performed such rage-driven, one-man attacks. They were called "berserkers."

THE TURNING POINT

The North Vietnamese had kept up the pressure for more than three weeks. Casualties were mounting on both sides, with no end to the stale-mate in sight. Con Thien had averaged fifty men wounded and two killed by incoming every day since the rains came September 16. Out-side the wire, 2/9 was suffering almost as many casualties. Most of the shrapnel wounds caused by incoming were not serious enough to require being medevaced. Those less seriously wounded were treated at the bat-talion aid station (BAS) by the battalion surgeon, Navy Lieutenant Donald Shortridge, and his corpsmen, and then sent back to their units; otherwise, the battalion would have been incapable of continuing its mission by this time. It was not unusual to find men with three or four Purple Hearts on The Hill. By III MAF policy, anyone with two Hearts was supposed to be pulled out of harm's way and serve out the remainder of his tour "in the rear with the gear." The III MAF had to look the other way, though, as neither 2/9 nor 3/9 could afford to comply with that mandate.

On the morning of September 25, Con Thien was astir with morning chores. Black smoke curled skyward from the fifty-five-gallon drum halves that were pulled out from beneath sandbagged wooden commodes, partially filled with diesel fuel, and burned every morning. Men washed their hands and faces and shaved with water poured in their steel pot helmets. The lucky ones either had heat tabs or burned a small chunk of C-4 plastic explosive to warm the water; others, the "hard core," shaved in cold water.

Another morning ritual was emptying the rat traps. Con Thien was overrun with the vile, loathsome creatures. As soon as all lights and movement ceased inside the bunkers after dark, they could be heard rustling through trash, squeaking their displeasure at rivals competing for the same bits of food. Occasionally, a sleeping Marine would be awakened by a rat bouncing across him. Stories were told of some desperate Marines putting peanut butter or cheese on their toes and fingers at night, hoping a rat would chew on them. If it did happen, they would be evacuated to the rear and have to undergo a painful series of rabies shots. To their way of thinking, a few needles in the stomach were better than a rocket in their fighting hole.

At 7:15, the peaceful morning routine abruptly changed to a screeching, crashing, earth-shaking cacophony from hell, as hundreds of rockets, mortars, artillery shells, and recoilless rifle rounds commenced the worst bombardment yet experienced at Con Thien. It was a time-on-target bombardment coming from nearly every direction of the compass.

Lieutenant Coan was sitting in the tank commander's seat of A-11. He was still dozing after his two-hour watch had ended at 6:00 a.m. when he was jolted back to reality by an ear-splitting explosion behind A-11. The tank rocked and shuddered from near misses. His first instinct was to lock the overhead hatches, but as a wise old veteran had advised him once, "Close your hatches but never lock 'em when you're taking incoming, because the concussion from a direct hit will clobber everyone inside." Coan watched in awe through his cupola vision blocks as impacting shells blasted across the length and breadth of Con Thien. He wanted to retaliate, shoot back, but where? Better to sit tight and wait it out. Round after round shrieked in, coming from many different directions. Survival for the grunts meant hugging the ground while praying for the bombardment to lift soon.

The driver of A-11, DuBose, noticed that the new kid, PFC Williams (not his real name), was not in the turret. "Where the hell is that new guy?" Nobody knew. A chill came over Second Lieutenant Coan. A massive ground assault might be coming, and PFC Williams was outside the tank somewhere, maybe dead or wounded. Climbing out of the tank to look for him, though, was out of the question.

"Stay alert! This could be the one we've been waiting for," said Coan to no one in particular, pulling down hard on his .50-caliber charging handle to chamber a round. It was 7:45 a.m.—thirty minutes of nonstop shelling without letup. A shrieking rocket whacked into the mud beside the tank. They waited, but there was no blast—it was a dud. Coan looked to his left as a direct hit blew a bunker to pieces; sandbags and lumber flew in all directions. Miraculously, two grunts scrambled out from amid the shambles of their former shelter and dove headfirst into a nearby trench.

As suddenly as it began, the avalanche of incoming subsided. The silence was profound; no one dared breathe lest the hellish ordeal resume. A pall of dark gray smoke hung in the air over Con Thien. Coan surveyed the battered hillsides, expecting to find every bunker and privy smashed. Incredibly, nearly every structure was still intact despite that tremendous show of NVA firepower.

The loader's hatch flipped open suddenly, and PFC Williams wriggled through it, dropping to the turret deck. "Where were you?" asked Coan, noticing the dried remnants of shaving cream on his eyebrows, nose, and ears.

"I was outside shaving, standing beside the tank. That first salvo came in before I could duck. Something socked me in the back, and I dove under the tank."

The young Marine was pale and trembling. Coan did not dare ask what went through his mind when the dud rocket impacted next to him. "Let me see your back," said Coan, as he gently turned him around. His entire lower back and trouser seat were soaking wet with blood. A piece of jagged shrapnel had struck him just below the edge of his flak jacket, one inch from his spine. He began to faint, saying his legs were numb. He was going into shock. "Crank her up, DuBose! Get us to the aid station," shouted Coan to his driver.

A stream of stretcher-bearing corpsmen and grunts bore their casualties through the BAS entrance. A few stretcher bearers congregated outside, catching their breath before sprinting back whence they had come. A-11 roared to a halt in the mud outside the BAS, which was next to the LZ.

PFC Williams's legs would not move; his eyes were wide with fear that he was paralyzed. Coan could almost feel his tank sinking in the spongy clay outside the BAS as he and the gunner struggled to hoist the young man up through the loader's hatch. In another minute they would be too bogged down to move. Medevac helicopters might not be able to land because a tank was stuck in the LZ. "Damn it!" Coan bellowed. "You're no more paralyzed than I am! . . . Start moving those legs and get your butt outta here!" The young Marine's "paralyzed" lower limbs began probing for a toehold as he pulled himself up through the loader's hatch. The last that 1st Platoon ever saw of PFC Williams was his blood-soaked trouser seat as he stumbled through the BAS entrance.

The men of Lt. Col. John Peeler's 2/9 had been enjoying their C-ration coffee and warming themselves in the morning sun when the first of dozens of screaming 122mm rockets impacted in their midst. More than two hundred more rounds of artillery and mortars followed in less than an hour. When the shelling lifted, helmeted heads poked up slowly from hundreds of fighting holes and trenches, seeing but not believing the cratered landscape full of dirt mounds that had only an hour earlier been their company or battalion area. Surprisingly, considering the sheer volume of incoming, casualties were light. The men of 2/9 were well dug in. However, for the unlucky few who took direct hits, the corpsmen had their work cut out for them. Jack Hartzel from E/2/9 remembered the carnage:

> The thing about September 25 that really sticks in my mind is a picture of a Marine sitting in a puddle of blood and battle dressings on a poncho with his legs blown off from the waist down. He was numb from morphine and in shock from loss of blood. He was

smoking a cigarette very calmly as if nothing had even happened. He was waiting for a medevac. He probably died on the chopper ride back. . . . Our platoon arrived at Con Thien with 45 men. When we left we only had 12. Now you know why we called it "The Meatgrinder!"[11]

Situated east of Con Thien was 2/4. Lieutenant Colonel Hammond had relocated the 2/4 CP four hundred meters closer to Con Thien on September 23 because snipers had zeroed in on his former CP. Patrols and night ambushes were conducted toward Phu Phuong and Phu An to the southeast. The Phu Oc area was being avoided until the time was right to go back after their dead. Simultaneously with 3/9 on The Hill and 2/9 outside the perimeter, hundreds of incoming artillery, rockets, and mortars also hit Hammond's battalion.[12]

One particularly alarming development that afternoon was the sighting of an enemy tank thirty-five-hundred meters southwest of Con Thien. An artillery mission was called in on the target, and a secondary explosion resulted. The tank, probably an amphibious, Russian-made PT-76, was blown on its side, completely destroyed. Tanks were rarely encountered south of the Ben Hai River. Because tanks hardly ever went out alone, the Marines were justifiably concerned that others were hidden nearby.

A precise total of incoming rounds received by the three battalions that day was impossible to count. The first hour of bombardment was the worst, but heavy shelling continued intermittently the rest of the day and into the evening. Easily twelve hundred, and even as many as fifteen hundred, rounds of incoming were fired at the three battalions defending Con Thien on the twenty-fifth.

Perhaps the NVA were emptying their ammunition stores, preparing to pull back from the DMZ, because from that day forward the amount of incoming slacked off significantly. No more NVA tanks were spotted, and the urgency of that threat passed. Daily life was still hazardous but not nearly as bad as it had been in previous weeks. The Marines on the ground began to experience glimmers of hope that maybe the bombing campaign was working, that maybe they would survive the siege after all.

RETURN OF THE WALKING DEAD

A new dude joined our team, but we lost him right away. I don't remember his name. Sadly, most of the dead I can't and really don't want to remember. His replacement named Mike joined us, but he lost an arm. By that time, I didn't really talk to anyone much anymore, especially new guys. I closed the doors early in my tour. The cry of "corpsman" came early, often, and everywhere.
—Robert Brosa, Bravo Company, 1/9

For the remainder of September, the NVA pressure continued to diminish. September 26 was the first day that no one was killed on Con Thien since the rains came on the sixteenth. Lt. Col. John Peeler's 2/9 was pulled out of the Con Thien TAOR on September 27 and returned to Dong Ha, where they would assume the role of base defense and Rough Rider reaction force. It was a more-than-welcome respite for the battle-weary grunts of 2/9 who had been out in the field on Operation Kingfisher for more than two months.

During that abominable month of September, 2/9 incurred losses of 31 KIA (including three who later died of wounds) and 239 WIA. One corpsman died due to drowning. Some of the wounded included "battle fatigue" cases that were treated and, in most cases, returned to the field. Corpsmen also treated 370 cutaneous fungus infections and 106 cases of diarrhea that month. Hot showers, cold beer, and steak dinners were a little bit of heaven offered to those 2/9 grunts when they arrived back at Dong Ha.

Hunkered down inside Con Thien's perimeter, the 3d Battalion, 9th Marines had also endured the worst the NVA had to throw at them, short of an all-out ground assault. On October 4, MACV headquarters in Saigon announced that Operation Neutralize had broken the back of the month-long siege of Con Thien and that the enemy was in full retreat. Calling it a "Dien Bien Phu in reverse," General Westmoreland stated that the enemy had suffered "a crushing defeat," having some two thousand men killed.[13]

A heavy price had been paid in blood by the U.S. Marines and their attached units to hold Con Thien during the September siege. The combined total of Marines and corpsmen killed in action at The Hill that month was 140, which includes casualty figures from 2/9, 3/9, 2/4, 3/4, 2/12, 11th Engineers, amtracs, and Ontos. Well over a thousand Marines and their corpsmen were wounded, many more than once.

Precipitation still fell intermittently; otherwise, the weather was fair. On most days, visibility was excellent for spotting NVA artillery and rocket sites. Daily life on The Hill settled into routines only occasionally interrupted by incoming. With the easing of the constant tension and fear came humor, albeit twisted, but the Marines were finding a few things to laugh about again.

One evening, the following exchange of dialogue was heard over the 3/9 radio net: " . . . and tell your Actual to report over here ASAP, over."

"Roger dodger."

" . . . Listen up, Marine! You'd better start using proper radio procedure, or you're gonna find your ass in serious hot water! Do you roger *that!?*"

"Roger dodger, . . . sir. Out."[14]

Two tank crewmen were sitting outside their tank next to a bunker on the southwest portion of the perimeter. An incoming 60mm mortar shell exploded nearby with a loud *WHAM!* Both men dove head first into a nearby trench. Two grunts piled in on top of them. A second round impacted closer, twenty meters away. Two seconds later, another shell exploded ten meters away; and a fourth shell impacted only meters from their trench. An NVA mortar crew was walking the rounds in toward them. Terror wrenched their guts; they only had seconds to live! *Whoosh-BAMM!!* Another shell detonated a foot from the edge of the trench, showering the huddled men with mud.

As they lay there hugging the earth or the man under them, some cursing, some praying, another shell impacted near the bunker. Bright, whitish globs rained down on them like sleet. "My God! They're shootin' 'Willy Peter' at us!" screamed one of the tankers hysterically. Several of the men undoubtedly peed on themselves when they saw the white globs resting on their skin. After a moment of panic, they fully realized nothing was burning them. Peeking cautiously over the edge of the trench, they saw a punctured can of aerosol shave cream lying on the ground. It was many months before that particular tank crewman heard the last of the Willy Peter incident.

One bit of bad news troubled the support troops on The Hill, the ones who would remain behind when 3/9's turn in the barrel was over and another battalion replaced them. The word went out in early October that 1/9 was coming back—the infamous Walking Dead. "If it could go wrong, it would go wrong. Wherever they went, they stepped into the shit."[15] Unfortunately, that was their reputation. Deserved or undeserved, other Marines believed that to be true about 1/9. The support troops on The Hill were no different. Operation Buffalo was still too fresh in their memories. Just when it seemed that they might survive Con Thien and all of its horrors, a new twist of fate was going to place them right back beneath the sword of Damocles.

The 1st Battalion, 9th Marines had been at Camp Carroll since July 13, having been replaced at Con Thien by the 3d Battalion, 4th Marines after Operation Buffalo. Thoroughly decimated on July 2 at the Marketplace, 1/9 was gradually rebuilt into a viable Marine infantry battalion as their wounded were treated and returned. New replacements filtered in, resigned to having to fill slots left vacant by the dead or maimed Marines who had preceded them. Used flak jackets issued to them at company supply still bore blood stains left by the previous wearer—an ominous welcome aboard.

The former battalion commander, Lieutenant Colonel Schening, a cloud hanging over his head in the aftermath of Operation Buffalo, was reassigned as the USMC liaison officer to the Korean Marine Corps brigade. Schening's replacement, Lt. Col. John F. Mitchell, assumed command of 1/9 on September 25 and was ordered to make preparations for a return to Con Thien in early October. The actual relief of 3/9 by 1/9 would commence October 7.

September had been a grueling month for 3/9. They were not exactly sad to be leaving Con Thien's muddy, shell-cratered slopes. They had incurred losses of 27 Marines and corpsmen killed and 683 wounded (many of those wounds recorded were second, third, and even fourth Purple Hearts). One quad-fifty, one LVT, and two of the three observation posts were knocked out (OP#2 was demolished by direct hits four times). Even on their final, long-awaited departure day, as the tail end of 3/9's column departed through Con Thien's minefield exit and headed south along the MSR, their trial by fire was not over. Long-range

130mm artillery sniped at the column rear until they were well beyond Yankee Station.[16]

October 7, the long-awaited day of departure for 3/9, and the dreaded day of return to Con Thien by 1/9, was bright and sunny, with hardly a cloud in the sky. That was a mixed blessing for the Marines. Aerial observers circling overhead could better detect enemy guns firing in the DMZ, but no way could the exposed columns of Marines marching in both directions alongside the MSR hide from the ever-present NVA FOs.

Private Robert Brosa, a twenty-year-old machine gunner with Bravo Company, 1st Battalion, 9th Marines, had arrived in country after undergoing one summary court martial for insubordination and an Article 15 for disobeying a direct order. "I was a two-year 'J' reservist with an attitude," Brosa said later. Brosa remembered the first glimpse he had of Con Thien's muddy slopes: "Walking in was bad news. We suffered WIAs just getting there. I recall looking up at the hill, which was cluttered with debris; blown up, lopsided, falling over bunkers; huge stacks of equipment. It appeared at first nobody was home. Walking by, guys just looked at you, not a word. Barbed wire was everywhere. You knew this was a bad place. When Marines don't housekeep, it is not a good sign."[17]

Helmets and Flak Jackets
The XO of A/1/9 was 2d Lieutenant Ted Christian, nicknamed "Warthog" by his classmates at the Basic School because of his stocky build, pug nose, and acne-scarred face. He had come to Alpha in July, right after Buffalo, one of hundreds of replacements needed to replenish 1/9's losses. Lieutenant Christian had performed his job as platoon leader of 1st Platoon well and was recently made the company XO. His company commander, Capt. John A. Ryan, had replaced that hard-nosed warrior Capt. Albert Slater shortly after Buffalo.

Christian and Second Lieutenant Coan had lived across the hall from each other at the Basic School and were good friends, so when they bumped into each other by the south gate on October 12, it was a happy reunion. Alpha Company and Coan's tank shared the same portion of the perimeter.

Five days had passed since 1/9 had taken over The Hill from 3/9. The afternoon sun shone brightly in a cloudless, azure sky. No incoming had hit since early morning, and that was only a few 60mm mortar rounds landing by OP#3. An artillery fire mission was called in on two elephants spotted north of the Ben Hai, and that bit of bizarre news had the CP crowd buzzing.

Lieutenant Coan had noticed that some of the 1/9 grunts were walking around out in the open not wearing helmets or flak jackets. He walked over to the Alpha Company CP to recommend that Christian have his men keep their flak jackets and helmets on, no matter how quiet the day was. However, Coan was dismayed to find that both Christian and his CO, Captain Ryan, were standing outside their bunker, chatting with the battalion chaplain, and none of them were wearing flak jackets or helmets. He called Christian over to him. "Ted, this place is like living on a bull's-eye. The whole damned hill is ground zero. You guys are taking a big chance out sunbathing like that. Flak jackets and helmets at all times—that's the best way to make sure you stay alive up here."

"Yeah, sure, okay," said Christian. "This place is not so bad. We haven't seen nothin' yet to be that concerned about."

Coan walked away, rationalizing that they would learn after their first close call, and no one would have to remind them again about wearing helmets and flak jackets. He was a few feet from his tank when he heard *Wheeww-*BAMM!! A sharp explosion socked his eardrums as he dove for a nearby trench. A greasy black cloud of smoke hung in the air where he had just been moments earlier. A recoilless rifle airburst had detonated right above the Alpha Company CP. Despite the ringing in his ears, he heard the anguished cries for help: "Corpsman! Corpsman up!" A handful of corpsmen carrying stretchers sprinted in that direction. Knowing that one round of incoming was likely followed by another, Coan stayed put. Several spectators from 1/9 could not resist the temptation to see what havoc the mystery blast had wrought and rushed on over. *Wheeww-*BAMM!! Again, that evil black cloud of smoke hung in the air right where the first round had detonated. Counter-battery fire began as

81s, 4.2-inch mortars, and 105s started blasting back. Our FOs must have spotted the NVA weapon site.

An hour later, while hiking up to the battalion CP for the evening briefing, Lieutenant Coan happened to glance over and notice three blanket-draped bodies lying on stretchers outside the BAS bunker entrance, their jungle-boot toes pointing skyward. He recognized the watchband on the arm of one of the dead Marines. It was just like the one worn by his friend Ted Christian.

Coan inquired as to the dead man's identity. A nearby corpsman stated, "We don't know who he is. He didn't have no dog tags. He was with a bunch of guys that took a direct hit down by the south gate this afternoon." Coan lifted the blanket up slowly, dreading, but somehow knowing, what he might find. It was his friend, Ted Christian, his ashen-gray face frozen in that instantly recognizable look of death. He had been killed by the first airburst, and his company commander, Captain Ryan, had been critically wounded (Captain Ryan would succumb to his grievous wounds a week later). Corpsman Richard V. Smith and PFC James E. Canidate had been killed by the second airburst. Another half-dozen men had been wounded.

When the stricken Lieutenant Coan reached the CP bunker, Lieutenant Colonel Mitchell was standing alone outside the bunker entrance. He noticed the look on Coan's face and asked whether there was anything wrong. The lieutenant struggled to maintain a stoic demeanor as he quietly informed the colonel that he had just identified one of the dead Marines outside the BAS as Lieutenant Ted Christian. A look of pain crossed the battalion commander's face, and he spun abruptly on his heels, disappearing into his quarters. The CO's briefing was postponed until later that day.

The battalion S-2 was Capt. Henry Radcliffe, who had led the reaction force out to rescue Bravo Company on July 2 at the Marketplace massacre. Now he was cast in a similar role, taking over a company devastated by the sudden loss of its key leaders. Captain Radcliffe possessed a rare quality that distinguished the good combat leader from the outstanding. He could sense the grief and uncertainty that few men showed outwardly but that most of them felt. He and the company gunny went along the Alpha perimeter that evening, stopping to talk quietly with each Marine in the company, reassuring them and making sure they were okay. After the captain and gunny departed each group, they were all wearing their helmets and flak jackets.[18]

The TPQ Incident

A common experience at Con Thien was hearing the nighttime stillness broken by a sudden shrill whistle followed by several bomb blasts. Then, one heard the faint sound of a jet plane traveling away from the site of the bomb drop. Marines on watch during the night often noted secondary explosions resulting from the TPQ strikes and were in awe of their deadly accuracy.

Grunts on the northern perimeter were determined to do something about a little ritual the NVA had developed in recent weeks. Just after dusk, teams of NVA hidden in a tree line would fire a few rounds from a recoilless rifle or 60mm mortar, knowing they could pick up their weapons and run away before the grunts could locate them after dark. The remainder of the night was then usually quiet. On the evening of Friday the thirteenth, something went terribly wrong with a TPQ strike intended for that tree line.

Men on The Hill were winding down for the day, writing letters home by candlelight, reading, or otherwise preparing for another quiet night at Con Thien. Nocturnal incoming was a rare occurrence since the arrival of 1/9, so it was a good time to try to relax. The evening tranquility was shattered by the sound of a low-flying jet screaming overhead, followed immediately by four enormous explosions, shaking The Hill violently. Then, quiet . . . as if everyone on Con Thien had stopped to listen at once. The faint whine of a rapidly departing jet aircraft could be heard fading into the distance.

Private Robert Brosa and his friend Lance Jenkins ("a good Catholic boy from New Jersey") were standing outside their bunker smoking cigars when the bombs came down.

> The first blast literally blew me into the side of our bunker entrance, and the next bomb blast hurled me into the bunker. I never knew the sky could turn so red, so intensely, so quickly. All I suf-

fered was a few hours of deadhead. Lance wasn't so lucky. The concussion blew Lance over the bunker. He didn't know what planet he was on, or his name for that matter. Every time you asked him if he was okay, he'd say 'yeah,' then stare off into space. He came back to earth a few days later.[19]

Former sergeant Barry Lombardo was a squad leader with 3d Platoon of Delta Company on the northern perimeter that night. He recalled: "We heard the plane and then we heard the bombs. We immediately knew exactly what it was. I tried to drop to the bottom of my fighting hole, but when the bomb exploded it kind of lifted me up, and I landed flat on my back looking straight up at the sky. A dirt clod about the size of a truck came right down on my position. It missed."[20]

Capt. Francis L. Shafer, CO of Delta Company, was in his CP bunker when the bombs landed on his portion of the perimeter, lifting him off his cot and throwing him to the ground. He was horrified to learn that one bomb had landed near a 3d Platoon bunker. Several dead and wounded men were trapped inside. Another bomb had impacted in the minefield, scattering trip flares and unexploded mines all over Delta Company's area. Shafer yelled at everyone around him to start digging by hand, using anything they could find to attempt to rescue the trapped men. A bulldozer was brought to the scene, but even with the aid of that heavy equipment, it still took hours to reach the pinned men. By that time, corpsman George E. Slade and PFC Herman B. Gailliard were dead. Seventeen other Marines were injured, several critically.

Word began to fly around the perimeter that four TPQ bombs had accidentally landed inside the perimeter north of OP#2. The momentary shock passed, only to be replaced by disgust and then anger. That should never have happened. Who was to blame? Was it pilot error, or did the radar operator screw up? Then it began to sink in to the distraught Marines looking for answers. A scapegoat was unanimously divined—it was 1/9 itself. If any doubts still lingered in anyone's mind that 1/9 was a hard-luck outfit, they were permanently erased by this disaster.

The NVA had to have noticed the calamity that happened to 1/9 on the northern perimeter. A ground attack to take advantage of the breach in the perimeter's devastated defenses was a distinct possibility. The rest of Con Thien was placed on high alert, waiting to see what the NVA did in response to the accidental bombing. But nothing major happened at Con Thien. The NVA had other things to do that night; they were already in place around Washout Bridge, preparing for an all-out attack.

15

The "Magnificent Bastards"

Marines will do exactly what you expect them to do. If you expect them to do nothing, they'll do nothing. If you expect them to do great things, they'll do great things.

—Lt. Col. William Weise, former battalion commander, 2d Battalion, 4th Marines

The 2d Battalion, 4th Marines had been known as the "Magnificent Bastards" since World War II. The nickname was resurrected after they had decimated an NVA regiment two years earlier during Operation Starlite. Since their costly encounter at Phu Oc on September 21, having left fifteen dead comrades behind on the battlefield, morale was rock bottom. They were not feeling like they were magnificent—just plain, miserable bastards. The men of 2/4 had fought bravely and valiantly at Phu Oc, but that battle and the month of constant shelling and chilling rains had taken its toll, both on their spirit and on their numbers. From a "foxhole strength" of 952, the battalion was down to less than 500 effectives.

THE RECOVERY MISSION

The vital land route to Con Thien had to be kept open. The Marines needed assurance that the NVA had not returned to their old positions south of Con Thien. BLT 2/3, commanded by Lt. Col. Henry Englisch,

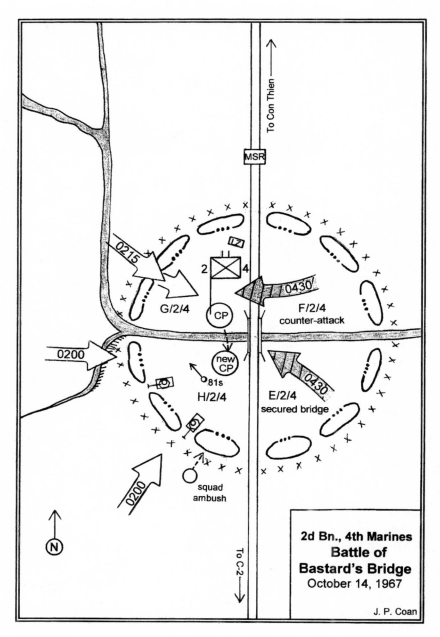

2/4 Battle of Bastard's Bridge

came ashore in early October to participate in a joint search-and-clear operation with 2/4. The BLT initially set up in a defensive perimeter around the Rocky Ford Washout, where engineers from the 3d Platoon, 3d Bridge Company, 11th Engineer Battalion had been hard at work for more than a week constructing a steel girder bridge that could support tanks.

At first light on October 4, after three days of artillery and air preparation, 2/4 and BLT 2/3 teamed up and swept through the often-contested, destroyed hamlets south of Con Thien: Thon Trung An, Thon An Nha, Nha Tho An Hoa, and Nha Tho Bai An. The NVA had obviously made a hasty retreat. A number of abandoned mortar positions were discovered with loose mortar rounds and powder-charge increments lying about. Outside of one abandoned bunker complex, the putrid odor of decaying human flesh led Marines from G/2/4 to a hastily dug gravesite containing the bodies of twenty NVA.

Good news awaited 2/4 at the end of their successful search-and-clear operation with BLT 2/3. The division commander had finally ordered a multibattalion attack on Phu Oc to recover their dead. On October 6, the attack commenced with a systematic, round-the-clock bombardment. Artillery and fixed-wing air strikes hit the area during daylight, followed by TPQs at night. BLT 2/3 and 2/4 were set to launch the ground attack with tank support on October 9, but torrential rains the evening of the eighth forced a postponement by one day to the tenth. Again, tank support had to be canceled because of the sodden paddy terrain.

On October 10, at first light, five hundred grim-faced grunts from 2/4 moved into position east of Con Thien for the attack on Phu Oc to retrieve their dead. Companies E and F of 2/4 crossed the line of departure at six thirty and attacked directly east toward Phu Oc. Company G followed in trace of Company E, though slightly to the north; their mission was to secure an LZ and protect Echo's left flank. An AO circled overhead, as all friendly artillery positions in range of the DMZ were poised to deliver instant counter-battery fire. BLT 2/3 was in position south of Phu Oc, prepared to counterattack if necessary, but this was intended to be 2/4's show. They had to be the ones to put their own dead in body bags.

The attack encountered little resistance, with only some sparse artillery and mortar fire resulting in a few casualties. The massive, ingeniously laid-out bunker complex, built to house a battalion, had been recently deserted. The Marines found several bunkers smashed by direct hits from bombs and artillery, but no sign of the NVA. Interconnected fighting positions and bunkers were situated so that their maximum observation and fields of fire were aimed directly west toward Con Thien. In that ill-fated sweep on September 21, 2/4 had walked right into the teeth of the complex.

Marines from each company claimed their own dead and completed the grisly task of placing the rotting corpses of their friends into body bags. One of the most distasteful chores of corpsmen and infantrymen is retrieval of their dead, especially after decomposition has begun, after the bodies have alternately cooked in the sun and then soaked in the rain for weeks. No eighteen- or nineteen-year-olds should have to endure that horror, but it had to be done. Especially tormenting was finding that the enemy had mutilated the bodies of their former buddies, who had once shared with them their hopes and dreams on returning to "the world." Cpl. Carlton Sherwood, a scout-sniper with G/2/4 recalled:

> The only time I ever took anything personally [the NVA] did was when we discovered that they'd mutilated the bodies of guys we left behind during the fight on September 21, 1967. They skinned one guy, took the USMC tattoo he had on his chest and displayed it on a tree trunk. There was no call for that sort of thing. We never did it to them. We didn't even collect ears from NVA corpses. That was just sheer meanness.[1]

On finding their fellow Marines mutilated, the battalion's hate for the NVA began to build. That suppressed rage corrodes the soul, as revenge is uppermost in everyone's mind, never far from their thoughts. Woe be to the unfortunate who is wounded or otherwise evacuated from the battlefield before he has had a chance to extract his revenge. His personal demons will fester and never give him peace. At the conclusion of the day, BLT 2/3 returned to their positions around Washout Bridge, and 2/4, in a collectively sullen, dark mood, moved back into their former location south of Con Thien.

BATTLE AT BASTARD'S BRIDGE

On the morning of October 12, BLT 2/3 vacated its positions around Washout Bridge and resumed its role as Special Landing Force (SLF) aboard ship. Lieutenant Colonel Hammond got the welcome news that his 2d Battalion, 4th Marines was moving out of the accursed Con Thien area at last and would replace BLT 2/3 at the Washout.

Initially, the drastically understrength 2/4 had difficulty manning the perimeter positions that the larger BLT had nearly two weeks to prepare. The perimeter had to be compressed accordingly. Two tanks from Alpha Company, 3d Tank Battalion came up from Charlie-2 to reinforce 2/4 and were integrated into the defense scheme.

The Washout stream, which was still chest deep and flowing fast, intersected the north-south MSR at right angles from west to east. A forest green steel bridge resting on two piers on either side of the stream was situated at the center of the perimeter. Thus, the perimeter was logically divided into four quadrants with a company assigned to defend each one. The ground on all four quadrants sloped gradually upward from the stream into bald knolls that leveled off at the top.

Company F occupied the northeast quadrant; Echo had the southeast. On the other side of the bridge, Hotel had the southwest quadrant, which included the 81mm mortars and the two tanks. The battalion CP and LZ were located in Golf Company's area inside the northwest quadrant.

For the remainder of the day, the men took turns bathing in the cold stream, washing off the mud and grime accumulated from a month of operations around Con Thien. Morale was markedly improved. Their next stop would be hot showers and chow at Dong Ha as soon as they were relieved of bridge security duty by the 3d Battalion, 3d Marines. Hopes were high that it would be only a few days. Some of the rocket men and grenadiers in Golf Company even had a little diversion that evening, target shooting at a burned-out tank retriever hulk sitting just outside their lines.

On Friday, October 13, 2/4 got familiar with the neighborhood. Company E patrolled east as far as Phu An, detecting no sign of the enemy. Golf Company sent a platoon patrol north all the way to Yankee Station, again finding no indications the enemy was in the area. However, Hotel Company's patrol to the southwest discovered an aiming stake near the church at Nha Tho Bai An, aimed directly at a tank in Hotel's portion of the perimeter. The two tanks were subsequently repositioned after dark.

A most welcome meal of steaks and cold milk was brought up to the Washout, courtesy of 3/4 at Charlie-2. Even more good news was the arrival of eleven new officers and several dozen enlisted replacements to add to the battalion's strength. Things were finally looking up for 2/4.

The newfound good cheer changed abruptly on the morning of October 14. At 1:25 a.m., two dozen artillery shells and rockets screamed in, impacting generally south of Hotel Company. Then, 82mm mortars fired from near Hill 48 dropped on Hotel's lines. A few minutes later, an ambush squad out in front of Hotel's lines reported NVA moving toward them and opened fire. The squad leader reported three friendly casualties and requested to bring his seriously outnumbered squad back into the perimeter. Capt. Arthur P. Brill Jr. ordered the squad to pull back and called for night defensive fires to interdict avenues of approach to his position.

At 1:55 a.m., just as the ambush squad reached Hotel's lines with their three wounded, a thunderous prep fire barrage of 150 mortar rounds fired from Thon An Hoa landed a few hundred meters west of the battalion perimeter. The firefight with the ambush squad had probably thrown the NVA off as to the battalion's defenses, because their expert mortar crews were rarely off target.

Marine sniper teams, using unmounted Starlight scopes, spotted a large group of NVA massing for an attack only fifty meters in front of Hotel Company. The sniper teams and two tanks opened fire, forcing the NVA to commence their attack prematurely. The rest of the company held their fire until the enemy entered a clearing twenty meters away and then slaughtered them in a murderous volley of small arms and automatic weapons. Rapid-fire 90mm tank cannister rounds delivered the *coups de grace* to the carnage. Only two NVA made it to the wire, and both were killed before they could crawl through.

The battered NVA company withdrew, leaving many dead behind, but the NVA were not finished. Fifteen minutes after the attack started on Hotel Company, enemy mortars found the range and commenced a punishing bombardment of Golf Company north of the stream. As the pre-assault barrage lifted, Company G's Marines peered over the edges of their fighting holes at the shocking sight of dozens of NVA charging directly at them out of the blackness.

PFC David A. Hamilton and PFC Gary C. Griswold were a machine-gun team with Golf. When the human-wave assault came toward the wire, Hamilton kept his machine gun blazing away, with Griswold feed-ing the ammunition. RPGs and automatic weapons fire erupted all around them. An enemy RPG round hit their position directly, wound-ing them both and knocking out their vital weapon. Ignoring their wounds, the two Marines joined in with their squad leader in vicious hand-to-hand combat, closing the breach in their lines before being fa-tally wounded by automatic weapons fire.

More concentrated RPG fire flashed out of the darkness, destroying another key machine-gun emplacement and several adjacent fighting po-sitions and opening a path through the wire. In all the confusion, smoke, and blinding flashes came the terrifying cry: "Gas!" The NVA had fired tear-gas shells, forcing the Marines to stop and don gas masks. The ef-fects diminished within minutes, but that was all the time the NVA needed to exploit their second breach in the wire.

Silhouetted by the light of 81mm illumination rounds, shadowy figures tossing satchel charges and spraying AK-47s on full automatic overran the Golf Company CP, killing the new CO, Capt. Jack W. Phillips, and his FO, 1st Lt. Bill Mullins. It was kill or be killed: hand-to-hand combat with rifle butts, bayonets, k-bars, e-tools, screaming, and cursing—total chaos. Two of the newly arrived platoon leaders, 2d Lt. Eric Egge and 1st Lt. Charles Yaghoobian, were also killed in the no-holds-barred melee.

Lieutenant Colonel Hammond ordered his S-3A, newly arrived Capt. James W. McCarter, to take over Golf Company. McCarter fought his way across fifty meters of hotly contested terrain to reach Golf's hard-pressed warriors. He had reestablished communication with his platoons and was consolidating their positions when an enemy grenade killed him.

In all the confused, hand-to-hand fighting, surviving elements of the attacking force had advanced to within hand-grenade range of the bat-talion CP. As Sgt. Paul H. Foster, a member of the battalion FSCC, continued to call in artillery and mortar fire missions around the perimeter, he was wounded by an enemy grenade. He continued to call down deadly accurate mortar fire on the attacking forces. Sergeant Foster then spotted another grenade rolling toward him and the six other Marines in the FSCC. He threw his flak jacket on the grenade and jumped on it. The blast mortally wounded him, but his heroic actions saved the lives of the other Marines. He was awarded the Medal of Honor posthumously. Also killed or wounded in the melee was the entire forward air control team. The battalion's chief corpsman was killed; the artillery liaison officer, headquarters commandant, and battalion sergeant major were all wounded.

At 3:50 a.m., Lieutenant Colonel Hammond made a command decision to order Foxtrot Company to counterattack west across the MSR into Golf's portion of the perimeter despite the potential threat of attack from the east. Company E was ordered to move a platoon to the bridge, engage any enemy who approached, and hold it at all costs. Then Hammond moved his CP south across the stream to the Hotel Company area.

At four thirty, Foxtrot Company jumped off in a counterattack, advancing across Golf Company's front. "Puff" and friendly artillery final defensive fires effectively blocked all NVA avenues of retreat or approach. Foxtrot's timely counterattack caught the retreating NVA attempting to drag off their dead comrades and retrieve weapons. In their haste to flee, the NVA dumped several bodies into the stream and ran.

At the coming of dawn, Lieutenant Colonel Hammond moved his command post back across the stream to its former position within Golf's portion of the battalion perimeter. Hammond was greeted by the gruesome sight of a dozen bloody NVA bodies lying sprawled on the ground within Golf's perimeter. Another eighty drag marks indicated the number of NVA dead hauled off.

One company from the 3d Battalion, 4th Marines at Charlie-2 arrived as reinforcements. They were emplaced around the bridge while Echo Company went outside the bridge perimeter in pursuit of the retreating enemy. Hotel Company also left on a hunt to the west, finding one wounded NVA and taking him prisoner.

The Marines found numerous footbridges crossing the stream where it divided north and south just outside the western portion of the battalion perimeter. Communication wire strung by sappers had led the attackers into 2/4's lines. The fresh condition of the uniforms and equipment indicated that the two attacking NVA companies were newly arrived in the area. Officially, 2/4 was credited with twenty-four NVA killed because that was the number of dead left behind. In reality, probably another one hundred paid with their lives in that all-out attack.

Company G, which had borne the brunt of the fighting, was now commanded by its only surviving officer, one of the new second lieutenants who had arrived the day before. The night's toll for 2/4 was twenty-one Marines killed and twenty-three wounded (evacuated).

The bridge had been saved from destruction by the valiant efforts of 2/4's Magnificent Bastards. They had borne the legacy of their nickname well that night. Lieutenant General Cushman, Major General Hochmuth, and the 9th Marines CO, Col. R. B. Smith, arrived by helicopter later that morning to survey the scene. In accordance with a request by Lieutenant Colonel Hammond, the new bridge was renamed Bastard's Bridge to honor the men from 2/4 who had lost their lives in its defense. Later that afternoon, Lieutenant Colonel Hammond turned responsibility for the bridge defense over to Lt. Col. Robert C. Needham's 3d Battalion, 3d Marines. After a month of combat, 2/4 would finally leave the field and return to Dong Ha for some much-deserved rest and rehabilitation.

The repugnant duty of administering the disposal of the NVA dead fell to 3/3. They laid the bodies on top of each other in previously dug fighting holes and then threw dirt in on top of them. But 3/3 had not seen the last of the grim reaper's handiwork at Bastard's Bridge. At about three o'clock in the morning on the fifteenth, another TPQ drop went astray with tragic results. A single bomb dropped silently out of the starlit night sky, exploding directly on 3/3's position. Four more Marines were killed, and six were wounded.[2]

"ONCE MORE UNTO THE BREACH"

The last major action of Operation Kingfisher occurred October 25–28. It would involve the much-used 2d Battalion, 4th Marines (minus Golf

Company, which was attached to 3/4) in a sweep west of Route 561 from Cam Lo to Con Thien. Regimental and division staff believed that the NVA were gearing up for another attempt to sever the MSR and possibly attack the Washout Bridge. The regimental frag order directed Lieutenant Colonel Hammond's 2/4(-) to sweep north, paralleling the MSR, while 1/9 at Con Thien and 3/3 at Washout Bridge would provide blocking forces.

At 6:00 a.m. on October 25, 2/4(-) moved north from Cam Lo. The battalion's objective was to reach Hill 48 southwest of the Washout Bridge area before dark. The distance from Cam Lo to the initial objective was a little more than three miles, which would ordinarily be easy for any infantry unit. However, thick and nearly impenetrable brush along the way slowed the battalion's progress. As they advanced slowly northward, a moonscape of B-52 bomb-churned earth between them and the mountains to the west was a constant, nagging reminder that they were out in what the Marines at the time called "Indian Country," that is, any forbidding, hostile territory. While 2/4 had been dealing with Viet Cong booby traps and snipers prior to their move north to the DMZ in September, other Marine battalions had been fighting battalion- and regiment-sized NVA forces in the same area they were moving into.

On September 10, 3/26 had tangled with the 812th NVA Regiment at Nui Ho Khe and Hill 48. Prior to that murderous encounter, the 3d Battalion, 9th Marines had fought large-scale battles in that same area during Prairie III in March, Hickory in May, and Cimarron on June 1. Lieutenant Colonel Hammond was blindly leading his under-strength battalion right into that same lion's den, where every square meter was targeted by NVA forward observers.

Just before dark, with his spent battalion about one thousand meters south of their day's objective, Lieutenant Colonel Hammond decided to halt and request an ammunition resupply. That was a calculated risk because the arriving helicopters would signal his battalion's location to the NVA. He decided to take the chance, however, because additional ammunition could partially compensate for the absence of Company G. Without Golf Company, his depleted battalion was not much larger in number than a reinforced rifle company. He believed logically that his battalion could accomplish its resupply and be on the way before the NVA could respond.

Hammond gambled and lost. Through no fault of the battalion commander or his staff, the rear-area supply types struck again. In addition to not getting everything they requested, 2/4 also received a lot of unnecessary ammunition and supplies they had no use for, including three pallets of tactical wire. Stymied by rear-area ignorance, Lieutenant Colonel Hammond would be forced to spend the night guarding the worthless junk-ammo pile.

The late-dusk arrival of helicopters did not go unnoticed by the NVA. They had every key spot in that area east of Nui Ho Khe preregistered. At eleven thirty that night, ten rounds of artillery smashed into the battalion perimeter. The battalion XO, Major John J. Lawendowski, was killed, and Lieutenant Colonel Hammond and two others were seriously wounded.

At three in the morning, Lt. Col. John C. Studt, regimental operations officer, was ordered to fly out to 2/4 the following morning and take command of the battalion. Instead, Lieutenant Colonel Studt went immediately to the Dong Ha airstrip and convinced Lieutenant Colonel Allgood to chopper him out to the battalion, despite the fog and inclement weather moving in.

The absent Company G arrived in the battalion perimeter the morning of the twenty-sixth, which was a welcome boost. But even with the addition of Golf Company, the battalion still had fewer than four hundred men, less than half the number a full-strength battalion should field.

Lieutenant Colonel Studt was unable to requisition helicopters to come back and retrieve the unwanted ammunition. Only emergency medevacs were authorized. Thoroughly frustrated, he decided to leave Foxtrot Company behind to guard the pile while the remainder of the battalion moved out toward its objective near Hill 48, which they reached by one o'clock in the afternoon. Before the battalion could organize its defensive perimeter, a barrage of 60mm mortars hit, wounding several men. An hour later, an even heavier artillery and mortar bombardment hit 2/4, followed by small-arms fire coming from the west and northwest. The Magnificent Bastards were in deep trouble again.

The Marines requested medevacs to evacuate priority casualties. Capt. Ronald D. Bennett, pilot of a Sikorsky UH-34D from HMM-363, responded to the call. Flying behind him was Capt. Frank T. Grassi. Captain Bennett and his crew knew the LZ was hot, but critically wounded men could die if they did not try to land. Bennett spun his UH-34 into a steep downward spiral, attempting to come down fast right on the LZ. Enemy tracers from several heavy machine guns zeroed in on the downward hurtling craft, ripping into the fuselage. Horrified grunts on the ground saw the tail pylon break completely off. The shot-up chopper crashed 150 meters outside the perimeter and then rolled over and burst into flames. Black smoke billowed into the sky. Captain Bennett and his crew chief, Corporal Clem, died in the crash. The copilot and gunner crawled out of the wreckage, badly injured but alive.

Captain Grassi felt compelled to help his section leader. He dove his craft down over the crash site, but NVA machine gunners found the range on him, too. Grassi, his gunner, and a corpsman were all hit. The uninjured copilot aborted the landing and wrestled his stricken craft skyward. He managed to limp back to C-2 and just clear the minefield before making a hard landing inside the perimeter.

Close air support had arrived on station, three flights of F-4B Phantoms and one of A-4s. The air liaison officer for 2/4, Captain James E. Murphy, was calling in air strikes in front of Company E when he saw Captain Bennett's helicopter go down. With his radio still on his back and armed only with his pistol, Murphy dashed out to the helicopter crash site, at times crawling through brush past groups of NVA soldiers. He reached the burning helicopter and pulled its two survivors to a concealed defilade position in some thick bushes. For more than an hour, Captain Murphy shielded them with his body as he called in air strikes to within fifty meters of the crash site.

A Marine A-4 came in and laid down a line of smoke. Under cover of the smoke screen, an Army Huey that happened to be in the neighborhood zipped in and landed. Captain Murphy disabled his radio and then carried both wounded survivors to the chopper. The gutsy Huey pilot was struck by small-arms fire during the rescue, but he managed to steer his shot-up bird to Charlie-2, where he, too, made a forced landing.

Captain Murphy would receive the Navy Cross for his remarkable feat of heroism that day.

Lieutenant Colonel Studt recognized the need for reinforcements. His mini-battalion was being attacked by a numerically superior NVA force and needed help. The 9th Marines ordered 3/3 at Washout Bridge to send two companies to the aid of 2/4.

Meanwhile, Company F had been left behind in a vulnerable position guarding the unwanted ammunition pile. Studt said to hell with that and ordered them to blow the ammunition in place and join the rest of the battalion. Try as they might, though, the engineers could not get their wet explosive charges to detonate. Exasperated after an hour of unsuccessful attempts, Studt ordered Foxtrot to forget the ammo and move out. He had the ammo pile in sight from his position and would be able to cover it by fire. Foxtrot was able to fight their way into the battalion perimeter before dusk.

The situation was quickly changing from bad to worse. NVA artillery and mortars were wreaking havoc as the Marines attempted to both dig fighting holes and return the enemy fire. Rain was pelting down, and the runoff was filling their fighting holes. A misty ground fog reduced visibility even further. Jumpy grunts from 2/4 opened fire on the lead platoon from 3/3 coming to join them. The two units engaged in a brief firefight before the mess got straightened out. Captain James Williams, S-3A for 2/4, was ordered to relieve a company commander who had "become irrational" when the order was given to keep everyone in their holes and consider anyone up moving as NVA and shoot them.[3]

Due to the chaotic situation, 3/3's two companies were never fully integrated into the 2/4 perimeter. They had to dig in and crouch in their water-filled holes within earshot of 2/4, with both 3/3 and 2/4 being shelled by enemy mortars and artillery and fighting off one probe after another. If anything good could be said about the situation, the positive aspect was that in all the confusion of trying to discern the good guys from the bad in the fog-shrouded darkness, the NVA were not able to figure out what the Marines were doing either.

Throughout the night and until two in the morning, the NVA dropped hundreds of mortars and launched one ground attack after another, probing here and attacking there, but Studt's people held together, throwing back every NVA attack. Friendly artillery boxed them in, undoubtedly saving them from being overrun. Casualties had begun to mount. Every time a medevac attempted to land, intense enemy machine-gun fire drove the helicopter off. A plan was devised that, on signal, everyone on the perimeter would open fire for a "mad minute." It worked long enough for one helicopter to zoom in and evacuate several emergency casualties.

After the NVA onslaught ceased about 2:00 a.m., the grunts could hear continued activity outside their lines as the NVA sunk meat hooks into their dead and dragged them away. At dawn, the Marines counted nineteen North Vietnamese bodies left behind. That was the body count sent up the command chain. After medevacs had carried away 2/4's seriously wounded, the remaining walking wounded and able-bodied grunts bagged up their eight dead and trudged wearily toward C-2. Medevacs came only for the wounded, not the dead.

Once the exhausted 2/4 Marines arrived back at Dong Ha, a head count revealed that a little more than three hundred men were still fit for duty in the battalion. The Magnificent Bastards had lost better than half their number in fierce fighting over the killing fields of Con Thien that September. A message received from Lieutenant General Cushman read in part: "2/4 has met and beaten the best the enemy had to offer. Well done."[4]

In retrospect, the Magnificent Bastards of 2/4 had defeated the enemy in three major battles over a six-week period in abominable weather conditions, always within range of numerous batteries of artillery ensconced within the DMZ. The September 21 battle at Phu Oc uncovered and subsequently deterred a sizeable enemy force poised for an attack on Con Thien. The Washout Bridge battle thwarted an NVA attempt to sever the main artery to Con Thien. Finally, the battle at Hill 48 revealed that General Giap's forces were still present in strength, posing a continued threat to the installation and ultimate completion of McNamara's Wall.

Operation Kingfisher ended on October 31 with the Marines claiming 1,117 enemy dead and 5 captured. Marine casualties were 340 killed and 1,461 wounded. Con Thien was still a dangerous place. Artillery, rockets, and mortars periodically shelled its cratered, muddy slopes. During the interminable nights, anxious Marines on the lines strained their eyes to peer through drizzle and fog, expecting to see the enemy at the wire at any moment. Resupply convoys headed up to Con Thien were always prepared for an ambush. A subsequent operation would follow on the heels of Kingfisher. Commencing November 1, the next operation would be called Kentucky.

PART SEVEN

KENTUCKY

Every Marine journeyed through each night in his own way, with stops at memories of home, plans for the future, and fantasy after fantasy where every chrome-plated deal worked. He lived in the sustaining world of a combat infantryman's imagination, shielded and reassured by the silent presence of another Marine in the trench beside him, or the next foxhole, whose dreams were probably interchangeable with his own.

—David Douglas Duncan, *War without Heroes*

16

Winter Battles: 1967–68

The fall-winter monsoon misery continued without letup. The badly battered North Vietnamese withdrew many of their units into DMZ sanctuaries for some rest and refitting. They had suffered an appalling number of casualties at the hands of the Marines that fall. General Westmoreland was quoted in the press as stating that the attempted siege of Con Thien had cost the NVA more than two thousand dead. For the Americans along the DMZ, it was war as usual—Dyemarker bunker building, endless patrolling, and dodging incoming—they did not get a break.

Periodic shelling attacks continued to plague the Marines, despite the ongoing efforts of Operation Neutralize. The NVA had endured a terrific pounding from air, land, and sea. Nevertheless, their persistence and determination to rebound after each setback were amazing to Westerners who could not fathom such dedication in the face of staggering losses. MACV staffers must have imagined that they were dealing with a multi-headed Hydra—slice off one serpent head, and two more took its place. "I never thought it would go on like this," once commented a bewildered Secretary McNamara. "I didn't think these people had the capacity to fight this way, to take this punishment."[1]

There were some notable successes, however. On October 16, in a stunning coup, 1/9's FAC ran a series of air strikes on an NVA position to the north that resulted in eleven secondary explosions. For the next several days, incoming on The Hill was noticeably infrequent. In early November, a devastating B-52 Arc Light strike fatally smashed the 812th NVA Regiment headquarters three miles southwest of Con Thien, forcing the few dazed survivors to retreat into North Vietnam. That unit was never heard from in the Con Thien area again.

GAINING THE UPPER HAND

Lt. Col. John Mitchell's 1st Battalion, 9th Marines conducted sweeps daily in all directions out of Con Thien but primarily to the northwest and southwest. Enemy troop sightings in those areas indicated that a well-used trail was being utilized to infiltrate small units south across the DMZ. Evidence of the enemy's continued presence was frequently encountered, such as freshly dug graves and empty harbor sites, but 1/9 made little actual contact until November 1, the first day of Operation Kentucky.

Elements of Delta Company had a brief firefight with an NVA unit one thousand meters northwest of Con Thien. They quickly gained the upper hand and overwhelmed the NVA, killing ten and capturing one. They were hot on the trail of the retreating enemy, having chased them through the trees for two hundred meters, when the AO overhead spotted something that brought Delta to an abrupt halt. A large force of NVA had set up an ambush and was waiting for them. Capt. Francis L. Shafer wisely held his Delta hard chargers back and then covered his company's withdrawal by supporting fires from Con Thien's 81s and 4.2-inch mortars.

NVA from the 803d NVA Regiment attempted to draw 1/9 into another trap a week later in almost the same location. Companies A and D, accompanied by a command group, departed the Con Thien perimeter at five o'clock in the morning on November 7 under cover of darkness. Moving quietly, Captain Henry Radcliffe's Company A established a blocking position one thousand meters west of Con Thien. Delta continued searching to the south.

Before Alpha could set up in position, their plan was interrupted by fifteen NVA who opened fire wildly and then broke contact and ran. They expected Alpha to pursue them because green, hard-charging Marine assault troops usually did when they caught the enemy's scent. Instead, 1/9 pulled the old "snowball fight" tactic on the NVA: lob one snowball high to the right and, while their attention was diverted in that direction, hit them with a low, hard snowball toss from the left.

Captain Radcliffe held Alpha back and made a visible show of preparing to pursue, while Captain Shafer's Company D stealthily approached the hedgerow into which the NVA had retreated and attacked unexpectedly from the south. The NVA, waiting in battalion strength for Alpha, had been caught totally off guard by Delta. A fierce three-hour battle ensued. Delta finally broke contact under covering fire provided by Alpha and supporting fires from mortars, artillery, and fixed-wing air strikes.

The battle had quickly turned into a rout. Lieutenant Colonel Mitchell's two companies claimed seventeen enemy dead and forty-two probables. Friendly losses were one killed and nineteen WIA (eleven medevaced). To first deceive and then engage an NVA battalion in a three-hour battle, while having only one man killed, spoke volumes about 1/9's success at renovation since Buffalo, as well as the direction and leadership provided by Lieutenant Colonel Mitchell and his staff.

Reports were filtering in from Allied agents that the NVA had designs on Con Thien again, with possibly an attempt to cut the MSR and overrun the base. The battle on November 7 had proved that the NVA were out there again in strength. The III MAF ordered a search-and-clear operation to be conducted around Con Thien.

Early on the morning of November 11, the 192nd birthday of the Marine Corps, BLT 1/3 moved out of its positions at Cam Lo and headed north toward Con Thien on Phase II of Operation Kentucky. The 1st Battalion, 1st Marines (two companies plus a command group) was on their right flank. The mission involved sweeping around the northern face of Con Thien from east to west in a spoiling attack to disrupt NVA plans in the area.

At 8:30 a.m., Company D of BLT 1/3 came at the Communists' notorious Phu Oc fortifications from an easterly direction, the enemy's blind side, and launched a skillfully orchestrated attack. In two sharp battles with the dug-in NVA, Company D killed thirteen of the enemy, ran off the rest, and destroyed the bunker complex they had rebuilt. A captured prisoner later told interrogators that his battalion had been secreted in the area for weeks awaiting further orders to attack Con Thien.

Those two decisive Marine victories on the seventh and eleventh in which two NVA battalions were soundly trounced went largely unnoticed in the press. But any plans that General Giap might have had for another attempt to isolate and overrun Con Thien that November had been thoroughly derailed.

Death of a General

Vice President Hubert Humphrey visited the 3d Marine Division headquarters at Phu Bai on November 1. After a flight over the division's area of operations, he landed at Da Nang, where he presented a Presidential Unit Citation to the 3d Marine Division for "extraordinary heroism and outstanding performance of duty in action against North Vietnamese and insurgent Communist forces in the Republic of Vietnam from 8 March 1965 to 15 September 1967."[2] After pinning the streamer on the division colors, the vice president proudly congratulated Maj. Gen. Bruno Hochmuth, division commander. It was the last official ceremony the general would attend. On November 14, General Hochmuth's UH-1E helicopter exploded in midair on a routine flight from Hue to Dong Ha, killing him and everyone on board.

The exact cause of the helicopter crash remained a mystery. An elite investigating team examined every inch of the helicopter carcass once it was ferried back to Phu Bai, and all maintenance records were looked at in great detail, searching for any clues as to the reason for the helicopter's demise. No official explanation was ever given as to the cause of the crash. Maj. Gen. Rathvon McC. Tompkins, holder of the Navy Cross as a battalion commander at Saipan during World War II, was tabbed to succeed Major General Hochmuth, who was the first commander of a Marine Corps division to be killed in action in any of our country's wars.

The 1st Marines Take Over

General Westmoreland had kept his word to the Marines. He seemed to recognize that the tactical situation in northern I Corps had made it nearly impossible to build the barrier and fight the enemy simultaneously with existing manpower resources. Westmoreland ordered the deployment of a brigade from the Army's 1st Cavalry north to the Da Nang area, which permitted Lieutenant General Cushman to move the 1st Marine Regiment from Da Nang north to Quang Tri Province.

After their disastrous first week on The Hill, the 1st Battalion, 9th Marines had finished out their remaining "time in the barrel" without any major setbacks. During their stay at Con Thien, the battalion had incurred losses of 14 Marines and corpsmen killed and 217 wounded. They claimed thirty-five NVA confirmed killed (seventy-two probable) and captured one POW.

On November 20, 1/9 turned over control of Con Thien to Lt. Col. Marcus J. Gravel's 1st Battalion, 1st Marines of World War II and Korean War fame and relocated to Camp Evans. The Walking Dead had seen the last of the Con Thien area for a while, but they would soon be going from a bad situation into one that was worse. In a few months, they would be headed up to Khe Sanh in support of the 26th Marine Regiment.

After the middle of November, with the marked lessening of pressure on Con Thien and Gio Linh, coanchors of the Trace, Dyemarker construction efforts accelerated. Incredibly, the minefield outside Con Thien's northernmost section of the perimeter did not contain any mines. This most vulnerable portion of the base, which had to be considered a major attack route for NVA ground forces because of their bases and fire support in the DMZ north of Con Thien, was the last portion of the perimeter minefield to be completed. Understandably, when the southern minefield installation had been undertaken the previous spring, incoming was infrequent. However, as the NVA came to recognize Con Thien's key role in the barrier plan, they had focused their attention there, making the cost of further minefield installation prohibitive in terms of American casualties.

Taking advantage of the monsoon fog and reduced visibility, engineers from the 11th Engineer Battalion under Capt. Randolph Brinkley worked feverishly from Thanksgiving to Christmas putting in the northern perimeter minefield. One grotesque obstacle had to be overcome. The common grave holding the bodies of the more than two hundred NVA killed in the abortive attack on May 8, 1967, was situated right in the middle of the minefield.

PFC Al Sansone was a "nail bender" with 2d Platoon, Delta Company, 11th Engineers, installing those deadly antipersonnel mines. He recalled that skeletonized appendages protruded whenever the engineers dug more than a foot beneath the surface. Heavy earth-moving equipment was used to scrape more dirt over the area, and the engineers put their mines in place right atop the mass grave site.

That much activity right under the noses of the NVA would have seen heavy enemy fire a month earlier. The 1st Battalion, 1st Marines were fortunate to have drawn the short straw to pick who went up to man the meat grinder at a time when the NVA were not focused on Con Thien.

With less incoming to contend with, the Marines had more time to think about the unpleasant side of life on Con Thien. The rat population was thriving. Dave Granger, one of only twenty-seven Marines from Bravo 1/9 who had walked out unscathed from the July 2 Marketplace massacre, recalled: "We had a real battle with the rats. They'd keep you from sleeping, they'd piss all over your gear, fight you when you confronted them—they were a real pain in the ass."[3]

Contests were held between neighboring bunkers to see who had trapped the most rats at night. Each morning, the previous night's catches were hung outside the bunker entrances like hunting trophies. Some enterprising Marines even devised a pool to make bets on how many rats would be killed overnight. Besides the rats, mud was another adversity the Marines had to endure. Cpl. Orley VanEngelenhoven of A/1/1 remembered his nemesis:

> The mud—it was just as much an enemy as the NVA. It just always worked against you, never worked tactically for you, or physically for you, or mentally for you, or spiritually for you. It was a constant bother, nagging at you; there was no relief. You wanted to stay clean, but there was no way. Avoid the mud as much as possible, don't succumb, don't give in, don't let it win. At Con Thien, the mud was cursed at more than the enemy.[4]

DYEMARKER BLUES

General Westmoreland was not satisfied with the effort the Marines were putting into making the barrier plan operational. At the end of October, he radioed General Cushman that he was unhappy with the quality control provided by III MAF during construction of the Dyemarker strongpoints and that the project had "not been accorded a priority consistent with its operational importance."[5]

Marine brass were taken aback at the general's seemingly unconscious perspective. For the previous two months, the Marines had been embroiled in some of the heaviest fighting of the war along the DMZ, further complicated by an early monsoon and a disastrous shelling attack on Dong Ha that had wiped out almost an entire ammunition dump and bulk fuel depot. Had the general forgotten that the MSR was washed out, that 3/9 and 2/9 had suffered more than a thousand casualties sitting on Con Thien to keep it from being overrun during the siege? And what about 2/4 being chewed up while going it alone in a series of major battles? Apparently he did, or else his higher-ups back in Washington, far removed from the realities of Vietnam, were putting pressure on him to get the barrier plan moving again.

The III MAF reacted to MACV's persistence by appointing Maj. Gen. Raymond L. Murray to develop a high-ranking staff team to oversee the entire barrier project. But Murray himself had expressed doubts about the project: "How in the hell were you going to build this thing when you had to fight people off while you were building it?"[6] Nevertheless, the Marines went full-speed ahead on the project again, once the enemy pressure slackened in mid-October.

By the end of the year, despite abominable weather conditions, the 11th Engineer Battalion had resurfaced the MSR with crushed rock and asphalt. Assisted by Marine infantry and Navy Seabees, the engineers had completed 167 SPOS bunkers, with another 234 ready except for overhead cover. More than 67,000 meters of tactical wire had been laid, and 120,000 meters of minefields had been emplaced.

Lt. Col. John Mitchell, 1/9's commander at Con Thien, later remarked that his engineer detachment showed enormous courage working in daylight hours, mostly in the open with heavy equipment. Mitchell further remarked that the engineer detachment at Con Thien suffered a higher percentage of casualties than his infantry Marines. Randolph Brinkley, former commander of Delta Company, 11th Engineer Battalion, recalled that, out of 156 men in his company, he incurred losses of 30 killed and 121 wounded during the September/October siege. Of those wounded, forty-seven received two or more Purple Hearts. He was one of only five engineers in the entire company to leave Con Thien unscathed.

Westmoreland was still not satisfied. In mid-December, after two trips to visit the DMZ fortifications, he was particularly unhappy with Con Thien when he saw that the bunkers there were built to house a nine-hundred-man Marine battalion rather than the typical four-hundred-man ARVN battalion that was scheduled to take over the base in the spring. General Westmoreland concluded that the Marines had "little experience in construction of fortifications and therefore lacked the know-how to establish them in the way I had visualized them."[7]

In a strongly worded memorandum to Lieutenant General Cushman, Westmoreland laid out in detail that each strongpoint was to be virtually impregnable. An ARVN battalion with supporting arms would be able to hold off an enemy division. He wanted the primary defense to be two-man fighting bunkers covered in hardened concrete, mutually supporting, and protected by dense wire and mine obstacles.

The Marine command was stung by Westmoreland's criticism. Contrary to Westmoreland and MACV, Marine generals had viewed the strongpoint bunkers as living areas for the troops, and the actual fighting positions would be located outside the bunkers.

There may have been some justification for General Westmoreland's concerns about the strongpoint construction. Marines were traditionally an offensive organization, and organizing defenses in depth was not their forte. Marine Corps generals perceived the barrier plan as a constant irritant, preventing them from conducting the pacification programs they truly believed had merit. And being tied down holding static positions prevented them from sending out more Marines after the enemy's infiltration routes and harbor sites.

Maj. Gen. Rathvon McC. Tompkins, the new commanding general of the 3d Marine Division, referred to the entire barrier plan as "absurd." He pointed out that the original barrier plan was designed to halt infiltration. By the time actual construction began, the NVA were established in force in the DMZ and supported by artillery. "It was perfectly obvious," said Tompkins, "that if there would be an incursion, it would be by NVA divisions and not by sneaky-peekies coming through at night." His boss, Lieutenant General Cushman, later admitted, "We just weren't going out getting everybody killed building that stupid fence."[8]

As if they did not already have their hands full, another firebase was deemed necessary for the 9th Marines to construct. This new firebase, labeled A-3, would be located approximately halfway between Con Thien (A-4) and Gio Linh (A-2) on the southern edge of the Trace. In order to secure the area prior to construction, three Marine battalions commenced search-and-clear operations on November 29. The ARVN were tasked with guarding the eastern approaches to A-3, primarily along Highway 1.

THE CHRISTMAS/NEW YEAR'S TRUCE HOAX

In mid-December, the 2d Battalion, 1st Marines, commanded by Lt. Col. Evan L. Parker Jr., took over responsibility for Con Thien's defenses from 1/1. Work continued on the bunkers as the Marines raced to reach the deadline for completion of the barrier strongpoint at Con Thien, also called A-4.

In a surprising turn of events, the North Vietnamese and Americans agreed on a holiday truce. For a twenty-four-hour period over Christmas, no hostile actions were to be taken by either side. Over the New Year holiday, a thirty-six-hour truce would be observed. The Marines at Con Thien took advantage of the cease-fires to put in eleven additional bunkers on the exposed north side of the perimeter and complete a trench line around the base of the most forward slope.

At the end of Christmas Day, Marines all along the DMZ had a few peaceful moments to reflect on home, think about family and loved ones, and pull out their short-timer calendars for the umpteenth time to recalculate the number of days they had left to serve in 'Nam. No one knows who started it, but sometime during the middle of the night, green flares and red star clusters could be seen popping up into the sky over nearly every firebase in northern I Corps. One former Marine engineer recalled: "The lifers were going nuts trying to stop us—they couldn't."[9] The view from Con Thien was especially spectacular that night.

We always had the irreverent few who made the holiday memorable in their own way. At the C-2 Bridge, where K/3/4 was responsible for guarding the bridge, Artillery FO Philip J. Stoner recalled the company supply man, Pancho, careening around the perimeter on his motorized "mechanical mule" vehicle with three other grunts, singing, "Jingle bells, shotgun shells, Charlie's in the grass. We wish you a Merry Christmas, and shove it up your ass!"[10]

Taking full advantage of the cease-fires and the cessation of U.S. air operations, the NVA were able to resupply all of their units. Over Christmas Day alone, aerial observers above the DMZ counted between six hundred and eight hundred military vehicles and boats transporting provisions and equipment south. MACV recorded 118 enemy violations over Christmas and 170 during the New Year's truce period. An old military cliché states that about 10 percent of the troops "don't get the word." That might explain a few of those incidents, but not this debacle. The U.S. command called both stand-downs a "hoax," recommending that any further cease-fires for Tet or the Vietnamese lunar new year be cut short.[11]

By the end of the year, 2/1 and the 11th Engineers had installed waterproof membranes over all of the completed bunkers at Con Thien. Dyemarker bunker construction had to meet rigid specifications. A "burster layer," usually steel airfield runway matting, was installed in the roof to detonate delayed fuze rounds. Sandbags had to be laid in a prescribed fashion, and then a heavy rubberized tarp ("membrane") was placed over the bunker roof for rain proofing. New German razor wire was also added to the perimeter's defenses. The Marines were feeling fairly secure as the new year began.

Within days, however, it became all too obvious that the cease-fire had permitted the NVA to restock their ammunition supplies completely. Once again, Con Thien was being bombarded regularly, though not with the same intensity experienced in September and October. On

January 5, a direct hit on the battalion CP by a 120mm mortar shell killed one Marine and wounded eight, including the battalion commander, Lieutenant Colonel Parker.

The Marines assigned to the 106s were fed up. It seemed to happen as soon as a mechanical mule–mounted 106mm recoilless rifle was set into its firing position for the night that the NVA dropped a half-dozen mortar rounds in on them. Some grunts came up with a ploy to outfox the NVA gunners. Right at dusk, some distance from their true position, they would mount a straight tree log between two sandbags as a dummy 106mm, making it readily visible on the skyline. They even hung a helmet on the back end to represent the breech. It worked. The NVA clobbered the decoy recoilless rifle with mortars almost every evening. They never caught on to what the Marines were up to.

For the next two weeks, the northern perimeter and its new minefield were blasted by incoming. The Marines housed on that portion of the perimeter went through hell as the NVA gunners, with their freshly stocked ammo bins, attempted to dismantle Con Thien's newly built defenses. The NVA fired on Con Thien twenty-two out of the thirty-one days in the month of January, averaging thirty rounds a day when they did open fire.

The battalion was anxious to leave Con Thien at the end of the month and rejoin their parent regiment because their thirty days on The Hill were up, but the battalion received the following bad news: "With the present enemy threat . . . the relief of 2/1 at Con Thien is postponed until after Tet."[12] Something major was coming down the pike. Allied intelligence had warned that Khe Sanh and bases along the DMZ, possibly Con Thien and Gio Linh, could expect to be attacked during the Tet holiday.

ACTION ALONG THE TRACE

As 1967 came to a close, MACV and III MAF began shuffling U.S. ground units throughout the I Corps Tactical Zone in a high-level plan named Operation Checkers. The primary purpose was to relieve 3d Marine Division units of the responsibility for covering the western approaches to the capital city of Hue so that they could focus their attention on northernmost Quang Tri Province. The presence of the 324B Division along the eastern half of the DMZ, the fact that the 325C Division was threatening Khe Sanh to the west, and the movement south into the DMZ of the 304th and 320th NVA Divisions were the main reasons behind all of this movement of Marine and Army units.[13]

By the end of December, the new firebase designated A-3 was taking shape in record time. Of all the Dyemarker strongpoints, A-3 was the only one actually developed from a plan and carried out to completion. All of the others, such as Con Thien (A-4), had evolved under several separate battalion commands and reflected responses to the immediate tactical situation being faced at the time. Keeping Marines alive was the highest priority. Had MACV demanded that the Marines follow the original Dyemarker completion schedule for Con Thien that fall, few engineers or Navy Seabees would have survived to see that project completed.

The Marketplace Revisited

Lt. Col. Lee Bendell's 3d Battalion, 4th Marines left behind its cozy, dry Dyemarker bunkers at Charlie-2 in December to become one of three Marine battalions tasked to secure the new A-3 area between Con Thien and Gio Linh. In mid-January, Lieutenant Colonel Bendell relocated his battalion to An Phu, an abandoned, destroyed hamlet along the Trace and three thousand meters east of Con Thien. Recent probing actions along Con Thien's perimeter indicated another enemy buildup in the area, and this required Marine ground forces to flush them out.

In the misty predawn darkness of January 18, a two-company operation, with L/3/4 as the sweep company and M/3/4 as the blocking force, set out across the Trace and headed into the bombed-out no-man's-land northeast of Con Thien. The planned route would take Capt. John D. Carr's Lima Company through the infamous Marketplace area east of Route 561. The 2d Battalion, 9th Marines had fought a fierce, daylong battle at nearby Gia Binh six weeks earlier on November 30. However, the 3d Platoon of Lima, led by 2d Lt. Kenneth L. Christy, had patrolled through that same area recently and had not seen any signs of the enemy.

Company M, commanded by Capt. Raymond W. Kalm Jr., and a battalion command group set in their blocking positions amid the shrub- and tree-covered woods at Gia Binh. The first hint that something was amiss occurred at a quarter of nine that morning. A group of five NVA was observed to move hurriedly south across Mike's front and disappear into a tree line.

At a quarter of ten, just east of the Marketplace, the point platoon from Company L was attacked in a devastating ambush. In a manner eerily reminiscent of Bravo 1/9's July 2 massacre, NVA in skillfully camouflaged bunkers and spider holes opened up on the 1st Platoon with scattered small-arms fire. The Marines went to ground quickly to return fire, but tall grass blocked their view of the enemy positions. Lieu- tenant Thomas J. Hoare Jr. deployed his 1st Platoon to attack what was first believed to be an enemy squad. As the volume of enemy fire in- creased, Hoare's platoon then assumed they were up against an enemy platoon. Too late, the surrounded 1st Platoon found itself cut off from the rest of Lima and then divided into isolated groups under heavy at- tack by a reinforced NVA company. Lima's Captain Carr managed to link up his 2d Platoon with the rear squad from 1st Platoon, which had taken cover in a large bomb crater, before NVA artillery and mortars commenced shelling the pinned-down Marines.

Captain Carr ordered Second Lieutenant Christy to bring his 3d Pla- toon up. In a wild 180-meter charge, Christy led his platoon forward under heavy automatic weapons fire, leapfrogging by fire-team rushes from bomb crater to shell crater, until they reached Captain Carr. Mi- raculously, none of Christy's men were hit.

The NVA were using the two cutoff squads from Second Lieutenant Hoare's platoon as bait. The proximity of L-1's dead and wounded to the NVA positions ("hugging the belt") prevented the Marines from calling in air strikes to help break contact.

An artillery FO, Lance Cpl. Michael Madden, had been with the point platoon when the ambush commenced. He was pinned down in a bomb crater, still calling in artillery fire missions and directing Huey gunship fire on the NVA positions, when an AK-47 bullet struck a glancing blow on his forehead. Temporarily blinded by concussion from the bullet's impact, he continued calling in artillery fire missions, adjust- ing fire through his sense of hearing. Hospital corpsman Jeffrey Scott

Aker was shot and killed right in front of Madden while attempting to crawl out to aid his wounded Marines in the bomb crater.

Captain Carr ordered 2d Lt. Ken Christy to accompany him and take a squad forward to retrieve the dead and wounded so they could medevac them and get out of the area. Carr, Christy, and his squad sprinted through a deadly cross fire of small arms and automatic weapons to reach 1st Platoon. While Captain Carr covered him with his shotgun, Christy located four seriously wounded Marines in a bomb crater; one of them was the blinded Lance Corporal Madden. He lay on top of Madden to protect him from mortar and artillery shrapnel while he bandaged his head, and then he tied Madden's wrist to another wounded Marine's ankle and had them low crawl back to safety.

Christy then spotted the 1st Platoon commander, 2d Lt. Tom Hoare, lying dead fifty meters to his front. Braving a hailstorm of enemy fire, he charged to his side and hoisted the two-hundred-pound body of his friend across his shoulder and then reached down and retrieved a fully loaded M-60 machine gun. The adrenaline-charged Christy backed out of the kill zone carrying Lieutenant Hoare, pouring deadly accurate fire from the machine gun into the NVA positions. The heroic actions of Second Lieutenant Christy, plus the continuous artillery fire missions raining down on the NVA, allowed Christy's squad to retrieve all of 1st Platoon's dead and wounded.

By this time, reinforcements from India 3/4 and a company from 3/3 at A-3 had arrived on the scene, securing the flanks of Lima and Mike. Huey gunships circling overhead rained hot lead down on the NVA, who refused to give up the fight. A UH-34 medevac helicopter lifting off from Lima's LZ with four wounded was hit by ground fire and forced to crash-land at A-3. Though badly shaken by their close call, all aboard survived.

Shortly after noon, Lieutenant Colonel Bendell and his command group accompanied Mike Company as they moved forward to link up with the heavily engaged Lima. The AO overhead gave directions to assist Mike Company in negotiating the rough terrain. Small pockets of NVA were hidden in bomb craters between themselves and Lima. The AO aided Mike Company by pinpointing those positions with marking rockets. Once the linkup was made with Lima, the two companies overran three enemy mortar positions and several machine guns, forcing the surviving NVA to flee north.

Lima and Mike companies had sustained casualties of nine dead and twenty-two wounded. Enemy casualties were 116 KIA and another 46 killed by supporting air. What had started out as another well-orchestrated Marketplace ambush turned into an NVA slaughter.

Captain Carr had been seriously wounded by mortar fragments during the withdrawal and was evacuated. Lance Corporal Madden regained his eyesight and was awarded a Bronze Star with Combat V. Second Lieutenant Christy would not be officially recognized for his acts of heroism that day until twenty-six years later. On March 25, 1994, then-Colonel Kenneth L. Christy Jr. was presented with the Navy Cross by Brigadier General Lawrence H. Livingston, commanding general of Camp Lejeune, North Carolina.[14]

Renewed Pressure on Con Thien

Increased enemy activity along the Trace and intelligence reports of a major enemy buildup in the Khe Sanh area had MACV and III MAF concerned. General Westmoreland reluctantly agreed with Lieutenant General Cushman's request to suspend further work on the barrier until the enemy's intentions could be fully ascertained.

On January 21, the 2d Battalion, 1st Marines was hit by the heaviest bombardment since they had arrived at Con Thien in mid-December. Shortly after noon, 100 rounds of 82mm mortars and 130 rounds of 152mm "bunker busters" bombarded The Hill, killing two Marines and wounding sixteen. Thirty minutes later, Companies F and G were on a sweep one thousand meters north of the base when they ran into a company-sized force of NVA. A firefight developed, but the NVA pulled back under covering fire from their 60mm mortars. The Marines had losses of two men killed and eight wounded in that fight.

The NVA bombarded Con Thien again the night of January 23. Just before midnight, sixty rounds of mixed 60mm and 82mm mortar fire and ten rounds of 152mm artillery landed inside the Con Thien perimeter, wounding six more Marines. Real alarm began to be felt along the lines and in the foxholes that a major ground attack was coming any day.

On January 29, the value of holding Con Thien was validated once again when an NVA convoy was observed moving above the Ben Hai after midnight. The FO called in air and artillery. Flashing up out of the blackness, four or five SAM missiles fired from the DMZ launched hot on the trails of the American jets. The FO immediately ran a TPQ bombing mission on the SAM site. Nine secondary explosions and a huge fireball lit up the night sky.

As January drew to a close, Allied intelligence had indications that the enemy was poised to do something unusual over the Tet holiday. Reports trickled in from districts all over South Vietnam that should have sounded the alarm to put all American and South Vietnamese forces on alert. But Allied intelligence was unable to connect the dots and deduce that an all-out attack was coming. Besides, General Westmoreland was convinced that this increased enemy activity was only a ploy to shift attention away from the enemy's real target—Khe Sanh.

The CIA's station chief in Saigon, John Hovey, had warned of a major attack coming during Tet months earlier, but he was first discounted and then ignored. Hovey's superiors at Langley were skeptical, and the "number crunchers" at MACV and in Washington did not even remotely consider Hovey's warnings as having any credibility. His doomsday scenario did not fit with the universally shared, politically correct belief that the NVA/Viet Cong were a beaten army—the Americans were winning the war.[15]

17

After Tet

To say that we are closer to victory today is to believe, in the face of evidence, the optimists who have been wrong in the past. It seems now more certain than ever that the bloody experience of Vietnam is to end in a stalemate.
—Walter Cronkite, *CBS Evening News,* February 27, 1968

PHASE II: THE TET OFFENSIVE

Phase I of the "General Offensive, General Uprising" had met its objective of drawing U.S. forces away from the major population centers and into the remote mountains and borders of South Vietnam, especially the DMZ and Khe Sanh. According to the plan, the Viet Cong would have an easier time infiltrating South Vietnam's major cities when the right moment came to initiate Phase II, the takeover of population centers and attacks on ARVN and U.S. bases and communications facilities.

North Vietnam's generals at the DMZ Front Headquarters had to be pleased. The entire 3d Marine Division was moving north. Major General Tompkins, commanding general of the 3d Marine Division, had relocated his division headquarters from Phu Bai to Dong Ha.

As 1968 began, the Operation Kentucky area, which encompassed all of Leatherneck Square, was the responsibility of the 9th Marines. Defending Con Thien was 2/1; 1/4 held down C-2 and C-2 Bridge (C-2A); and 2/9 was at C-3 and C-3 Bridge (Cam Lo). Strongpoint A-3 at the Trace was defended by 3/3. Lieutenant Colonel Bendell's 3d

Battalion, 4th Marines was moved from the Trace to Camp Carroll at the end of January, replacing the 1st Battalion, 9th Marines sent to Khe Sanh to bolster the 26th Marines in Operation Scotland.

All of those moves were part of Operation Checkers. Battalions were hopscotched around in an effort to meet the recent threat posed by the large numbers of North Vietnamese forces moving into areas along Route 9 and around Khe Sanh and the Qua Viet.

Tet Nguyen Dan, the lunar New Year holiday, came on the last day of January and was traditionally a happy time of celebration for the Vietnamese people. Tet was like our Fourth of July, Thanksgiving, and Christmas all rolled into one. The Viet Cong announced a countrywide Tet truce from January 27 until February 3. Following suit, the South Vietnamese also offered a Tet cease-fire but only for thirty-six hours commencing on January 29. The I Corps was exempted from the cease-fire altogether due to recent intelligence reports that large numbers of NVA were infiltrating southward into I Corps. The recent Christmas/ New Year's truce fiasco was still fresh in the minds of the Allies. Few had any great expectations that this new truce would last.

On the night of January 29, any delusions of a Tet truce were rudely shattered. In a series of devastating strikes, first Da Nang was attacked, followed the next day by the ancient imperial capital of Hue, and then Quang Tri City. All major cities, provincial capitals, and district headquarters throughout South Vietnam were attacked by the NVA and Viet Cong during the Tet "truce." The Americans, largely ignorant of Vietnam's history, had assumed Tet was a peaceful holiday. That was not always the case; in a famous battle in January 1789, the Viets defeated a Chinese army and drove it out of Vietnam during Tet.

At 2:15 a.m. on February 2, the Cam Lo District Headquarters compound, located astride Route 9, was assaulted by two battalions of NVA plus a sapper company. The compound was defended by an understrength platoon of Marines—two squads from D/1/4 and a squad from E/2/9—and a Combined Action Program squad, a handful of combat engineers, some Popular Force Vietnamese, and a contingent of U.S. Army advisors. The enemy force was gunned down and blasted by artillery before they could penetrate the wire. At first light, a Marine armor/

infantry counterattack from C-3 and Cam Lo Bridge routed the attacking force. The official body count was 111 NVA/VC killed and 34 captured. Corporal Larry L. Maxam from D/1/4 was awarded the Medal of Honor posthumously. The district's deputy senior advisor, U.S. Army Capt. Raymond McMaken, said later, "The Marines just stacked them up on the wires. They were magnificent."[1]

After all of the warnings and preparations for an imminent attack somewhere along the Trace, the actual Tet truce period was anticlimactic at Con Thien. The pre-Tet pressure along the Trace had been a ruse to direct attention away from the real intended targets of the Tet Offensive, South Vietnam's major population centers and military bases. Other than the usual occasional shelling at Con Thien and Gio Linh, the Tet holiday passed by rather quietly along the Kentucky portion of the DMZ.

In the aftermath of the Tet Offensive, the battle for Hue City ended after twenty-six days of violent, bitter battle. The U.S. Marines combined with South Vietnamese military forces to win a decisive victory over the North Vietnamese invaders at Hue. The battle for Khe Sanh was still raging without letup, however. Despite the welcomed arrival of close-in B-52 strikes, enemy trenches were inching closer and closer to the perimeter wire with each passing day.

The American military took stock of what had transpired during the Tet Offensive and realized that it had been a disaster for the enemy, particularly the Viet Cong, who had lost tens of thousands of their most dedicated cadre in that ambitious surprise offensive. But the news media's perception of Tet was that it exposed America's military presence in Vietnam as a total failure, a house of cards, weak and vulnerable to attack. Thus, the Tet Offensive was a strategic psychological victory for the North Vietnamese despite being a staggering tactical defeat. At worst, the media pundits proclaimed, America was losing the war. At best, it was a stalemate. The old Pentagon rallying cry that "we can now see the light at the end of the tunnel" became a myth no longer believed by most Americans. Voices rang out loudly in Congress and in the halls of academia that America should cut bait and get out of Vietnam.

Many years later, one of North Vietnam's senior generals, Tran Do, admitted that "in all honesty, we failed to achieve our objective, which was to start a general uprising in the South. As for making a propaganda impact in the USA, it had not been our principal intention—but it worked out as a very fortunate result for us."[2]

At the end of February, a broken and distraught secretary of defense, Robert McNamara, attended a farewell luncheon given in his honor at the State Department. He astonished those present as he spoke tearfully of "the futility, the crushing futility, of the air war." Perceiving him as a growing liability, President Johnson had covertly arranged for the emotionally deteriorating McNamara to take over the presidency of the World Bank. McNamara later admitted he did not know whether he had been fired or whether he had merely been reassigned, because he learned of his sudden removal from Johnson's cabinet in the press. A trusted Johnson crony, Clark Clifford, took over as the new secretary of defense. McNamara's sudden departure was the first nail in the coffin for Operation Dyemarker.[3]

Turkey Shoot at the Trace

In mid-March, Lt. Col. Edwin A. Deptula's 1st Battalion, 4th Marines took over responsibility for The Hill from the 2d Battalion, 1st Marines. Deptula's battalion also assumed responsibility for Yankee Station and the C-2 Bridge. A former rifle platoon leader in Korea, Lieutenant Colonel Deptula was a taskmaster of a Marine officer. He was wiry, rawhide tough, and perhaps lacking some of the polish of the Naval Academy stereotype, but no nonsense when it came to getting the job done right.

Life on The Hill had improved significantly since the bad days of fall 1967. Men shared dry, roomy Dyemarker bunkers; fifty-five-gallon steel drums filled with rainwater provided crude showers. Some bunkers even had electricity powered by generators. Most remarkable was the lack of incoming. Entire weeks passed with nary a single round. And the infernal mud had dried up. Patrolling around Con Thien in April was routine business as usual, that is, occasional snipers and a few abandoned bunkers but no serious contacts. Still, Con Thien could still be a hellish venue for danger and death without warning.

On the first night 1/4 spent on The Hill, a freak accident befell a mortar crew. While unpacking equipment from a trailer and setting up in the new position, someone accidentally struck a box of primers, setting off the propellant charges in a roaring flash of fire. Four mortarmen were horribly burned before nearby grunts responding to their screams of agony were able to extinguish the flames.

In another fluke incident, the early morning quiet was shattered by the shrieking sound of an incoming missile, followed by an earthshaking blast near the counter-battery radar bunker by OP#3. A five-man working party filling sandbags outside the bunker had taken a direct hit, killing or maiming them all. Some Marines said the rocket had been launched from a delta-winged jet, leading them to believe initially that a MIG-21 had done it. Later investigation revealed that an American jet fighter-bomber's radar-detecting equipment had picked up a signal from Con Thien and mistakenly interpreted it as coming from a SAM site. The counterfeit signal originating from the high-tech counter-battery dish had inadvertently bounced a radar signal skyward off of a nearby pile of old discarded concertina wire, which is precisely where the air-ground missile impacted.

During the end of April and first three days in May, BLT 2/4 and the 320th NVA Division, in one of the major battles of the Vietnam War, tangled in the village of Dai Do, twenty-five hundred meters north of Dong Ha. Units from the South Vietnamese Army and U.S. Army fought alongside the Marines and ultimately decimated two NVA regiments. Thinking he had seen the last of the enemy for a while, Maj. Gen. Rathvon McC. Tompkins stated that "the 320th NVA Division would not pose a serious threat to the allied positions along the DMZ for some time to come."[4] The general's opinion was unfortunately myopic. Shortly after he was replaced by Maj. Gen. Raymond G. Davis as commander of the 3d Marine Division on May 21, the 320th was on the move south again.

Capt. Matthew G. McTiernan had recently assumed command of India 3/3. On May 22, his company left the perimeter of the Trace firebase at A-3 before daylight and headed southwest to establish a series of ambush positions along the TAOR borderline separating 1/4 at Con Thien from 3/3 at A-3. The NVA always seemed to know how to take advantage of such a seam and use it as an infiltration route.

India bumped into what they thought initially was a small NVA patrol but turned out to be at least a company. Captain McTiernan called for reinforcements, and the helicopter gunship support overwhelmed the enemy. The NVA, on the move and caught off guard, had no prepared positions from which to defend themselves. They withdrew and headed west toward Phu Oc in a desperate attempt to escape certain annihilation.

That same morning, a patrol from Alpha 1/4 searching the woods east of Con Thien had encountered an enemy unit of unknown size. A sudden wild firefight developed. As the intensity of enemy fire increased, the outnumbered Marines prudently chose to fall back toward their company lines at the Trace. The NVA were apparently up to their old tricks again in Leatherneck Square.

To exploit this contact further, Bravo 1/4, located at Yankee Station just outside of Con Thien, was loaded aboard eight Marine tanks. The mounted tank/infantry force roared east along the Trace, halting where it intersected with the former Route 561, two klicks from Con Thien.

The scheme of maneuver had Capt. Robert E. Harris align his Bravo Company from the edge of the Trace south along the tree-shaded, narrow dirt road shown as Route 561 on their maps. They would then attack east toward Captain McTiernan's company from 3/3 out in Leatherneck Square, trapping the fleeing NVA between them. Bravo's grunts, keyed for the hunt and sensing the kill, disembarked eagerly and proceeded to their line of departure. The tanks set in alongside Alpha 1/4, nestled among the trees at the southern edge of the Trace, awaiting any of the flushed NVA quarry who attempted to escape the trap and flee north across the Trace.

Unbeknown to Captain Harris and his Company B Marines, a reinforced company of NVA was hidden in a heavily fortified bunker complex north of Phu Oc, the scene of one bloody battle after another the previous year. The Marines had a short memory when it came to the Phu Oc area. Captain Harris would blindly lead his unsuspecting Marines into a murderous L-shaped ambush.

Once they were formed up along the road, Company B commenced the attack at 4:10 p.m., heading directly east through dense thickets and thickly vegetated hedgerow country toward Phu Oc. The lead platoon was commanded by 1st Lt. Victor David Westphall III, who was from

Albuquerque, New Mexico. Lieutenant Westphall was twenty-eight, a squared-away, recruiting-poster kind of junior officer, and highly respected by his young Marines. He had served a four-year hitch as an enlisted Marine before returning to graduate with honors from the University of Montana. He then rejoined the Marines to attend OCS. An honor graduate of the Basic School, First Lieutenant Westphall was one of the elite few selected for Recon Marine training at Camp Pendleton. After successfully completing that course, he had arrived in country in October, hoping for a coveted recon assignment, but was instead assigned a grunt officer billet in B/1/4. He had performed admirably, leading his platoon successfully for seven months. Westphall was a warrior, well versed in the art of DMZ warfare.

Captain Robert E. Harris, the thirty-three-year-old company commander from Russell, Kentucky, also a former enlisted man, had even more time out in the bush. Captain Harris had been warring for more than a year and was due to rotate home in less than a week. Staying true to his character, he would never opt out of a battle where his men were involved. He requested to go along on this operation and shadow his replacement, just to ensure that the new Bravo CO got properly schooled. May 22 would be his final battle and last day on this earth.

A disciplined force of NVA, crouched in their expertly camouflaged bunkers with firing apertures barely above ground level, gripped the triggers of their AK-47s and RPD machine guns tightly, watching the spread-out Marines from 1st Platoon cautiously traverse the open paddies to their front. They waited until the unsuspecting point men from Bravo were only a dozen yards away and then opened fire on command with a roaring fusillade of deadly missiles tearing into the shocked Marines.

Lieutenant Westphall, reacting instantly, sprang forward, intending to direct his platoon's return fire. He was ripped up the left side of his body by a burst of machine-gun fire, which killed him instantly.[5] His loyal-unto-the-death radioman, Lance Cpl. Charles Kirkland from Missouri, had followed right on Lieutenant Westphall's heels and was killed in the same burst of fire. Captain Harris rallied a group of Marines and attempted to lead a charge into the teeth of the enemy fortifications. He too fell dead, shot in the back by one of his own men. Then 82mm mortars dropped down on the two remaining squads of pinned-down 1st Platoon, adding to the carnage.

Bravo's 2d and 3d Platoons fought back valiantly. They managed to form up into a cohesive defensive posture and fight off several attempts by the NVA to launch an attack into their lines, all the while being pounded by enemy mortar fire. After only twenty minutes, from 5:20 p.m. to 5:40 p.m., every officer, radioman, and staff NCO in Bravo Company, except for two, were lying dead or wounded in the paddy grass.

As Company A and the 1/4 command group double-timed south from the Trace toward the ambush site, they too came under heavy 82mm mortar fire. Alpha's FO team finally got counter-mortar fire going, and that suppressed the enemy mortars. The tanks alongside Alpha laid down a blistering covering fire with their machine guns and 90mm cannister shells, enabling Alpha to close with the enemy and gain the upper hand in a wild, brutal, anything-goes brawl.

By seven thirty, it was growing dark. Alpha and Bravo were able to retrieve their wounded and some of their dead and break contact with the enemy for the night. Company A had incurred losses of two men killed and seven wounded medevaced. Bravo Company had twelve men killed (six bodies had to be left behind), nineteen wounded medevaced, and two missing in action (later accounted for). Two PRC/25 radios from Bravo were lost, compromising both the company and battalion frequencies. Company B claimed fifty-two enemy confirmed killed, plus one captured heavy machine gun, several light machine guns, three 60mm and two 82mm mortars, and twenty-eight rifles.

The lifeless body of Capt. Robert E. Harris was placed atop one of the tanks gently and with deliberate, even exaggerated, care by his men. They turned away in anger, disgusted and unable to make eye contact, when they heard the rumor that the M-16 bullets that ended their captain's life were not fired by accident. Apparently, some heartless, psychopathic cretin had seen the opportunity to collect on an old hit contract that some other twisted individual had put out on the captain many months earlier. Such was the warped value system of a few highly trained teenage killers who had seen too much death and dying and who knew full well that they were also doomed.

In the brutal and unforgiving kill-or-be-killed world of combat infantrymen, who trudged through each day like human beasts of burden, the grim reaper's hooded visage lurked just out of sight behind the next hedgerow, the next paddy dike, waiting to snuff out their young lives. A primal instinct for survival inevitably surfaced, and *anyone* who was perceived as preventing them from reaching that goal of survival must be eliminated. Somehow, in a cruel, twisted, perverted way—like it or not—the grunts understood that harsh reality.

The May 22 attack by 1/4 had not gone well. The NVA were out in Leatherneck Square again in force, determined to attack any Americans who came their way. Colonel Richard B. Smith, the 9th Marines CO, believed that at least a battalion of NVA was in his Kentucky sector. The following day, he asked permission of General Davis to release the 3d Battalion, 9th Marines from operational control of the 4th Marines, and they were lifted by helicopter into blocking positions south of Phu Oc. The 1st Battalion, 9th Marines were also brought in by helicopter to support the operation; they landed in blocking positions to the north. Combined with 3/3 pushing in from the east, twelve companies of Marines, a full regiment, were tightening the noose around the cornered NVA.

On the morning of May 23, Company A of 1/4, accompanied by five Alpha Company, 1st Platoon tanks, commenced attacking south from the Trace toward Phu Oc. When the company began receiving sniper fire, artillery and air support were brought down on the enemy positions. Realizing that they were being encircled, several groups of NVA attempted to make a break for it. They fled north across the Trace, only to be cut down by small-arms and tank gun fire. More artillery and air strikes were called in. The confused and panicked NVA were observed running from one impact area to another, all the while being pounded by the artillery from three separate batteries, plus 60mm and 81mm mortars. Tank cannister and beehive rounds added to the slaughter.

Viewed from Con Thien, the scraped-bare Trace was like looking down a golf course fairway that was six hundred yards wide. As each group of NVA made a desperate attempt to break out of the trees and sprint across the Trace, the Marines on OP#3 at Con Thien blasted them with their mechanical mule–mounted 106mm recoilless rifles. What the

106s did not get, the tanks, 4.2-inch mortars, gunships, and fixed-wing air strikes did; it was a real turkey shoot. Few of the estimated 150 NVA who broke from the woods and tried to run across the Trace made it across alive. When the NVA attempted to bring their 82mm mortars into play, the tanks destroyed them.

Company A had a mission: return to Phu Oc and retrieve the bodies of the dead Bravo Marines left behind the previous evening. Desiring no repeat of that debacle, they had artillery and mortar preparatory fires thoroughly saturate their route of advance. When Alpha reached the enemy bunker complex, it was deserted. The remains of all six MIA were recovered and evacuated.

An estimated 142 NVA squandered their young lives that day. Surrender was certainly an option, but rarely did the NVA choose to make that choice, preferring instead to slug it out with the Marines. Even when surrounded and cut off from retreat, their situation hopeless, the tenacious, courageous soldiers of the People's Army of North Vietnam would choose to go down fighting to the last man.

By noon on May 24, the battle was declared over in the 9th Marines sector. Since the morning of the twenty-second, when Alpha 1/4 and India 3/3 first encountered the NVA battalion, the Marines had suffered more than one hundred casualties, with twenty-three dead and another seventy-eight wounded and evacuated. Enemy losses were 225 dead and 3 prisoners taken. Taking that journey south across the Trace was becoming costly, perhaps too costly, as the North Vietnamese were finding out.

AMBUSH AT NAM DONG

Come on, you sons-o'-bitches! Do you want to live forever?
   —Dan Daly, gunnery sergeant, USMC

One black night on Hill 861A at Khe Sanh, Captain Earl Breeding's Company E, 2d Battalion, 26th Marines earned a special place in Marine Corps history. Shortly after four o'clock on the morning of February 5, 1968, an NVA battalion overran the company perimeter. Breeding's Marines launched a vicious counterattack, hand to hand with knives, e-tools, and bayonets, *mano a mano*. It was a massacre. Five Navy

Crosses were awarded to Breeding's men for their valor that night. Their costs in casualties were seven killed and thirty-five wounded. The NVA left more than 100 dead behind; some estimates went as high as 150.[6]

On May 27, 1968, the 2d Battalion, 26th Marines, under Lt. Col. Francis J. Heath Jr., was assigned responsibility for all of the Marine bases in the Con Thien vicinity, including C-2, A-3, and C-2 Bridge. Six months earlier, four battalions had defended the same area. In recent months, the war in this portion of the Operation Kentucky AO had slowed significantly, so those other battalions were shifted elsewhere.

On June 6, a reinforced platoon from Echo Company departed on a routine patrol southeast of Con Thien. Second Platoon's hard chargers were led by Staff Sergeant Allen J. Baker from Houston, Texas. About one thousand meters beyond Con Thien's southern minefield gate, a deeply gouged cart trail running east to west intersected the MSR. The platoon followed the eight-foot-wide trail east in the general direction of an abandoned airfield runway at Nam Dong, eighteen hundred meters southeast of Con Thien.

Echo's grunts had seen almost zero action around Con Thien since they had relieved 1st Battalion, 4th Marines at the end of May. They were not expecting any trouble on this hot and humid June day, either, as they trudged along the sun-baked, dusty earth that was once rice paddies bordered by thickly vegetated tree- and shrub-crowned hedgerows.

First and 3d Squads were on line abreast, followed by 2d Squad in a staggered column. Machine guns and mortars went with 2d Squad. The platoon resembled a T formation. At about eleven o'clock in the morning, when they were some five hundred meters beyond the last of three bombed-out Catholic church structures beside the dirt road, it happened. The entire right flank came under sudden heavy automatic weapons and RPG fire from a tree line to the south. Third Squad, the furthest south element of the T formation, had walked directly into the NVA's camouflaged ambush positions. Staff Sergeant Baker and his radioman, Lance Cpl. Daniel Prock, had been with 3d Squad. They were likely killed in the opening volley.

Second Squad returned the enemy's fire as they lay prostrate in the sunken cart trail that ran parallel to the enemy positions, twenty to thirty meters away. First Squad managed to join up with 2d Squad, but the fierce enemy fire was too heavy for those remaining two squads to maneuver out of the sunken dirt road where they had sought cover.

A 60mm mortarman, Lance Cpl. Leldon Barnett, detached the mortar tube from its bipod and fired his mortar while holding and aiming it with his hands. One round hit a running NVA soldier directly in the back. Lance Cpl. James N. Kaylor, a grenadier with 2d Squad, joined with Barnett in rapid firing his M-79 grenade launcher. He exhausted his supply of one hundred M-79 grenade rounds, obtained a resupply of ammo from a wounded grenadier, and continued moving up and down the sunken trail, firing at targets pointed out by other Marines.

Snipers picked off Marines attempting to rescue their downed comrades. PFC Daniel A. Staggs was a scout serving with 2d Platoon. He braved the enemy fire to pull several of 3d Squad's wounded men to cover in a bomb crater. He grabbed an M-60 machine gun and ran forward, blazing away at the NVA positions to retrieve a badly wounded man and drag him to safety. A radioman alongside PFC Staggs was not so lucky—a sniper's bullet found its mark. Staggs then got the badly wounded man's radio working and was able to establish communication with an aerial observer.

Corporal Kenneth Schauble, the squad leader of 2d Squad, stepped up and assumed the role of platoon leader. No one challenged him. He sent a fire team north to locate an avenue for a flanking movement, but they were forced to turn back by heavy small-arms fire, their team leader shot dead. Schauble realized then that his platoon was surrounded. He attempted to call in artillery, but the artillery FO, Lance Cpl. Steve McDonald, said they were in too close to the enemy. The NVA's favorite tactic—grabbing the belt—was working all too well. They were forced to direct their artillery support behind the NVA positions to prevent them from bringing in reinforcements. His attempts to call for gunship support went unanswered; the division's helicopters were all tied up elsewhere.[7]

Corporal Schauble's men fought back for hours in the sweltering high-noon heat, waiting in vain for reinforcements in the form of a tank/infantry reaction force from Con Thien or C-2 to arrive. His men had nearly exhausted their ammo, and they were about out of water.

Only one radio was still working. Dead and wounded were lying out in the open. The dead could wait, but not the wounded. Schauble decided that it was time to get aggressive.

Schauble deployed 1st Squad to the right of 2d Squad; they would lay down a base of fire while 2d Squad assaulted the enemy positions. Corporal Schauble placed himself in the middle of the skirmish line and yelled, "Fix bayonets!" Most thought, "Oh, shit, I don't believe this is happening," but they all complied with the order. Schauble raised his right hand and motioned forward, giving the command to attack. Second Squad leapt to its feet in unison and bravely rushed forward, firing all of its weapons furiously. It was old-fashioned Marine Corps tactics: "Hey diddle diddle, straight up the middle." Their momentum carried them right on through the first enemy-held hedgerow into another field approximately fifty meters across. Most of 2d Squad had made it that far unscathed.

Lance Corporal Kaylor spotted a helmeted head poking up from a hole and fired at him with his .45-caliber pistol. Fortunately he missed, because he then recognized the wounded man in the hole as Corporal Jerry Callaway, 3d Squad leader. Kaylor yelled, "Cease fire, he's one of ours!" Other Marines had also fired at Callaway as they ran past.

Continuing their hell-bent-for-leather advance across the open field, they realized too late that they had overrun their first objective and had charged blindly into a secondary enemy bunker/trench line system. Lance Corporal Kaylor and PFC Bill Hayes realized their predicament: they had to act fast, but they could not run back, and they could not stay prone. They exchanged a quick "this is where we die today" look. Resigned to their doomed fate, they launched a desperate two-man attack.

PFC Hayes, helmetless and bare chested, jumped up running with a primed grenade in each hand. He tossed his first grenade underhanded; then, just as he threw his second grenade, he was mortally wounded. His momentum carried him tumbling into the NVA position. Before they could push Hayes's body aside and swivel their machine gun around to get him, Kaylor ran up and with his pistol blasted at four enemy faces from six feet away, knowing he would surely be killed there. To his stunned surprise, the firing from the bunker stopped, and the machine-gun barrel pointed skyward. Kaylor did not know how many he had hit, but he had bought himself a few precious seconds to scramble back to a nearby bomb crater.

An explosion suddenly went off behind Kaylor, showering him with dirt. The surviving enemy in the bunker had recovered and was tossing stickhandle Chicom grenades at him. He was down to his last three rounds of .45-caliber ammo. Seeing PFC James Terry and another pinned-down Marine thirty meters to his rear, Kaylor yelled for them to throw him some of their hand grenades. To his dismay, all the grenades except a smoke grenade landed outside the crater. He first tossed the smoke grenade, blinding the NVA in the bunker long enough to jump out of his crater and retrieve the errantly thrown hand grenades. Before he could make it safely back to his crater, the smoke cleared. He heard Terry yell, "Don't stick your head up—one of them is looking out of the bunker!" An M-16 bullet cracked over Kaylor's head from Terry's position. Terry, one of the best shots in the company, yelled, "I got him!"

Back in the crater once again, Kaylor pulled the pins, let the handles fly off, and held the grenades for a few seconds before throwing, which made them detonate on target before the NVA could toss them back. Two of his grenades impacted harmlessly on either side of the enemy bunker, but the third took one bounce and went right through the bunker opening, killing all the remaining occupants.

Pulling back to the location of his other two comrades, Kaylor realized that they were the only men from 2d Squad not wounded or killed. Corporal Schauble lay dead where he fell during the charge, shot through the face.[8]

A platoon from Hotel 2/26, led by First Lieutenant Rudd, arrived on the scene at last and took over for the exhausted Echo-2 survivors, cleaning out the remaining NVA positions. Several CH-46 helicopters landed and evacuated the casualties. Fourteen Marines had been killed, and eleven were wounded—the majority of 2d Platoon. Fourteen NVA bodies were collected and tossed in a pile at the bottom of a large crater.

It was a typical DMZ-style dogfight, where neither force could claim a clear victory. The NVA had ambushed their prey in so close that the Marines could not disengage and pull back to employ their air strike and artillery trump cards without hitting their own casualties.

Back at Con Thien during the debriefing that evening, some battalion staff commenced second-guessing and finger pointing, upset over 2d Platoon's charge that day. Conversely, the exhausted, angry ambush survivors believed (justifiably so) that they should have been reinforced hours sooner by their company. Also, a fully loaded platoon of five Marine Corps tanks had been ignored back at Con Thien, never unleashed as a reaction force into an area they knew so well. The tanks would have made a substantial difference in the battle's outcome, and Marine lives would have been saved if someone in the CP bunker at Con Thien had thought to use them.[9]

OPERATION THOR

Important command changes had occurred in mid-1968. The 3d Marine Division received a new commander, Maj. Gen. Raymond G. Davis, a soft-spoken Georgian who had received the Navy Cross for his valor at the bloody battle at Peleliu in World War II. As a battalion commander at the famous Chosin Reservoir breakout in the Korean War, Davis was awarded the Medal of Honor. He brought with him the right stuff to break out of the DMZ stalemate that had trapped the Marines in their static defense role below the DMZ for more than a year.

General William C. Westmoreland was replaced on June 11 as the commander of MACV by U.S. Army general Creighton W. Abrams. The decision to sack Westmoreland had been made the previous March in the aftermath of the stunning Tet Offensive. Not only was the public's will for backing the war broken, but the Johnson administration itself had lost confidence in the wisdom of Westmoreland's war of attrition. He was permitted to hang around MACV for three more months as a lame-duck commander until he was essentially kicked upstairs to assume the position of the U.S. Army chief of staff. He left Vietnam still convinced that the Tet Offensive was an elaborate ruse to distract attention away from Khe Sanh, which he believed in his heart was the enemy's primary goal all along.

With the change of command at 3d Marine Division headquarters came two significant changes that would dramatically affect the way the Marines conducted the war in northern I Corps. The first change directly implemented by Major General Davis was to restore regimental integrity. Formerly, it was not uncommon for a regimental commander to have under his command several battalions and companies that were not part of his own regiment. Operation Checkers, which saw Marine battalions and even separate companies jumping from one area of operation to another, had contributed to the unwieldy command structure that General Davis inherited when he took over the reins from Major General Tompkins.

A second goal of General Davis was increased mobility of Marine ground forces. He was profoundly impressed by the Army 1st Air Cavalry's ability to move large numbers of soldiers around quickly by helicopter during the Khe Sanh relief operation called Pegasus. In the ensuing months of the war, the Marines would try their hand at breaking out of their strongpoint defense mentality, taking the war to the enemy by leapfrogging from one temporary firebase to another, leaving no former NVA sanctuaries untouched.

Planning had begun months earlier by III MAF staffers to neutralize the Cap Mui Lay sector of Vietnam, generally the eastern half of the DMZ ranging from the southern border up several kilometers into North Vietnam itself. Long-range shore batteries, artillery, and SAM missile sites ensconced within that area presented a continual threat to America's military presence at Dong Ha and along the Cua Viet. D-Day for this operation, code-named Thor after the Norse god of thunder, was July 1.

Coincidentally, an artillery attack from that Cap Mui Lay area struck the ammunition dump at Dong Ha on June 20, setting off a massive fireworks display of exploding ordnance and fuel that lasted for hours and could be both seen and felt at Con Thien, ten miles away. Despite that setback, Operation Thor went ahead as scheduled.

Operation Thor called for a weeklong bombardment effort against the Cap Mui Lay sector involving units of III MAF, the Seventh Fleet, and the Seventh Air Force. The primary objectives were twofold: first, destroy NVA antiaircraft, field artillery, and coastal batteries, and, second, facilitate further surveillance and destruction of targets in and north of the DMZ. It was hoped that this operation would preempt any of North Vietnam's preparations for an autumn offensive.

Phase I of the operation commenced with a massive bombing effort. Controlled by the Seventh Air Force, 664 Marine, Navy, and Air Force attack aircraft and 114 B-52 sorties delivered more than four thousand tons of ordnance against carefully plotted enemy targets during the first two days of the operation.

The next two phases of Thor involved the artillery component. Inadvertently, the catastrophic devastation of the Dong Ha ammo dump on June 20, which closed the logistic support area for six days, provided a perfect cover for the Marines bringing in additional shiploads of ammunition from the Quang Tri logistic support area in their buildup for Operation Thor.

As another deceit tactic, additional work being performed at strongpoints such as A-4 (Con Thien) and A-2 (Gio Linh) would be assumed to be a normal part of Dyemarker construction, when, in reality, the Marines were preparing additional artillery battery sites. An eight-inch gun battery was set into predug firing slots on the southern perimeter at Con Thien. All together, thirteen batteries of fifty-nine artillery pieces participated in the operation, including three batteries of 155mm from 4/12 and one battery from K/4/13.

The Seventh Fleet offshore provided two cruisers and six destroyers closing to within five thousand meters of the coast uncontested. They delivered more than twelve thousand rounds of various calibers against Communist positions on shore.

A pall of dust and smoke visible for a dozen miles hung over the Cap Mui Lay sector as day after day of merciless pounding from air, land, and sea continued without letup. Marines at Con Thien, A-3, and Gio Linh were intrigued by the sounds of round-the-clock naval gunfire shrieking inland from cruisers offshore and large-caliber artillery shells whooshing overhead, carrying death and destruction to the hated NVA artillerists. The *boom-ba-boom!* sounds were all friendly; nothing was coming back the other way, which was a welcomed change. But everyone knew it was only a temporary respite, because the next phase of Thor would involve a massive ground assault up to the DMZ, similar to Hickory the previous year.

After a week of uninterrupted blasting away at the enemy, all of the artillery batteries brought up to the forward firebases were withdrawn.

Air and naval attacks were halted to allow the smoke to clear for more accurate target analysis. The damage results were substantial: more than five hundred artillery and antiaircraft positions, numerous bunkers and storage areas, and two SAM sites were destroyed. Observers reported 352 secondary explosions and 236 secondary fires as a result of hits on ammunition and supply dumps.

On July 7, the 9th Marines commenced its ground offensive in the Kentucky AO. The operation involved the entire 9th Marine Regiment. With Con Thien as the hub, 2/9 and 3/9 wheeled abreast in a counterclockwise sweep that took 3/9, the outside battalion, all the way up to the southern boundary of the DMZ. The scheme of maneuver had 1/9 pushing north through Leatherneck Square to join 2/9 and 3/9 north of the Trace. Any NVA in the area would be caught in the squeeze.

The July heat was anticipated as a problem. To counter the high demand for water, U.S. Army ammunition trailers were filled with five-gallon water cans and hitched to ARVN personnel carriers to ensure an adequate water supply. Despite the precautions taken, the 9th Marines evacuated more casualties caused by the torrid heat and humidity than from enemy fire.

Action was surprisingly light in the Kentucky area. Knowing a major offensive was headed their way, the NVA chose by and large to move out of the way rather than do battle. One exception occurred July 11, when Lt. Col. Edward J. Lamontagne's 3/9, "Mister Outside," encountered a platoon of NVA in the open three thousand meters northeast of Con Thien in the Gia Binh area. With a combination of air, artillery, and tanks in direct support, 3/9 killed thirty of the enemy and seized twenty-six weapons. Sweeping through Gia Binh, the scene of numerous battles for various Marine units over the previous two years, Lamontagne's Marines were amazed when they came across a regiment-sized complex extending more than a square kilometer, with 242 artillery-proof bunkers. Supplies and equipment captured included 935 mortar rounds, 500 pounds of explosives, 55 antitank mines, and 500 pounds of rice.

Besides the Gia Binh complex, the major prize realized from Thor was the staggering quantities of weapons and munitions destroyed. Engineers with bulldozers followed in trace of the infantry battalions, punching through bunkers, filling in trenches, and blowing up whatever else they were unable to knock down. If something looked like it could be used for an observation post, it was knocked over. A scorched-earth policy of sorts was employed to deny the NVA the use of that land to launch more attacks against the Marines.

For the first time in several years, large numbers of Marines had swept all the way around Con Thien clear up into the DMZ, crossed the Trace, and roamed throughout Leatherneck Square with impunity. The week of punishing bombardment had worked—for the time being; no one had expectations that the NVA losses in men and material would be a permanent setback. The enemy would return to the eastern DMZ, but not in the same numbers as before and no longer with such a determined focus on Con Thien.

18

Parting Shots

Change was inevitable. Inertia had set in long ago at MACV and III MAF headquarters regarding the need to tie up whole battalions of Marines building and defending Operation Dyemarker strongpoints. With General Westmoreland out of the picture, Maj. Gen. Raymond Davis set out to change that mentality.

One of the first casualties of the new order was Colonel Richard B. Smith, CO of the 9th Marines for the past ten months. On July 13, Col. Robert H. Barrow, who had fought alongside General Davis in Korea at the Chosin Reservoir breakout, replaced Colonel Smith. The 9th Marines then vacated its Dong Ha headquarters and moved west to Landing Zone Stud in the Lancaster II area of the central DMZ.

General Davis had almost his entire 3d Division—the 9th Marines and 3d Marines, plus 2/26 and 1/4—out doing battle with the 320th NVA Division. Fierce combat raged in the hills and mountains around Mutter's Ridge, the Rockpile, and the central DMZ from mid-August through the end of October. With the withdrawal south of the 1st Marines to Da Nang on August 31, the U.S. Army's 1st Brigade, 5th Infantry Division assumed control of the Kentucky area of operation to free up Davis's Marines.

Both the Army and ARVN had taken up the slack behind the Marines committed to Operation Lancaster II. Leatherneck Square was no longer a Marine Corps enclave. It was not uncommon to see joint operations involving Marines, Army, and ARVN ground, air, and mechanized forces working in concert throughout the Kentucky area as the year drew to a close.

DYEMARKER'S DEMISE

The barrier, once the ironclad plan determining how the Marines would fight the enemy along the DMZ, had begun to lose favor in high places in the government due to several key factors. First was the sudden departure in February of Robert McNamara, primary advocate of the plan. Then, General Westmoreland went home in June. With his hands no longer tied by a fixed-strongpoint mentality, Major General Davis instituted a new mobile operation concept in September that was highly successful in soundly defeating the 320th NVA Division. One of the final nails in Dyemarker's coffin was hammered in on October 22, when General Abrams ordered all construction and planning efforts associated with the anti-infiltration barrier effort halted.

According to the original plan for Dyemarker, all of the strongpoints were to be taken over eventually by the South Vietnamese Army. By June 1968, only A-1, A-2, and C-1 had been secured by the 2d ARVN Regiment. U.S. Marine forces occupied the other bases. A revised plan code-named Project Duel Blade, submitted by III MAF in mid-June, called for the ARVN regiment to relieve the Marines at A-4 (Con Thien) and A-3 by the end of 1968. The new plan would eliminate two other strongpoints proposed for construction further east between Con Thien and the Rockpile.

Later that fall, the ARVN commander, Lieutenant General Lam, balked at taking over A-3 and A-4 from the Marines until all the sensors, minefields, and wire barriers originally intended for Dyemarker were installed along the Trace. This forced the hand of General Abrams and MACV. It was either put up or shut up. Do the barrier all the way, as it was originally planned, or else drop it. General Abrams dropped it. Then, as a result of that decision, General Cushman requested permission of General Abrams to close two strongpoints no longer seen as necessary in the revised scheme of things, A-3 and C-3 (Cam Lo). A-3 and the artillery support base at C-3 were now seen as superfluous, whereas a year earlier they were seen as crucial to the success of Dyemarker. One can only wonder how many American boys had shed their blood to establish and secure those now-expendable strongpoints.

The future fate of the former Operation Dyemarker was permanently sealed on November 1, 1968, when President Johnson announced a total bombing halt in the DMZ and North Vietnam. This edict included no artillery missions and naval gunfire missions. Marine units were under standing orders not to set foot or even fire into the DMZ. Thus, the entire strongpoint and obstacle barrier concept was no longer feasible.

Mobility was the new watchword. From that point onward in the war, hi-tech surveillance would replace the observation posts. Recon teams were still going to be used, but detection devices using laser technology would be relied on heavily. Such sensor fields had been installed south of the Ben Hai, throughout the southern DMZ, by the end of 1968. Much of the no-longer-needed Duel Blade construction material was then shifted south to Da Nang, where another anti-infiltration barrier was to be installed.

The Marine bases at Con Thien, C-2 Bridge, and C-2 would continue to be manned and defended by units of the 3d Marines in 1969. With the dissolution of Dyemarker, or Duel Blade, or whatever clever code name MACV and the Pentagon had invented for the now-defunct Strong Point Obstacle System that Robert McNamara and his whiz kids once believed in so fervently, Con Thien was no longer being contested. The North Vietnamese seemed to have heard the news, along with the Marines, that Dyemarker was dead, just one more lamentable casualty in a protracted, misguided struggle that had squandered thousands of human lives and billions of treasury—and to what end? The North Vietnamese merely concentrated their forces elsewhere, so they could continue their strategy of bleeding the Americans. Accordingly, the American war-fighting emphasis shifted to Quang Tri's mountainous border areas and into the A Shau Valley, where more savage fighting ensued.

What with the hot showers, electricity, nighttime movies, and hot food being brought up each day from C-2, the Marines manning the firebase at Con Thien in 1969 could not possibly have any clue as to the muddy hellhole that their predecessors had endured in years past. But if a pensive young Marine standing watch some quiet evening listened carefully, his absent gaze fixated on Con Thien's grassy slopes, the ghosts of more than a thousand dead Marines and corpsmen who had given up all of their tomorrows could be heard whispering in the wind. Their home for all of eternity . . . The Hill of Angels.

Requiem

Now, from the mirror the aging man peers at me, searching for an answer, but finds none. The question "what might they have done with their lives had they lived?" goes unresolved. Of their lives, I am certain only of the challenges of life untried, and of youthful aspirations unfulfilled. Still, within the weary eyes of the man in the mirror, I see thirty-year-old images as keen as yesterday's, images of forested mountains and endless seas of rice, barren hills of red earth, and the boys we left behind, the boys forever young.

—Salvatore Bafumo, 11th Engineer Battalion, USMC

On November 24, 1969, the last infantry battalion of the 3d Marine Division remaining in Vietnam, the 3d Battalion, 4th Marines, embarked on U.S. Navy ships for redeployment to Okinawa. An era had come to a close. President Nixon was carrying out his promise to get the Americans out of the war and turn it over to the Vietnamese. "Vietnamization" was the bureaucratic buzzword for that process; "peace with honor" was the goal of Nixon's administration.

In November 1971, the veteran 1st ARVN Division, responsible for defending the firebases along the DMZ as well as the rest of Quang Tri Province, was replaced by the untried 3d ARVN Division. The former Marine positions that had once made up Leatherneck Square were still there, though the ARVN referred to them by their Dyemarker alphanumeric designations. Con Thien was A-4.

Once Hanoi's leaders were certain that the Americans were both physically and psychologically removed from Vietnam, they unleashed their devastating Easter Offensive into South Vietnam at the end of March 1972. Twenty-five thousand well-armed NVA, backed by hundreds of Soviet- and Chinese-built tanks, rolled unimpeded across the DMZ. The rookie 3d ARVN Division folded like a house of cards, some too dazed to react and others literally running panic stricken from the battlefield.

On April 1, hordes of truck-mounted NVA infantry rode south alongside their PT-76 and T-54 tanks down Route 561, sneering with disdain at the white surrender flags flapping in the wind. Relentless and unstoppable, they cruised right on past A-4, blasted into shambles from days of thunderous rocket and artillery bombardment. The last Marine to see Con Thien was the former CO of M/3/26, Capt. Andrew DeBona, then an advisor to the Vietnamese Marine Corps, as he was lifted by helicopter out of the beleaguered Con Thien LZ.

Past Phu Oc and Phu An, through C-2 and Nui Ho Khe they rode, ever onward through Dong Ha and Cam Lo. Eventually, the North Vietnamese tidal wave exhausted its momentum. The South Vietnamese were able to make a stand, even recapture much of the territory they had lost to the North Vietnamese, but Con Thien no longer remained in Allied hands.

No one will ever know the exact number of Americans who lost their lives in the years of fighting around Con Thien and the area known to the Marines as Leatherneck Square. Official statistics for that specified area of operation, starting with Operations Prairie III/IV and including Hickory, Cimarron, Buffalo, Kingfisher, and Kentucky, list 1,419 Marines and Navy corpsmen killed in action from March 19, 1967, through February 28, 1969, when Kentucky ended. Another 9,265 were wounded seriously enough to require medical treatment. Official records kept by III MAF recorded 7,563 NVA killed by the Allies during the same time frame, but that figure is merely a guesstimate. The actual number of North Vietnamese who sacrificed their lives in three years of battle around the Con Thien/Leatherneck Square area is known only to their God.

❖

Today, located approximately halfway between the former outpost at Con Thien and the Ben Hai River is the Trung Son Cemetery, maintained by the Vietnamese government. More than ten thousand Vietnamese soldiers lie buried there in the Cemetery of the Martyrs. A memorial at the entrance is inscribed, "The Nation Honors its Glorious Dead." Once inside, unending rows of tombstones, perfectly aligned, remind one of our own Arlington National Cemetery in Washington, D.C.

Many of us old vets have made the pilgrimage back to Vietnam, perhaps to help ease the pain of our memories from the war or even to assuage the irrational guilt we long felt, having survived to come home when our comrades did not. Oliver North, a former platoon commander with Kilo Company, 3d Battalion, 3d Marines, and a famous Iran-Contra scandal figure in later years, had fought in several battles around Con Thien from 1968 to 1969. He described some memories of his 1993 return to the area: "Pineapples, tea, eucalyptus and rubber trees now cover the terrain that I had patrolled so carefully. Had I not recognized the distinctive, raised, flat profile of the firebase, I would have been hard-pressed to believe that I was standing where my old battalion once had its forward headquarters."[1]

Another visitor in 1994 was Kent Wonders, a former platoon commander with 2/26 in 1968. He wrote of his visit to Con Thien: "The guide warns when we leave the bus, 'Stay on paths. Still mines.' . . . The hill looked freshly plowed in parts by people looking for metal. Pieces of dark green sandbags were everywhere. I looked closely and soon found many things I recognized, such as a combat boot. . . . I wished the boot could talk to me. Where's the Marine? Where is his foot? How many years have you been here?"[2]

John "Doc" McNiff was a Navy corpsman with the 3d Battalion, 4th Marines in 1966–67, having survived both Hastings and Prairie. He recalled during his 1994 trip back to Vietnam how the scars of war had healed around the Con Thien area. "Farmers, their water buffalo and their entire families were busy at work tilling, planting, flooding, and harvesting the rice paddies. . . . Along the way, we passed a peasant plowing his field behind an ancient water buffalo. The man stopped the 'waterboo' long enough to stare at us as we made our way up the slope. I couldn't help but think that when we fought here he would have been a young boy."[3]

With each passing year, memories of the war grow more faded. The pain of losing friends remains, but the sharp edges have dulled. It does not take much, though, to bring it all back again. We Vietnam veterans ask ourselves why, but the answer never comes. To what end did we risk everything by subjecting ourselves to the trauma of Vietnam? Did our sacrifices mean anything? Or were we merely like autumn leaves blown hither and yon without real purpose or meaning, our brave sacrifices soon forgotten, never to be appreciated by future generations of Americans?

But former Marines always think back to the Corps. Until we take our last breath on this earth, we shall forever take a certain measure of pride in the knowledge that, no matter what, no matter how or why the war in Vietnam was lost, we gave everything we had to give, for the honor of the Corps and for each other. *Semper Fidelis!*

Appendix A

Medal of Honor and Navy Cross Recipients in the Con Thien Area of Operations, 1966–68

Name/Rank (*Posthumous)	Date	Unit	Operation
Medal of Honor			
Barker, Jedh Colby, Lance Cpl.*	Sept. 21, 1967	F/2/4	Kingfisher
Bobo, John Paul, 2d Lt.*	Mar. 30, 1967	I/3/9	Prairie III
Foster, Paul H., Sgt.*	Oct. 14, 1967	2/4	Kingfisher
Maxam, Larry L., Cpl.*	Feb. 2, 1968	D/1/4	Kentucky
Singleton, Walter K., Sgt.*	Mar. 24, 1967	A/1/9	Prairie III
Navy Cross			
Armstrong, Russell, Staff Sgt.	Sept. 7, 1967	I/3/26	Kingfisher
Ashby, James W., HM3*	June 1, 1967	L/3/9	Cimarron
Barrett, James J., Cpl.	Sept. 10, 1967	I/3/26	Kingfisher
Bendorf, David G., Lance Cpl.*	May 20, 1967	L/3/9	Hickory
Brown, David, Sgt.*	Sept. 10, 1967	L/3/26	Kingfisher
Browning, Randall A., Lance Cpl.	Sept. 10, 1967	A/3d AT	Kingfisher
Burns, Leon R., Staff Sgt.	July 2, 1967	B/1/9	Buffalo
Christy, Kenneth L., 2d Lt.	Jan. 18, 1968	L/3/4	Kentucky
Corsetti, Harry J., Cpl.	Aug. 15, 1968	3d Recon	Kentucky
Cousins, Merritt T., Lance Cpl.*	July 8, 1967	B/1/12	Buffalo
Crawford, Charles H., HM*	May 29, 1967	M/3/4	Prairie IV
Curley, Ronald T., Sgt.	May 16, 1967	F/2/26	Prairie IV
Danner, David J., Sgt.	May 8, 1967	A/3d Tank	Prairie IV
DeBona, Andrew D., Capt.	Sept. 10, 1967	M/3/26	Kingfisher
Dillard, Henry C., PFC	May 29, 1967	M/3/4	Prairie IV
Eades, Lawrence M., Cpl.	Feb. 2, 1968	CAC-P	Kentucky
Finley, Michael P., Lance Cpl.*	May 8, 1967	A/1/4	Prairie IV

Getlin, Michael P., Capt.*	Mar. 30, 1967	I/3/9	Prairie III
Gillingham, Richard K., Cpl.*	May 19, 1967	H/2/9	Hickory
Grant, Gollie L., HM*	Sept. 19, 1966	B/1/26	Prairie
Hartsoe, David E., PFC*	May 20, 1967	L/3/9	Hickory
Howell, Gatlin J., 1st Lt.*	July 2, 1967	1/9	Buffalo
Judge, Mark W., PFC*	Sept. 21, 1967	E/2/4	Kingfisher
Keys, William M., Capt.	Mar. 2, 1967	D/1/9	Prairie II
Kuzma, Marc J., Pvt.*	Apr. 26, 1968	A/1/4	Kentucky
Loweranitis, John L., Cpl.*	Mar. 30, 1967	I/3/9	Prairie III
Moffit, Richard E., Cpl.	May 16–17, 1967	G/2/26	Prairie IV
Monohan, Robert, Lance Cpl.*	May 28, 1967	D/1/9	Prairie IV
Murphy, James E., Capt.	Oct. 26, 1967	2/4	Kingfisher
Reis, Tiago, Cpl.*	Sept. 21, 1967	F/2/4	Kingfisher
Rivers, Jettie, Jr., 1st Sgt.*	May 14–15, 1967	D/1/9	Prairie IV
Rogers, Raymond G., 1st Sgt.	Mar. 30, 1967	I/3/9	Prairie III
Russell, Timothy W., Cpl.	Feb. 2, 1968	D/1/4	Kentucky
Slater, Albert C., Jr., Capt.	July 6–7, 1967	A/1/9	Buffalo
Sotomayer, Miguel R., Cpl.	July 29, 1967	F/2/9	Kingfisher
Stewart, Michael E., Lance Cpl.*	May 13, 1967	A/1/9	Prairie IV
Stuckey, James L., Lance Cpl.	July 6, 1967	C/1/9	Buffalo
Thatcher, Charles D., Lance Cpl.	May 8, 1967	A/3d Tank	Prairie IV
Thouvenell, Armand R., PFC*	May 29, 1967	M/3/4	Prairie IV

Appendix B

Con Thien/Leatherneck Square Area Casualties, March 19, 1967–February 28, 1969

Operation	USMC		NVA	
	KIA	WIA	KIA	POW
Prairie III (Mar. 19–Apr. 19, 1967)	56	530	252	4
Prairie IV (Apr. 20–May 31, 1967)	164	1,240	505	9
Hickory (May 18–28, 1967)	142	896	304	30
Cimarron (June 1–July 1, 1967)	38	470	245	2
Buffalo (July 2–15, 1967)	159	345	1,301	1
Kingfisher (July 16–Oct. 31, 1967)	340	3,086	1,117	5
Kentucky (Nov. 1, 1967–Feb. 28, 1969)	520	2,698	3,839	117
CASUALTY TOTALS	1,419	9,265	7,563	168

Sources: Jack Shulimson, L. A. Blasiol, D. A. Dawson, and C. R. Smith, *U.S. Marines in Vietnam: The Defining Year, 1968* (Washington, DC: History and Museums Division, Headquarters, U.S. Marine Corps, 1997); E. H. Simmons, ed., *The Marines in Vietnam, 1954–1973: An Anthology and Annotated Bibliography* (Washington, DC: History and Museums Division, Headquarters, U.S. Marine Corps, 1974); E. H. Simmons, *The United States Marines: A History,* 3d ed. (Washington, DC: Naval Institute Press, 1998); Gary L. Telfer, L. Rogers, and V. K. Fleming, *U.S. Marines in Vietnam: Fighting the North Vietnamese, 1967* (Washington, DC: History and Museums Division, Headquarters, U.S. Marine Corps, 1984).

Appendix C

Organization of U.S. Marine Corps Infantry Units—Vietnam

RANKS

Enlisted

E-1   Private
E-2   Private First Class
E-3   Lance Corporal
E-4   Corporal
E-5   Sergeant
E-6   Staff Sergeant
E-7   Gunnery Sergeant
E-8   Master Sergeant/First Sergeant
E-9   Master Gunnery Sergeant/Sergeant Major

Officer

Second Lieutenant
First Lieutenant
Captain
Major
Lieutenant Colonel
Colonel
Brigadier General
Major General
Lieutenant General
General

COMPONENTS

Fire team—A four-man team usually led by a corporal or lance corporal.
Squad—Consisted of three fire teams. The squad leader was a sergeant or corporal.

Platoon—Consisted of three squads. The platoon leader was a lieutenant; the platoon sergeant was a staff sergeant.

Weapons platoon—Consisted of the crews needed to man six M-60 machine guns, six 3.5-inch rocket launchers, and three 60mm mortars. Later in the war, the 3.5-inch rocket launchers were replaced by the Light Antitank Assault Weapon (LAAW). The platoon leader was a lieutenant; the platoon sergeant was a gunnery sergeant.

Company—Consisted of three platoons and a weapons platoon. The company commander was a captain, and the executive officer (XO) was a lieutenant. A first sergeant was responsible for administrative details, and a gunnery sergeant was the logistics/operations overseer.

Battalion—Consisted of four rifle companies as described above, plus a Headquarters and Service (H & S) Company. The companies were referred to by letters of the phonetic alphabet as Alpha, Bravo, Charlie, and so on. Companies A, B, C, and D always indicated that they were part of the 1st Battalion. Companies E, F, G, and H were 2d Battalion. Companies I (J was never used), K, L, and M were 3d Battalion. In addition to administrative and communications staff, H & S Company consisted of an 81mm mortar platoon (eight mortars plus crews), a 106mm recoilless rifle section (eight guns and their crews), and a flame section (eight flamethrowers and their crews). The battalion commander was a lieutenant colonel, and the XO was a major. The senior enlisted Marine was a sergeant major. The S-1 (administration) was a captain; S-2 (intelligence) was a captain; S-3 (operations) was a major or senior captain; and S-4 (logistics) was a captain. Other staff were the adjutant, chaplain, communications officer, motor transport officer, supply officer, and surgeon (lieutenant, U.S. Navy).

Regiment—Consisted of three battalions. The regimental commander was a colonel, the XO was a lieutenant colonel, and the senior enlisted Marine was the regimental sergeant major. Staff positions were generally the same as those on the battalion level except that each was filled by one rank higher than that at the battalion level.

Division—Consisted of three infantry regiments plus an artillery regiment. A division was commanded by a major general, and the assistant commander was a brigadier general. Staff organization was consistent with battalion and regiment except that staff officers were a grade higher and designated by a "G," as in G-1 rather than S-1.

Attachments—Other units and/or weapons systems that might have been attached to infantry units mentioned in this book were amtracs, Dusters (U.S. Army), engineers, forward air controllers (FACs), forward observers (FOs), motor transport, Ontos, quad-fifties (U.S. Army), reconnaissance (recon), snipers, and tanks.

Notes

EPIGRAPH

The epigraph to this book is drawn from Laurence Binyon, "For the Fallen," first published in 1914. The epigraph is the fourth verse of a seven-verse poem written to honor the English who died in World War I. Verse 4 is also known today by the title "The Ode" and is cited in various texts. See, for example, Arthur Quillen-Couch, ed., *Oxford Book of English Verse, 1250–1918* (Oxford: Oxford University Press, 1939).

PROLOGUE

1. Thanks to R. B. English, John Brock, and Howard Blum for sharing their recollections of that devastating incident. The author was later scolded by that same artillery officer for allowing three of his tanks to congregate in one place. The dialogue between the artillery officer and Gunny English is an approximation of a similar warning the lieutenant gave to the author six weeks later. The dialogue of the NVA FO was contrived by the author to illustrate the constant threat faced by the Marines at Con Thien by enemy artillery firing at them from the DMZ.

PART I: ROOTS OF CONFLICT

The epigraph to this part is drawn from Peter MacDonald, *Giap: The Victor in Vietnam* (New York: W. W. Norton, 1993), 197.

CHAPTER 1. BEFORE THE AMERICANS CAME

1. Ronald H. Spector, *After Tet* (New York: Vintage Press, 1994), 72.

2. Neil Sheehan, *A Bright Shining Lie: John Paul Vann and America in Vietnam* (New York: Vintage Books, 1989), 639.

3. Michael Lee Lanning and Dan Cragg, *Inside the VC and the NVA* (New York: Ivy Books, 1992), 32.

CHAPTER 2. THE GENERALS

The epigraph to this chapter is drawn from MacDonald, 91.

1. Spector, 72–73.

2. Eric Hammel, "Marines under Fire at Con Thien," *Vietnam* (December 1997): 42.

3. See Karnow's comprehensive comments in Stanley Karnow, *Vietnam: A History* (New York: Penguin Books, 1997), 20.

4. Robert Pisor, *The End of the Line: The Siege of Khe Sanh* (New York: Ballantine Books, 1983), 133.

5. Karnow, 20.

6. Sheehan, 630–31; also Pisor, 48.

7. Sheehan, 634–39. General Lew Walt's conflict with General Westmoreland is discussed in depth.

8. Ibid., 641–43.

CHAPTER 3. McNAMARA'S WALL

1. "MACV—Barrier and Dyemarker, 1967–68, 1/1/67" (Archives Document, USMC Historical Center, Washington, DC), 1073.

2. Gary L. Telfer, Lane Rogers, and V. Keith Fleming, *U.S. Marines in Vietnam: Fighting the Vietnamese, 1967* (Washington, DC: Headquarters, USMC, 1984), 87.

3. John Prados and Ray Stubbe, *Valley of Decision: The Siege of Khe Sanh* (Boston: Houghton Mifflin Co., 1991), 144.

4. Telfer, Rogers, and Fleming, 87.

5. Quotes are from various Marines I heard in Vietnam.

6. Edwin H. Simmons, ed., *The Marines in Vietnam, 1954–1973: An Anthology and Annotated Bibliography* (Washington, DC: Headquarters, USMC, 1974), 82.

7. Eric Hammel, "The DMZ Campaign of 1967," *Military History Guild* (Words to Go, Inc., 1994, Document 94-0005).

8. Shelby Stanton, *The Green Berets at War* (Novato, CA: Presidio Press, 1985), 153.

PART II: THE DMZ WAR UNFOLDS

The epigraph to this part is a verse from the Vietnamese national anthem.

CHAPTER 4. NGUYEN OF THE NORTH VERSUS PFC JONES

1. Lanning and Cragg, 46.

2. W. C. Westmoreland, *A Soldier Reports* (New York: Doubleday, 1976), 330.

3. Lanning and Cragg, 255.

4. Ibid., 258.

5. Keith W. Nolan, *Operation Buffalo: USMC Fight for the DMZ* (Novato, CA: Presidio Press, 1991), 77.

6. James H. Webb Jr., "Heroes of the Vietnam Generation," *The Proud Warrior, Newsletter of the 1/9 Network* (Winter 2000–01).

CHAPTER 5. SETTING THE STAGE

1. Jack Shulimson, *U.S. Marines in Vietnam: An Expanding War, 1966* (Washington, DC: History and Museums Division, Headquarters, U.S. Marine Corps, 1984), 176.

2. Marion F. Sturkey, *Bonnie-Sue: A Marine Corps Helicopter Squadron in Vietnam* (Plum Branch, SC: Heritage Press International, 1996), 173–74; also see 660925 KIA incident description on USMC Vietnam Helicopter Association Web site, www.popasmoke.com.

3. Edwin H. Simmons, *Illustrated History of the Vietnam War: Marines* (New York: Bantam Books, 1987), 70.

4. Archie Echols, personal communication with author, December 16, 2002.

5. Senator Mark Hatfield, "Marines Need Gear," U.S. Congress, *Congressional Record,* 90th Cong., 1st sess. (November 22, 1967): pt. 25:33690–91.

6. William L. Myers, *Honor the Warrior: The United States Marine Corps in Vietnam* (Lafayette, LA: Redoubt Press, 2000), 135.

7. "Rifle under Fire," *Newsweek,* September 10, 1967, 27–28.

8. Telfer, Rogers, and Fleming, 14–19.

PART III: THE BLOODY MONTH OF MAY

The epigraph to this part is drawn from Alan Seeger, *Poems* (New York: Charles Scribner's Sons, 1917). Seeger was an American volunteer in the French foreign legion. He was killed in France in 1916.

CHAPTER 6. BATTLE FOR CON THIEN

1. The Navy Cross citations for both Danner and Thatcher erroneously state that the battle occurred at Gio Linh. The confusion was because Con Thien is located in Gio Linh District and because Gio Linh was also attacked that night.

2. "Bloody Trial," *Newsweek,* May 22, 1967, 46.

3. David Lovewell, personal communication with author, February 10, 2002.

4. W. D. Ehrhart, *Ordinary Lives: Platoon 1005 and the Vietnam War* (Philadelphia: Temple Press, 1999), 279. Suffering from extreme post-traumatic stress syndrome, Stephen Summerscales would take his own life four and one-half years after returning home.

5. Stanton, 156.

6. Kenneth Bores, personal communication with author, August 21, 2001.

7. Sturkey, 371. However, the USMC Vietnam Helicopter Association Web site, www.popasmoke.com, listed the HMM-363 Command Chronology entry for May 12, 1967, and it does not support Sturkey's assertion that enemy ground fire brought down YZ-78. A subsequent interview many years later with the copilot of YZ-78, George

Hadcewycz, also contradicts Sturkey. Hadcewycz, personal communication with author, March 2002.

8. Nolan, 5; Prados and Stubbe, 85–89.

9. Nolan, 29.

10. Ibid., 28.

11. Ibid., 334–35.

12. Phil McCombs, "Peace Church, Vietnam," *Washington Post,* http://www. washingtonpost.com/wpsrv/national/longterm/vietnam/tripp.htm (accessed October 27, 1998).

13. Ibid.

14. Fred Rivero, personal communication with author, August 4, 2001, and Lloyd Reynolds, "Operation Hickory" (unpublished essay, March 2001).

CHAPTER 7. DMZ INVASION

1. Jim Cool, personal communication with author, November 30, 2001.

2. Clyde Petrella, M/3/4, confirmed that a squad from his company waded across the Ben Hai River on May 19. Refer to the Battalion Command Chronologies, Combat After Action Reports, Hickory, 3/4, p. 4(#10.g), which states: "Company 'M' called in an air strike on village in vicinity (078753). . . . At 1500H, Company 'M' searched village. Area appeared to be a major NVA harboring site." Grid coordinates given in the CAAR indicate the village was, in fact, on the northern side of the Ben Hai.

3. Reynolds, n. p.

4. Ms. Leroy fully recovered from her shrapnel wounds. Keith Nolan, *Battle for Hue: Tet, 1968* (Novato, CA: Presidio Press, 1983), 65–72, described how she and a fellow male French journalist were taken prisoner in Hue City during Tet, 1968. A French-speaking NVA officer ordered them released. The following day, just as an Ontos gunner lined up his six 106mm recoilless rifles for a broadside at a Catholic Church the Marines believed was a sniper hideout, Cathy ran up to the closest officer and grabbed him, beseeching him to stop the Ontos from firing. "There are four thousand refugees in there," she begged. "They aren't VC! They are just people!" The shocked Marines ceased fire. Killing civilians was not what they were about. She later said of the Marines: "The Leathernecks will always remind me of what we call the Foreign Legion . . . big mouths with hearts of gold."

5. Battalion Command Chronologies, Combat After Action Reports, Hickory, 3/4, May 67, #5; Robert McIntosh interview with the author.

6. Hugh Kelley, personal communication with author, November 10, 2001.

7. Telfer, Rogers, and Fleming, 29.

8. Spector, 224.

9. Telfer, Rogers, and Fleming, 30.

10. Hammel, "DMZ Campaign of 1967," 8–9.

11. Edward F. Murphy, *Semper Fi—Vietnam* (Novato, CA: Presidio Press, 2000), 120.

12. Clyde Petrella, personal communication with author, November 8, 2001.

13. Ibid.

14. Ibid.

15. Telfer, Rogers, and Fleming, 30.

PART IV: SUMMER IN HELL

The epigraph to this part is drawn from Sir John Bright (1811–89), speech to the House of Commons, Great Britain, February 25, 1855.

CHAPTER 8. BUFFALO

The epigraph to this chapter is drawn from Nolan, *Operation Buffalo*, 23.

1. "Ambush at Con Thien," *Newsweek*, July 17, 1967, 45.

2. Sturkey, 382–83.

3. Nolan, *Operation Buffalo*, 105.

4. Ibid., 109.

5. Ibid., 81.

6. "Ambush at Con Thien," *Newsweek*, 45.

7. Nolan, *Operation Buffalo*, 116.

8. Ibid., 122.

9. Gunnery Sgt. Norman Eckler comments, November 6, 1967, 3d Marine Division Historical Section—Infield Interviews, USMC Historical Center, Washington Navy Yard, Washington, DC.

10. Jack Wilder, personal communication with author, September 1, 2001.

11. Major Curtis Danielson comments, July 7, 1967, 3d Marine Division Historical Section—Infield Interviews.

12. Roger Liggon, ed., "Membership Directory, 1995–96" (mimeograph, 1st Battalion, 9th Marines Network Headquarters, Plainfield, NJ, September 5, 1996).

13. Nolan, *Operation Buffalo*, 177.

14. Ibid.; Battalion Command Chronologies, Combat After Action Reports, USMC Historical Center, Washington Navy Yard, Washington, DC, July 1967.

15. Staff Sgt. Leon Burns comments, July 7, 1967, 3d Marine Division Historical Section—Infield Interviews.

16. Telfer, Rogers, and Fleming, 100.

17. Otto J. Lehrack, *No Shining Armor: The Marines at War in Vietnam* (Lawrence: University Press of Kansas, 1992), 361.

18. Nolan, *Operation Buffalo*, 252.

19. Ibid.

20. Lance Corporal Wilson's status was officially changed from Missing in Action to Killed in Action, Body Not Recovered, in September 1974. In an after-action interview on July 7, the XO of 1/9, Major Danielson, stated that thirteen bodies at the Dong Ha morgue still had not been identified. Captain Warren O. Keneipp was initially listed as Missing in Action; however, his decapitated body was one of the thirteen subsequently positively identified. Major Danielson expressed his fear at the time that some of those

missing in action could have been taken prisoner. This proved later not to be the case. Major Danielson comments, July 7, 1967, 3d Marine Division Historical Section—Infield Interviews.

21. Telfer, Rogers, and Fleming, 102.

22. Nolan, *Operation Buffalo,* 285–87.

23. Ibid., 292.

24. Battalion Command Chronologies, Combat After Action Reports (1st Battalion, 9th Marines, 3d Marine Division), July 1967.

25. See Nolan, *Operation Buffalo,* 269–329, for complete descriptions of major July 6 battles around Con Thien during Operation Buffalo.

26. For a complete listing by name of all casualties in the CP Bunker disaster, see Nolan, *Operation Buffalo,* 333–40.

27. Telfer, Rogers, and Fleming, 104.

CHAPTER 9. RUNNING THE GAUNTLET

The epigraph to this chapter is drawn from Major Robert Rogers, *Standing Orders, Rogers' Rangers* (1759), quoted in David H. Hackworth, *About Face* (New York: Simon and Schuster, 1989), 835.

1. Telfer, Rogers, and Fleming, 125–28.

2. Frank Southard, personal communication with author, February 22, 2001.

3. Ibid.

4. Myers, 153.

5. Jack Hartzell, "Fighting Forces," *Vietnam,* April 2001, 18–20.

PART V: GENERAL OFFENSIVE, PHASE I

The epigraph to this part is drawn from a quote from "Chesty" Puller, quoted in Eric Hammel, *Khe Sanh: Siege in the Clouds* (New York: Crown Publishers, 1989), 2. Lieutenant Colonel Puller said this when his battalion was surrounded by the Japanese on Guadalcanal in 1942.

CHAPTER 10. THE "THUNDERING THIRD"

The epigraph in this chapter is drawn from Michael Herr, *Dispatches* (New York: Alfred A. Knopf, 1978), 102–3.

1. Jack Shulimson et al., *U.S. Marines in Vietnam: The Defining Year, 1968* (Washington, DC: Headquarters, U.S. Marine Corps, 1997), 10–11.

2. Shulimson et al., 13.

3. Charles R. Anderson, *The Grunts* (New York: Berkley Books, 1985), 165.

4. Tim O'Brien, *If I Die in a Combat Zone: Box Me Up and Ship Me Home* (New York: Broadway Books, 1999), 123–24.

5. Ron Smith, "Perspectives," *Vietnam* (June 1997): 62–65. On November 10, 1993, in a ceremony held at the Pentagon, Ron "Doc" Smith and Bob Wilson were awarded the Bronze Star Medal with Combat "V" by Secretary of the Navy John S. Dalton.

6. John Wear, "My Two Days at Con Thien," *Sponson Box*, May 2003, 13. Bill Carroll would spend five weeks in the hospital and return to Con Thien in October. He retired from the Marine Corps as a sergeant major.

7. Ibid.

8. Lee R. Bendell, "Marine Patrol," *Marine Corps Gazette*, November 1968, 99–100.

9. Tom Barry, personal communication with author, June 18, 2001.

10. Al Hemingway, "A Place of Angels," *Vietnam* (Feb. 1991): 31.

11. Ron Smith, personal communication with author, December 12, 2001.

12. Dominic Bilotta, personal communication with author, November 11, 2002.

Chapter 11. Into the Valley of Death

1. The Third Battalion, Fourth Marines command group at Con Thien had already commenced setting up a new CP at C-2 on September 10.

2. Eric Hammel, *Ambush Valley* (Novato, CA: Presidio Press, 1990), 53.

3. Ibid., 60.

4. In a group interview conducted by the author in 2001, Guy Wolfenbarger, Jack Wilder, and Charles Witkamp, former tank crewmen present September 7 with India Company, all concurred that, if given permission by Lieutenant Drnek to fire the flame tank at that moment, it could have dealt a fatal blow to the NVA and permitted India to load up casualties on the tanks and make it back to the battalion perimeter only five hundred meters away.

5. Hammel, *Ambush Valley*, 64.

6. Ibid., 76.

7. Peter Fossel, personal communication with author, January 20, 2002.

8. Hammel, *Ambush Valley*, 92–93.

9. Ibid., 99.

10. Ibid., 131–33.

11. Richard D. Camp, *Lima-6* (New York: Macmillan, 1989), 123.

12. Hammel, *Ambush Valley*, 196. John Prince attended the University of Arizona at the same time as the author, and they signed their OCS contracts in a meeting with the Officer Selection Officer at the Sands Motel in Tucson.

13. Camp, 130.

14. Matthew P. Caulfield, "India Six," *Marine Corps Gazette*, July 1969, 28.

15. Hammel, *Ambush Valley*, 202.

16. Ibid., 190.

17. Caulfield, 29.

18. Guy Wolfenbarger, personal communication with author, December 12, 2001.

19. Hammel, *Ambush Valley*, 218–22.

20. Paul Drew Stevens, ed., *The Navy Cross* (Forest Ranch, CA: Sharp and Dunnigan Publications, 1987), 25.

21. Camp, 136.

22. Caulfield, 28.

23. Hammel, *Ambush Valley*, 230.

24. Gunnery Sergeant Gleason Norris received a Silver Star Medal in a ceremony held thirty-three years later on September 15, 2000. He had retired from the Marine Corps in 1970 with a 90 percent disability rating due to the severity of his wounds from the September 10, 1967, battle.

25. Hammel, *Ambush Valley*, 237.

26. Stevens, 43.

27. Charles Witkamp, personal communication with author, September 21, 2001.

28. Hammel, *Ambush Valley*, 255.

29. Caulfield, 29–30.

30. Hammel, *Ambush Valley*, 280. Both burned tankers survived through the night and were medevaced out to the hospital ship *Repose* in the morning. Gunnery Sergeant Harold D. Tatum succumbed to his burns on September 21, 1967. He was awarded a Silver Star Medal posthumously. Corporal Gary Young died September 20, 1967, also on the *Repose*.

31. Hammel, *Ambush Valley*, 292.

32. Ibid., 322–33.

Part VI: The Siege

The excerpt to this part is drawn from a letter written by 1st Lt. Victor David Westphall III, B/1/4, to his brother. Westphall was killed in action May 22, 1968, at Con Thien. Reprinted with permission.

Chapter 12. 3/9's Turn in the Barrel

1. Sheehan, 649–50.

2. Frank Breth, personal communication with author, July 21, 2003.

3. I conducted an exhaustive records search but could not determine the name of the drowned corpsman and when (or if) his body was ever recovered.

Chapter 13. Monsoon Misery

1. Gene Miller, personal communication with author, July 30, 2003.

2. Jack Hartzel, personal communication with author, November 1, 2001.

3. Ibid.

4. Stevens, 176.

5. J. W. Hammond Jr., "Combat Journal, Part I," *Marine Corps Gazette,* July 1968, 27.

6. Ibid., 23.

7. The total of sixteen dead included five Navy corpsmen.

Chapter 14. Living in the "V" Ring

The epigraph to this chapter is drawn from John H. Edwards, "Trench Warfare" (unpublished essay, 2003), 3. The epigraph in the text is drawn from Robert Brosa, personal communication with author, April 9, 1994.

1. Congressman Schweiker, speaking on a newspaper editorial from the *Sunbury Daily Item* by Mr. H. H. Haddon about a visit to Con Thien by Karl H. Purnell ("Purnell Writes of Hapless Plight of Marines, Victims of Dubious Policy"), 89th Cong., 1st sess., *Congressional Record* H13384.

2. Associated Press News Dispatch, September 25, 1967.

3. Ibid.

4. Pisor, 53.

5. Telfer, Rogers, and Fleming, 135.

6. Spector, 119.

7. Moyers S. Shore, *The Battle for Khe Sanh* (Washington, DC: Headquarters, USMC, 1969), 103–4.

8. Telfer, Rogers, and Fleming, 203.

9. Edwards, 4.

10. It was the author's experience that those who harbored this foolhardy belief soon became casualties.

11. Hartzel, personal communication with author.

12. Hammond, 27.

13. Simmons, *Marines in Vietnam,* 83.

14. Overheard by the author while monitoring battalion radio net.

15. A veteran tank crewman who had been attached to 1/9 in May 1967 and had carried dead B/1/9 Marines on the back of his tank during Operation Buffalo shared this belief with the author at that time.

16. Richard B. Smith, "Leatherneck Square," *Marine Corps Gazette,* August 1969, 37.

17. Robert Brosa, personal communication with author.

18. On February 8, 1968, when the First Platoon of Alpha Company had been overrun on Hill 64 at Khe Sanh, Captain Radcliffe led a platoon from his company in a spirited counterattack that retook the hill from the NVA. He would receive a second Silver Star Medal for his gallant leadership in that action—Operation Buffalo was his first. He retired from the Marine Corps as a colonel.

19. Brosa, ibid.

20. Barry Lombardo, personal communication with author, February 10, 2003.

CHAPTER 15. THE "MAGNIFICENT BASTARDS"

The epigraph to this chapter is drawn from Keith W. Nolan, *The Magnificent Bastards* (Novato, CA: Presidio Press, 1994), 1.

1. Lanning and Cragg, 260.
2. Lehrack, 184–85.
3. Nolan, *The Magnificent Bastards*, 29.
4. Telfer, Rogers, and Fleming, 139.

PART VII: KENTUCKY

The epigraph to this part is drawn from David Douglas Duncan, *War without Heroes* (New York: Harper and Row, 1970), 106.

CHAPTER 16. WINTER BATTLES: 1967–68

1. Pisor, 47.
2. Telfer, Rogers, and Fleming, 143.
3. Dave Granger, personal communication with author, May 11, 1994.
4. Orley VanEngelenhoven, personal communication with author, November 7, 2001.
5. Shulimson et al., 27.
6. Ibid., 28.
7. Ibid., 29.
8. Ibid., 13.
9. Al Sansone, personal communication with author, October 12, 2001.
10. Philip J. Stoner, personal communication with author, January 14, 1999.
11. Shulimson et al., 17.
12. Ibid., 126.
13. Simmons, *Marines in Vietnam*, 92–93.
14. John S. Jamison, "Brothers in Arms Relive Past," *Camp Lejeune Globe*, March 26, 1994. Soon after his return to the States, then-sergeant Madden submitted a reward recommendation for Lieutenant Christy, but it was lost, misplaced, or discarded; no one really knew. In 1986, their paths crossed again. Mike Madden was dismayed to learn that Christy had not received official recognition for his heroism that day. Despite Ken Christy's advice to forget about it, Madden embarked on a personal crusade to see that the man who had saved his life as well as the lives of many others would be recognized.
15. John Hughes-Wilson, *Military Intelligence Blunders* (New York: Carroll and Graff, 1999), 210–11.

CHAPTER 17. AFTER TET

The epigraph to this chapter is drawn from comments by Walter Cronkite, Anchor, *CBS Evening News*, February 27, 1968, quoted in Pisor, 212. For additional insight into

Walter Cronkite's growing criticism of America's involvement in Vietnam, see also Karnow, 560–61. The epigraph in the text is drawn from memory; every Marine Corps veteran has heard at one time or another about Gunnery Sgt. Dan Daly and this famous battle cry when he led a charge during the World War I battle at Belleau Wood, France, June 6, 1918.

1. "Cam Lo Battle Won Despite Odds," *Pacific Stars and Stripes,* February 24, 1968.

2. Hughes-Wilson, 210.

3. Karnow, 525.

4. Shulimson et al., 307.

5. Victor Westphall, *David's Story: A Casualty of Vietnam* (Springer, NM: Center for the Advancement of Human Dignity). Dr. Victor Westphall, a history professor at the University of New Mexico, and his wife, Jeanne, decided to commemorate their son David's short life with a memorial chapel. Begun in the fall of 1968, the memorial was finally dedicated in 1971. In 1987, President Ronald Reagan proclaimed the Angel Fire, New Mexico, site as the DAV Vietnam Veterans National Memorial, dedicated to all who lost their lives in the Vietnam War.

6. Prados and Stubbe, 306–9.

7. Shulimson et al., 320–22. Operation Robin was being carried out in the rugged mountains south of Khe Sanh on June 6, involving the 1st and 4th Marine Regiments. This multiregiment operation was being supported entirely by helicopter. That would explain the unavailability of helicopter support for E/2/26.

8. Lance Cpl. James N. Kaylor, PFC Daniel A. Staggs, and PFC William A. Hayes were awarded Silver Star Medals for their heroism. On June 3, 2000, the city of Closter, New Jersey, rededicated a park named for Corporal Kenneth Schauble. As of this writing, a group of former 2/26 Marines, led by James Kaylor, was lobbying to have a Navy Cross awarded to Kenneth Schauble posthumously.

9. Special thanks to James N. Kaylor for permission to reprint excerpts from his original manuscript about this battle.

REQUIEM

The epigraph to this chapter is drawn from Salvatore Bafumo, personal communication with author, May 7, 2001. Sal was also kind enough to share his personal papers written about his service in Vietnam.

1. Oliver L. North, *One More Mission* (Grand Rapids, MI: Zondervan Publishing House, 1993), 246.

2. Kent Wonders, "Con Thien," *Khe Sanh Veteran,* November 1994, 8.

3. J. "Doc" McNiff, *Hell Looks Different Now* (Atlanta, GA: Protea Publishing, 2001), 107–8.

Glossary of Terms and Abbreviations

A-1 Douglas Skyraider; single-engine, propeller-driven attack aircraft.

A-4 Douglas Skyhawk; single-seat, delta-winged jet.

A-6A Grumman Intruder; twin-jet, twin-seat, all-weather jet.

air panels Bright orange cloth markers about four feet wide by ten feet long laid on the ground to alert pilots to where the friendly positions are.

amtrac USMC amphibious tractor.

AO Aerial observer; also area of operations.

Arc Light Code name for B-52 bombing missions.

ARVN Army of the Republic of Vietnam (South Vietnam).

B-52 Boeing Stratofortress; U.S. Air Force eight-engine jet bomber.

Bangalore torpedo A long, hollow pipe or tube, often bamboo, filled with explosives for clearing barbed-wire obstacles.

BAS Battalion aid station; battalion surgeon's location.

beehive Antipersonnel cannon shell carrying thousands of steel darts called flechettes.

Bird Dog 0-1E observation plane.

"blooper" gun M79 grenade launcher, nicknamed "blooper" by the troops; it is fired like a shotgun and launches a 40mm projectile.

BLT Battalion Landing Team.

bouncing betty Antipersonnel mine; later called "tomato can."

bracketed Shells impacting on two or more sides of a target.

Brig. Gen. Brigadier general.

bush time Out in the field on operations as opposed to being back at base camp or in a rear area.

button bomblet Small antipersonnel mine sown by aircraft, carpeting the area.

C-4 Plastic explosive.

Capt. Captain.

CH-46 Boeing Vertol Sea Knight; medium transport helicopter, tandem rotors.

CH-53 Sikorsky Sea Stallion; heavy transport helicopter, 12,800-pound payload.

Chicom Chinese Communist, usually refers to hand grenade.

CIDG Civilian Irregular Defense Group; South Vietnamese paramilitary force, composed largely of Montagnards.

claymore Command-detonated, directional, antipersonnel mine.

CO Commanding officer.

COC Command operations center.

Col. Colonel.

com-helmet Hard-shell plastic helmet with radio transmitter and built-in receiver.

Conex box Steel crate or box used to carry large loads aboard a truck or ship or even a helicopter.

CP Command post.

Cpl. Corporal.

Delta Med. Emergency medical hospital unit at Dong Ha Marine base.

deuce-and-a-half truck Standard two and one-half ton military truck.

DMZ Demilitarized zone dividing North from South Vietnam.

Dyemarker Code name for the Strong Point Obstacle System.

e-tool Entrenching tool; a small folding shovel.

F-4B McDonnell Phantom II; Navy and USMC twin-jet, twin-seat fighter/attack bomber.

F-8 Vought Crusader; Navy and USMC single-jet, single-seat jet fighter/attack bomber.

FAC Forward air controller. (FAC [A] is airborne.)

flame tanker A crewman on a USMC M-67 flame tank.

FO Forward observer; a spotter trained to direct artillery and mortar fire.

frag grenade M-26 hand grenade used by U.S. troops.

frag order Written order from a superior to subordinates detailing how an attack or patrol is to be carried out.

FSCC Fire support coordination center.

gook Derogatory slang name for any Vietnamese or Asian.

"grease gun," M-3A1 U.S., .45-caliber submachine gun; thirty-round magazine; carried by tank crewmen to defend their tank.

grenade launcher, M-79 U.S., single shot, break open, breech loaded, fires 40mm projectiles.

grunt Slang term for infantryman.

gun, 100mm, M1944 Soviet-built, towed cannon; twenty-one thousand meters maximum range.

gun, 130mm, M-46 Soviet-built, towed cannon; thirty-one thousand meters maximum range.

gun, 155mm, M53 U.S., self-propelled gun; twenty-three thousand meters maximum range.

gun, 175mm, M107 U.S., self-propelled gun; 32,800 meters maximum range.

Gunny USMC gunnery sergeant.

gypsy rack Steel bar assembly welded to the rear of a tank turret for carrying gear.

H & I fires Harassing and interdiction artillery fire.

HE High explosive.

HEAT High-explosive antitank.

heat tabs Small chemical briquettes that burn intensely for several minutes; used to heat C rations.

HM Hospitalman.

HMM Marine medium helicopter squadron.

howitzer, eight-inch, M-110 U.S., self-propelled gun; 16,930 meters maximum range.

howitzer, 105mm, M2A1 U.S., towed light artillery; 11,155 meters maximum range.

howitzer, 155mm, M1 U.S., towed medium artillery; 15,080 meters maximum range.

"Huey" Popular name for UH-1 helicopter.

"hugging the belt" NVA tactic for negating U.S. supporting arms by inflicting casualties in proximity to themselves, especially during an ambush.

hump Tote all gear on foot during patrols or operations.

k-bar Large bladed combat knife used by Marines.

KIA Killed in action.

kilometer One kilometer equals 0.62 miles (⅝ of a mile); 1.61 kilometers equals 1 mile.

klick One thousand meters or one kilometer.

LAAW U.S., light antitank assault weapon.

Leatherneck Square Area below the eastern DMZ delineated by Marine bases at Con Thien, Gio Linh, Dong Ha, and Cam Lo.

LP Listening post.

LST Landing ship, tank.

Lt. Lieutenant.

Lt. Col. Lieutenant colonel.

Lt. Gen. Lieutenant general.

LVT Landing vehicle, tracked.

LZ Landing zone.

M-42 Duster U.S. Army tracked vehicle; antiaircraft; twin 40mm automatic cannons.

M-48A3 tank USMC and U.S. Army tracked vehicle; fifty-two tons, 90mm cannon, .30-caliber coaxially mounted machine gun, .50-caliber cupola-mounted machine gun.

machine gun, M-60 7.62mm, U.S., belt fed, gas operated, six hundred rpm; maximum range eleven hundred meters.

machine gun, RPD 7.62mm, Soviet built; drum fed; gas operated, 150 rpm; maximum range eight hundred meters.

machine gun, 12.7mm Soviet or Chinese heavy machine gun, wheel mounted, antiaircraft.

machine gun, .30-caliber U.S., disintegrating link, belt fed; 450 rpm; maximum range eight hundred meters.

machine gun, .50-caliber U.S., belt fed; recoil operated, one hundred rpm; maximum range 1,450 meters.

MACV Military Assistance Command, Vietnam.

"mad minute" All weapons firing simultaneously at no particular targets.

MAG Marine aircraft group.

Maj. Major.

Maj. Gen. Major general.

mechanical mule Small four-wheel cargo carrier able to negotiate rough terrain.

medevac Transport of casualties via helicopter to a medical facility.

meter, meters One meter equals 39.37 inches; 1,000 meters equals 1,093 yards.

MIA Missing in action.

millimeter One millimeter equals .039 inch.

mortar, 60mm, M19 U.S., forty-five pounds; maximum rate of fire thirty rpm; maximum range two thousand meters.

mortar, 81mm, M29 U.S., 115 pounds; maximum rate of fire two rpm; maximum range 2,300–3,650 meters.

mortar, 82mm Soviet built, 123 pounds; maximum rate of fire twenty-five rpm; maximum range 3,040 meters.

mortar, 120mm Soviet built, six hundred pounds; maximum rate of fire fifteen rpm; maximum range fifty-seven hundred meters.

mortar, 4.2-inch, M30 U.S., rifled bore, 330 pounds; maximum rate twenty rpm; maximum range 4,020 meters.

MSR Main supply route.

NCO Noncommissioned officer.

NLF National Liberation Front; political arm of the Communist-led insurgency against the South Vietnamese government.

Nung Vietnamese of Chinese extraction; tend to dwell in remote mountainous areas.

NVA North Vietnamese Army; term for soldiers in that army.

OCS Officer Candidate School at Quantico, Virginia.

Ontos M-50; USMC lightly armored tracked vehicle with six 106mm recoilless rifles; thirty mph top speed; three crewmen.

OP Outpost or observer post.

OPCON Operational control.

Otters Marine Corps tracked amphibious vehicles.

PF Popular Force.

PFC Private first class.

pickled Released bombs from an aircraft.

pistol, .45-caliber, M1911A1 Standard sidearm of U.S. military.

Practice Nine Code name for planning the anti-infiltration barrier across the DMZ.

PRC/25 Radio carried by radio operator in the field.

preregister Plot the coordinates on a map to indicate a specific target area.

PT-76 tank Amphibious tank, Soviet made.

"Puff"gunship Nickname for an AC-47 minigun armed aircraft.

quad-fifty U.S. Army, antiaircraft, four .50-caliber machine guns.

R&R Rest and relaxation.

recoilless rifle, 106mm U.S. built, single shot, breech loaded, 438 pounds; sustained rate of fire of six rounds per minute and an effective range of 1,365 meters.

recon Reconnaissance.

register Mark a target's location on a military map or grid.

rifle, AK-47, 7.62mm Soviet-designed, Chinese-built assault rifle; semiautomatic or fully automatic; cyclic rate of fire six hundred rpm; effective range 350 meters.

rifle, M-14, 7.62mm U.S., semiautomatic; twenty-round magazine; effective range 460 meters.

rifle, M-16, 5.56mm U.S., semiautomatic or fully automatic; cyclic rate of fire seven hundred to nine hundred rpm; effective range 460 meters.

rocket, 122mm Soviet built; fin stabilized, nine feet long, 125 pounds; seventeen thousand meters maximum range.

Rough Rider Vehicle supply convoy escorted by tanks.

RPD *See* machine gun, RPD.

RPG Rocket-propelled grenade.

RPG-2, rocket-propelled grenade Soviet/Chinese-designed, 40mm HEAT round; infantry shoulder-fired antitank weapon; effective range one hundred meters. (RPG-7 had five-hundred-meter range.)

SAM Soviet-made surface-to-air missile.

Sappers NVA engineer troops highly trained in breaching wire obstacles and minefields.

Sav-A-Plane Radio procedure for requesting that the artillery fire control center halt all artillery and mortar fire into a battle zone where aircraft are flying.

Seabees U.S. Naval Construction Battalion.

Sgt. Sergeant.

short-timer American serviceman close to going home.

SLF Special landing force.

Snake-eye Bombs equipped with pop-out braking fins to slow their descent so jet aircraft could avoid blast damage during low-altitude bomb runs.

spider hole Camouflaged fighting hole dug in the ground.

sponson box Equipment box on both sides of an M-48A3 tank.

SPOS Strong Point Obstacle System.

Starlight scope Light-gathering scope for night vision.

tanker Tank crewman.

TAOR Tactical area of responsibility.

TC Tank commander.

time-on-target bombardment *See* TOT.

TOT Time on target; one or more artillery batteries fire all guns simultaneously so all shells arrive at the target at the same instant.

TPQ AN/TPQ-10 ground-based radar system; guides aircraft to bombing mission targets in darkness and inclement weather.

Trace Official term used to describe the bulldozed six-hundred-meter-wide strip between Con Thien and Gio Linh.

UH-1E Bell "Huey"; light attack/observation helicopter.

UH-34 Sikorsky Sea Horse; smallest troop-carrying helicopter.

USMC United States Marine Corps.

VC Viet Cong.

VMFA Marine fighter attack squadron.

VT fuze Variable-timed fuze for artillery shell airbursts.

walk, walking Advancing pattern of impacting artillery or mortar shells.

WIA (E) Wounded in action, evacuated.

WIA (NE) Wounded in action, not evacuated.

"Willy Peter" Military slang for any explosive shell or grenade that contains white phosphorus.

WP White phosphorus.

XO Executive officer.

"Zippo" Military slang for the M-67 flame tank; carries a ninety-second load of napalm propelled by compressed air, ignited as it leaves the barrel.

Bibliography

Alsop, Joseph. "Aiming for a Dien Bien Phu." *Washington Post,* September 29, 1967.

"Ambush at Con Thien." *Newsweek,* July 17, 1967, 45.

Anderson, Charles R. *The Grunts.* New York: Berkley Books, 1985.

Battalion Command Chronologies. Combat After Action Reports, MACV, and III MAF declassified documents. Washington, DC: Archives, USMC Historical Center, Washington Navy Yard.

Bendell, Lee R. "Marine Patrol." *Marine Corps Gazette,* November 1968, 99–102.

"Bloody Trial." *Newsweek,* May 22, 1967, 46.

Buckley, Tom. "Monsoon Rains Cut Off Marines Near Buffer Zone." *New York Times,* September 19, 1967.

Camp, Richard D. *Lima-6.* New York: Macmillan, 1989.

Caulfield, M. P. "India Six." *Marine Corps Gazette,* July 1969, 28–29.

Corley, Francis J. "Viet-Nam since Geneva." *Fordham University Quarterly* 33 (Winter 1958–59): 515–58.

Davidson, Phillip B. *Vietnam at War.* Novato, CA: Presidio Press, 1988.

Doleman, Edgar C., Jr. *The Vietnam Experience: Tools of War.* Boston: Boston Publishing Co., 1985.

Duncan, David Douglas. *War without Heroes.* New York: Harper and Row, 1970.

Edelman, Bernard, ed. *Dear America: Letters Home from Vietnam.* New York: Simon and Schuster, 1988.

Ehrhart, W. D. *Ordinary Lives: Platoon 1005 and the Vietnam War.* Philadelphia: Temple University Press, 1999.

Giap, Vo Nguyen. *Big Victory, Great Task.* New York: Frederick A. Praeger, 1968.

Guidry, Richard A. *The War in I Corps.* New York: Ivy Books, 1998.

Hammel, Eric. *Ambush Valley.* Novato, CA: Presidio Press, 1990.

———. "The DMZ Campaign of 1967." *Military History Guild.* Words to Go, Inc., 1994 (Document 94-0005).

———. *Khe Sanh: Siege in the Clouds.* New York: Crown Publishers, 1989.

———. "Marines under Fire at Con Thien." *Vietnam* (December 1997): 38–44.

Hammond, J. W., Jr. "Combat Journal, Part I." *Marine Corps Gazette,* July 1968, 20–29.

———. "Combat Journal, Conclusion." *Marine Corps Gazette,* August 1968, 46–51.

Hartzel, Jack T. "Fighting Forces." *Vietnam* (April 2001): 18–20.

Hemingway, Al. "A Place of Angels." *Vietnam* (February 1991): 27–32.

Herr, Michael. *Dispatches.* New York: Alfred A. Knopf, 1978.

Hughes-Wilson, John. *Military Intelligence Blunders.* New York: Carroll and Graff Publishers, 1999.

Jamison, John S., Jr. "'Brothers in Arms' Relive Past." *Camp Lejeune Globe,* March 26, 1994.

Kaizer, Kenneth E. "Perspectives." *Vietnam* (August 2001): 58–61.

Karnow, Stanley. *Vietnam: A History.* New York: Penguin Books, 1997.

Lanning, Michael. *Inside the Crosshairs: Snipers in Vietnam.* New York: Ivy Books, 1998.

Lanning, Michael Lee, and Dan Cragg. *Inside the VC and the NVA.* New York: Ivy Books, 1992.

Lehrack, Otto J. *No Shining Armor: The Marines at War in Vietnam.* Lawrence: University Press of Kansas, 1992.

Liggon, Roger, ed. "Membership Directory, 1995–96." Mimeograph. Plainfield, NJ: 1st Battalion, 9th Marines Network Headquarters, September 5, 1996.

MacDonald, Peter. *Giap: The Victor in Vietnam.* New York: W. W. Norton, 1993.

Martin, Bruce. "Time in the Barrel." *Leatherneck,* November 1971, 71–75.

McCombs, Phil. "Peace Church, Vietnam." *Washington Post,* October 27, 1998.

McNiff, J. "Doc." *Hell Looks Different Now.* Atlanta: Protea Publishing, 2001.

McQuillan, J. F. "Indochina." *Marine Corps Gazette,* December 1954, 14–21.

———. "Indochina, Part II." *Marine Corps Gazette,* January 1955, 48–59.

Murphy, Edward F. *Semper Fi—Vietnam.* Novato, CA: Presidio Press, 2000.

Myers, William L. *Honor the Warrior: The United States Marine Corps in Vietnam.* Lafayette, LA: Redoubt Press, 2000.

Nolan, Keith W. *Battle for Hue: Tet, 1968.* New York: Dell Publishing Co., 1983.

———. *The Magnificent Bastards.* Novato, CA: Presidio Press, 1994.

———. *Operation Buffalo: USMC Fight for the DMZ.* Novato, CA: Presidio Press, 1991.

North, Oliver L. *One More Mission.* Grand Rapids, MI: Zondervan Publishing House, 1993.

O'Brien, Tim. *If I Die in a Combat Zone: Box Me Up and Ship Me Home.* New York: Broadway Books, 1999.

Olson, James S., ed. *Dictionary of the Vietnam War.* New York: Greenwood Press, 1988.

Pisor, Robert. *The End of the Line: The Siege of Khe Sanh.* New York: Ballantine Books, 1983.

Prados, John, and Ray W. Stubbe. *Valley of Decision: The Siege of Khe Sanh.* Boston: Houghton Mifflin Co., 1991.

"Rifle under Fire." *Newsweek,* September 10, 1967, 27–28.

Shaplen, Robert. *The Road from War.* New York: Harper and Row, 1970.

Sheehan, Neil. *A Bright Shining Lie: John Paul Vann and America in Vietnam.* New York: Vintage Books, 1989.

Shore, Moyers S. *The Battle for Khe Sanh.* Washington, DC: Historical Branch, G-3 Division, Headquarters, U.S. Marine Corps, 1969.

Shulimson, Jack. *U.S. Marines in Vietnam: An Expanding War, 1966.* Washington, DC: History and Museums Division, Headquarters, U.S. Marine Corps, 1984.

Shulimson, Jack, Leonard A. Blasiol, Charles R. Smith, and David A. Dawson. *U.S. Marines in Vietnam: The Defining Year, 1968.* Washington, DC: History and Museums Division, Headquarters, U.S. Marine Corps, 1997.

Simmons, E. H. *Marines (Illustrated History of the Vietnam War).* New York: Bantam Books, 1987.

———. *The United States Marines: A History.* 3rd ed. Washington, DC: Naval Institute Press, 1998.

———, ed. *The Marines in Vietnam, 1954–1973: An Anthology and Annotated Bibliography.* Washington, DC: History and Museums Division, Headquarters, U.S. Marine Corps, 1974.

Smith, Charles R. *U.S. Marines in Vietnam: High Mobility and Standdown, 1969.* Washington, DC: History and Museums Division, Headquarters, U.S. Marine Corps, 1988.

Smith, Richard B. "Leatherneck Square." *Marine Corps Gazette,* August 1969, 34–42.

Smith, Ron. "Perspectives." *Vietnam* (June 1997): 62–6.

Spector, Ronald H. *After Tet.* New York: Vintage Press, 1994.

Stanton, Shelby L. *The Green Berets at War.* Novato, CA: Presidio Press, 1985.

Stevens, Paul Drew, ed. *The Navy Cross.* Forest Ranch, CA: Sharp and Dunnigan Publications, 1987.

Sturkey, Marion F. *Bonnie-Sue: A Marine Corps Helicopter Squadron in Vietnam.* Plum Branch, SC: Heritage Press International, 1996.

Telfer, Gary L., Lane Rogers, and V. Keith Fleming. *U.S. Marines in Vietnam: Fighting the Vietnamese, 1967.* Washington, DC: History and Museums Division, Headquarters, U.S. Marine Corps, 1984.

Third Marine Division Historical Section. Infield Interviews. Washington, DC: USMC Historical Center, Washington Navy Yard. Reel-to-reel tapes: Staff Sgt. Leon Burns, B/1/9 (Dong Ha, July 7, 1967); Major D. Curtis Danielson, 1/9 (Dong Ha, July 7, 1967); Gunnery Sgt. Norman E. Eckler, Bravo Company, 3d Tank Bn. (Dong Ha, November 6, 1967).

U.S. Congress. *Congressional Record.* 89th Cong., 1st sess. (H13384).

U.S. Congress. *Congressional Record.* 90th Cong., 1st sess. (November 22, 1967): 33690–91-pt. 25.

Walt, Lewis W. *Strange War, Strange Strategy.* New York: Funk and Wagnalls, 1970.

"The War: The Bitterest Battlefield." *Time,* September 22, 1967, 14–15.

"The War: Demilitarizing the Zone." *Time,* May 26, 1967, 24–5.

"The War: Thunder from a Distant Hill." *Time,* October 6, 1967, 7–12.

Warner, Denis. "Bearing the Brunt at Con Thien." *The Reporter,* October 19, 1967, 18–21.

Webb, James. "Heroes of the Vietnam Generation." *The Proud Warrior, Newsletter of the 1/9 Network,* Winter 2000–1, 10–12.

Westmoreland, William Childs. *A Soldier Reports.* New York: Doubleday, 1976.

Westphall, Victor. *David's Story: A Casualty of Vietnam.* Springer, NM: Center for the Advancement of Human Dignity, 1981.

Wonders, Kent. "Con Thien." *Khe Sanh Veteran,* November 1994, 8.

Index